GRAPHIC DESIGN

Julian Wehr. A scratch-drawing on a black crayon background.

GRAPHIC DESIGN

A LIBRARY OF OLD

AND NEW MASTERS IN

THE GRAPHIC ARTS BY

LEON FRIEND, M.A., AND

JOSEPH HEFTER, Ph. D.

WHITTLESEY HOUSE

McGRAW-HILL BOOK CO.

NEW YORK AND LONDON

Copyright, 1936, by
McGraw-Hill Book Company, Inc.
All rights reserved. This book, or parts thereof, may not be reproduced in any form without the permission of the publishers.
Printed in the United States of America.

SECOND PRINTING

Published by
Whittlesey House, a Division of
McGraw-Hill Book Company, Inc.

AUTHORS' PREFACE

GRAPHIC design, as treated in this book, is that creative endeavor which finds expression through the medium of printing ink. It is the design used in the make-up of daily papers, magazines, and books; in display cards, package goods, and advertising literature; and in the reproduced or original prints that adorn our walls.

The essential factors in successful graphic expression are a knowledge of the *tradition* of the craft (though not a slavish nor an academic one), a consideration of the *purpose* for which the design is intended, *imagination*, and a control of the requisite *skill* which will leave the artist free for self-expression. The presentation in this book is based on these essentials.

The book's aim is to mirror good taste in the productions that collectively make up the graphic arts. With this in view, the authors have minimized text and emphasized pertinent illustrations with appropriate critical legends. That such a mirror is possible is due to the cooperation of internationally known artists and craftsmen. Credit lines accompanying the illustrations indicate to those who so generously helped a small measure of the authors' appreciation. Help was also given by F. C. Kendall of *Advertising Arts*; Dr. M. F. Agha, of the Condé Nast Publications; L. D. Siegfried, of the *American Printer*; H. W. Kent and D. F. Williams, of the Metropolitan

Museum of Art; and H. M. Lydenberg and F. Weitenkampf, of the New York Public Library. Valuable, too, was the aid of T. Hoinko, of the American-Polish Chamber of Commerce; D'Alton Valentine, of the Society of Illustrators; George Macy, of the Limited Editions Club; W. G. Lownds and Paul A. Bennett, of the Mergenthaler Linotype Company; E. Leipprand, of the Bauer Type Foundry; Franklin Fischer, of the National Geographic Society; J. L. Frazier of the *Inland Printer;* and Douglas C. McMurtrie, of the Ludlow Typograph Company. Among the European contributors are Lord Riddel, late of the London School of Printing; J. H. Whitney, of the British Museum; Eric Maclazar, of the Victoria and Albert Museum; B. L. Warde, of the Monotype Corporation; T. H. Richardson, of the General Post Office, London; R. H. Hill, of the Bodleian Library; N. H. Holden, of the Birmingham School of Art; H. P. Huggill, of the Liverpool School of Art; E. P. Bates, of the Technical College, Hull; Stanislaw Dabrowski, of the Graphic Industries School, Warsaw; L. Tcherniavsky, of the Voks, Moscow; A. Ruppel, of the Gutenberg Museum, Mainz; Prof. Dr. Julius Zeitler, of the Leipzig State Academy of Arts and Book-crafts; Dr. Hugo Eberhardt, of the Offenbach School of Arts; and M. Mair, of the Swiss Post Office.

The authors are particularly appreciative of the criticism and suggestions that were made by the following specialists: Professor Sallie B. Tannahill, *Lettering;* Harry L. Gage, *Printing;* Harry A. Groesbeck, Jr., *Reproductive Arts;* Anton Bruehl, *Photography;* Douglas C. McMurtrie, *The Book;* Earnest Elmo Calkins, *Advertising Art;* Leonard London, *The Poster;* and James C. Boudreau, *Graphic Arts Education.*

NEW YORK CITY, DECEMBER, 1935.
LEON FRIEND AND JOSEPH HEFTER

TABLE OF CONTENTS

FRONTISPIECE............ii

AUTHORS' PREFACE.......v

LETTERING..............1

PRINTING...............29

REPRODUCTIVE ARTS....71

PHOTOGRAPHY.........115

THE BOOK.............151

ADVERTISING ART......245

THE POSTER...........299

ART EDUCATION.......357

GLOSSARY OF TERMS..384

BIBLIOGRAPHY.........396

INDEX.................399

LETTERING CHAPTER 1

LETTERING

LETTERING IS Used either to convey a meaning or to decorate a surface or both. It is a means of registering visibly what speech records audibly. As a vehicle for expressing meaning, therefore, the importance of lettering is obvious. The letterer, by means of skill and good taste, lends life and character to the lettered symbol, just as the speaker enlivens and accentuates the spoken word through modulation of voice, facial expression, and gesticulation. The written word gains through permanency what it lacks in the absence of the live concomitant of speech—the speaker.

Lettering is a versatile art. It functions in behalf of our everyday needs. Although in practice one finds a wealth of type styles to contest the use of lettering, the most painstaking efforts of type designers (letterers, by the way) cannot lend to type the pliability, the decorativeness, or the individuality that we associate with successfully designed lettering. After all, it is made to order, while the needs that a type face must fill are multifarious. This is evident from a comparison of the lettering and type designs of Johnston, Hewitt, Gill, Larisch, Simons, Ehmcke, Koch, Van Krimpen, Goudy, or Dwiggins.

Lettering is used at times for the enrichment of surfaces. It is difficult to decipher the ecclesiastic calligraphy on the heavily ornamented cape of a Greek-Orthodox priest. The fact that the contorted frills are embroidered in gold on a rich background contributes nothing to its legibility. Its beauty is its justification. The same may be said of the lettering on an incised Persian vase, a raised heraldic shield, or the more familiar engraved jewelry. Here lettering is the excuse, and decoration the final desideratum.

The characters of the alphabet are simplified equivalents of picture writing. They are the natural outgrowth of ancient prototypes following a slow process of evolution. Historically, all lettering and most types are

CHAPTER DECORATION designed by Prof. Erberto Carboni, Parma. CHAPTER FRONTISPIECE: "The Annunciation," a full-page miniature from the Ruskin Hours, North Eastern France, early fourteenth century. From a catalogue issued by Sotheby & Co., London. (*Reproduced by courtesy of Herbert Reiach, Ltd., London.*)

developments of writing. In *italics* this relationship is still noticeable. It can also be seen by overlapping a lettered form over its written equivalent (see page 10).

Edicraft Products are the only electrical appliances developed in my laboratories, made in my factories, and authorized to carry my signature

Thos A Edison.

FAMOUS EXAMPLE of the close relation between writing and lettering. Which is this? (*Courtesy of Thomas A. Edison, Inc., Orange, N. J.*)

The major influences in styles of lettering are:
1. The necessity for legibility.
2. The choice of the tool used and the material upon which the lettering is inscribed.
3. The desire for economy of time and effort through simplification.
4. The need to arrange harmoniously the various letters of a family in all sorts of combinations.
5. The demand that lettering reflect modernity in design and harmonize with it.

HE · HE · ђє · ђe

SHOWING RELATION between Roman and rustic capitals and pen-made uncials and half uncials (lower case).

To be more specific, a *wedge-shaped instrument* and clay gave us the cuneiform writing of the Assyrians. A *brush*, as tool, encourages the freedom and flow of line that characterize Chinese lettering. The *chisel*, following the lines of least resistance—thick when hammered downward, thin when hammered right to left—gave us the relationship of the thick and thin parts of Roman characters (see formal letters from Trajan column on page 32).

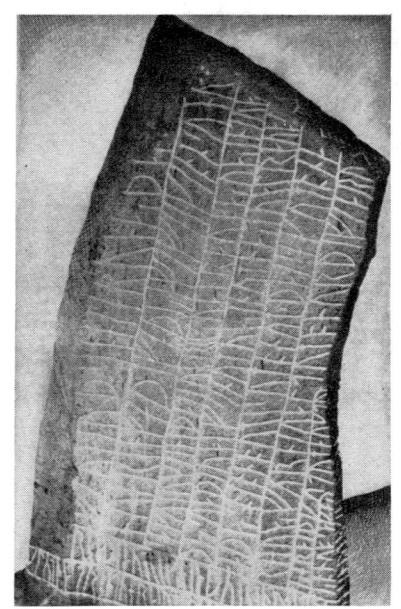

HISTORIC LETTERING. ABOVE, left: Egyptian hieroglyphics; symbolic lettering in limestone; stela on the back of a statue of Yuni and his wife, nineteenth dynasty (*Metropolitan Museum of Art, New York.*) Right: Runic inscription. (*Courtesy of Gustav Heurlin, Stockholm, and the National Geographic Magazine.*) BELOW, left: Syro-Egyptian script writing on brass. (*Metropolitan Museum of Art, New York.*) Right: Ecclesiastical use of ornamental lettering. Photograph by Captain V. Perfilieff. (*Times Wide World Photos, New York.*)

DESIGN 5

26   31

HOUSE ✠ LORDS
WAR·MEMORIAL
UNVEILING·BY
H·R·H

THREE MAJOR lettering styles: *Black-face Gothic, Sans serif,* and *Roman.* Two attractive pages from "St. Elizabeth"; the hand lettering by Keller shows a modernized black-face minus any attempt to justify the lines in imitation of type. (*Reichsdruckerei, Berlin.*) Title page of *Efter Storhetstiden,* lettered in free one-stroke style by Akke Kumlien. (*P. A. Norstedt & Söners, Stockholm.*) Formal lettering, fittingly designed for a cover of a booklet commemorating a solemn occasion by H. I. F. Badeley. (*Baynard Press, London.*)

Likewise the *quill*, *reed*, or *flat-nib steel pen* explains the German black-face or manuscript writing, and the modern *ball-shaped steel pen* accounts for the form of so-called Gothic (sans serif) letters.

With the Chinese, the Mohammedan, and the medieval illuminator, writing was a fine art. With many moderns, and with the best type designers, it still is. The incentive, however, has changed. While the colophon of the Book of Lindisfarne indicates that that Celtic masterpiece was done for "the love of God and St. Cuthbert," the lettering of today is more likely to be made to the order of commerce.

Chronologically, the capital letters (majuscules) of the alphabet antedate the lower case (minuscules). Perhaps that is why many authors and most pedagogues recommend the study of capital letters for beginners. Because the transition for the average amateur from writing to lower-case lettering is more natural, and because the small letter is more frequently seen and hence more familiar than its parent, the authors have preferred it as a starting point. In the following pages the high lights of lettering are illustrated with lettered plates.

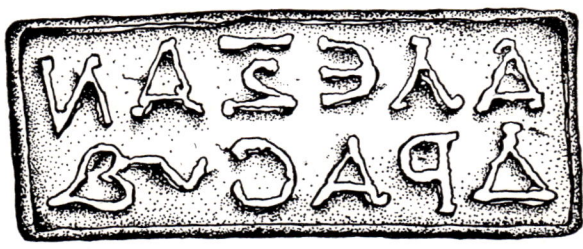

GREEK SEAL and Eric Gill lettering. Both show high regard for legibility and design. (*Courtesy of Metropolitan Museum of Art, New York, and the Fabian Society, London, respectively.*)

DESIGN

ORIGINS OF LETTERING · I
A presentation of its evolution

  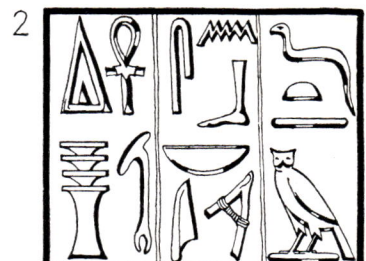 

1. Paleolithic pictographs on caves and tools were a prehistoric form of recording thoughts and deeds. Drawings in France and Spain still exist

2. Egyptian hieroglyphics, a decorative form of picture writing, developed into a system of lettering symbols in which each represented a word.

 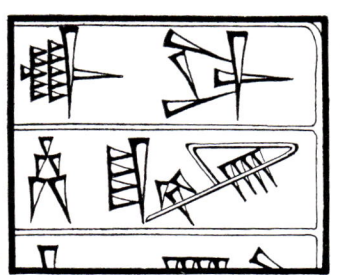  

3. Cuneiform, or wedge-shaped symbols of the Babylonian epoch; a syllabic "shorthand" version of hieroglyphics, simplified for easy inscription on clay

4. Chinese ideographs are brush signs based on pictographic methods, with each character representing a definite idea and a sound...

  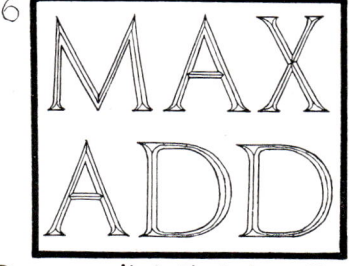 

5. Greek script on wax or papyrus evolved its alphabet from the Sinaitic adaptation of Egyptian hieroglyphics...

6. Roman capitals that show the "serifs"—chisel-made endings to stone-cut letters—and the fine design of the letters (TRAJAN COL) UMN

8 ——————————————————————— GRAPHIC

ORIGINS OF LETTERING · II
Showing the art and the artist

7. Roman pen letters that show the thick and thin strokes peculiar to the tool used. Excerpt, from a manuscript by Virgil, shows classical form

8. Uncials of the 6th century, showing angles rounded out by continuous use of reed or quill pen on parchment, becoming later, half-uncials

 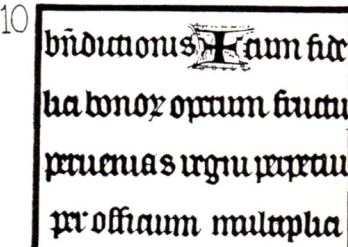 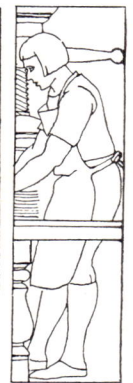

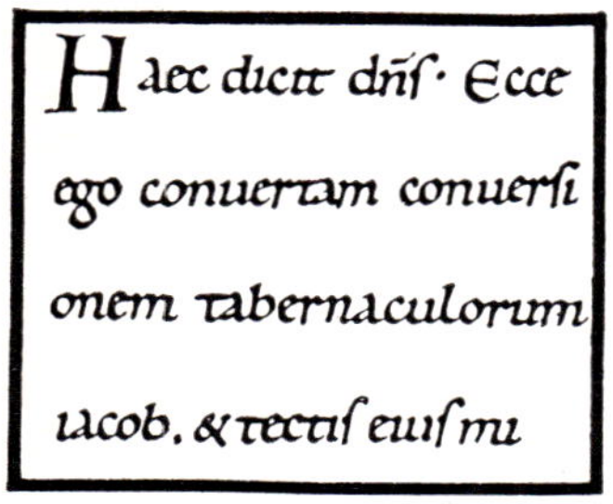

9. Carolingian minuscules, which developed from uncials, in the 9th century, are regarded as the prototype of present-day alphabets

10. Blackface Gothic characters, based on early German scripts and used in documentary, ecclesiastic, and general lettering during 1300-1500

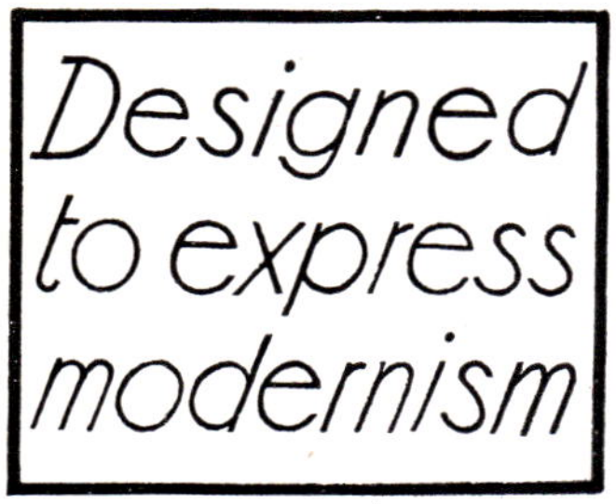

11. Sans serif "Gothic" letters exemplify the simplicity and avoidance of non-essentials that characterize everything modern...

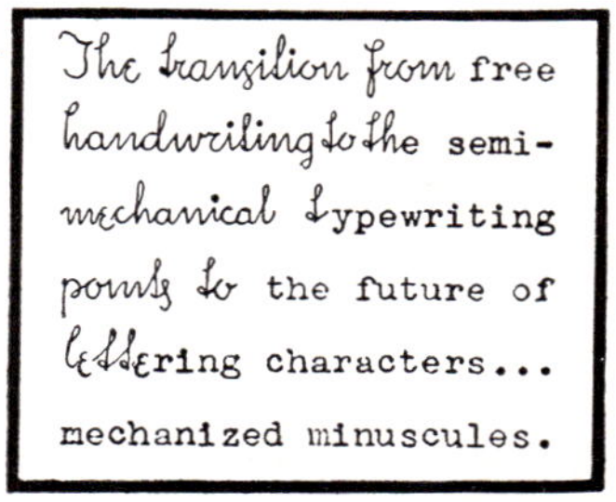

12. Typewritten lettering may point to the form toward which most alphabets are now developing — a hand-controlled mechanical script

DESIGN　　　　　9

WRITING and ITALICS

*a b c d e f g h i
j k l m n o p q r
s t u v w x y z*

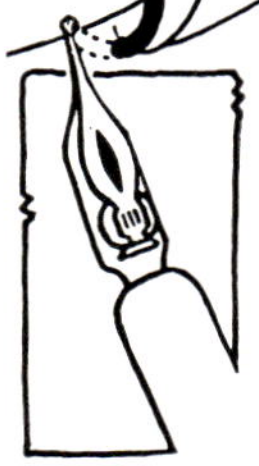

1. THE SLANT AND GENERAL SHAPE OF LETTERS IN ITALICS AND WRITING ARE SIMILAR.
2. THE THICKNESS IS DEPENDENT ON THE TOOL USED.
3. MOST LETTERS HAVE "O" OR "I" FORM IN COMMON~

a b e f g h l m n etc.

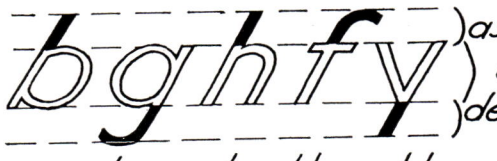
) ascender: upper part of letter
) waist: major part of letter
) descender: lower part of letter

variety can be obtained by exaggerating both the ascenders and the descenders.

MATERIALS: graph paper, ball-pointed lettering pen and India ink are necessary. The Tankpen, number 15 is also good. Practice is essential to success.

GRAPHIC

CLASSIC WRITING

E glie' manifesto Egregio lettore, che' le' lettere' Cancellaresche sono de uarie sorti, si come poi ueder nelle scritte tabelle, le quali to scritto con mesura e arte, Et per satisfatione de' cui apitisse una sorte, et cui unaltra, Io to scritto questa altra uariatione de lettere la qual uolendo imparare osserua la regula del sottoscritto Alphabeto:

A a. b. c. d. e e. ff. g. h. i. k. l. m. n. o. p p.
. q. g. r. s. t. u. x. y. z. &.

Le lettere cancellaresche sopranominate se fanno tonde longe large tratizzate e non tratizate ET per che io to scritto questa uariacione de lettera la qual imparerai secundo li nostri precetti et opere

A a a b. c. d. e. f. g. h. i. k. l. m. n. o. p q. r. s. t. u. x. y. z. &.

PAGE OF WRITING from Tagliente, *Opera che Insigna a Scrivere*, Venice, 1524; a beautiful example of free lettering showing discriminate use of decorative swirls. (Victoria and Albert Museum, London.)

DESIGN 11

ROMAN ALPHABET

abcdefghi
jklmnopq
rstuvwxyz
ABCDEFG
HIJKLMN
OPQRSTU
VWXYZ&1
23456789

BUILT-UP LETTERS; OUTLINE WITH PEN, THEN FILL IN (see 'a')

12 — GRAPHIC

BLACK-FACE GOTHIC

𝔄𝔄𝐴𝐴𝐴 𝔥𝔥𝔥𝔥· 𝔰𝔰𝔰𝔰𝔰𝔰
𝔅𝔅𝔅𝔅𝔅 𝔍𝔍𝔍𝔍𝔍· 𝔗𝔗𝔗𝔗𝔗
ℭℭℭℭℭ· 𝔎𝔎𝔎𝔏𝔏 𝔘𝔘𝔙𝔙·
𝔇𝔇𝔇𝔇𝔇 𝔐𝔐𝔐𝔐𝔐 𝔚𝔚𝔚𝔚
𝔈𝔈𝔈𝔈𝔈 𝔑𝔑𝔑𝔒𝔒 𝔛𝔛𝔜𝔜𝔜·
𝔉𝔉𝔉𝔉𝔉𝔉 𝔓𝔓𝔓𝔔𝔔𝔲 𝔍𝔍𝔍𝔍𝔍𝔍
𝔊𝔊𝔊𝔊𝔊 𝔑𝔑𝔑𝔑𝔨

VARIATIONS OF GOTHIC 'CAPS'
BY PROFESSOR RUDOLF KOCH

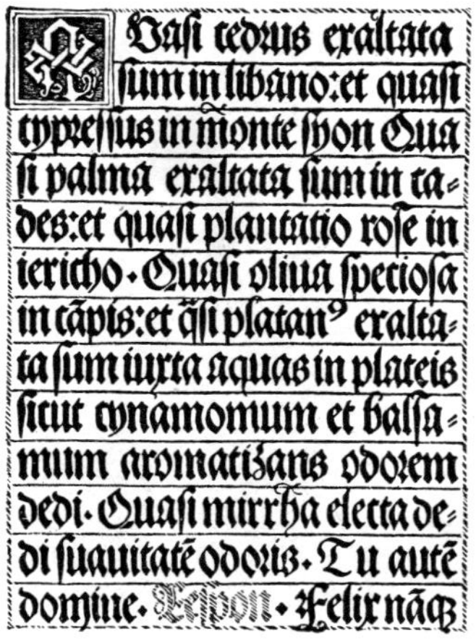

abcdefghijklmn
opqrstuvwxyz:

16TH CENTURY GERMAN BLACK-FACE GOTHIC BY A. DÜRER

MODERN MODIFIED, BLACK-FACE GOTHIC BY H. RHODE

DESIGN ═══════ 13

1, 3, and 4, Robert Foster, Walt Harris, and Friedrich Heinrichsen, respectively, for "Inness Alphabet." (*Courtesy of Century-Standard Vincent Edward, New York.*) 2. Willi Schumann, for Wezel & Naumann A. G., Leipzig. 5. Eric Gill, England. (*Courtesy of Arts et Métiers Graphiques, Paris.*)

SPACING

LETTERS AND NOT LETTERS

GOOD TASTE AND DISCRIMINATING EYE — *NOT THE RULER* — SHOULD BE THE CRITERIA OF SPACING BETWEEN LETTERS, WORDS, LINES, TEXT, AND BACKGROUND AREAS. STRAIGHT, CLOSED LETTERS (H, I, M, N, ETC.) SHOULD BE PLACED FARTHER APART THAN "OPEN" LETTERS, (A, C, J, L, T, ETC.). E.G. MNEMONIC

"RIVERS" BETWEEN WORDS IN A PARAGRAPH DESTROY THE UNITY OF THE LETTERED MASS AS THIS ILLUSTRATES → ←

 For a centered effect, the optical center, (a), is used instead of the measured one, (b).

a.   b

A·C·G·O·Q·S·J·N·U·V·W extend either above or below the guide lines, as indicated; otherwise they seem not "to line up"

A·CLOSED·ARRANGEMENT· ADDS·TONE·TO·THE·LETTER· ED·MASS·&·HARMONIZES WITH·A·HEAVY·DESIGN

WIDE·INTERLINEAR·SPAC

ING·LENDS·STYLE·TO·THE

LETTERED·COMPOSITION

c   d

 fig. e, f, g, show relation of letters to a square: like 'E' are B·F·J·L·P·S;  like 'A' are D·H·K·N·R· T·U·V·X·Y·Z; like 'W', C·G·M·O·Q

e   f   g

DESIGN ═══════════ 15

APPROPRIATENESS

fig. 1 Cancellation stamps (courtesy German Reichspostminister); as simple, legible, and decorative as the purpose demands.

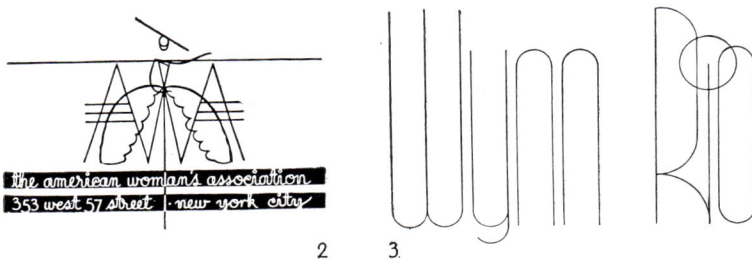

2.   3.

4.

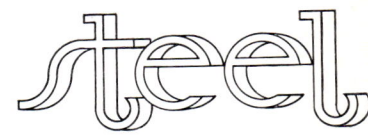

Creative lettering ought to convey, in its very construction, the character of the object it seeks to describe. The strength of steel, the delicacy of perfume, and the massiveness of weight are inherent in *appropriate* letters.

2-3 .. Appropriate use of dainty, well-proportioned letters. (Courtesy George Switzer, artist.)

4 ... Designed for a motorcycle company, the letters give some idea of the speed of the article advertised. (Courtesy Reimann School Berlin.)

5 ... Letters, as clear-cut and as crisp as Steel itself..

16 ———————————————— GRAPHIC

APPLICATION. ABOVE, left: *Das Insel Schiff*, by E. R. Weiss; lettering dominant. (*Poeschel & Trepte, Leipzig.*) Right: Prof. Hermann Virl; lettering subordinated to decoration. (*From Ehmcke's "Das Zelt," Munich.*) BELOW, left: Max Fritz; an all-lettered design. (*From Ehmcke's "Das Zelt."*) Right: Morris Goldsholle; a student's solution. Original colors were black, yellow, and gold. (*Abraham Lincoln High School, Brooklyn.*)

DESIGN

INVENTIVENESS

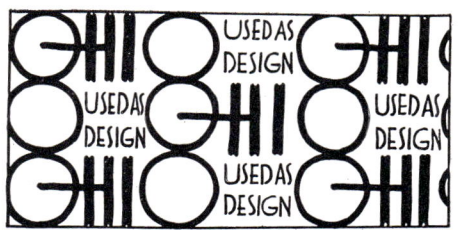 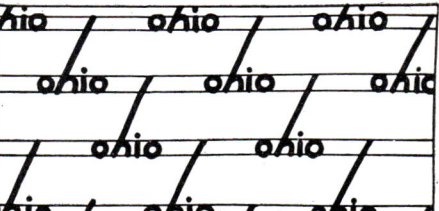

PATTERN is often best obtained by emphasizing and by repeating certain lettering-forms, as above.

MONOGRAMS: frequent repetition, limited appeal and supplementary information permit letter-combinations which are unique and not always easily intelligible.

WESTMINSTER PRESS · GIMMI & CO., ZURICH · MUSTER-MESSE, LEIPZIG · FUTURO FILM - HEFTER · VERLAG RECKENDORF

FARRAR·RINEHART · PROF. F. H. EHMCKE · OTTO V. HOLTEN

SEIBERLING CO. · A. CECIL WADE · OLEG ZINGHER · 'MAX' CLOTHES - FRIEND · "W.M."-WADE

END-PIECES ∮ DECORATIVE UNITS ∮ ORNAMENTS ∮

These are most successful when open like lettering... The use of the lettering pen helps to relate lettering and decoration.

18 GRAPHIC

1. From Ehmcke's *Das Zelt*, Munich. 2 and 6. Courtesy of Heintze & Blanckertz, Berlin. 3 and 4. Elsnerdruck, Berlin. 5. Cryptogram by Andreas Niessen, Berlin. 7. Savings bank motto by Charal, Berlin.

DESIGN 19

INVENTIVENESS

STUDENTS' WORK. The grained effect is obtained by working with a crayon on rough paper. (*Courtesy of Prof. Sallie B. Tannahill, Chairman of the Art Department, Teachers College, Columbia University, New York City.*)

20 ══════════════════════════════ GRAPHIC

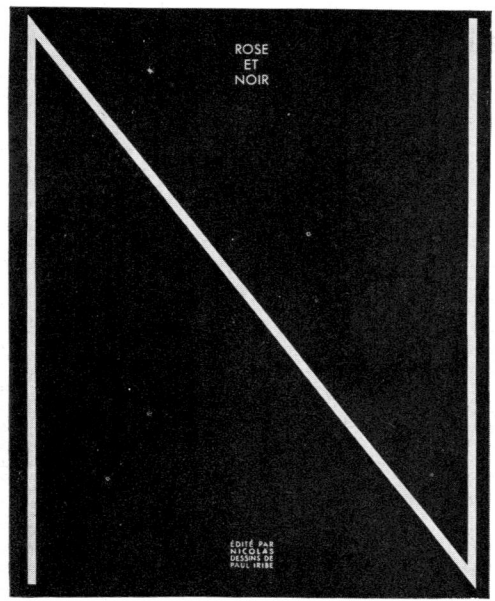
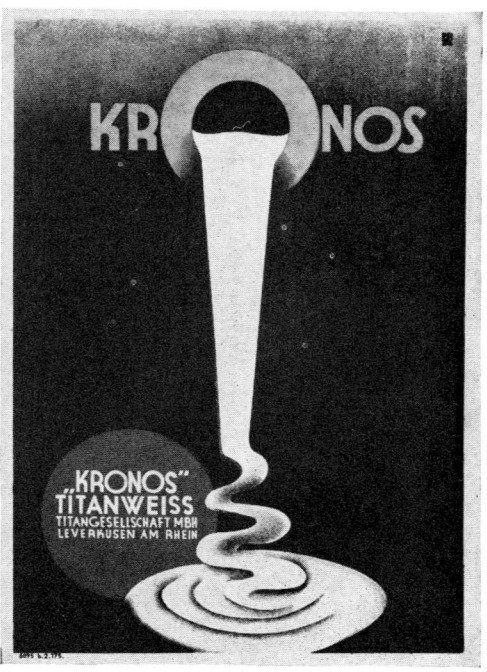

POSTER-LIKE announcements in which lettering plays the dominant role. Designed by Iribe, Erbe, Shep, and Mondaini. (*Courtesy of Draeger Frères, Titangesellschaft, Baynard Press, and Milan Fair, respectively.*)

COVER FOR *Grafika*, leading organ of Polish graphicists, which attains dignity by its simplicity, its architectural plan, and its disposition of lettering. (*Designed by W. Suwalski, student of Graphic Industries School, Warsaw.*)

DYNAMIC BOOKLET cover by Paul Iribe showing striking use of diagonal line with script lettering excellently juxtaposed. (*Courtesy of Draeger Frères, Paris.*)

DESIGN 23

HERALDIC TRADE-MARKS: 1. Haus Neuerburg, Prof. Hadank. 2. Pynson's device. 3. George W. Jones, A. A. Turbayne. 4. Curwen Press, Percy Smith. 5. Cluett, Peabody & Company. 6. City of Cologne, A. Niessen. 7. The Baynard Press, Fred Richards. 8. A student, courtesy of Heintze & Blanckertz. 9. Wezel & Naumann, Schulpig. 10. Joseph Feinhals, Prof. Ehmcke. 11. Eugen Diederich.

GRAPHIC

TRADE-MARKS: 1. Rupprecht Press, Prof. Ehmcke. 2. Charal. 3. Rissling & Rissling, Friend. 4. A. J. Petroleum Industry, Charal. 5. North German Lloyd. 6. F. Wolff & Son, Elsnerdruck. 7. Weber & Heilbronner, Hans Schleger (Zeró). 8. Deutsche Ostmesse Königsberg, Charal. 9. Union of German Advertising Artists, Schulpig. 10. John of Cologne and Jenson; earliest printer's mark. Courtesy of Lanston Monotype. 11. Universum Film A. G., Bernhard. 12. American Printer, Foster.

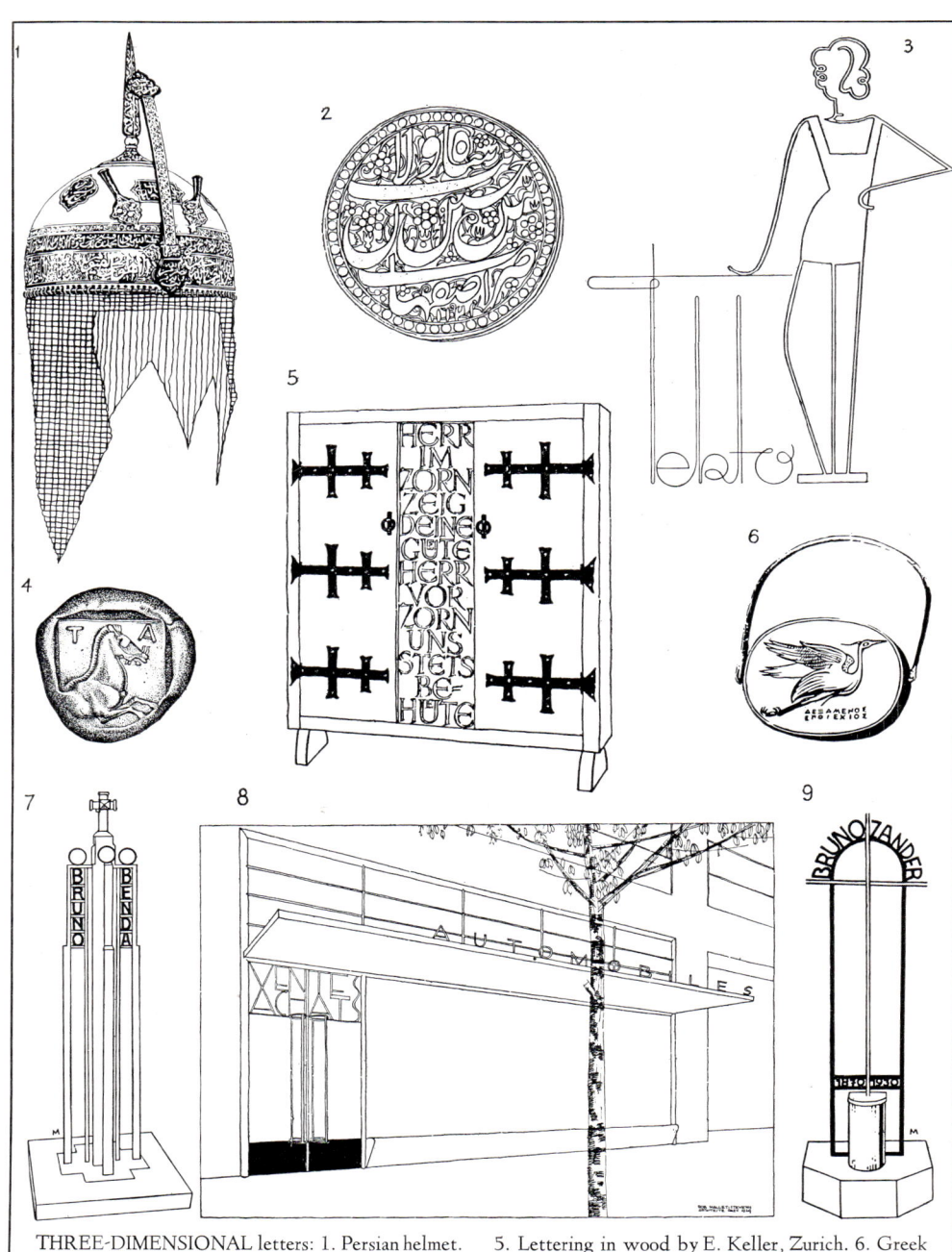

THREE-DIMENSIONAL letters: 1. Persian helmet. (*Metropolitan Museum of Art, New York.*) 2. Eighteenth century Persian silver coin with rhythmic lettering. 3. Wrought-metal display by Walter Holz, Berlin. 4. Greek coin. (*Metropolitan Museum of Art, New York.*) 5. Lettering in wood by E. Keller, Zurich. 6. Greek cameo by Dexamenos. (*Hermitage, Leningrad.*) 7 and 9. Grave markers by Land and Brum, respectively. (*Heintze & Blanckertz.*) 8. Shop front by Robert Mallet-Stevens, with cutout letters. (*Devambez, Paris.*)

26 GRAPHIC

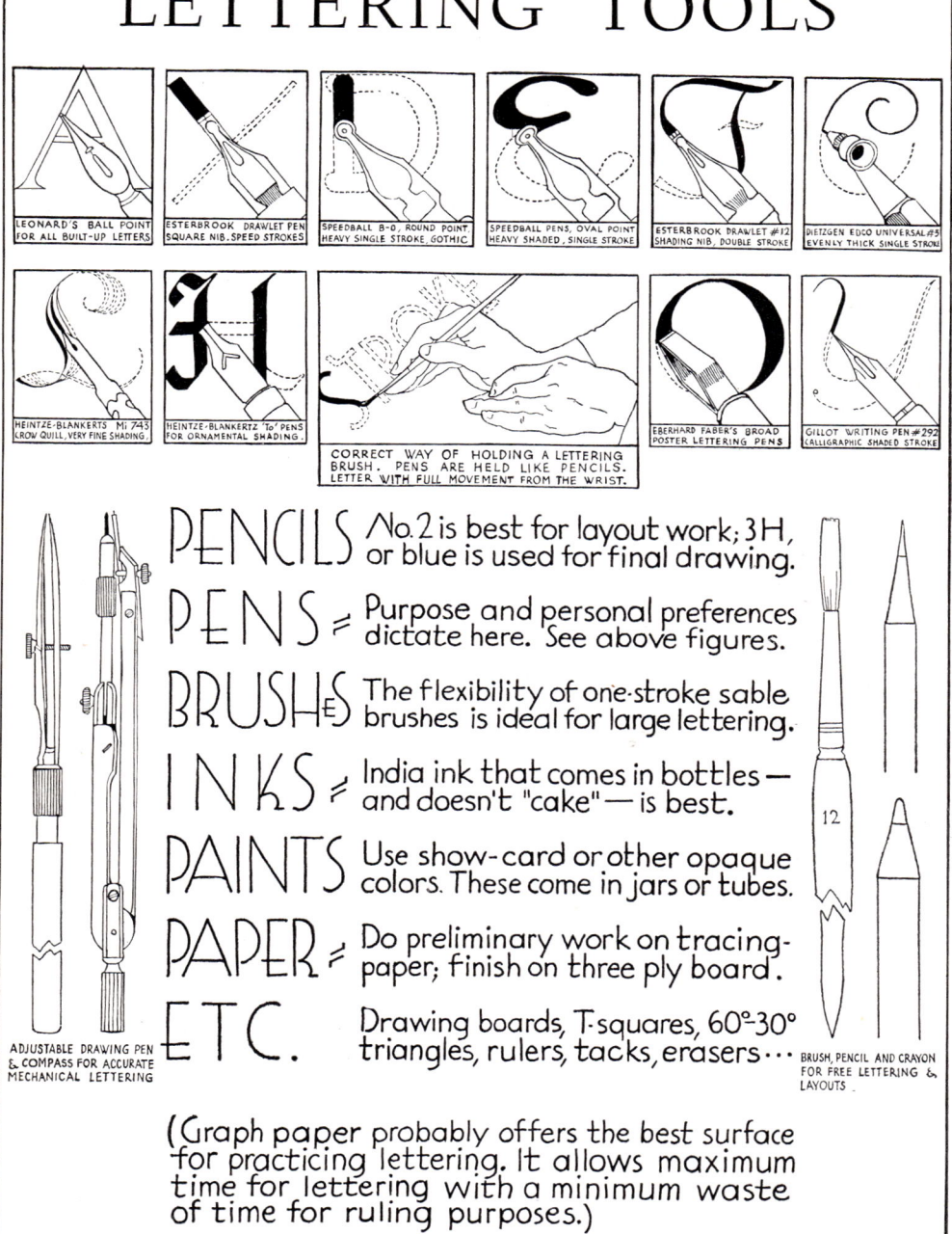

LETTERING TOOLS

- LEONARD'S BALL POINT FOR ALL BUILT-UP LETTERS
- ESTERBROOK DRAWLET PEN SQUARE NIB, SPEED STROKES
- SPEEDBALL B-0, ROUND POINT HEAVY SINGLE STROKE, GOTHIC
- SPEEDBALL PENS, OVAL POINT HEAVY SHADED, SINGLE STROKE
- ESTERBROOK DRAWLET #12 SHADING NIB, DOUBLE STROKE
- DIETZGEN EDCO UNIVERSAL #5 EVENLY THICK SINGLE STROKE
- HEINTZE-BLANKERTS Mi 743 CROW QUILL, VERY FINE SHADING
- HEINTZE-BLANKERTZ 'to' PENS FOR ORNAMENTAL SHADING
- CORRECT WAY OF HOLDING A LETTERING BRUSH. PENS ARE HELD LIKE PENCILS. LETTER WITH FULL MOVEMENT FROM THE WRIST.
- EBERHARD FABER'S BROAD POSTER LETTERING PENS
- GILLOT WRITING PEN #292 CALLIGRAPHIC SHADED STROKE

PENCILS No. 2 is best for layout work; 3H, or blue is used for final drawing.

PENS Purpose and personal preferences dictate here. See above figures.

BRUSHES The flexibility of one-stroke sable brushes is ideal for large lettering.

INKS India ink that comes in bottles — and doesn't "cake" — is best.

PAINTS Use show-card or other opaque colors. These come in jars or tubes.

PAPER Do preliminary work on tracing-paper; finish on three ply board.

ETC. Drawing boards, T-squares, 60°-30° triangles, rulers, tacks, erasers...

ADJUSTABLE DRAWING PEN & COMPASS FOR ACCURATE MECHANICAL LETTERING

BRUSH, PENCIL AND CRAYON FOR FREE LETTERING & LAYOUTS

(Graph paper probably offers the best surface for practicing lettering. It allows maximum time for lettering with a minimum waste of time for ruling purposes.)

DESIGN

LETTERING PROBLEM

Exhibition of Graphic Arts in the Lincoln Round Hall on September 2 1:00 to 5:00

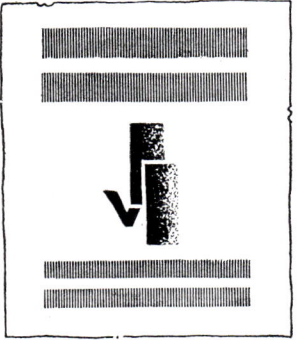

a. Material for poster.   b. Dark and light plan..   c. Formal-static layout..

1. Many dark and light schemes—in proportion to the final announcement—should be tried before finishing a poster.

2. Emphasize important ideas by using an extra color, by suitable spacing or by subordinating minor information by using smaller lettering.

3. A simple silhouette (see fig 'b') is easier to read than an irregular one.

4. Unnecessary punctuation may be omitted; and phrases may replace sentences.

5. Use soft pencil (2) and tracing paper to design your layouts.

d.

6. Fig 'd' is an informal-dynamic design. A plan off the vertical tends to suggest movement and hence has strong attraction-value.

28   GRAPHIC

PRINTING CHAPTER 2

dicens loqueris deus ego sum coram
interficientibz te cū sis homo τ nō de9
In manu occidentiū te morte incircū-
cisoɀ morieris:in manu alienoɀ: qa
ego locut9 sum ait dns deus. Et sact9
est sermo dnī ad me dicens. Fili hoīs
leua planctum sup regem tyri et dice-
ri. Hec dicit domin9 deus. Tu signacu-
lum similitudinis plenus sapientia
pfectus decore:in delicijs paradisi dī
fuisti. Omnis lapis pciosus opercmē-
tum tuū: sardius thopazius τ iaspis
crisolitus et onix τ berillus saphirus
et carbunculus τ smaragdus. Aurū
quoqɀ decoris tui τ foramina tua in
die qua conditus es pparata sunt. Tu
cherub extentus et pregens: τ posui te
in mōte sancto dei. In medio lapidū
ignitorū ambulasti: perfectus in vijs
tuis a die conditionis tue: donec in-
uenta est iniquitas in te. In multitudine negociationis tue repleta sunt
interiora tua iniquitate τ peccasti: et
eieci te de mōte dei:τ pdidi te o cherub
protegens de medio lapidū ignitorū.
Et eleuatum est cor tuū in decore tuo.
Perdidi sapientia tuā in decore tuo:
in terrā pieci te: ante faciem regū dedi
te ut cernerēt te. In multitudine iniqui
tatū tuarū τ iniquitate negociationis
tue polluisti sanctificationē tuā. Pro-
ducam ergo ignem de medio tui qui
comedat te: τ dabo te in cinerem sup
terrā in conspectu omniū videntiū te.
Omnes qui viderint te in gentibus
obstupescent sup te. Nichili factus es:
et non eris in pperuum. Et factus est
sermo dnī ad me dicens. Fili hominis:
pone faciē tuā contra sydonem τ phetabis de ea:τ dices. Hec dicit domin9
deus. Ecce ego ad te sydon et gloria-
bor ī medio tui:τ scient quia ego dns

cum fecero in ea iudicia: τ sanctificat9
fuero in ea. Et immittā ei pestilentiā et
sanguinē in plateis eius: et corruent
interfecti in medio eius gladio p circu-
itum: τ scient quia ego domin9. Et nō
erit ultra domui israhel offendiculū
amaritudinis et spina dolorem infe-
rens undiqɀ per circuitū eorū qui adū-
santur eis: et scient quia ego domin9
deus. Hec dicit domin9 deus. Quādo
congregauero domū israhel de pplis
in qbus dispsi sunt sanctificabor ī eis
corā gētibz:τ habitabūt ī terra sua quā
dedi seruo meo iacob:τ habitabūt in
ea securi. Et edificabūt domos τ plā-
tabūt vineas: τ habitabūt confidēter
cum fecero iudicia in omnibus q ad-
uersantur eis p circuitū: τ scient quia
ego dominus deus eorū. XXIX
In anno decimo in duodecimo mēse
una die mensis factū est verbū dnī ad
me dicens. Fili hominis pone faciem
tuā contra pharaonem regem egipti:
et phetabis de eo:τ de egipto uniūsa
loquere τ dices. Hec dicit domin9 de9.
Ecce ego ad te pharao rex egipti dra-
co magne q cubas in medio fluminū
tuorū τ dicis. meus est fluuius:τ ego
feci memetipm. Et ponā frenū ī maxil-
lis tuis:τ cōglutinabo pisces fluminū
tuorū squamis tuis. Et extraham te
de medio fluminū tuorū: et uniūsi pisces tui squamis tuis adherebūt. Et p-
iciā te in desertū: τ omnes pisces flumi-
nis tui. Super faciem terre cades. Nō
colligeris: neqɀ congregaberis. Bestijs
terre τ volatilibus celi dedi te ad deuo-
randum: τ scient omnes habitatores
egipti quia ego domin9. Pro eo qɀ fuisti baculus arundineus domui israhel quādo apphenderunt te manu et
confract9 es τ lacerasti omnē humerū

PRINTING

PRINTING FROM types as we now know it was developed by Gutenberg after 1450. He sought, undoubtedly, to imitate the scribe-written books and possibly to sell the printed variety at prices that the calligraphic examples of that time commanded. Relief printing had been known to the Chinese before 900 A.D., as were paper and carbon ink, but it was not until after Gutenberg's discovery that metal type was cast singly from molds.

In the recording of man's ideas the natural progression seems to have been from pictorial woodcut (xylograph) to blocks of wood with words cut upon their surfaces, followed finally by the isolation and cutting of the individual letters by Gutenberg. The prevailing face was the black-face Gothic. Dark and architectural in appearance, this style and its immediate successors have been almost entirely superseded by the lighter Roman designs that first appeared in Jenson's books about 1470. It is from these that all modern Roman types are said to derive, despite the near perfection of such masterpieces of Gothic printing as the Gutenberg Bibles. The minor changes that have modified these Roman prototypes have been due to the tools used and to the individual preferences or limitations of the designers. Thus, when seventeenth century copper engravers used a burin or graver instead of a pen, a fine crisp letter resulted, and when the tools used were the compass, ruler, and triangle, the so-called constructivistic, modern type materialized. Now designers are striving to impress on type something of the strength and conciseness which we associate with still another type-maker's tool, the steel punch cutter. "Honesty to materials" has been found as desirable in type designing as it has proved to be in every art.

The twenty-three capital letters which formed the earliest Latin alphabet were evolved from Greek and Phoenician examples. The phonetic distinctions associated with the letters J, U, and W were seventeenth and eighteenth

CHAPTER DECORATION: Removal notice designed by Piero Bernardini for Bertieri & Vanzetti, Milan.
CHAPTER FRONTISPIECE: A page from the 42-line Gutenberg Bible, from an original owned by Edward L. Stone, Roanoke, Va. This early typographic creation has not been excelled in the four hundred years intervening.

ABCDEF
GIMPRS

THE DIGNIFIED, well-proportioned Roman letters of the Trajan column have been an inspiration to letterers and type designers and the source of many modern type faces.

century accessions. Together, they give us the twenty-six capitals that are part of every type case. Of type, a craftsman once said: "With twenty-five soldiers of lead, I have conquered the world." With the aid of the latest recruit, the W, as much might be said today.

Admitting that new times and new conditions demand new solutions, typographers, who heretofore designed letters exclusively for book composition, now distinguish between body type and display type, or plan for both purposes. Types, whatever their style, have much in common. All are type-high, .918 inch in America from foot to printing surface. The faces, which run the gamut of styles, rest on bodies which are fairly well standardized. These in turn are arranged in type cases in much the same layout both here and abroad. Even the *point* system of measurement used in America, where seventy-two points approximately equal an inch, is used in the foreign type which is popular enough to have international demand.

The machine with which type is impressed on paper is called a printing press. This was changed in form from a lever-and-screw propelled wooden

TWO LINES from *Weltgericht*, original size, earliest Gutenberg example. Note how closely these first types resembled manuscript writing. (*Gutenberg Museum, Mainz.*)

THE INDULGENCE of Nicholas V, printed in Mainz in 1454, is considered by many to be the earliest printed document to have a printed date. It is institutional typography of a high order. (*Museum Meermanno, The Hague.*)

press which, in 1480, was capable of printing some three hundred pages a day to Koenig's power-driven cylinder press which in 1814 was able to make over a thousand impressions an hour. Later followed the form similar to the Washington hand press in which pressure was applied by a lever on to a metal bed which was moved under and out of the platen as the printing progressed. These inventions and that of a paper-making machine by the Foudrinier Brothers (1803), Hoe's cylinder press (1827), and Gordon's platen press (about 1838) went a long way toward increasing the number of impressions a minute. Then Mergenthaler's linotype machine (1884-1885), which sets one-line slugs utilizing a keyboard similar to a typewriter, and Lanston's monotype (1888), which sets type singly through a perforated roll, as in a pianola, were invented. Intertype, a later invention, is similar to the linotype in style and use and, like it, casts lines of type on slugs. These and other keyboard typesetting machines make it possible to compose type fast enough to keep up with the speed dictated by the capacity of the presses. They are able to set type three to six times as fast as the hand compositor.

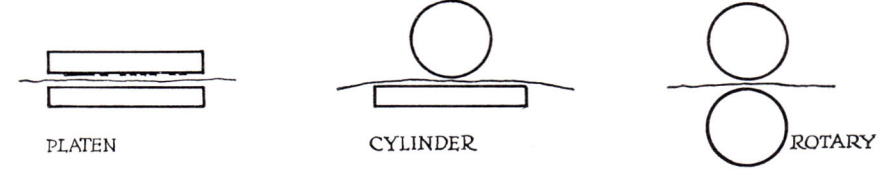

PLATEN   CYLINDER   ROTARY

These sketches give a diagrammatic picture of the three forms of pressure which are most commonly used in the production of printing. The source of motivation, however, may be either hand power or machine power.

DESIGN 33

GUTENBERG TAKING the first proof, engraved after a painting by Hillemacher. (*Courtesy New York Public Library.*) It shows with what limited means and unlimited devotion printer-artists created their work.

TYPE WAS MADE TO READ *by* Berton Braley

"Type," said the Foreman, "was made to read,
And that is a maxim it's well to heed,
For the printer frequently gets a start
With a craze for 'beauty,' a bug for 'art,'
Which holds him fast in a fearful gripe
And keeps him trying mad stunts with type,
With seventeen fonts and seventy styles
And borders by thousands and rules by miles.

"Type," said the Foreman, "was made to read,
But the printer, oftentimes, in his greed
For novel features and 'class' and 'tone,'
Forgets this fact he has always known
And sends out work that is fine to see
As 'smart' and 'natty' as it can be,
A job with a swagger and high-bred look,
But hard to read as a Chinese book!

"Type," said the Foreman, "was made to read,
And that should serve as the printers' creed,
For work on the Linotype machine
Or hand-set jobs should be clear and clean,
Not ornamental, obscure, bizarre,
Composed of all of the fonts there are,
But simple, legible, quiet, plain,
A joy alike to the eye and brain!

"For art in printing is not the way
Of wild extravagance, weird display,
But rather the unobtrusive thrall
Of type that gives you no shock at all,
But draws your eyes to the page with zest
And holds your mind to the thought expressed;
We must keep ourselves to this simple creed,
Type was made—and is meant—to READ!"

(*Written for and published in the Linotype Bulletin for March, 1915. Courtesy Mergenthaler Linotype Company, Brooklyn.*)

MAJOR TYPE STYLES

Earl
72 point Caslon Old Style showing wedge-shaped serifs and letters of generous width. The influence of pen construction is obvious.

Earl
72 point Bodoni modern showing sharp and precise serifs, condensed in proportion, and strong contrast between thick and thin parts—influence of the burin.

Earl
72 point Elegant Grotesk, sans serif, showing modern tendency in elimination of unessentials—influence of mechanical-drafting tools.

TYPE RULE

showing relationship of *point* to inch (72 points = 1 inch). Note that type size refers to height of face and shoulder, *not* of letter. In fact, the same sizes of different type faces frequently differ.

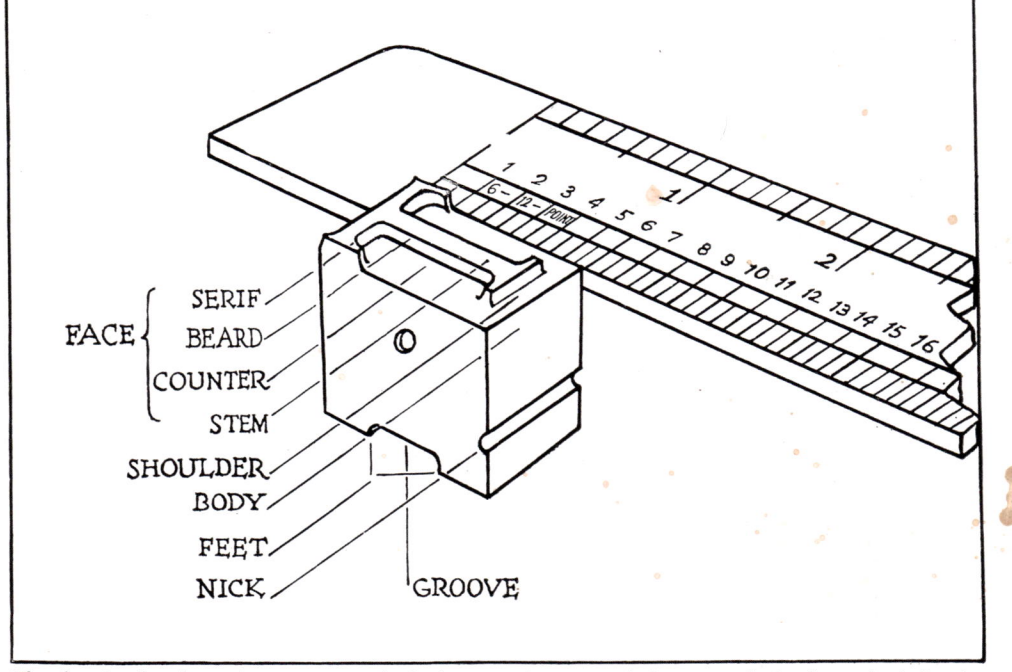

FACE { SERIF, BEARD, COUNTER, STEM } SHOULDER, BODY, FEET, NICK, GROOVE

The drawing by the authors represents both the type character and the type rule in almost facsimile size.

DESIGN 35

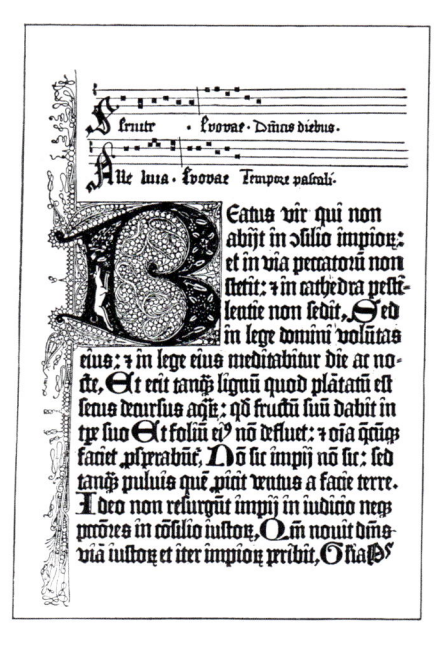

Since each casting furnishes new, clearly defined type in lieu of the familiar battered variety, much make-ready time is saved, and the wasteful process of substituting new for broken type is avoided. Even more time is saved by melting down the dead type matter (used type). Heretofore it had to be distributed.

Presses for relief printing are designed to give one of three forms of printing pressure. The commonest form is the platen, the so-called job press, where two flat surfaces are forced together. In the cylinder press the flat bed is still retained for the type, but the paper is fed around a cylinder. In the rotary machine, cylinders bearing type and paper are adjusted to produce the requisite pressure. This form is used in lithographic presses, where metal plates

ABOVE. Page from Gregorii Frates's *Herodotus*, 1494, showing how provision was made for initial letter H. (Victoria and Albert Museum, London.) CENTER. Page of Fust and Schoeffer's *Psalter*, 1457, characterized by a marked dependence on manuscript writing in use and disposition of initial. (Cuneo Press, Inc., Chicago.) BELOW. Four contemporary initial letter arrangements: *a* and *b* are correct solutions, *c* and *d* are decorative but incorrect.

FACING PAGE: From G. Savonarola, *Sermone della Oratione a M. A. d. S.*, Florence, circa 1497; a beautiful symphony of tonal quality. The indented decoration is a daring and successful departure from the more common oblong silhouette. Distinction within the limits of simple type and simple layout is no ordinary achievement. In its objectification of fine typographic design it has attained that timeless beauty that helps us to enjoy it as much today as it must have been enjoyed four hundred years ago. (Victoria and Albert Museum, London.)

a. Es war ein König von Kurneval mit Namen Markus, der hatte einmal lange mächtig

b. SIMPLE initial decorations which are definitely tied-up with the rest of the text are the best solution to

c. IT IS FOUND IN BOOKS THAT PURPORT TO WRITE ON GOOD BOOK DESIGN—THIS UNRELATIONSHIP BETWEEN INITIAL & TEXT.

d. THIS INITIAL is unsatisfactory. It does not "line-up" at all possible points (e.g. bottom of T)..

36 GRAPHIC

⸿ Sermone della oratione a.M.A.d.S. composto da frate Hieronymo da Ferrara dellordine de frati predicatori.
Prohemio.

Portet semper orare. Lucæ.xviii.cap. Auenga che la prouidentia di Dio sia ineffabile , & lauolōta īmutabile dilectissima ī Xp̄o Iesu madōna: nietedimeno il cōsigliare & fare puisione alle cose future & pregare iDio che ledispona bene & optimamente leriduca alloro destinato fine , nō er cosa uana: pche lomnipotēte Dio & imutabile nostro creatore non solamēte ha cō lasua infinita sapientia ordinato qual fine debba hauere ogni creatura : ma etiam ha disposto limezi per liquali debbe alpreordinato fine peruenire. Hauendo adunque iDio ordinato alla sua creatura rationale uno altissimo fine , ilquale er lauisione & fruitione della sua es

a

PSYCHE BORNE OFF BY ZE-
PHYRUS, DRAWN BY EDWARD
BURNE-JONES & ENGRAVED
BY WILLIAM MORRIS

now largely replace the former stone. By printing from the cylindrical plates on to a rubber blanket and by reprinting from the blanket, we obtain *offset* reproduction. Despite these ingenious devices, it has proved more difficult to surpass the handiwork of the mediaeval craftsman qualitatively than it has been to surpass him quantitatively. Perhaps the time will come when a need for excellence in workmanship elicits as many conferences and as much enthusiasm as are prompted by a desire for increase in wages and profits. However, the introduction of photomechanical processes has made available new techniques and new standards for which there is no comparable basis in the earlier centuries of printing.

Progress in typographic design has only recently attempted to parallel mechanical advancement in the field. The tenacity with which printing art has held to tradition can be shown in a small measure by some notes on initial letters. Originally, in the manuscript form, these were intended to serve as a device for varying the monotony of straight lettering, for adding color and contrast to the grayness of

ABOVE: ERHARD RATDOLT'S title page for the *Calendarium*, printed in Venice in 1476. BELOW: *Book of Hours* designed and printed by Geoffroy Tory in Paris in 1530. FACING PAGE: A William Morris page, with a Burne-Jones illustration, which carries about as much ornamentation as a fine page could possibly accommodate. The marginal whites are an essential antidote for the art work and a great aid in the legibility of the page.

DESIGN 39

THE STICK, a device for composing type to measure. Illustration was set entirely with type matter by Prof. Frans Marten, Königsberg. This demonstrates, incidentally, how well type and decoration of a type character combine. It substitutes the virile quality of the type line for the uneven scratches of the pen line.

written matter, and for pointing out chapter headings. With the invention of movable type, space was provided where initial decorations might be put in by hand. Later still, a small type — an H, for example — was printed where a large initial was to be made. Some illuminators used the small H for the purpose for which it was intended. Others, susceptible to the apparent perfection of the printed letter, decorated around the small type form with the poor result with which we are all familiar. To this day type founders still issue initial letters that are lost in a large, highly decorated box and that are totally unrelated to the letters with which they are supposed to form a word. Another foible, the contribution of psychologists, deserves mention. It was found by covering in turn the lower and upper half of lower- and upper-case letters, that the lower part of the lower cases was more legible than the corresponding part of the capitals. Therefore, it was concluded that lower cases ("l. c'.s") were more legible than capitals ("caps"). One wonders. Even if this were true, might it not be due rather to our greater familiarity with lower-case letters and to the greater spacing between solid lines of these letters than unleaded capitals permit? Some of the best uses of lower case and capitals have been those least true to rule, from which it may safely be deduced that in this era of a thousand legible types *how type is used* is just as important as *what type is used*. Precisely for this reason the authors agree with those schools of thought that emphasize type design over type identification.

BIFUR EMPHASIZES IN BOLD BARS THE CHARACTER OF EACH LETTER. THE LIGHT *filiforme* ADDS COLOR **LETAN**

AN UNUSUAL display type designed by Cassandre (A. Mouron) for Deberny et Peignot, Paris. It lends surprise and distinction to *brief* headlines or slogans. In its use, however, brevity is not a matter of choice.

In spite of individual expression in printing, due to the person's training or idiosyncrasies, there are certain principles that are generally accepted in practice. These are recommended for the guidance of the beginner, not for the limitation of the craftsman:

1. The rules of design—spacing, dominance, harmony, rhythm, variety, balance, etc.—that are true for lettering apply to type in equal measure.

2. That style of type and that layout should be used which does not attract to form, the attention that is desired for contents.

3. Lettering ought to be combined with type only when greater flexibility is needed than type alone can give.

4. Type harmonizes better with type and type matter than it does with process plates.

5. Type size is dependent on measure of line: The smaller the type the shorter the line must be. Leading permits greater license than is possible with solid type matter (the Pelican Press recommends from eight to thirteen words to a line). Type that is too large for a given measure results in a great many hyphenated words.

6. The width to which type is to be set should partly influence the choice of a face—wide, full letters like Goudy for a long measure; and narrow, almost condensed letters like Garamond for a short measure.

7. Familiar type ought to be used for body text. Familiar or eccentric type may be used for display. A short heading or a desire to challenge the reader will permit the eccentric; a long heading or an intention to inform only will require the familiar type.

8. Type should be appropriate to the purpose for which it is to be used and for the background in which it is to appear.

9. For a modernistic note it is wiser to use a readable though unusual layout than an unusual but illegible type.

10. The thick and thin strokes of type, as in Caslon, or the uniform thickness, as in Vogue, ought to influence the treatment of the drawing that may be used; e. g., the black letter and the woodcut go well together.

11. Decoration should be used sparingly—preferably to fulfill a real need. As previously suggested, type rule and decorative type units are the best forms of ornamentation to use with type. They have a blood relationship.

DESIGN

12. The more virile the type used the rougher the texture of the printing surface may be; dainty and small type dictates the use of smooth or semi-smooth paper. The obverse is also true.

13. When two colors are used in a layout, the lighter color should be set in a heavier type so that the tonal unity of the type mass is retained.

14. Every attempt should be made to keep the corners of the text, and especially the outside corners of facing pages, intact. This is why fine craftsmen seek to prevent a paragraph's opening on the upper or lower corner of even pages. Similarly, a short sentence in the upper or lower corner of odd pages mars the rectangular appearance of the text mass of the page.

15. The white space of the margins contributes as much quality or tone to a page as does the type itself.

Experience will dictate other principles that the craftsman may find desirable to observe.

Outstanding contributors to the development of type, besides Gutenberg, were Fust and Schoeffer of Germany (whose *Psalter* of 1457, on page 36, is a typographical monument that has remained a continued source of inspiration), Jenson (a Frenchman who added lower case to Roman caps), and

OMINOUS HOUSE

The door dark whispered woe, the panes blank fire,

The rearing gable like a reptile's head—

For fiend or nightmare would you fain inquire?

Enter, and hark the dithering of the dead!

A PAGE from a booklet *Emblems and Electra*, illustrated by W. A. Dwiggins, announcing a new type face "within the 'modern' family of type styles" designed by this letter-draftsman. In the original printing, the use of color rather than black prevents the illustration from overbalancing the text. (Copyright by Mergenthaler Linotype Company, Brooklyn, and the Saturday Review of Literature.)

Manutius (who introduced italics), Bodoni of Italy (designer of "modern" type); Froben of Switzerland and the Estiennes, Tory, and Didot of France. The Elzevirs of Holland and Caxton, Pynson, Caslon, Baskerville, and Morris of England were other masters. Contemporary designers of note are Goudy, Koch, Bernhard, Weiss, Ehmcke, Renner, Jones, Gill, and a host of others of great promise though not yet of so great a reputation.

    The plates in the book will better illustrate type and its potentialities than the text. Included among the examples of fine printing is the work of the students of the Leipziger Technikum für Buchdrucker, the Leicester College, the London and Birmingham Schools of Printing, and the Warsaw School of Graphic Arts. Such thorough training as these schools offer gives promise of a finer craftsmanship tomorrow than we have any reason to expect today. The plates and the legends tell their own story.

    Francis Meynell, in his stimulating booklet *Typography*, says of the implications of type letters: "... All the heights and depths and breadths of tangible and natural things—landscapes, sunsets, the scent of hay, the hum of bees, the beauty which belongs to eye-lids (and is falsely ascribed to eyes); all the immeasurable emotions and motions of the human mind, to which there seems no bound; ugly and terrible and mysterious thoughts and things as well as beautiful—all are compassed, restrained, ordered in a trifling jumble of letters. Twenty-six signs!"

IMPRESSION FROM a 72-point Erbar Grotesk slug, a Ludwig & Mayer type face ... (*Arrangement by the authors.*)

DESIGN

GARAMOND characters, a Ludlow type face of today, based on the Berner Specimen Sheet of 1592....

BERNER SPECIMEN Sheet and three lines of Garamond type, a successful modern adaptation. This illustrates better than words the interdependence of old and contemporary typographic art. (*Courtesy of the Ludlow Typograph Company, Chicago.*)

Fourscore and seven *years ago our fathers br* ought forth on this conti nent a new nation, conceive **d in liberty and dedic** ated to the propositio *n that all men are create* d equal. Now we are e ngaged in a great civ *il war, testing wheth* **er that nation, o** r any nation, so conceived a *nd so dedicated, can long e* ndure. We are met on a gr eat battlefield of tha *t war. We have co* me to dedicate a portio *n of that field as a final* resting-place of thos **e who here gav** e their lives that that NATION MIGHT LIVE. IT IS AL together fitting and prope *r that we should do this. But* in a large sense, we cannot *dedicate, we cannot conse* crate, we cannot ha llow this ground. T he brave men living a nd *dead who struggled* HERE HAVE CON secrated it, far abo ve our poor power to add or detract. The world will little **note, nor long re** member what we say here, but it can never f ORGET WHAT THEY DID HERE. IT IS FOR

VERSATILE

No one really needs the 68 type faces here used—yet it is certain that someone wants each. Versatility in type faces is only one advantage of the many that are yours when Beck-Gerlach does your composition and printing.

THE BECK-GERLACH PRINTING COMPANY

548 Commercial · Garfield 6763 · San Francisco

us, the living, rat her to be dedica TED HERE TO the unfinished work *which they who fought here have thus far so nobly advanced. I t is rather for us to be he re dedicated to the great* **task remaining be**

FORE US That from these honored dead we take in **CREASED DEV otion to that cau** se for which they gave th e last full measure of devotion. That we h ere highly resolve *that these dead shall not have*

died in vain. Tha *t this nation under God, shall hav* e a new birth of free dom and that governme *nt of the people, by the peopl* e, For the People E, SHALL NOT PERISH FROM **THE EARTH**

TYPE SPECIMEN sheet. A contemporary printer's presentation of a problem similar to Berner's broadside. To keep sixty-eight type faces subordinate to the design as a whole is indeed an accomplishment. While the example is splendidly appropriate for the purpose it serves, it is nevertheless worth remembering that the average printing creation is not a specimen sheet. It must emphasize thought, not type. (*Beck-Gerlach Printing Company.*)

DESIGN 45

ABCDEFGHIJKLMNOPQRST!
UVWXYZÆŒ ABCDEFGHIJJ
abcdefghijklmnopqrstuvwxyzeæœ
fiffflffiffl abcdefghijklmnopqrstuvw
12345 àê&ɛtffft.,;:''!?()[]— 67890

ABCDEFGHIJKLMNOPQR!
STUVWXYZÆŒ.ABCDEFG
abcdefghijklmnopqrstuvwxyzææ:fiff
flffifflàéê,abcdefghijklmnopqrstuvwx
12345 &ſſſſtſſɩ&,;:''!?[]() 67890

TWO FACING pages from *Monotype*, a Lanston Monotype Machine Company publication. They show Goudy's version of a sixteenth century Garamond type, and Bruce Rogers' ability to create a symphony with pure type matter. BELOW: A Lanston revival of a classic old face designed by Pierre Simon Fournier (1712-1768) and now used because of the condensed character of the type. It shows the timelessness of good design. (*Lanston Monotype Machine Company, London.*)

FACING PAGE: Above, two layouts using similar basic space divisions. Unity of type and decoration is obtained by repeating the line quality of the type in the decoration. Note the uniform grayness of the total mass in both examples. (Futura Light and Weiss Roman, respectively.) (*Bauer Type Foundry, Inc., New York.*) IN THE LAYOUT of the folder below, a dark spot is used to gain a punctuating note—emphasis—for the message. Compare the attraction value of this dark note in the Bertieri folder with the restrained character of the Bauer advertisements. (*Courtesy Bertieri, Milan.*)

46 GRAPHIC

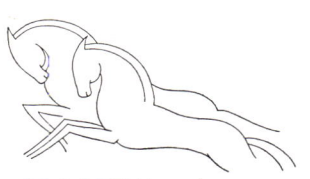

GRACEFUL and charming — simple and sincere are the silver pieces created by our skilled craftsmen who sense a keen delight in bringing their work to perfection. Spirited, rhythmic, sparkling is our civilization. And this modern production bearing the mark of the Diana Studios combines subdued mysterious beauty of silver with the subtle lines we call modern. The sculpturesque quality of every piece of exquisite silverware in our extensive display is evident, and quite in harmony with the exciting graduations of light grouped around it. Every piece is as different in appearance as one person from another and certainly a thorough spirit of simplicity pervades these fine pieces of silverware for the modern home. For your holiday gifts select from the exquisite Diana Collection, for few gifts have the long-lived charm and beauty. Whether it will be a decorative piece or a set of table silver, it will be received with pleasure. Any Diana creation of today will be amongst the heirlooms of tomorrow.

DIANA SILVER

MANUFACTURED BY THE DIANA STUDIOS · NEW YORK, N.Y.

The creations of the Diana Studios are on display and for sale at all prominent jewelers and department stores in your city.

WEISS ROMAN
ITALIC, BOLD AND INITIALS

The Weiss Family is the greatest creation of Germany's most celebrated designer of type faces. Keenly, incisively modern, it nevertheless evokes a subtle memory of the noble past. No type is so dignified, yet so fresh and youthful. No type is so expressive of

The perfect type-companion for any quality product

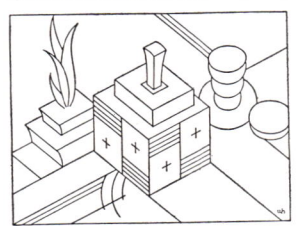

luxurious things, yet so simple and unassuming. • If you are plotting a super-campaign for a quality product...an expensive multi-cylindered motor car...a delicate French perfume...or perhaps a sophisticated accessory of the feminine boudoir...one of the Weiss faces will magically convey the intimate and elusive personality of your subject. • Specimen showings of this group, in roman, italic, bold and initials, will be forwarded upon request.

THE BAUER TYPE FOUNDRY · INC
TWO THIRTY-FIVE EAST FORTY-FIFTH STREET · NEW YORK CITY

Gli stampati di Bertieri non invecchiano....

DESIGN ══════════════ 47

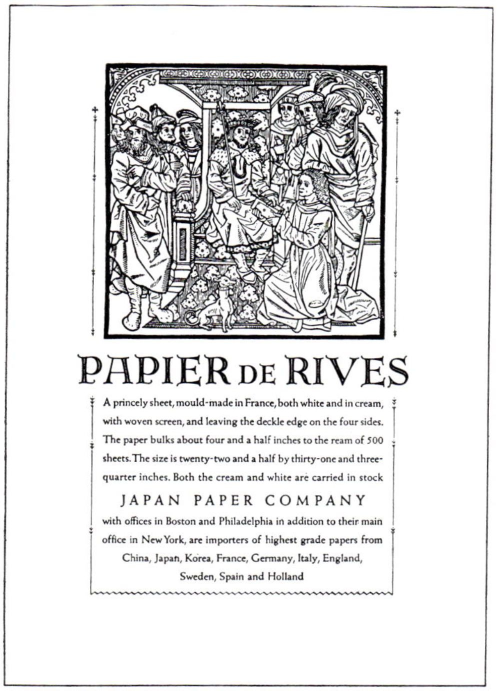

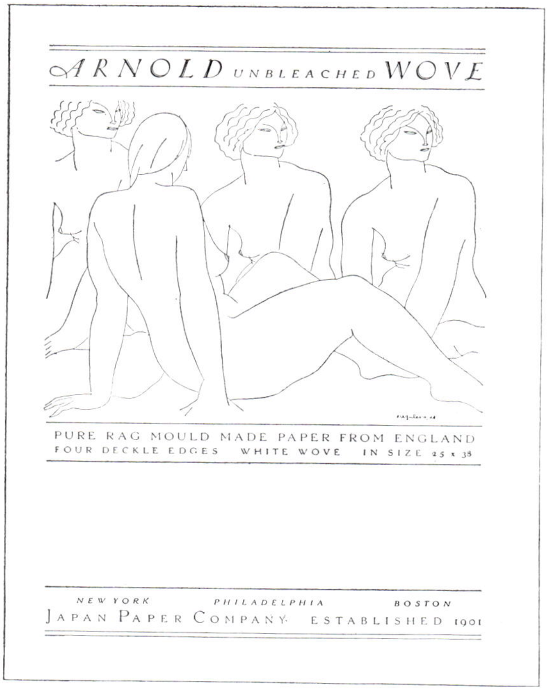

THREE ADVERTISING folders for a paper house that recognizes art as a business aid. (*Japan Paper Company, New York.*) PAPIER DE RIVES: Title set in Erbar type; text in a face designed by E. R. Weiss; woodcut from a fifteenth century French book. Designed and arranged by Pynson Printers, New York. The Erbar type serves as a transitional note between the fifteenth century design and the twentieth century type. LOMBARDIA "CREMONA": Original printed by John Henry Nash, San Francisco, from Caslon Old Style types and Caslon Old Style initial. It shows that modern designers do not feel that the twentieth century necessarily has a monopoly on art motifs.

ARNOLD WOVE: Title in Koch Antiqua; text in Bernhard, cast in Germany; drawing by Jean Negulesco. Planned and produced by Pynson Printers. The contour line of the figures carries out the light key of the layout as a whole. The repetition of the figure forms in the drawing evokes the same response as does the repetition of a theme in music.

FACING PAGE: Mailer designed by Walter Dorwin Teague for and produced by Pynson Printers. The definite character of the border and headpiece shows a fine understanding of the like quality in the type used (Garamond Old Style). The whole is characterized by good use of line.

RICHARD PYNSON — MASTER PRINTER

RICHARD PYNSON
PRINTER TO HIS MAJESTY KING HENRY VIII 1510-1529

LIKE so many of the early "English" printers, Richard Pynson was not an Englishman. The time and circumstances of his emigration from his native Normandy are uncertain. A theory that he was brought as an employé of Caxton is founded chiefly on a reference in Pynson's introduction to his edition of the *Canterbury Tales:* *"whiche boke diligently ouirsen & duely examined by the pollitike reason and ouirsight of my worshipful master william Caxton."* But as this obviously paraphrases a statement in the introduction to Caxton's original edition of the same work, it would seem to be merely an acknowledgment (unusually candid for the period) of the source of Pynson's text, together with a graceful compliment to a late illustrious colleague.

The probabilities are that Pynson came to London in 1490, thirteen years after Caxton began to print there, and that he came from Rouen. "Wherever he came from," says Mr. Henry R. Plomer in his *Short History of*

PORTRAIT REPRODUCED FROM AMES' "TYPOGRAPHICAL ANTIQUITIES"

The Restful Car

*„The supreme combination of
all that is fine in motor cars."*

Luxury. The improved Packard Eight is the supremely luxurious car. It is designed and built for those favored few who may and do demand the comfort and ease of their own drawing rooms in motor travel. Fast or slow, flashing through the maze of metropolitan congestion, or smoothly annihilating distance at almost aircraft speed in the open, Packard passengers know the luxury of truly restful transportation. The graceful beauty of Packard lines, the roominess of the car's interior, the quiet good taste of its upholstery and appointments, the silent ease of motion, and the sense of security which comes with tremendous power under sure control — all contribute to the mental satisfaction and the physical repose of the Packard Eight owner.

PACKARD
ASK THE MAN WHO OWNS ONE

Fancier typographic compositions than this one have been made, but more satisfactory ones rarely. See page 51.

BENVENUTO CELLINI

TWO EXAMPLES of type arrangement. In the Cellini folder, the type (Caslon Old Face Open) is subordinated to the picture. Decorative line and outline type are dovetailed into a single related unity. Movement is contributed to an otherwise formal design by the diagonal line of the tipped pitcher. (*Printing House of Rudge, New York City.*)

FACING PAGE: While type plays the major role here, a small decorative unit lends interest to the display. Bernhard Roman and Bernhard Cursive are combined to make a dignified layout that suggests a like quality in the object advertised. Generous leading and margins are consistent with the word "Luxury." (*Bauer Type Foundry, New York.*)

OUR LATE HOLY FATHER
POPE PIVS X
EXHORTATION ADDRESSED TO THE WHOLE WORLD FROM OUT THE PALACE OF THE VATICAN THIS THE SECOND DAY OF AUGUST IN THE YEAR MDCCCCXIV ❧ AT THESE MOMENTS WHEN NEARLY THE WHOLE WORLD IS BEING DRAGGED INTO THE VORTEX OF A MOST TERRIBLE WAR WITH ITS PRESENT DANGERS AND MISERIES AND THE CONSEQUENCES TO FOLLOW, THE VERY THOUGHT OF WHICH MUST STRIKE EVERYONE WITH GRIEF AND HORROR, WE WHOSE CARE IS THE LIFE AND WELFARE OF MANY CITIZENS AND MANY PEOPLES, WE CANNOT BUT BE STRONGLY MOVED AND OUR HEART WRUNG WITH MOST BITTER SORROW AND SHAME THAT THE WORLD, BLIND TO

TORY BORDER combined with contemporary type to exemplify that restraint, color relationship, and good judgment that people nowadays are learning to expect of fine printing. (*Pelican Press, London.*) FACING PAGE: Cover of a limited-edition book which combines type with illustration most successfully; both are fairly free in character and, excepting the title, related in tonal value. Decoration by Anthony de Witt; printed in Humanistic type by Bertieri & Vanzetti. Familiarity with Italian is not essential to the universal appreciation of its design.

AMBRA
POEMETTO DI LORENZO DE' MEDICI
IL MAGNIFICO

ISTITUTO DI EDIZIONI ARTISTICHE
FRATELLI ALINARI
FIRENZE

Published by Fratelli Alinari, Florence. See facing page for mention of the qualities that make this book outstanding.

DESIGN 53

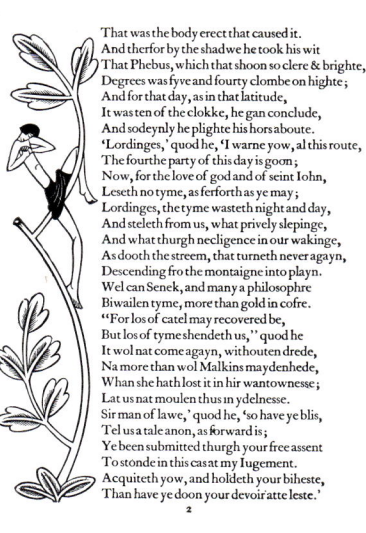

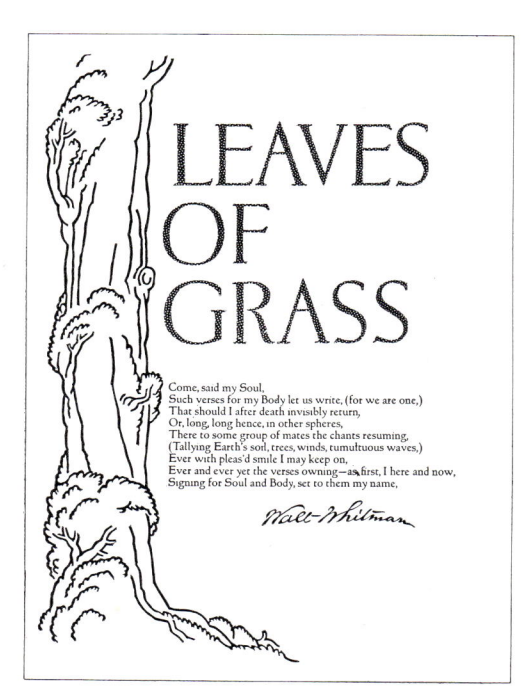

TYPOGRAPHIC SOLUTIONS which are completely satisfying: In the two pages from the *Canterbury Tales*, the artist makes the irregular measure of the right page balance the regular beginning of the left by purposeful use of line decorations. (*Eric Gill for the Golden Cockerel Press, Waltham Saint Lawrence.*) The page from *Leaves of Grass* breaks away from hard and fast rules to convey the freedom of the subject of the book—proof again, if one needs it, that rules are not masters of artists. Goudy New Style type; woodcut by Valenti Angelo. (*Designed and printed by the Grabhorn Press, San Francisco, for Random House, New York.*)

FACING PAGE: The opening page of *Fritiofs Saga* strikes a happy mean between the tight and too-conservative and the loose and too-liberal view of typographic expression. (*P. A. Norstedt and Sons, Stockholm.*) *Horns in Velvet*, a classic disposition of type and type decoration, is as unexciting as a Doric column—and almost as lasting! (*The Harbor Press, New York.*) *Parables from the Holy Bible* pages are shown here as normally planned—two at a time. The use of a touch of red in initial and rule of the original helps to avoid undue somberness. Black rules would have divided the page area into too many segments. (*Conceived and executed by students of the Birmingham School of Arts and Crafts, England, H. H. Holden, director.*)

54 GRAPHIC

FRITIOFS SAGA.
Litteraturanmälan 1824.

MORGONBLADET tillkännagav i nummer etthundrasextiofem, 1822, en ny behandling av dessa djärva, friska, nordiska sägner, som den geniale Tegnér gripit sig an med. De små dikterna, som där presenterades, lyckligt översatta av fru von Helwig, tjäna som en inledning till det hela och föra därjämte handlingen framåt. Eftersom de äro tillgängliga för alla, återgiva vi här endast i all korthet deras innehåll.

1. Fritiof och Björn, två djärva vikingar, ha mitt i vintern drivits genom isen till ett land, där en åldrad konung vid namn Ring härskar vida om kring. Denne kung Ring har tidigare vunnit Fritiofs trolovade, Ingeborg, till maka. Fritiof jagas av en obetvinglig längtan efter att än en gång få se den älskade och beger sig för den skull, djupt upprörd men likväl i försonlig sinnesstämning, till hovet, där julen just skall firas med stora festligheter. 2. Han kommer dit, höljd i björnfällar, förklädd till en gammal man, en tiggare. Hovfolket hånar honom och driver gäck med honom; upptänd av vrede ger han då prov på sin styrka, och fram ur den grova förklädnaden träder en ung

---

HORNS IN VELVET

JOAN RAMSAY

NEW YORK
THE HARBOR PRESS
1930

PARABLES FROM THE HOLY BIBLE   13

with me, and I will pay thee all. Then the lord of that servant was moved with compassion, and loosed him, and forgave him the debt. But the same servant went out, and found one of his fellowservants, which owed him an hundred pence: and he laid hands on him, and took him by the throat, saying, Pay me that thou owest. And his fellowservant fell down at his feet, and besought him, saying, Have patience with me, and I will pay thee all. And he would not: but went and cast him into prison, till he should pay the debt. So when his fellowservants saw what was done, they were very sorry, and came and told unto their lord all that was done. Then his lord, after that he had called him, said unto him, O thou wicked servant, I forgave thee all that debt, because thou desiredst me: shouldest not thou also have had compassion on thy fellowservant, even as I had pity on thee? And his lord was wroth, and delivered him to the tormentors, till he should pay all that was due unto him. So likewise shall my heavenly Father do also unto you, if ye from your hearts forgive not every one his brother their trespasses.

A CERTAIN MAN MADE A GREAT SUPPER and bade many: and sent his servant at supper time to say to them that were bidden, Come; for all things are now ready. And they all with one consent began to make excuse. The first said unto him, I have bought a piece of ground, and I must needs go and see it: I pray thee have me excused. And another said, I have bought five yoke of oxen, and I go to prove them: I pray thee have me excused. And another said, I have married a wife, and therefore I cannot come. So that servant came, and shewed his lord these things. Then the master of the house being angry said to his servant, Go out quickly into the

THE GREAT SUPPER

DESIGN ═══ 55

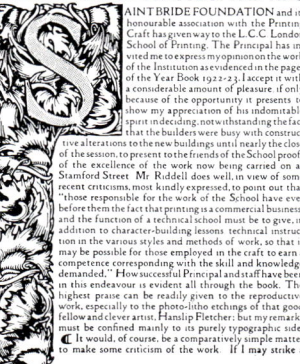

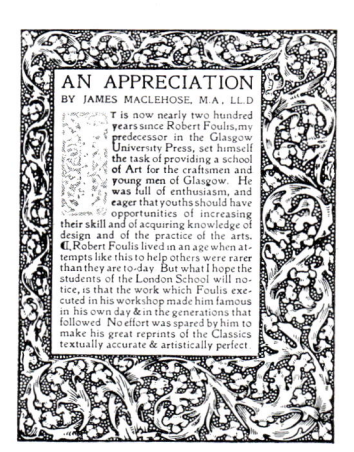

TWO EXAMPLES of layout, composition, and printing by students; they show sympathetic understanding of printing traditions. (*London School of Printing.*) BELOW and facing page: Three solutions of layout, composition, and printing problems by students. The style of the work is a departure from the common-place and is in keeping with the inventive spirit that characterizes our time. Compare the irregular silhouettes of these layouts with the above. Which is the more exciting; which the more restful? (*Technikum für Buchdrucker, Leipzig;* students W. Bachmann, D. I. Popescu, and H. Affolter, respectively.)

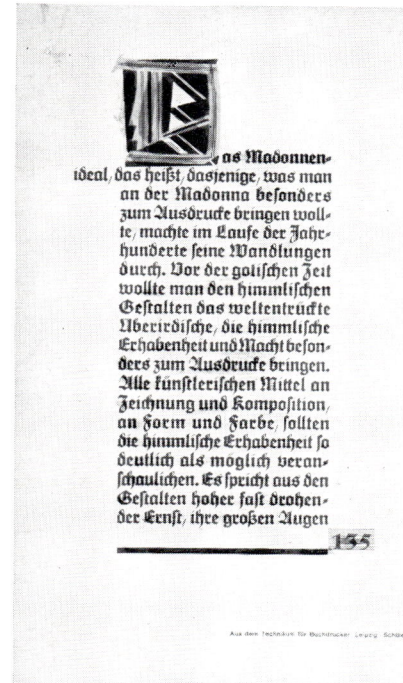

Als der Mond ihm nun gerade ins Gesicht leuchtete, erwachte unser Freund. Die Flut hatte sich verlaufen und zwischen ihm und dem Dorfe lag nur die schlammige Fläche, auf der er sich leicht zurecht finden konnte. Man sah jetzt kein Licht mehr in den Häusern und soweit er nach dem Stande des Mondes urteilen konnte, mußte bereits die Mitternachtsstunde vorüber sein. Das Meer sah schwarz und unheimlich aus und brauste dumpf. Peter zitterte und fühlte etwas von jenem seltsamen Grauen, das uns in der Dunkelheit beschleicht. Eben wollte er sich aufmachen, um über den Damm zurückzukehren. Da hörte er unter sich ein Geräusch. Vorsichtig beugte er sich vor über den Rand des Dammes und erkannte

CAFÉ BLUM
WIESBADEN / WILHELMSTR. 46

GEGRÜNDET 1878

WARME GETRÄNKE

1 Tasse Kaffee mit Sahne	0.40
1 Kännchen Kaffee mit Sahne	0.80
1 Glas Wiener Melange	0.50
1 Tasse Kaffee-Hag mit Sahne	0.50
1 Kännchen Mokka mit Sahne	1.00
1 Kännchen Mokka-Hag mit Sahne	1.20
1 Tasse Schokolade mit Schlagsahne	0.60
1 Glas Tee mit Sahne oder Zitrone	0.50
1 Glas Tee mit echtem Jamaika-Rum	1.00
1 Portion Tee mit Sahne oder Zitrone	0.80
1 Portion Tee mit echtem Jamaika-Rum	1.20
1 Glas Milch, kalt oder warm	0.30
1 Glas Grog von Arrac oder Cognac	1.00
1 Glas Grog von echtem Jamaika-Rum (75 Prozent)	1.20
1 Glas Burgunder-Punsch	1.00
1 Glas Glühwein von altem Burgunder	1.00
1 Glas Hindenburg-Punsch	1.50

GEFROR

ERFRISCHUNGEN

1 Limonade Amer Gentiane mit Citron	0.80
1 Limonade Vermouth mit Cassis	0.80
1 Limonade Grenadin Cusenier mit Kirsch	0.90
1 Zitrone oder Orange, naturell	0.60

THE DOUBLE CROWN CLUB

MENU
XXIX APRIL MCMXXV

¶ Hors d'oeuvre variés. ¶ Consommé aux légumes or Crème de tomate. ¶ Filet de Sole frite, sauce tartare. ¶ Caneton à la Bordelaise and petits pois, pommes château, and salade. ¶ Biscuit Porto Rico and langues de chat
¶ Canapé aux laitances
¶ Café

MENUS: A most attractive invitation to lunch at the Café Blum. The drawing and deliberate spacing of the light-dark units show a strong regard for the unity of the whole. The shorthand-like notes help one to identify the courses easily. Original in black, red, and a tint color. (*Stempel Type Foundry.*) The Double Crown Club menu is not unlike a Picasso in the effective use of line quality. The free character of the title (French Sylvan type) serves as a transitional note between the spontaneous drawing and the crisp type face. (*Pelican Press, London.*)

FACING PAGE: A minister's greeting, appropriate in spirit and in treatment. (*Rudge Press for Rev. and Mrs. William Harold Weigle.*) The greeting card "The Word" is composed purely of type materials and is as devoid of unessentials as a well-designed bridge. (*Frederick Warde for Gabriel Wells, courtesy Rudge, New York.*) The type and type ornaments that make up Vojtech Preissig's unique card were designed and cast by this artist. The printing house of Seix y Barral, Barcelona, wishes us well with type—a strong, related unit that graphically portrays the printer's appreciation of his tools of trade.

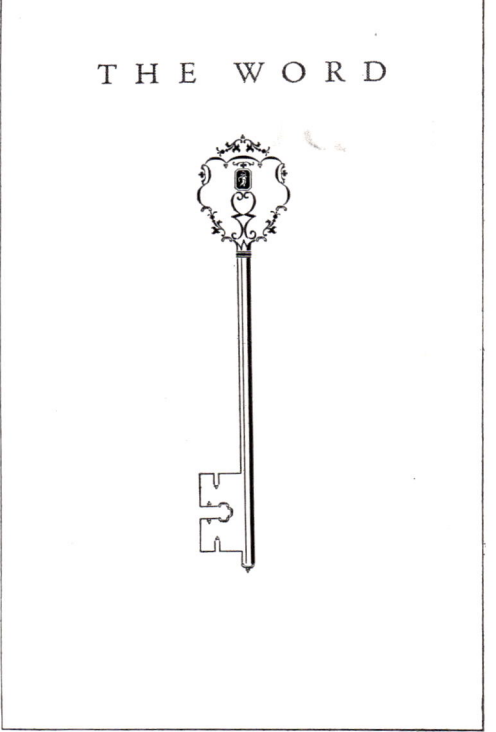

Verily He that Receiveth the Divine Peace Is Blessed

THE WORD

Vojtěch Preissig
p. f. 1930

GREETING CARDS that bring a wealth of variety into a field commonly limited in its symbolism. No trees, no Santa, no holly! See facing page for identification.

DESIGN 59

VARIED USE of type rules. (*Deberny et Peignot*, type founders and printers, Paris.)

60 GRAPHIC

TYPE BORDERS and some of their uses: 1, 2, 5, and 7 designed by Prof. Ehmcke for Stempel, Frankfort; 3 set by Erasmusdruck, Berlin; 4, Ludwig & Mayer, Frankfort; 6, Deberny et Peignot, Paris. Borders have taken endless forms and served a million uses since their supposed introduction in typography by Erhard Ratdolt, Venice, 1476. White space itself, type rule, vine and bird effects, etc., have served to enhance type. The reproductions suggest some of the possibilities. The modern tendency is to replace ornate borders with broken bands or rule as more in keeping with type. By breaking the uniform grayness of a layout, they add color to printed matter. In the advertisements of the crowded newspaper, borders may also serve to make an announcement outstanding, as in the *Rekord*, fig. 4.

DESIGN 61

PRINTERS DEVICES AND ENVELOPES

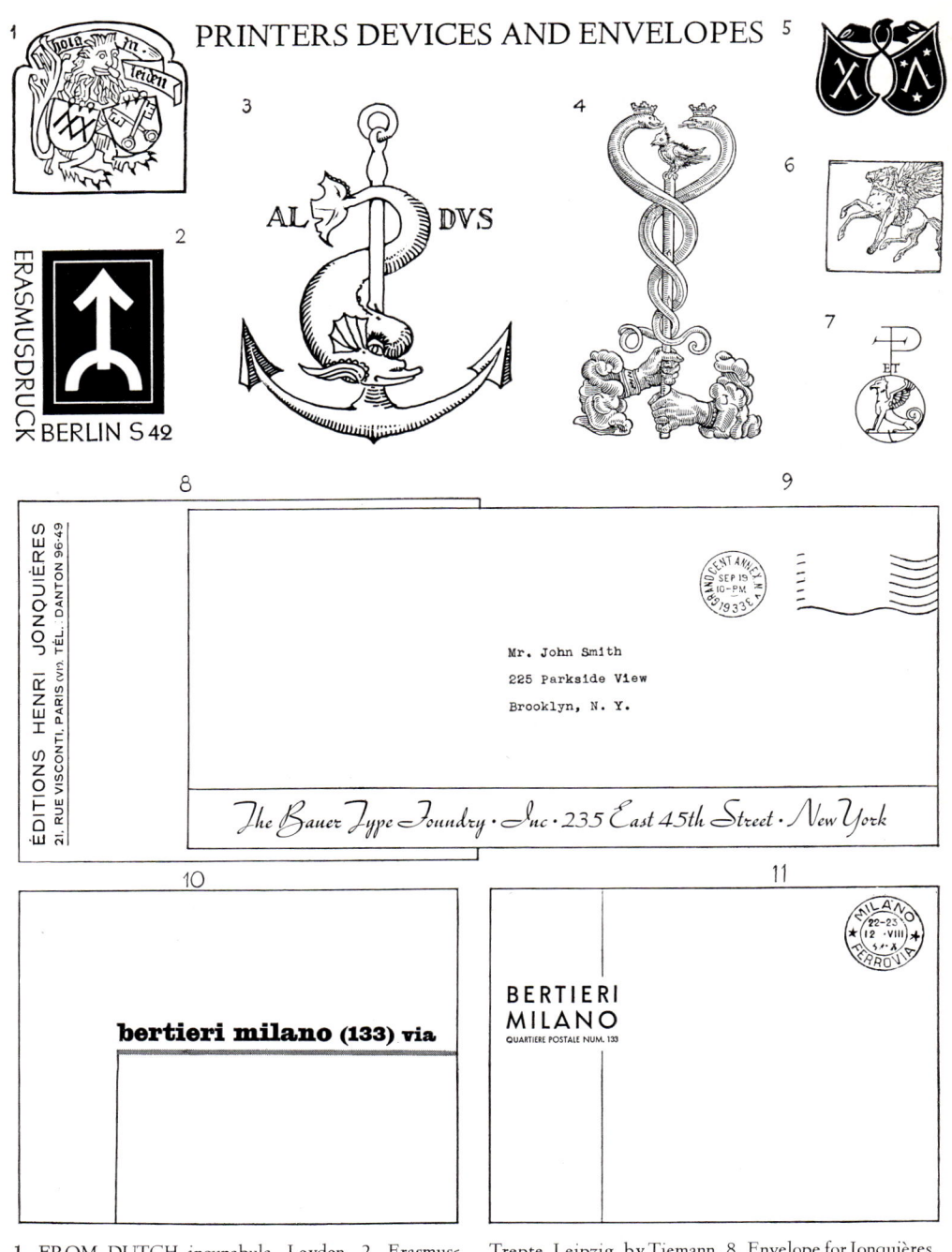

1. FROM DUTCH incunabula, Leyden. 2. Erasmusdruck, Berlin. 3. Dolphin device of Aldus Manutius. 4. J. Froben's caduceus. 5. Colophon of Fust and Schoeffer. 6. Pynson Printers, New York, by Cleland. 7. Poeschel & Trepte, Leipzig, by Tiemann. 8. Envelope for Jonquières, Paris. 9. Envelope for Bauer Type Foundry, New York, with Trafton Script. 10 and 11. Envelopes for Bertieri, Milan. In 10, the return address continues on the reverse.

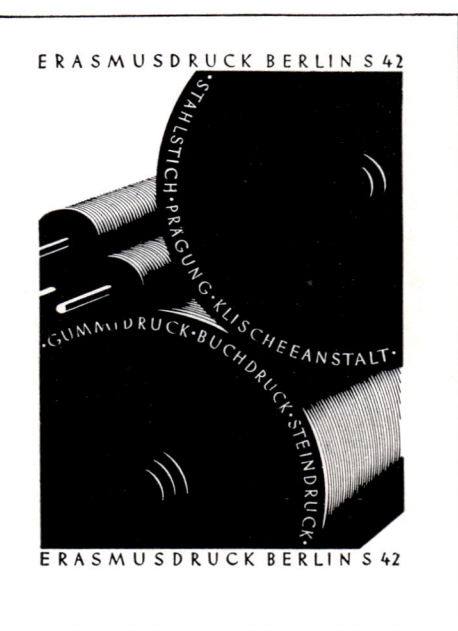

ERBAR-GROTESK
DIE GROTESK-SCHRIFT IN KÜNSTLERISCHER FORM

WITH COMPLIMENTS FROM
THE WESTMINSTER PRESS
GERRARDS LIMITED
411A HARROW ROAD
LONDON
W 9

From D. B. Updike
The Merrymount Press
712 Beacon Street
Boston, Mass.

ABOVE ARE two of a series of printer's announcements. In the original they were black on yellow and they illustrated the skill and good taste that the printer endeavored to sell. They also indicate an understanding of the elements of design—unity, dominance, variety. The strong display line of Grotesk was designed by Erbar for Ludwig & Mayer, Frankfort. The three printers' labels are functional and typical of the style of the printing shops represented. (They are reproduced by courtesy of Westminster Press, London; D. B. Updike Press, Boston; Monotype, London, respectively.)

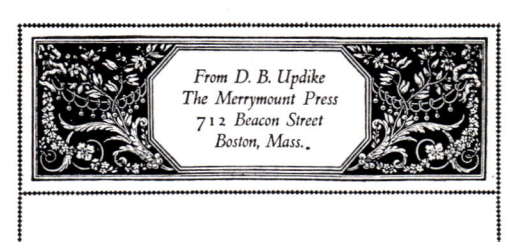

IF NOT DELIVERED PLEASE RETURN TO
Monotype
43 FETTER LANE, E.C 4 LONDON

DESIGN

FORMS PRODUCED with typographic rules, circles, squares, etc.—frank experimentation for honest invention. 1 and 2 by Prof. Frans Marten, Königsberg; 3 and ocean liner, courtesy Deberny et Peignot, Paris; alphabet and its elements by Prof. J. Albers, Black Mountain College, North Carolina; other units by the authors. FACING PAGE. A set of related printed matter, bill, brochure, tag, label, and invitation for a hotel, which is distinguished by the repetition of a single motif. Constructed by means of type material by Prof. Frans Marten.

GRAPHIC

DESIGN 65

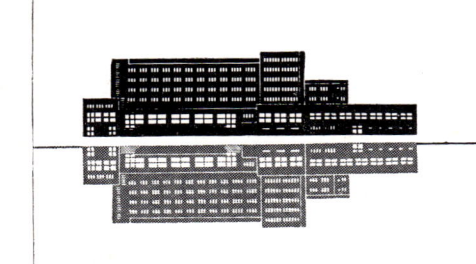

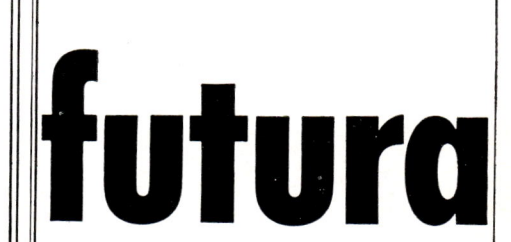

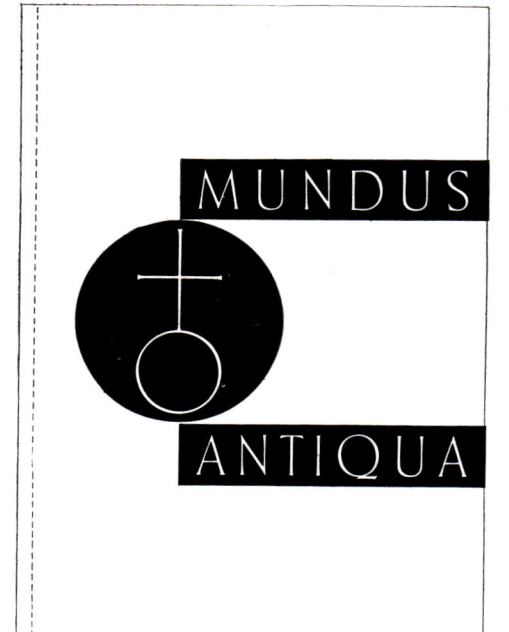

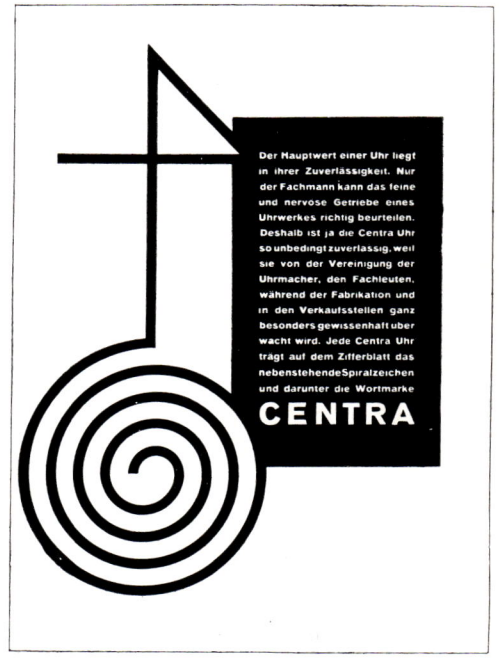

TYPE FOUNDERS' catalogue covers, boldly designed. For explanation see description on bottom of facing page.

PRESS-ROOM EQUIPMENT

PRESSES. ABOVE. A linotype machine. Keys controlled like a typewriter cast type in lines. Pressing a lever starts an assembled line of matrices and space bands on its automatic journey. (*Mergenthaler Linotype Company, Brooklyn.*) RIGHT. A proof press with moving cylinder and rigid bed on steel cabinet. (*Vandercook & Sons., Inc., Chicago.*) CENTER. A platen press. (*Chandler & Price, Cleveland.*) BELOW. Proof press with moving bed for placing on table. (*Challenge Machinery Company, Grand Haven.*)

FACING PAGE: Catalogue Covers: Unorthodox composition of type and rule gives a relievingly fresh appearance to the "Latein" cover. (*Stempel, Frankfort.*) Bold Futura type and bold border to harmonize with it produce a striking effect with simple means. (*Bauer Type Foundry, New York.*) The lines, Mundus and Antiqua, are reversed in color to produce more definitely geometric forms; the circle adds an attention-getting spot. (*Stempel Type Foundry, Frankfort.*) Reversing the Centra text in color translates it from a neutral gray mass to a strong dominant shape. The watch-spring drawing enlivens the otherwise severe and heavy composition (*Designed by Wilhelm Metzig, Hannover.*)

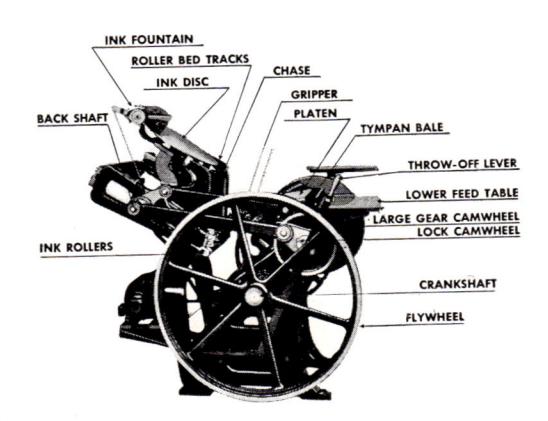

DESIGN 67

Case 312   36-pt. Kennerley Bold 269, 2691   (M = 26-pt. face)   Mono, job

ABCDEFGHIJKLM |M

abcdefghijklmnopq 12345

ABCDEFGHIJKLMNO

abcdefghijklmnopq 12345

Œ&ŒUG gjpq ctst ctst ( )

Case 313   42-pt. Kennerley Bold 269   (M = 30-pt. face)   Mono, job

ABCDEFGHIJKL|M

abcdefghijklnctst 123

Case 314   48-pt. Kennerley Bold 269   (M = 34-pt. face)   Mono, job

ABCDEFGHIJ |M

abcdefghijkctst 123

Case 315   60-pt. Kennerley Bold 269   (M = 44-pt. face)   Mono, job

ABCDEFG |M

abcdefg ctst 123

68 ═══════ GRAPHIC

[Advertisement 1 — left panel:]

IN BABYLON five thousand years ago were carts with wheels. That is the earliest knowledge we possess of man's chief mechanical wonder.

IN BABYLON two thousand five hundred years ago was the first known Bank.

The wheels of progress began to move.

IN GREAT BRITAIN to-day the most important Banking Business is the London Joint City and Midland Bank Ltd., with its affiliations the Belfast Banking Co., in Ireland, and the Clydesdale Bank in Scotland, commanding total resources of four hundred millions of pounds.

It keeps ever turning a myriad wheels of industry.

LONDON JOINT CITY & MIDLAND BANK LTD.

Chairman: Rt. Hon. R. McKenna
Over 1600 Offices

FREE HANDBOOK FROM 5 THREADNEEDLE ST. E.C.

[Advertisement 2 — right panel:]

A week's tour to
PARIS
£6-6s.

Inclusive fares, providing travel tickets, accommodation, three auto drives with local guides, gratuities, sight-seeing fees, guide book, etc. Departure on Saturday each week.

BESTWAY TRAVEL AGENCY
HIGH STREET, MORTON

The white space above has intentionally been left free to show how like a gray wash the finely set type mass at the right appears. Contrast the value of its grayness, too, with the lighter tone of this legend or with the dark tone of the "A Week's Tour to Paris" advertisement.

COMPARE THE tonal weights of these fairly similar layouts. Both advertisements were designed and set in the typography classes of the Leicester College of Arts and Crafts, England. The line illustrations by D. Cooper and Joy Williams, respectively, repeat the color value of the type. The caliber of a student's work is not always easily distinguished from that of the professional. FACING PAGE: A method of forecasting the number of letters in any area. Black vertical lines, spaced 12 points apart and red in the original, are used in determining the number of letters in any given width. Figures on right indicate the number of letters in a 34-pica line. The figures in parentheses, following the name of type face, show the actual point size of face of roman M. The 4-point rule, which precedes the roman M at the end of the line of roman, shows the point size of type body and position of face on body. Slightly reduced from two color original. (*Courtesy of the U. S. Government Printing Office, Washington, D. C.*)

DESIGN ═══════════════ 69

1

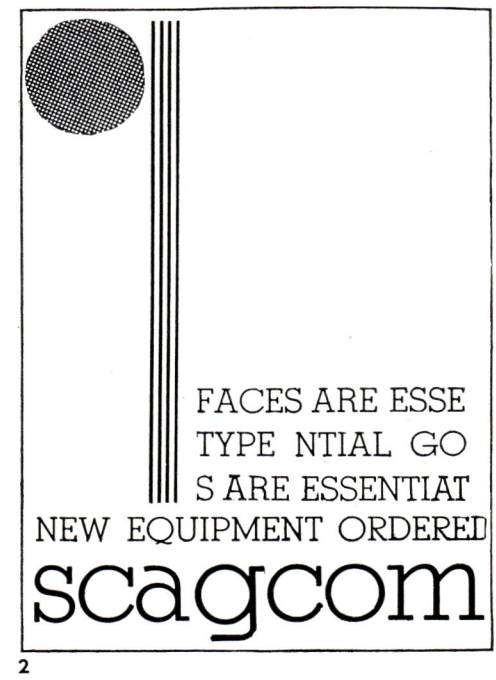

HERE'S MUSIC
FOR YOU & FOR
YOUR FRIENDS
A LITERARY & ART BOOK
cargoes

2

FACES ARE ESSE
TYPE NTIAL GO
S ARE ESSENTIA
NEW EQUIPMENT ORDERED
scagcom

3

HERE'S MUSIC
FOR YOU & FOR
YOUR FRIENDS
A LITERARY & ART BOOK
cargoes

TYPOGRAPHIC PROBLEM: Design an announcement for insertion in a school publication, advertising the merits of a school magazine. Or better still, give design and plan to the advertisements that appear in your school newspaper. For suggestions of alternate problems, see Course of Study in the chapter on Graphic Art Education; also Advertising Art chapter.

MAJOR STEPS in designing a typographic announcement: 1. Pencilled layout shows the content of the advertisement and indicates the disposition of the type. Note that the important line is outstanding in size—is dominant. 2. Any text matter using face and size of ultimate "ad" is cut up and pasted to help forecast the appearance of the finished advertisement. This form is judged for legibility, tonal color, and silhouette. 3. Final proof. When this follows sequential thought rather than guesswork, the result can be anticipated. Designed by Nat Super.

REPRODUCTIVE ARTS CHAPTER 3

A KNOWLEDGE of reproductive processes helped the artist Hans Schleger, known as Zéro, to obtain this unusual result. The original may have been rendered white on black, or black on white, and a positive plate made.

(Crawford's Berlin office for Hudnut, New York.)

REPRODUCTIVE ARTS

THE PHOTOMEchanical process of reproduction has done for the artist what movable type has done for the author and the screen for the actor. It has increased a thousandfold the number of those who appreciate art, and in like measure it has increased the impetus for good work.

Since commercial art, and most fine arts for that matter, are judged in reproduction rather than in the original state, an ability to forecast printed results is an essential tool of the successful graphicist. That is why the artist ought to understand not alone the artistic aspect of his work but also the mechanical means whereby it is multiplied. There are two major methods of multiplying art, *direct* and *indirect*. In the direct method, the artist sees the job through from the drawing to the cutting, scratching, or etching of the plate and often even through the printing of it. A woodcut or etching is likely to be such an example. A far simpler means of reproduction, from the artist's point of view, is the photomechanical or the indirect method. Here the artist is through when his drawing is completed. The photoengraver and the printer combine to finish the job. The line plate and the halftone, examples of mechanical reproduction, are indirect methods. Lithography may be either direct or indirect. The three main printing divisions of the reproductive arts are:

DIRECT (artistic)	INDIRECT (mechanical)
1. Relief or raised printing: Woodcut, linoleum, and composition cut	1. Relief or raised printing: Line plate, halftone, and their electroplates
2. Intaglio or subway printing: Etching, drypoint, engraving, aquatint, mezzotint	2. Intaglio or subway printing: Photogravure (heliogravure, rotogravure)
3. Surface or flat printing: Lithograph, stencil	3. Surface or flat printing: Lithograph—offset, aquatone, etc.

For each of the three major printing divisions, some one form of pressure

CHAPTER DECORATION: Bears; trade mark in line and Ben Day. (*Porzellan Baer; Ludwig & Mayer, Frankfort.*)

DESIGN

CONTRASTING WOODCUTS WITH METAL ENGRAVING

1. "ST. CHRISTOPHER" by an unknown artist, is one of the earliest dated woodcuts (1423). Possibly crude in drawing, it is nevertheless forceful in execution. The omission of crosshatching by the artist shows a respect for the medium which is absent in Van Leyden's print.

2. "CHRIST AND WOMAN of Samaria" by Van Leyden (1494-1533), a woodcut, is an early equivalent of a design that would today be reproduced by a line plate. It is quite free of the characteristics—stiffness and dominance of blacks—which are more commonly associated with woodcuts. (*M. Knoedler & Company, Inc., New York.*)

3. "THE ANNUNCIATION" by Schongauer (1440-1491). The labored line of the engraving furnishes a decided contrast with the free line play of an etching, "Annie Haden" by Whistler, for example (page 94). The line character of Schongauer antedates and suggests Dürer. Note also the surface tint of the block in the engraving and its absence in the woodcut. (*Boston Museum of Art.*)

FACING PAGE: "Man and Wife," a design done in the big and broad manner that gives woodcuts their strong appeal. Instead of finicky detail, the artist uses vigorous black-grey contrast, and white most sparingly. (*Courtesy of the artist, Fritz Richter, Berchtesgaden.*)

DESIGN 75

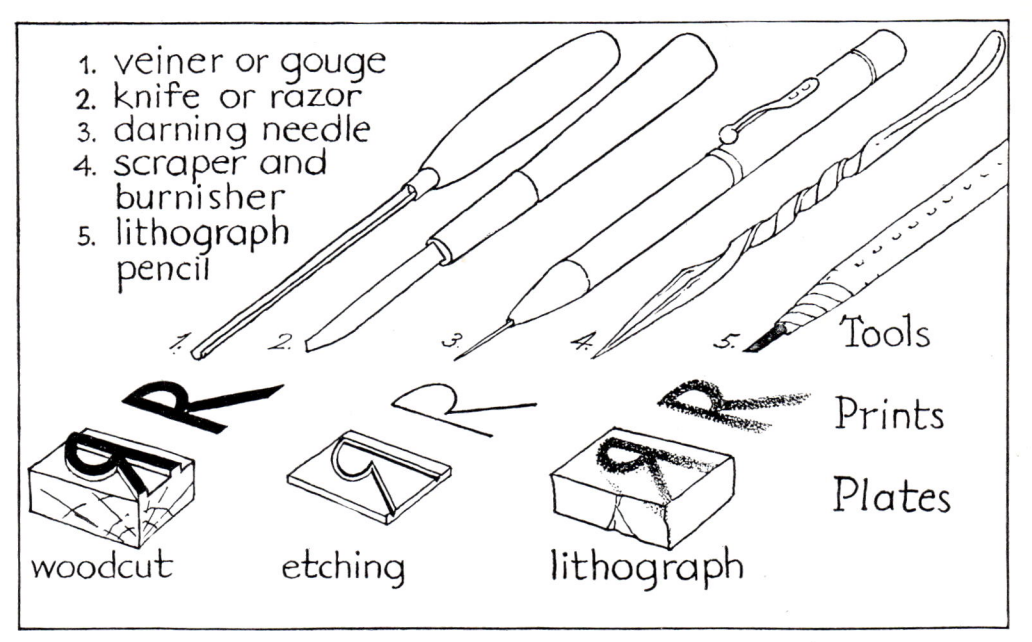

```
1. veiner or gouge
2. knife or razor
3. darning needle
4. scraper and
    burnisher
5. lithograph
    pencil
```

Tools

Prints

Plates

woodcut   etching   lithograph

ABOVE: Typical tools for working in wood, in metal, and on stone.

BELOW: 1 to 5 are gouges, chisels, etc.; 6 to 10 are gravers or burins.

gives best printing results. A platen or letter press, giving vertical pressure, is used for relief printing; a cylinder press gives the most successful form of pressure for intaglio printing, and a cylinder or rotary press is best for surface or planographic printing.

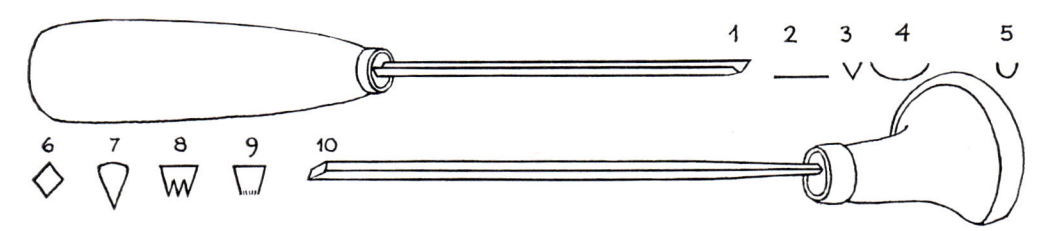

Historically, direct preceded indirect duplication. The potency of duplicating devices may be said to have been first manifest nearly fifty years after the appearance of the first dated woodcuts, the "Virgin and Child with Four Virgin Saints," 1418, or the "St. Christopher," 1423. Later (1470 to 1540), Schongauer, Dürer, and Holbein issued artistic mementoes, prints, that included among their audience the illiterate and literate alike. And even antedating them, Andrea Mantegna (1431-1506), the Paduan, printed from metal-engraved

"ST. ANDREW, CHRIST, and St. Longinus," an engraving in metal by the master of economic line, Andrea Mantegna (1431-1506). "The Climbers," a precise statement in metal by Marcantonio Raimondi (1488-1534) after Michelangelo. (Both prints from Engravings and Woodcuts by Old Masters, published by Bernhard Quaritch, London.)

plates compositions of such classic correctness that even Dürer sought to imitate them. The first truly "graphic" newspapers or tabloids were these prints. Human complacency was certainly jarred, and thought was crystallized by Goya's attack, with prints, on the French invaders of Spain. Similarly effective were Daumier's satiric lithographs picturing aristocracy's abuse of all that should have been considered fair and decent. Contemporary caricaturists' comment on political sleight-of-hand with plebeian line cuts has been equally poignant.

The Woodcut is one of the oldest of reproductive media. The stiffness and seeming archaic simplicity that are its characteristics are occasioned by the nature of wood. Uncut, the block offers maximum printing area—a black solid. The artist's problem, as in all printing, is to secure nonprinting areas by removing parts of this solid. After obtaining a design, a tracing in reverse is transferred on to the polished and whitened surface of the block. Frequently, a thin tracing paper is glued, Japanese-print fashion, face down, or, as often, the design is drawn directly on the wood. In the cutting, U- and V-shaped gouges, chisels, knives, and razor blades are used to remove the whites of the design. This is done by first outlining the parts to be cut with a thin gouge called a

DESIGN

ABOVE: "Margaret and Faust," a woodcut that indicates a judicious use of woodcutting and wood-engraving tools. See with what economy of means the figures are rendered. Note especially the few lines used to depict the doorway and the figures there and see how sparing has been the artist's use of white. The parallel lines were made with a threading tool for greater uniformity. (*Kalman Gaborjani-Szabó, Debreczen, Hungary.*)

SIDE: "Faust's Duel with Margaret's Brother" as interpreted by another artist. Contrast this straightforward woodcut with the above treatment. The artist effectively lends interest to his large black areas by use of suggestive line and by contrasting minute cutting, as in the church steeple, with sparse cutting, as in the left foreground. The figures are treated as a unit and nicely placed against the least interesting part of the design to avoid conflict in interest. (*Joseph von Divéki, artist, Bethis, Switzerland.*)

ABOVE: "Goodspeed," a woodcut by Rockwell Kent, is distinguished by fine deliberate design. Its decorative quality suggests still another treatment of the woodblock. Nothing is left to accident. By reserving the whites for the figure and by surrounding this with unbroken blacks, the artist has intensified his "color." Compare Kent's flying figure with a similar subject by Blake on page 169. (*Calkins & Holden, New York, for American Car and Foundry Company.*)

SIDE: "Faust and Marguerite" as seen by Lynd Ward. Decorative, imaginative, and sparkling in treatment, its fine pattern combines good woodcut technique with good figure drawing. (*Reprinted from Vanity Fair; copyright by the Condé Nast Publications, Inc., New York.*)

THE FOUR woodcuts show that the variety in the results is limited only by the creative power and the technical skill of the artist.

DESIGN 79

veiner. The fewer, finer, and shallower the incisions are the darker the print will be, since the printing surface is only slightly reduced by the whites of the design. Unless the wider expanses of the cut areas are made proportionately deeper the excavated parts will take ink and smudge the sagging paper. Undercutting, which shortens the life of a block, can be avoided by maintaining such a bevel as one obtains incidentally by using the V gouge.

The grain of wood used, its relative hardness (boxwood, apple, pine, pear, or cherry), and the way it is cut (cross grain, end grain, or plankwise) influence the quality of the print. An impression obtained from boxwood is uniform in texture; the proof from a pine block is likely to show the artist's work modified by the more conspicuous grain that distinguishes the wood. In making the woodcut, the knife or chisel is normally employed on the plank end of the block. Unfortunately, contemporary artists often work on the end grain to eliminate the danger of the graver's following the grain, but in so doing, they miss precisely those characteristics that help to give the wood-block print its individuality and appealing quality.

The composition, linoleum, or *rubber cuts* are good substitutes for the woodcut for those who prefer the easy give of these substances to the resistance offered by the grain in cutting the wood. The freedom which accompanies easy cutting makes up, in part at least, for the archaic quality that is contributed by the plank. Battleship linoleum and composition plates are also used in conjunction with woodcuts or line cuts, as tint blocks. Aside from this, the printed results are similar to the wood-block impression in character. A note of novelty and surprise—because the print cannot be fully controlled—can be obtained by using a paraffin block instead of wood. The amateur may go a step farther and rubber-cement successive layers of paper on a thick cardboard base, allowing this to dry in the press. Simple designs can then be cut as in linoleum. Shellacked and inked, the improvised block is ready for printing. Whatever medium is used, the procedure in printing will be much the same.

In color work, the main block, usually the black one, is called the key plate. This is marked with registering crosses (+) on the extreme top and lower left-hand points of the block. The key plate is then proofed on oily or clay-coated paper or gelatin sheets and offset on what are to be the successive color blocks. For offsetting, it is advisable to use a good grade of proofing black.

The number of transfers to be made is dictated by the number of printings that are necessary to produce the picture—one for each shade and color. The blocks are then temporarily tinted in their appropriate parts with the color that they will convey in the printing. Water color ought to be used, since it can be washed off readily. Its transparency permits the original offset lines to serve as a guide for careful registry. Next, by cutting away the untinted surface, the colored parts and the registering marks are left in relief, preparing the blocks for their respective inks. Inking may be done with a brayer (roller) or with a brush. The sequence of printings usually followed is from the lightest tint to the darkest shade. This procedure is especially desirable, where, to allow a margin of safety, a slight overlap or fringe is provided for in the darker blocks.

The printing may be as simple as inking the blocks and rubbing the back of the antique paper with the bowl of a spoon. For the same purpose the Japanese use a baren, a flat circular disk encased in a smooth covering. Or, again, the printing may be as comparatively complex as using a letter press or a latest model proof press. With either form of pressure, it is sometimes necessary to build up and "true" a block with the aid of make-ready. Here the block is proofed on tissue paper and tested for evenness of color. The light parts of the proof are cut out and pasted on the back of the corresponding parts of the block to provide additional thickness. The process of building up is continued until uniform color is obtained.

The number of impressions that one may get from a block varies with the material used and the degree of pressure necessary for printing. A large rubber block with few whites and large printing surfaces will stand up for many thousands of impressions even on roughly textured paper. Terminating each job is the unavoidable cleaning. This is best accomplished by using an ink solvent like gasoline, benzene or kerosene. The solvent as well as the waste should be kept in a fireproof container for safety and for cleanliness.

Block printing offers an opportunity for complete graphic-art experience within the means of the poorest student. The popularity of the process attests to the general recognition of this fact.

Wood engraving differs from the woodcut in the kind of tools employed to arrive at the image. The engraving on wood is in relief—the lines that print

ABOVE: One must see the colored original to appreciate the color register of "The Wave" by Hokusai (1760-1849). It is one of the most familiar examples of Japanese mastery of the block print. The power and rhythm of the sea are strongly pictured in this asymmetrically balanced composition although the artist has used only a fragment of the sea's expanse to do so.

SIDE: "Dante and Virgil in Hell," a Doré design engraved by Pisan for Cassell's edition of "Dante's Inferno." In its technique and in the placing of the various figures, the illustration is painstakingly correct. (*Metropolitan Museum of Art, New York.*)

FACING PAGE: Timothy Cole's wood engraving of the El Greco portrait of Fray Feliz Hortensio Palavicino shows the tonal niceties that are obtainable in the hands of a craftsman. This print was made from the block engraved by Mr. Cole for the Boston Museum's motion picture "The Last of the Wood Engravers," produced by the University Film Foundation.

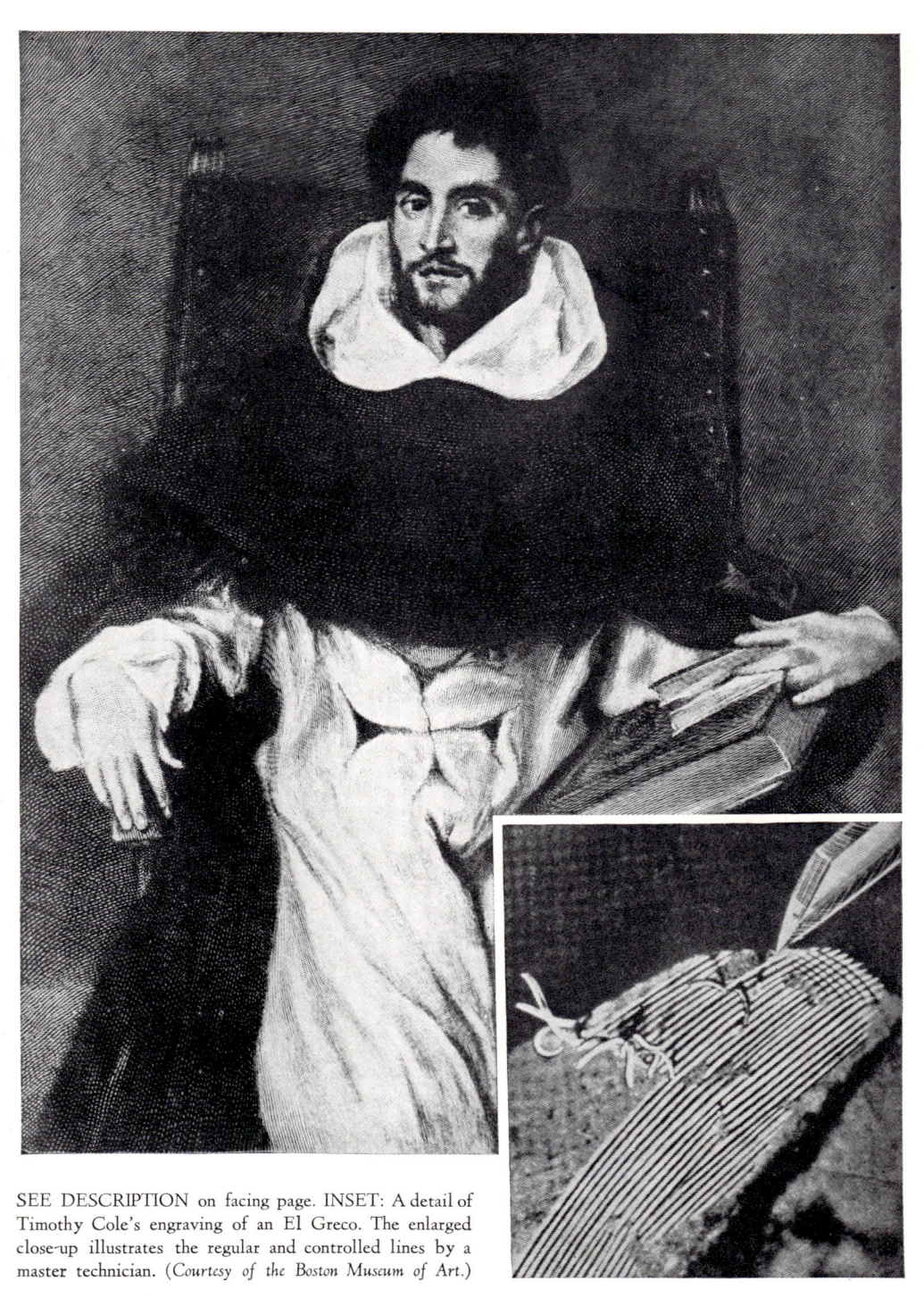

SEE DESCRIPTION on facing page. INSET: A detail of Timothy Cole's engraving of an El Greco. The enlarged close-up illustrates the regular and controlled lines by a master technician. (*Courtesy of the Boston Museum of Art.*)

DESIGN 83

ABOVE: Letterhead design cut in wood by Fritz Richter, Berchtesgaden, and originally printed in red and black. Note particularly the background of the letters—a natural result of cutting one way, then crosswise. BELOW: Steel-engraved letterhead for the city of Nuremberg. This form of reproduction is commonly used for formal stationery. (*Emil Bach & Company, Nuremberg.*) FACING PAGE: "ST. JEROME in His Study," by Albrecht Dürer (1471-1528). This halftone was made from a facsimile reproduction by the Reichsdruckerei, Berlin. Aside from its newness, the facsimile could not normally be distinguished from the 400-year-old original. Of this austere line engraving, Vasari is said to have said: "Nothing more and nothing better could be done in this field of art."

stand out—while in engraving on metal the lines that print are in intaglio, sunken. Here, too, the design may be transferred, as in the woodcut, by tracing or projected on to a sensitized block by photography. In this case effects suggestive of oil painting, in the Timothy Cole manner, may be obtained. Instead of the open U-shaped gouges, solid V and W gravers are employed to push the whites out that help to make the design. Because the tools are small, large white areas are uncommon; because they are varied, the engraving is further characterized by rich surface results.

On the other hand, by using steel or copper instead of wood, it is possible to produce a result as precise as an American postage stamp. Other direct methods of reproduction which are at the command and within the complete control of the artist are etching, drypoint, aquatint, mezzotint, monotint, and lithography. Explanations of these processes follow.

Etching is said to date from Dürer's time. Rembrandt, Goya, Meryon, and Whistler were masters in it. The process is based on the action of acid on metal. For zinc, the acid is usually nitric mixed with water (1:4). In this proportion, the acid bath yellows but does not burn the fingers. Perchloride of

"LE STRYGE," by Meryon. The reproduction on the left was made from an impression of the plate printed in intaglio, as an etching, with the surface ink wiped off before printing. On the right is a print in relief, in which a brayer is used to ink the surface alone. It is a masterly composition contrasting a strong gargoyle, treated broadly, against a detailed city. The design is like a mosaic in its interrelated elements. (*Courtesy Boston Museum of Art.*)

iron or a strong nitric solution is used for copper etching. A metal plate of the desired proportion is beveled along the edges with a file. In printing, these edges account for the "plate mark." The metal is then cleaned with whiting and water. A thin coat of acid resist (wax ground) is used to cover the face of a warmed plate, and asphaltum is painted on all other unprotected parts. Smoking the ground with tapers better enables the artist to see the progress of his drawing. The picture is next drawn with a needle or other sharp instrument, the ground being thus removed and the plate exposed to the action of the mordant (acid bath). The first "bite" lasts less than a minute and gives but the shallowest lines of the picture—sky, clouds, or other light parts. These lines are then protected from further action by drying and painting with asphaltum. The plate is then again immersed for the deeper lines which produce the blacks of an etching, the deeper lines holding more ink. Biting and stopping-out are continued as many times as the number of planes in the picture warrant. Following this, the acid resist (wax and asphaltum) is removed by slight friction with a rag saturated with benzol, turpentine, or naphtha.

If a medium-soft, grained paper is placed over the plate coated with a ground a little softer than before, and a drawing made on the overlay, its removal takes with it the wax where the pencil has impressed itself through the paper. The result, if etched, is called a soft ground etching. A print obtained in this fashion looks very much like a pencil drawing.

To print an etching, special etching ink is rubbed into the sunken lines of a

ABOVE: Two etchings by Rembrandt (1606-1669). "The Descent from the Cross" conveys within the limits of a small plate the grandiose sweep of a large canvas. Note the effects, both light and dark, obtainable in a single impression. (*British Museum, London.*) "Jan Lutma," considered by Hamerton as one of Rembrandt's finest portraits, is a good example of the tonal color, the breadth of chiaroscuro, obtainable by use of line. (*Boston Museum of Art.*) BELOW: "Love and Death" by Goya. An outstanding aquatint over an etched drawing by the most famous master of the rosin process. With lighting, composition, directness, and simplicity, the artist obtains dramatic quality and dominance with a capital D. The process was appropriately used. (*British Museum, London.*)

DESIGN 87

ABOVE: "No se puede mirar," from Goya's "Disasters of War" series. The granular effect of the aquatint is lost in reduction. The print, a combination of line and aquatint, shows the chiaroscuro obtainable with this medium. The suggestion of the soldiery is brief, but sufficiently gripping to be preferred to a literal exposition.

BELOW: "Three Ballet Graces" by Dame Laura Knight, D. B. E., A. R. A., London. The soft ground is used here with something of the spontaneity of a sketch. The lighting is original and does not follow a stereotyped pattern. Neither does it slavishly follow the implications of naturalistic lighting.

FACING PAGE: "La Galerie," an etching by Meryon (1821-1868), is a dramatic play of the lace of architecture against the expanse of sky. Compare Meryon's precise line with that of Piranesi and of Muirhead Bone (pages 92 and 93). Note also how its controlled drawing resembles an engraving. (*Victoria and Albert Museum, London.*)

GRAPHIC

SEE
opposite
page.

DESIGN 89

warmed plate with a rotating twist of the wrist. For this, a soft cloth dabber is used. The superfluous ink is then wiped off the surface with a hard cloth, and the plate is further cleaned by a slight sweep of the open hand over the inked area. The plate with damp paper is placed on a sheet of metal, covered with felt blankets, and forced with tremendous pressure through a special etcher's press. The process is repeated for each print.

It ought to be emphasized that etching always implies the *use of acid* on metal. Therefore, drypoints are not so classified by the well informed.

Drypoint. The name is self-explanatory. Upon a clean, unscratched, but beveled plate, the artist draws with a very sharp needle or diamond point. It is not now sufficient merely to draw, but one must actually dig into the metal. A needle held at a slant of 60 degrees throws up a burr on one side of the furrow. In printing, it is this burr that gives the feathery, rich line which the initiated have learned to associate with the drypoint. Because the burr will stand but a few impressions a fine edition of drypoints rarely exceeds some fifteen to twenty prints. Steel facing the metal increases the edition appreciably but with the loss of the very quality which gives the drypoint its charm. The drypoint is often used to give variety and to supplement the character of lines in etching proper or even to retouch the design. In this case, the burr is removed with a scraper to get a line more in harmony with the etched line.

The aquatint is a tone rather than a line technique. The first step in its production is coating the plate with rosin dust. This is accomplished by shaking an ordinary box (15 by 15 by 15 inches, for example) which contains a handful of powdered rosin. Following this, the plate is inserted into an opening at the bottom of the container to permit a film of the dust to settle on its face. For a very fine grain, some moments are allowed to elapse before exposing the plate to the lighter dust which remains suspended in the air in the box. The plate is then carefully withdrawn and heated to melt the rosin into tiny, fairly uniform globules which form an acid resist. As with the etching, the back is painted with asphaltum. The plate is then dipped into the mordant (acid bath) for a slight bite that gives even the whites of an aquatint a granular effect. The lightest areas are then painted out with asphaltum and protected from further chemical action. The biting is repeated until all the tonal distinctions that mark the design are obtained. The darkest tones are protected last of all.

Designs to be reproduced by this method must be treated broadly, in flat values, indeed almost as posters. Goya's "Caprichos" prints are the best known aquatints. Dame Laura Knight is an outstanding contemporary exponent. See pages 87 and 88.

Sand-grain etching is a variety of the aquatint where a sheet of sandpaper is used instead of a dust-box. The sheet of sandpaper is placed face down on a plate covered with a thin veneer of ordinary etching ground. Pressure is applied, causing perforations which expose the copper. The next steps are the same as for the aquatint, although the result is not so fine, uniform, or easily controlled.

The mezzotint is similar to but richer in depth of color than the aquatint. The principle of the process is that a roughened surface will hold more ink and hence print a richer black than a smooth one will. The roughening is done with a rocker, a cylindrical metal form with sharp projections on its surface. This is worked lengthwise and crosswise over the metal plate until a uniformly grained surface results. A fairly good imitation, which lacks, however, the velvety depth of the genuine mezzotint, can be produced by facing a plate with a sheet of sandpaper. The grain is neither so uniform nor so deep as that resulting from the genuine method. The whites of the design, in either case, are obtained by scraping and burnishing with a sharp steel tool called a scraper. And, only designs in flat treatment ought to be duplicated by this method.

The monotint is also called a monotype. A newly beveled plate is inked with a brayer. If printed, this would give a black rectangle. The chiaroscuro of the design is developed by rubbing with rags or fingers. A single print only is possible for each new "drawing." Because the metal plate is only externally affected, it may be used over and over again.

The lithograph process was discovered by Alois Senefelder about 1796. It is based on the affinity of one greasy substance for another and on the absence of this affinity between grease and water. Originally, a drawing was made on stone with a greasy crayon which contained soap among its ingredients. The drawing was fixed with gum arabic, and the whole was then saturated with water. The water was repelled by the greasy drawing but readily sucked up by the absorbent stone. Ink, which adhered to the drawing only, was next applied by a roller and passed together with a sheet of paper through a press. Today,

FOR DESCRIPTION of the etching by Piranesi and the soft-ground by Cotman see the legend on the facing page.

"DEMOLITION of St. James Hall; Interior." Muirhead Bone tackles the architectural motifs of Piranesi and Meryon with the drypoint. The large area covered is successfully unified by this master of the burr. (*British Museum, London.*)

BELOW: TWO STATES of a single design, "Wehlen," by Albert Heckman, Woodstock. The first state carries light tones. To give it a richer quality, the artist simply "drew it directly on the copper plate with one roulette, made several proofs, and then worked over the plate and pulled an edition of twenty prints." It was not, of course, so simple as it sounds. (*Courtesy Ferargil Galleries, New York.*)

FACING PAGE: An early state of an etching from the "Carceri" series by Piranesi (1720-1778) in the Boston Museum of Art. In a later state (*Batsford, London*) darker notes were used to enrich the pattern and as a framework to hold the composition together. "Trees Near Twickenham" by Cotman (1782-1842). This, a soft-ground etching, illustrates one of the best methods for reproducing the subtleness of the pencil sketch. The freedom of the artist's original and the absence of overrefinement combine with oneness of design to make a strong, terse record of an artist's observation. (*British Museum, London.*)

DESIGN 93

"ANNIE HADEN," by Whistler (1834-1903), is as light and airy an etching as the subject would warrant. Compare the free treatment here with the more labored line of a Schongauer engraving (page 74). (*British Museum, London.*) A successful solution of a difficult problem.

"A ROMAN MADONNA," an etching by Robert Austin, a contemporary artist, furnishes in its sureness of line a strong contrast with Whistler's creation. Lines here are ordered; there are no accidental lines. The circular basis of the composition is easily apparent. (*Courtesy the XXI Gallery, London.*)

FACING PAGE: "Spanish Good Friday, Ronda" by Muirhead Bone (1876-   ). The drypoint depicts very effectively, in this case, the indefiniteness and velvety blackness of figures in night procession. The black of the silhouetted building in the right foreground helps to unify the composition. (*M. Knoedler & Company, Inc., New York.*)

specially treated metal plates replace the cumbersome stones. The artist can, in fact, make a lithograph by drawing on a litho paper which is prepared for easy transfer to the stone. Or, again, he need not worry about the technique at all and yet rest assured that modern processes of photography can make up for this want of information. When, as in color reproduction, many blocks are used, the process is called chromolithography.

An incomparable master of the lithograph was Daumier. Brangwyn, too, has done strong work in this medium. Its present-day popular application includes posters, stationery, labels, packages, etc. See pages 96 and 98.

Photolithography, an offset process and an offshoot of lithography proper, permits the printing of fine-screenlike pictures on antique-finished papers.

The silk screen is a modern version of the stenciling process and another

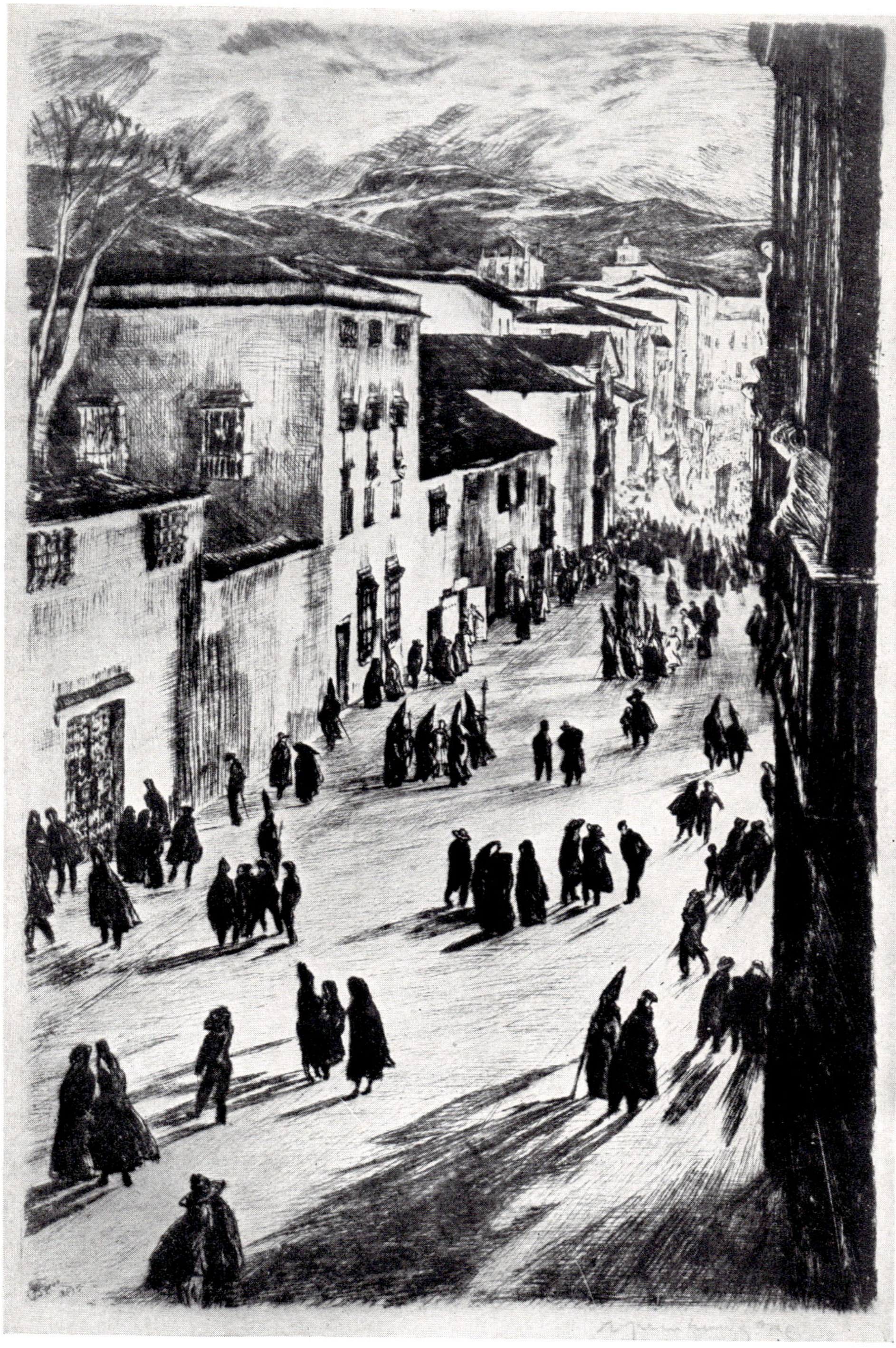

FOR DESCRIPTION of these lithographs by H. Daumier, A. Heckman, and A. Alexeïeff, respectively, see page 98.

DESIGN 97

THE LITHOGRAPH by Frank Brangwyn, above, is an example of the sweeping free style to which the litho pencil lends itself. Compare this with the closer handling of page 97 which is also a lithograph. (*Courtesy London and North Eastern Railway, London.*)

BELOW: Unusual perspective and tonal contrast make Arnold Ronnebeck's lithograph, "Wall Street," a striking presentation of an otherwise commonplace scene. The dramatic quality in the picture is intensified by the wise placing of the blacks, the black of Trinity Church for example. (*Weyhe Gallery, New York.*)

PAGE 96. ABOVE: "Rue Transnonain, le 15 avril 1834," a lithograph by Honoré Daumier. The play of light and its use suggest Goya. The barest hint of caricature is employed to emphasize the gruesomeness of the scene. (*From Jean Laran's Cent Vingt Lithographies de H. Daumier; courtesy Les Beaux-Arts Éditions d'Études et de Documents, Paris.*) BELOW: This Spirited lithograph, drawn with a No. 2 Rancon crayon on French-India paper, was made in Paris by Albert Heckman, Woodstock. The geometric simplifications of buildings are arranged to suggest an elliptical form and are tastefully contrasted with a restful mid-ground. (*Courtesy Ferargil Galleries, New York.*)

PAGE 97. The lithograph by A. Alexeïeff for Dostoevski's "Les Frères Karamazov" shows the stone-like texture that is the most common characteristic of lithography. Its composition and the artist's regard for our imagination make this a striking work of art. (*Éditions de la Pléiade, Paris.*)

"FOUR FIGURES" by Hofer is an example of a brief and personal expression. The line simplification offers a sermon on drawing to the observant artist. (*From a portfolio of Hofer lithographs published by Piper & Company, Munich, for the Marees Society.*) THE HARMONIOUS line character of the distinctive advertisement below could hardly have been reproduced as well as by anything but a line plate. (*Ashley Havinden for J. C. Eno, Ltd., London.*)

example of direct reproduction. It excels in duplicating a limited number of flat, poster-like designs. Here a drawing which is made the size of the stencil is transferred to a screen. This consists of silk material, bolting cloth or organdy, which is fastened to the four sides of a frame. Then the background of the design is made impenetrable to paint by blocking out with shellac or a similar resist. A color, mixed in japan, is poured into the frame and forced over the surface of the screen with a squeegee. The paint which passes through the porous (unvarnished) part of the silk produces the image. This duplication can be made on almost any kind of surface. Additional screens must be used for extra colors. Rich, flat colors characterize good examples of silk screen work.

The line plate is an indirect method of reproduction and the photomechanical equivalent of the woodcut. It is in everyday use in newspaper, magazine, and direct advertising. Any really black ink drawing can be reproduced by this process. The gradation of a normal pencil line, however, loses the grays in reproduction, retaining only the blacks.

Sketches are made in proportion to the size of the desired repro-

DESIGN 99

PRECISENESS OF LINE characterizes the illustrations on these pages. There is something clear-cut, something inevitable, in the placing of the lines and in the patterns which their combination makes possible.

ABOVE: The fine pen-and-ink work of Rosa Brothers borrows its crispness and textural effects from the wood block. Actually the work is drawn for line reproduction in zinc. (*American Telephone and Telegraph Company, New York.*)

BELOW: For reproducing the sharpness and polish of machinery, the line cut is often exceptionally good. The whole gamut from hair line to heavy shade can be truly rendered. (*F. Werkmeister for Meissenbach, Riffarth & Company, Berlin.*)

FACING PAGE: Here Jefferson Clark achieves a wealth of pattern. Even the faces are used as so many decorative notes. It is another superb example of the possibilities of the line cut. (*Decoration for Dodd, Mead & Company; courtesy Linweave Limited Editions, New York.*)

100 GRAPHIC

DESIGN 101

REDUCING OR ENLARGING

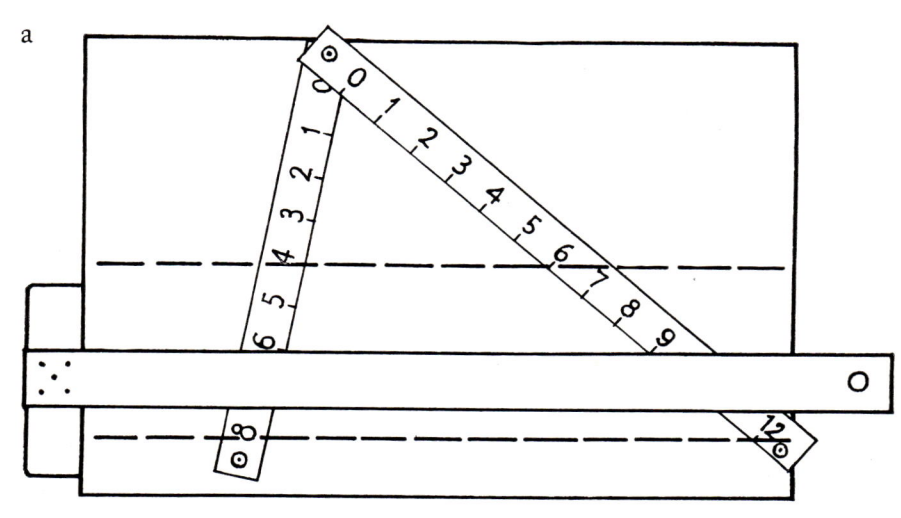

a

a. Tack two cardboard strips with ruler-like markings to show dimensions of original drawing, 6 by 9 inches, for example, where the T-square crosses both strips. To find new length for a contemplated reduction to a width of 4 inches, slide T-square to

4 inches. On a line with this is the new length, 6 inches. For 8 inches it will be 12 inches, etc.

b. This shows an approximate device for enlarging or reducing the various parts of a drawing in correct proportion.

c. A drawing like this, outlined on transparent tracing cloth, can be used over an illustration to test correctness of proportion for reduction to any given size. For general use and accuracy in measurements, however, a professional reducing and enlarging device—engraver's slide rule—is most reliable.

b

c

GRAPHIC

A JOHN AUSTEN LINE ILLUSTRATION FROM THE COLLECTED TALES OF PIERRE LOUŸS

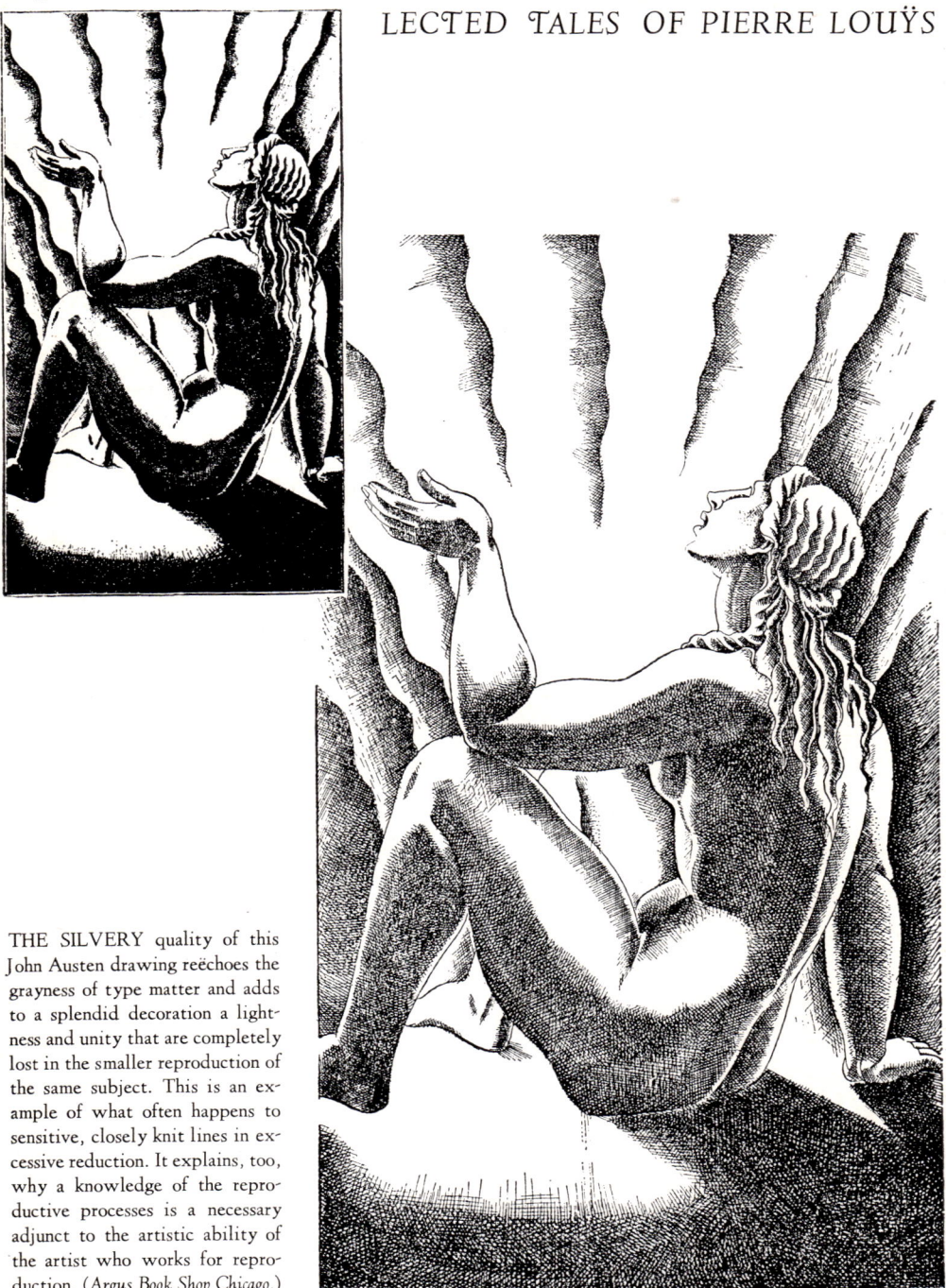

THE SILVERY quality of this John Austen drawing reëchoes the grayness of type matter and adds to a splendid decoration a lightness and unity that are completely lost in the smaller reproduction of the same subject. This is an example of what often happens to sensitive, closely knit lines in excessive reduction. It explains, too, why a knowledge of the reproductive processes is a necessary adjunct to the artistic ability of the artist who works for reproduction. (*Argus Book Shop, Chicago.*)

DESIGN 103

duction, "to scale." One can gauge the correct proportion by the use of a common diagonal for the original and the final sizes of art work (page 102b). This can also be done by using the geometric device for finding proportional lines, which is illustrated on page 102a. Thus, what will the new width of the reproduction be of a 9 by 6-inch picture if the reduced length must be 6 inches?

Where many uniform reproductions must be used, it is wise to draw on tracing paper (page 102c) a dozen or more proportional possibilities. This may be placed over any drawing to test correctness of relationship. The size of the artist's drawing will depend on the result wanted in reproduction—extra large for fine work and 1 inch = 1 inch for that spontaneity that marks an original creation. Mistakes may be painted out with white pigment or scratched out with a razor blade. Some artists use a blue pencil (because it does not usually reproduce) for preliminary sketching and for instructions to the engraver.

The major steps in making a line plate are these: A pane of glass, which has been cleaned and coated with the white of an egg, is allowed to dry. A film of negative collodion is then distributed over the plate. This is taken to the dark room and dipped into a lightproof tank of nitrate of silver. The plate, which is now sensitive to light, is placed into the plate holder and attached to an engraver's camera, in other words "loaded." The exposure that is then obtained on the wet plate is developed and fixed in the dark room. A coating of rubber cement is next applied to the developed negative, and the plate is further covered with stripping collodion. The required area of film is cut, loosened from the glass in a bath of acetic acid, and reversed (stripped) on its base so that the final image will print "right side up." A copper or zinc plate is now cleaned and sensitized (albumen, water, and bichromate of ammonia) in somewhat the same fashion as the glass. It is dried over a gas stove. The glass and metal plates are then locked together in a printing frame and exposed to the light of powerful arc lamps for a few minutes. The "printed" zinc plate is covered with an ink preparation which becomes insoluble in water where the arc lights have previously "baked" the emulsion on the metal. Subjected to the friction of running water, the coating upon the unexposed metal washes off. The enamel-like residue, which is first made "sticky" by slight warming, is

A SUPERBLY COLORED aquatint is the original by Grinevsky for Gogol's *Tarass Boulba*. Even in the half-tone one can see that in aquatints tonal distinctions rather than lines are used to bring out contours. (*La Pléiade, Paris.*)

DESIGN 105

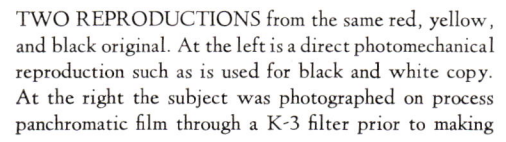

TWO REPRODUCTIONS from the same red, yellow, and black original. At the left is a direct photomechanical reproduction such as is used for black and white copy. At the right the subject was photographed on process panchromatic film through a K-3 filter prior to making the halftone. Note how in the first case, when filters were not used, the black lettering is lost against a red background, and the red figure against the yellow sky because all three colors photographed as black. (Design by E. Dryden, Paris, for Meissenbach, Riffarth & Company, Berlin.)

inked and then dusted over with dragon's blood—a rosin. This adheres only to the inked part of the plate. The plate is again heated over gas until the coating melts to a straw color. The hot plate is chilled in water, producing the acid resist that protects the image from the etching that follows. Etching by hand-

THE ORIGINAL by E. A. Georgi illustrated a happy combination of red, green, and black. The reproduction suggests the variety of textures obtainable by using a crayon drawing on surfaced board together with water color. BELOW: These strips illustrate two ways of obtaining tone effects in line engraving: the top strip was shaded with crayon on surfaced paper; the lower four segments were covered with transparent sheets of Ben Day patterns. Still other devices are available to the artist who prefers subtle gradations to harsh contrasts.

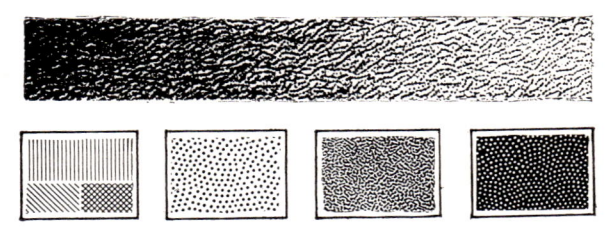

rocked bath or by machine eats away the uncoated metal to an almost imperceptible depth. Three or four successive coatings and etchings—protecting the shoulders of the relief areas with additional coatings of dragon's blood—

DESIGN 107

"LORENZO DI MEDICI," a detail of a painting in the Ricardi Gallery by Benozzo Gozzoli (1420-1498). By comparing the four sections of the reproduction, one can readily see the advantage of a fine 133 screen in obtaining delicate line or tonal distinctions in the main panel, over coarse screens of 50, 85, or 100 (left, top to bottom). Only the difficulty of printing on coarse paper prevents the wider use of the finer screens. (*Fratelli Alinari, Florence.*)

complete the necessary relief except in the larger open spaces. These must be routed out, by a drill-like machine. Often, after a photoengraver's proof is compared with the original drawing, additional hand tooling (retouching) is found necessary. The final plate is then beveled and mounted on wood to make it type high. This plate and proofs are then sent to the printer.

When color plates are wanted in photomechanical work, they are indicated with appropriate markings on a tracing-paper flap which covers the drawing. In not too complicated registry work, separate flaps may be made for each color. The complete "color separation" may be made by the artist if a slight overlap, consistent with safety, is provided on each color tracing. These are made in black and, when reproduced, printed in the appropriate inks.

Of course, a safer but more expensive method is available. A complete colored drawing may be sent to the engraver. Complicated color schemes may eas-

ABOVE: The fine line character of this illustration calls for reproduction in line cut. Ben Day screen indicates what was originally the second color. (Francesco Carnevali, Urbino, for Settimana di Passione published by Bertieri, Milan.) SIDE: In this newspaper advertisement, what would otherwise have been black solids are broken up into grays, without use of screens, by drawing on grained paper. (E. Dryden, Paris, for Haus Neuerburg, Cologne.)

ily be separated into the component elements of yellow, red, and blue by color filters. (Mechanically perfect registry can be taken for granted.) In such filters, the combined color of two primaries is used to filter through the third color. Thus:

Red-blue (violet) filter secures the yellow.

Blue-yellow (green) filter secures the red.

Yellow-red (orange) filter secures the blue.

The halftone is made on cop-

Nun beginnt die Zeit der Wochenend-Fahrten!

Fern von der Stadt irgendwo in schöner Gegend ein noch schöneres Fleckchen aufstöbern! Den Alltag vergessen und was man zurücklässt! — Geniessen, was man mitnimmt für diese schönsten Stunden der Woche, die gute Kameradin:

RAVEN KLAU

per or zinc following the steps used in the making of a line plate. Its invention is ascribed to Georg Meissenbach in the early eighties. The major distinction in production lies in photographing the copy. There, a screen is placed in front of the photographic plate in the camera. The screen consists of two glasses with opaque lines so placed that they cross each other at right angles. The number of lines ruled to the inch determines whether it is a 60-, 70-, 85-, 100-, 120-, 133-, 150-, or 175-screen halftone. It is the metal between the dots which is etched away. The dark parts are then protected from the re-etching which is continued in the high lights. The coarser screens 60, 70, 85 are used on antique stock, and the finer screens on coated paper. In newspaper and magazine reproductions the tonal gradations which are

THE CRISPNESS of the paper and the sparkle of Kees Van Dongen's sketch are both retained unmarred by any unnecessary screen in this high-light halftone. (*Cheney Brothers, New York.*)

FACING PAGE: Unique presentation makes for the attraction of this drawing. It is a halftone reproduction with the high lights etched away to effect vigorous tonal contrasts. (*Vladimir Bobritsky, New York, for Saks Fifth Avenue.*)

associated with photographs and paintings are reproduced almost exclusively by this method. The rare exceptions are those where dry brush, Ben Day, patterned sheets, or surfaced boards, employed in conjunction with line cuts, are found practical. The patterned sheets employed in this work come in transparent paper or celluloid form. The films in either case are laid over the drawing, and the superfluous part cut or scraped away. Copy and transparent sheets are photographed together. Editorial cartoons and comic strips are frequently so reproduced.

When it is desired to show the gradation of a pencil against the sparkling white of a paper background, a high-light halftone is used. Here the dots of the screen are dropped out by the overexposure or re-etching of those parts

DESIGN 111

ABOVE: An English student's wood engraving, with a finish more usually associated with professional work. For cutting the sky, a knife and gouge were used instead of a graver. (*Esther Forbes, Camberwell School of Arts and Crafts, London.*) SIDE: To the student, these two wood blocks show what striking results may be obtained with economy of cutting and also show the importance of background spaces. (*By Rak, student of the Warsaw School of Fine Arts; courtesy Grafika.*)

of the picture which represent the paper. Normally, the white of the paper is reproduced in the form of a light-gray screen. A high-light halftone may be obtained from a photograph, too, if the parts to be etched clean are indicated on a tissue flap which is made to serve the purpose of a frisket.

A "blowup" halftone is similar to the high-light halftone but more easily controlled by the artist. This is especially suitable for fine newspaper reproduction. An enlarged silver or Velox print is made from a halftone one-half the size of the desired plate (60-line screen instead of 120-line screen). The high lights are painted out, the shadows are darkened, and the retouched print is then rephotographed and etched on zinc or copper.

*Aquatone** is a planographic method of printing. The plate used is zinc, coated with a thin layer of

*Contributed by M. N. Weyl of E. Stern & Co., Inc., Philadelphia.

112 GRAPHIC

STUDIO IN THE Graphic Industries School, Warsaw, with stones, rollers, presses, used in lithographic work.

gelatin. The method of printing is similar to offset; and an offset press is employed. The image to be printed is hardened and made waterproof. This part of the plate takes ink and transmits it to the offset cylinder. The rest of the plate absorbs water and rejects ink. Owing to the extraordinary sensitivity of gelatin, very fine screens may be used. In practice, screens yielding from 40,000 to 90,000 dots to the square inch are used (a 150-screen halftone has 22,500 dots to the square inch). Aquatone permits reproduction of fine detail and wide tonal gradation on rough or mat paper.

Rotogravure is primarily an adaptation of photogravure to cylinder printing. We are familar with the process in the form of sepia-colored Sunday supplements. It reproduces tone pictures or photographs with results similar to the halftone but without its conspicuous screen. Engraved cylinders print image and type matter on both sides of the paper, which is fed into the press from rolls. The printed sheets, cut, dried, stacked, and counted, issue from another end of the machine. The rotary feature of the press permits minimum makeready, a large printing per hour, and, withal, a softer result than is possible with the more generally used halftone.

Stereotyping, electrotyping, and other "typings" are not treated in this book

DESIGN

because they are not within the control or influence of the artist. They serve to multiply the number of cuts from an original plate and so permit the economical and simultaneous printing of a single display in any desired number of places. With them it is also possible to reduce the cost of production through printing an identical unit many times with each impression.

Inventions are being made every day that make it more and more difficult to distinguish an original work of art from the reproduction of such a work. To most of us whose enjoyment of a picture is based on something more substantial than the item of exclusiveness alone, a modern facsimile reproduction is the source of much pleasure. The limitations set by the format of a book do not always permit facsimiles, but even in their reduced forms, the plates in this book for instance, give in a substantial measure the effects achieved by the originals. This can be furthered if neighboring pictures are compared, and then if all except the picture being analyzed are covered with a sheet of paper to minimize distraction. "Finders," formed by the overlapping of two L-shaped cardboards, serve such a purpose admirably.

PROBLEM in reproduction. Paint a piece of battleship linoleum, 5 by 7 inches, with white tempera. On it brush a free design in black to illustrate some favorite character about whom you have read and suggest just enough background (see page 112) to give atmosphere to your sketch. Cut out the white spaces with knives, razor blades, and linoleum-cutting tools.

ALTERNATE PROBLEM: Make a second solution for your favorite character. Now, however, make several layouts for your finished job, developing your best idea. This time plan your drawing to be reproduced to harmonize with type. Will it be linoleum again? See John Austen's work on page 103. See also the model illustrations in the chapter on the Book.

MORAL: Woe to the artist who depends on the next fellow for his craft. (Franklin Printing Company, Philadelphia.)

PHOTOGRAPHY CHAPTER 4

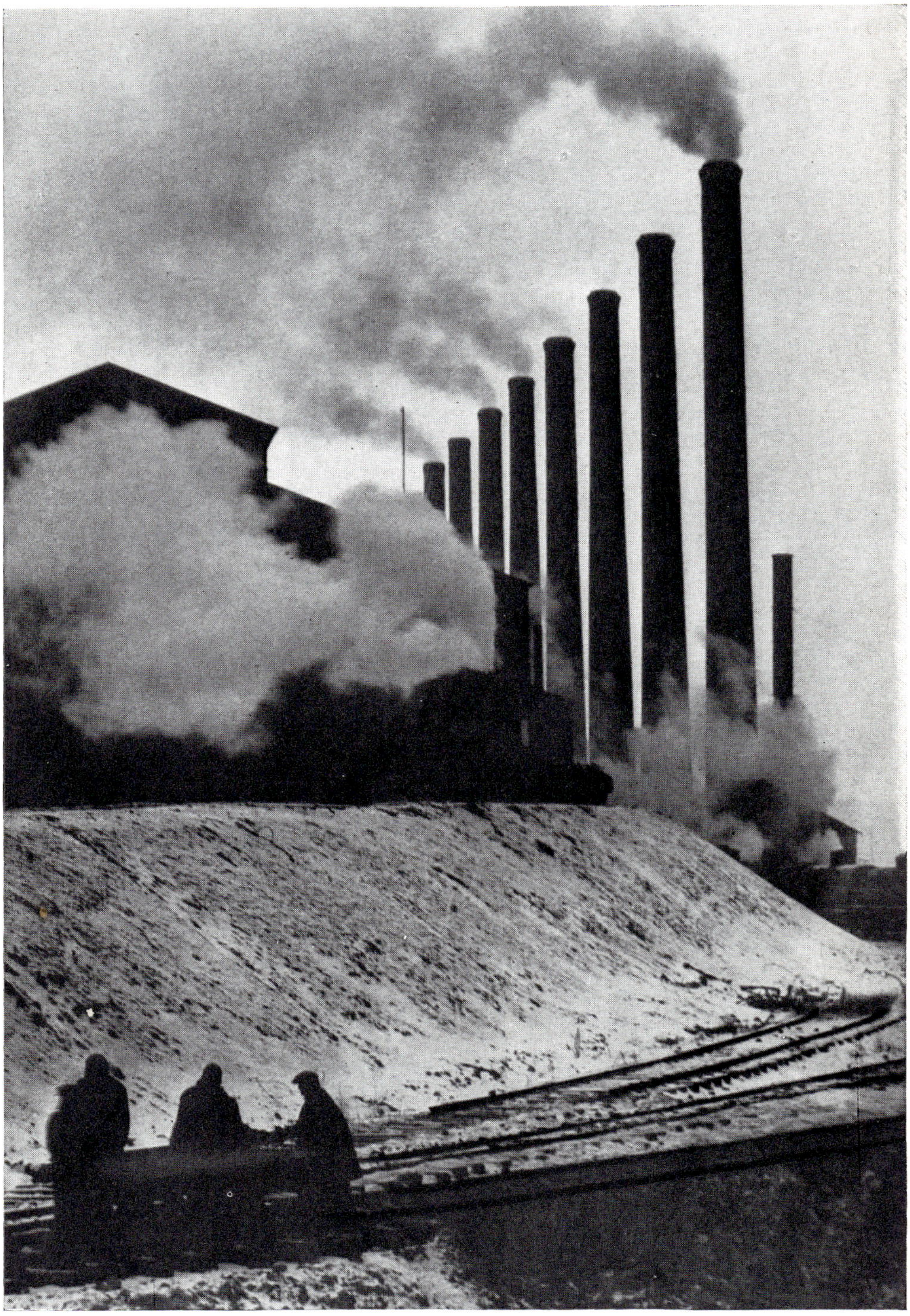

PHOTOGRAPHY

AS EARLY AS 1520, Leonardo da Vinci (and even before him Roger Bacon) had observed that images of objects could be reflected in a dark chamber. In 1556, Fabricius discovered the second fundamental law of photography, namely, that silver chloride turns black under the influence of light. In the course of the following three centuries, Porta of Naples, Schulze of Halle, the Swede Scheele, the Frenchman Charles, and the Englishman Wedgwood contributed discoveries and improvements to the method of arresting images by means of light. But it was only in 1822-1826 that the Frenchmen Nicéphore Niépce and Louis Jacques Daguerre perfected methods which are the prototypes of contemporary photogravure and photography. The present highly developed photographic processes were inaugurated in 1829 by Niépce de Saint-Victor and elaborated during the following thirty years by Archer and Fry, Major Russell and R. L. Maddox, Poitevin and Gandieu. In 1888, Eastman introduced celluloid film which was invented the previous year by Goodman, making photography economically accessible to the general public.

The appeal of realism, the desire to obtain accurate likeness, supplied the impetus for the development of photography. As a fine art, it has progressed from the simple objective of recording nature to the wider range that camera angles, ultraclose-ups, photograms, and photomontage have made possible. Today the lens penetrates beyond mere externals. Instead of depending upon accidental results, the contemporary photographer has learned to select, to arrange, and to interpret. Like other contemporary artists, he has dared to employ unusual points of view, to free himself from set dicta, and to emphasize expressionism, or impressionism if the artist preferred, over literal transcription.

Modern photography should be studied with the same thoroughness as painting. Its art employs the same principles of composition. It is necessary to

CHAPTER DECORATION: Vignette, combination line and halftone plate, by Brigdens, Ltd., Toronto.
CHAPTER FRONTISPIECE: Margaret Bourke-White has sought out a symbolic segment from the industrial landscape of the Otis Steel Company plant to suggest the impressiveness of the whole. Artistry is shown in the repetition of the smoke stacks and in the subordination of all that is pictorially extraneous to the problem at hand.

divide a given space, whether canvas or photographic plate, into parts that form an interesting and harmonious whole; to arrange the pattern of dark and light pleasingly; and to maintain a dominant point of interest with well-correlated subordinates. One learns through repeated efforts, with the use of the utmost care in both mechanical processes and composition, although many genuinely great photographers are impressed as much by subject appeal as by composition. In the words of one of them, "a beautiful photograph of a field of grass (referring to a Stieglitz photograph) without any so-called composition is still great art to me." Still, it is undeniable that the best results will accrue to the best artist. The general practice of employing photographic tricks, such as unnatural lighting and the overuse of mirrors and fog effects, does not necessarily displace good design. Knowledge of techniques is valuable, but superior skill cannot cover up inferior art. The result must still be judged, for its artistic merit, largely by the principles of composition.

Because developing and printing, important steps in this art, call for expert and painstaking application, the neophyte in illustrative photography may find it profitable to leave the chemical processes to a professional laboratory. To the student the bibliography offers a selected list of books on the mechanics of photography, the variety of lenses, emulsions, papers, and chemicals.

We recommend the professional view camera to the beginner, for its ease of

USED TO advertise Ivory Soap in 1883, this is considered the first composite photograph to have been enlarged to twenty-four-sheet poster size. (*Strobridge Lithographing Company, Boston, for Procter & Gamble Company, Cincinnati.*)

SIMILAR SUBJECTS interpreted by man (pen) and machine (camera). Fidelity to detail, attractive grouping, and sound mastery of the mediums are common to both. (Pen drawing prepared by F. C. Pritchard, Wood & Partners, Ltd., London. Photograph by Draeger Frères, Paris, for Tremlett.)

handling and low cost of required materials; and the 4- by 5-inch size of negatives because they enlarge naturally to the usual 8- by 10-inch size. To photograph with such a camera, these few simple manipulations should be observed:

1. Load the plate holder in a completely darkened room, or with the aid of a small ruby light, by removing the cut film carefully from its package and inserting it into the holder so that the dull-coated emulsion side will later face the lens.

2. Place the object at the required distance, anywhere from 3 to 10 feet in front of the camera, moving the camera until what you want is on the ground glass, taking care that sufficient light falls upon the object to effect an exposure.

3. Adjust the diameter of the lens opening to the existing conditions.

4. Focus the picture to the required sharpness on the ground glass back of the camera by extending or contracting the bellows, thus advancing or retarding the lens.

5. Close the shutter and insert the plate holder between the ground glass and the camera frame.

6. Pull out the lid that covers the film in the plate holder.

7. Again make sure that the object is well placed and well lighted and

A NEWS PHOTOGRAPH, sincere in its realism, tense with arrested motion and free from an artist's personal interpretation. General Francesco de Pinedo, right foreground, his arms outstretched in fiery death, perishes in an attempted solo flight from New York to Baghdad, 1933. (Casselman, copyright News Syndicate Co., New York.)

BELOW: A diagrammatic explanation of the relation of the camera both to group arrangement and to lighting.

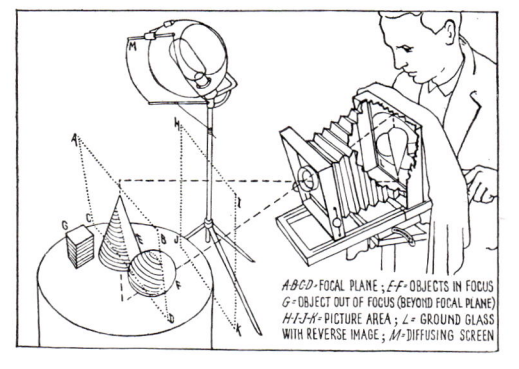

ABCD=FOCAL PLANE; *EF*=OBJECTS IN FOCUS
G=OBJECT OUT OF FOCUS (BEYOND FOCAL PLANE)
H-I-J-K=PICTURE AREA; *L*=GROUND GLASS WITH REVERSE IMAGE; *M*=DIFFUSING SCREEN

then open the shutter for the required length of exposure time.

8. Close the shutter, switch off the light, replace the lid in the plate holder, and remove the holder from the camera.

9. Take the plate holder back into the dark room, remove and develop the exposed film, or wrap it carefully into a few layers of black paper and keep it there until ready for the developing bath.

By placing the object before the lens, we have brought it into the camera's vision. The nearer we bring the object to the camera the larger it looms on the ground glass. Moving the camera away from the object reduces its size or area but includes more of the background. This is called a semiclose-up or a long shot.

With the area satisfactorily determined, the next step is to provide sufficient illumination for an exposure. For most purposes, full sunlight is the ideal condition. Direct window light indoors is also practical. As a rule, however, illustrative photography relies on artificial light. A 1000-watt electric daylight bulb will be bright enough for pictures of the close-up or semiclose-up variety, although, with longer exposure (for subjects other than the figure) or with sufficiently fast lenses and emulsions,

120 GRAPHIC

BALANCED SPACING and transparent clarity enliven the quaint atmosphere of this still life whose major contrasting note is suggested by the moving line of the slanted rifle. It is reminiscent of a Chardin. (*Studio Sun, London.*)

two 10-watt lamps will also be adequately bright. Two 500-watt or one 1000-watt light may be safely attached to the ordinary home or office current, but stronger fuses will have to be provided for lights of greater wattage.

DESIGN 121

MODERN CAMERA design: the 8 by 10-inch Century Imperial studio model. The sliding ground-glass carriage, devised for quick change of plates, is a convenient feature. (*A product of the Eastman Kodak Company of Rochester, N. Y.*)

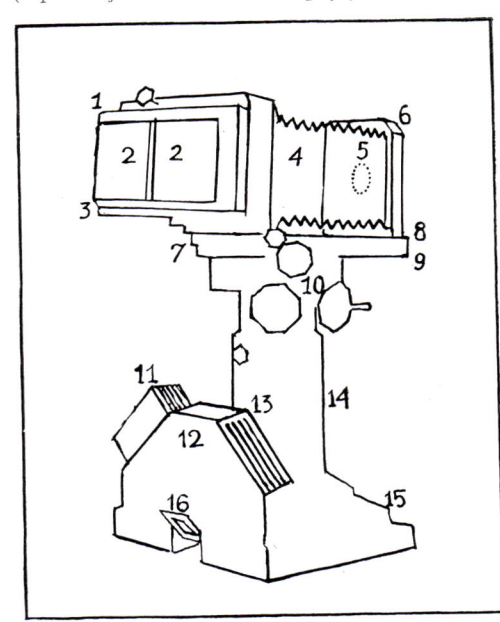

One of the latest devices to simplify the problem of lighting is the "floodlight" bulb, a home-current lamp of ordinary size, producing an extremely strong light for limited exposure-time. Combined use of fast lenses and emulsions sensitive to red, yellow, and green rays—not only violet and blue ones—makes night exposures possible at as little as 1/32 of a second and with only weak light (dim lamps and stage and screen reflections, for example). As a further step, experiments with infra-red photography are proving that images of objects can be recorded in what appears to be complete darkness to the unaided eye. Shadows on the object, unless intentionally created, may be eliminated

DIAGRAM OF PARTS OF CENTURY CAMERA
1. Reversible adapter back.
2. Ground-glass back.
3. Sliding ground-glass carriage.
4. Bellows.
5. Lens.
6. Lens board.
7. Camera bed.
8. Traveling frame-support bed.
9. Extension bed.
10. Controls to elevate or lower the camera, to swing it horizontally or vertically as the problem demands.
11. Plate holders before exposure.
12. Built-in holder compartment.
13. Compartment for exposed plate holders.
14. Stand: pedestal.
15. Stand: pedestal base.
16. Treadle to lift pedestal base and facilitate change of camera's position.

by reflectors, sheets, of white linen or paper placed opposite the source of light and facing the shadowed area. The intensity of the light can be diffused and its range arrested by the use of a white diffusing screen placed closely in front of the lamp. The light may be strong enough to effect exposures in seconds or fractions of seconds or mellow enough to require minutes or even hours of exposure. Prolonged exposure, or the so-called "painting-with-light" method—directing the illumination at certain portions of the object while the exposure is going on—are often necessary to produce a clear and detailed picture.

Area and light determined, the next task is to focus the image on the ground glass. This image should not only show the object itself in as clear and sharp contours as are required by the particular problem; but, what is more important, it should show the pictorial composition of the photograph and the distribution of light—thus prognosticating the expected result.

ABOVE: A composite photograph of the set at the Studio Sun, Ltd., London. The chains are part of the overhead lighting equipment and have been superimposed over an angle shot of the stage where a model was posing for a fashion photograph. Light and lines of chains and beams help to direct attention to the center of interest—the model. BELOW: A cleverly lighted interior photograph that shows also something of the equipment that forms an important part of the contemporary photographer's laboratory—his palette. (*Studio of Deberny & Peignot, Paris.*)

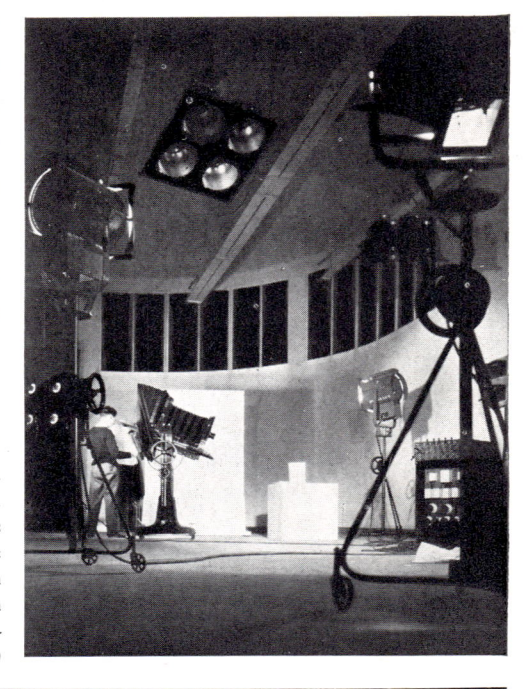

DESIGN 123

ANIMAL PICTURES: "Cat" by Moholy Nagy. The negative image, an unusual view, helps to impart an expression of stealthiness to this harmless kitten. (From Moholy Nagy, vol. 1 of the Fototek series published by Klinkhardt & Bierman, Berlin.) "Snake." The effectiveness of Unguentine as an antiseptic for scratches and possible poisoning is implied through association by this photograph of a snake. (Courtesy the Norwich Pharmacal Company, Norwich.)

Exposure is the time allowed for the action of light upon the emulsion and is one of the most difficult steps in the making of a photographic illustration. It varies for almost every problem. The following formula may serve as a guide:

With a wide-open $f\,4.5$ lens,
a 1000-watt light,
the lamp 3 feet away from the object,
the camera 6 feet away from the object,
an indoor picture requires an exposure of 1 second.

With a slower lens, the time will increase to 3, 5, 10, or more seconds. A larger distance between light, camera, and object will also double or treble the exposure time necessary to secure a clear negative.

Care should be taken to avoid accidental double exposures by always marking the exposed part of the plate holder. Exposure time of more than one second is controlled by the watch or counted. The count of "one and two and three..." approaches more nearly the actual duration of seconds than "one,

"CALF." With philosophical calm the young cow faces the distinction of being awarded to a champion woman worker on a collective Russian farm. A worm's-eye view and straightforward composition enhance the documentary value of this scene. Photographed by Sergei Eisenstein for one of his motion pictures. (*Kultsviaz-Voks, Moscow.*)

"BEACH COMBER" by Lucca Chmel of the Graphic Art and Research School, Vienna. The textural quality of water, the mist of morn, and the dark and light pattern of a work of art are encompassed within the small confines of a 5 by 7-inch print. "Coast of Portugal," an amateur's composition, combines aerial perspective with classic simplicity—two vertical, two horizontal, and two diagonal lines. (*Small snapshot taken by Anna Friend, Brooklyn.*) "Milan Cathedral" shows an interesting design achieved by the rapidly descending view of the stairway and the rapidly rising perspective of the inclosed courtyard. (*Walter Kerst for Seven Seas, house organ of the North German Lloyd, New York.*)

FACING PAGE: The tree study "Cypress—1931" is a typical Weston, transfiguring a fragment of nature into an intimate picturesque composition of irresistible appeal. A wealth of minute detail is brought to our attention by juxtaposing the bark against the uninterrupted flatness of the sky. (*Edward Weston, Carmel.*)

126 GRAPHIC

two, three...." and it is better to expose too long than too briefly. An underexposed negative is a total failure. There are a few helpful exposure meters on the market, but exposing should be mastered by diligent practice rather than by the application of, or too much dependence on, mechanical contrivances.

DESIGN 127

Lenses are combinations of concave or convex disks of glass which serve to concentrate light rays. The distance between the central point of the lens and the focused point on the film is called focal length f. The speed of a lens is expressed in a fraction derived from dividing the lens diameter by the focal length. The smaller the denominator of this fraction the brighter and faster the lens; e.g., the 1:6.5 lens is about half as fast as the 1:4.5. A larger denominator stands for decreased light capacity and longer exposure time in square proportion. Thus, an $f/8$ lens requires not twice but four times as much exposure as an $f/4$. The more general gradations are $f/4, f/8, f/16, f/32$.

Retouching should be unnecessary in a good negative. The appeal and the correct lighting should be on the negative before the latter leaves the camera. However, retouching may be of value as a corrective for unexpected faults or as a means of emphasizing shadows and high lights. For retouching, the negative is placed on a slightly tilted plate of ground glass. A 75-watt daylight bulb, standing or hanging directly behind the glass plate, supplies the light. Finer details are retouched on the emulsion side of the film, while larger areas are retouched on the celluloid side. Emulsion-side retouching is done with a medium-hard, finely pointed pencil and a great deal of patience. Occasionally, a

"HANDS." In these four studies, photographers, with the artistry of dramatists, have captured the telltale expressiveness of the human hand.

"THE GHOST TOAST." Its production required great skill and patience. Effective design is obtained by the use of the recurring motif. (*Victor Keppler, New York, for Hoffman Beverage Company, Newark, through Batten, Barton, Durstine & Osborn.*)

FACING PAGE: "Bread," a lens study in sociology. Coarse hands, crude knife, calico apron, and black bread combine to tell a story from the life of the "little people." Note the feel of the varied textures. (*Trude Hamburg, Berlin.*) "The Tailor." Utmost simplicity of means was employed to arrive at this striking result—a heraldic symbol for the ancient and honorable craft of the clothier. (*Anton Bruehl, New York, for Weber & Heilbronner.*) "Stop!" We deduce this command as an automotive-conscious people familiar with the gesture of the upright hand. The composition derives its eye-arresting effect from the strong diagonal lines of the fingers accentuating the compact message in the palm of the hand. (*Herbert Bayer for Dorland, Berlin; courtesy "Penrose's Annual," London.*)

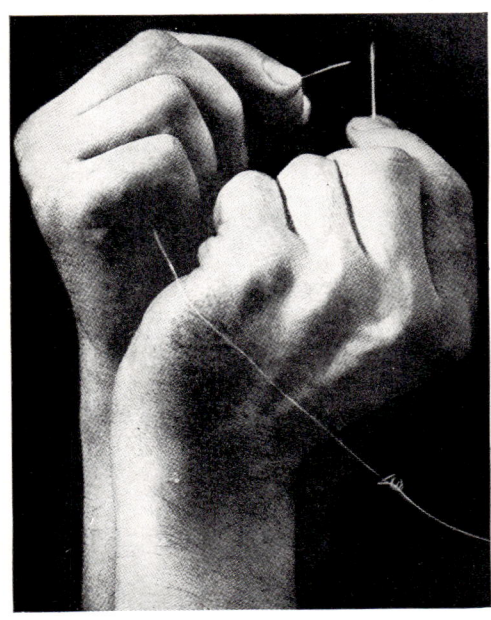

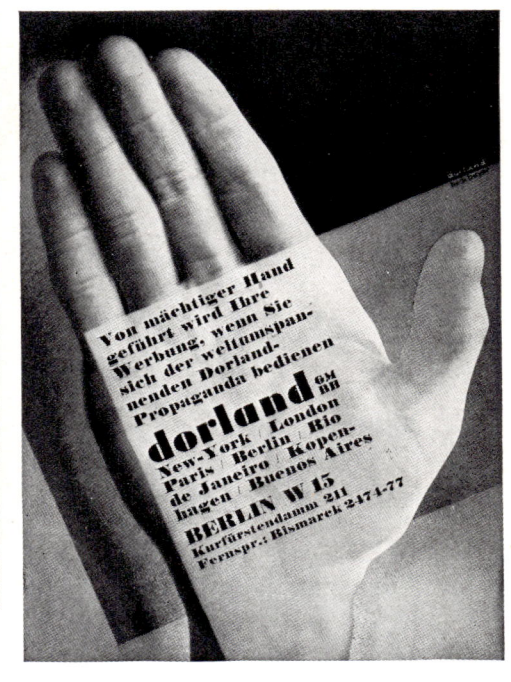

For description of these compositions see facing page.

DESIGN ═══════════════ 129

CHARNAUX

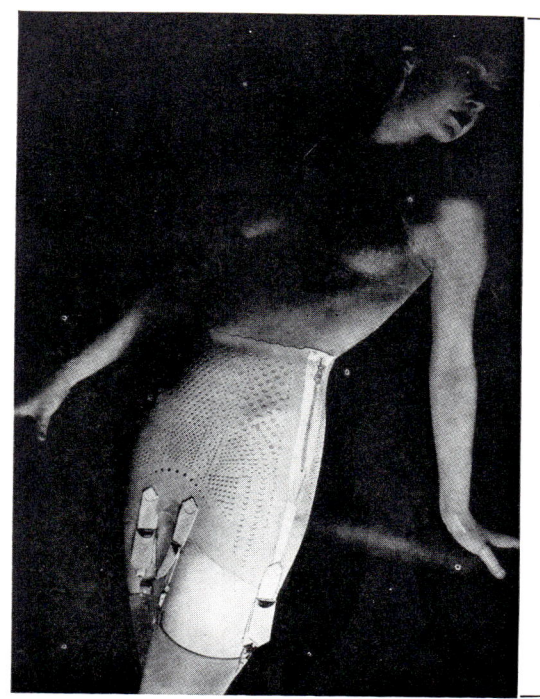

CORSETS AND BELTS ARE MADE FROM AN ANOTEX product, a wonderful new material deposited direct from the milk of the rubber tree, yet far removed from the established conception of rubber. Electro-deposition eliminates the usual rubber smell. Thousands of perforations pattern the corset, scientifically arranged to give ventilation and support.

THE CHARNAUX CORSET IS AS LIGHT AS LACE. Hygienic. Washable. Cool and exquisite to wear. It is like a new skin gently moulding your body into soft uncorseted loveliness.

"CUSTOM WEAVING." A truly creative approach to the more or less hackneyed task of fashion photography; nice play of dark against light. (*Anton Bruehl for Bonwit Teller, New York.*) "Lady in Black." Severe restraint of the pose and simple silhouette of the dress, uninterrupted by unessentials, make this an outstandingly fine fashion illustration. (*Von Horn for Bergdorf Goodman, through Kenyon & Eckhardt, New York.*) Further description on page 131.

GRAPHIC

"ELECTRICITY." Jagged white flashes are contrasted with the mystic lines of the torsos to symbolize the power of electrical energy. (One of a series of plates from Man Ray's portfolio Électricité, published by Jarach & Chambry for the Compagnie Parisienne de Distribution d'Électricité; courtesy of the Julien Levy Galleries, New York.)

FACING PAGE: Double-page, spread from a finely conceived and executed booklet. The treatment of the photograph excels in freshness and subtlety. (Photograph by Maurice Beck; layout and design by E. McKnight-Kauffer; printed by Percy Lund Humphries & Company, Ltd., for the Charnaux Patent Corset Company, Ltd., all of London.)

DESIGN 131

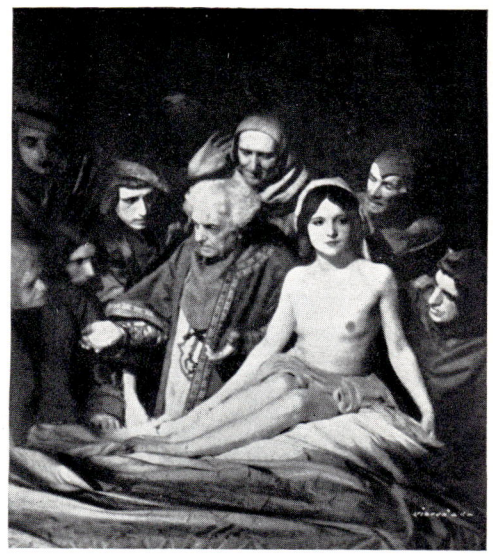

ABOVE: "Henri de Mondeville" and "Lafranchi of Milan," two units of a series of photographic compositions illustrating the development of surgery. Historic accuracy, careful costuming, appropriate models, fine lighting, dramatic staging, and good design were necessary to assure the success of this series. (Photographs by Léjaren a Hiller of Underwood and Underwood, for Davis & Geck, Inc., Brooklyn.)

SIDE: Hand and eyes are posed and lighted to register fear, which the black background accentuates. The terse exclamation gives point to the emotion expressed by posture and high lights. A concentrated bit of dramatics. (John Scott for the Johns-Manville Corporation, of New York.)

very fine thin brush and solid India ink are employed. With a clean piece of linen, a drop of retoucher's varnish is cautiously rubbed over the required spot. Very fine dots, dashes, or circles are then applied close to each other, until good coverage of the spot is obtained. It will be futile to use heavier pencil or brush marks where deeper coverage is necessary. Only layer over layer of very fine strokes will produce a good surface in printing. Celluloid-side retouching balances out the tonal values of the photograph as a whole by creating large light areas, toning down shadows which are too deep, etc. The surface is first cleaned, then covered with varnish as above and rubbed over with soft black chalk or with carmine-colored liquid crayon sauce. However, for most satisfactory results, photo retouching is best left to those who do it professionally.

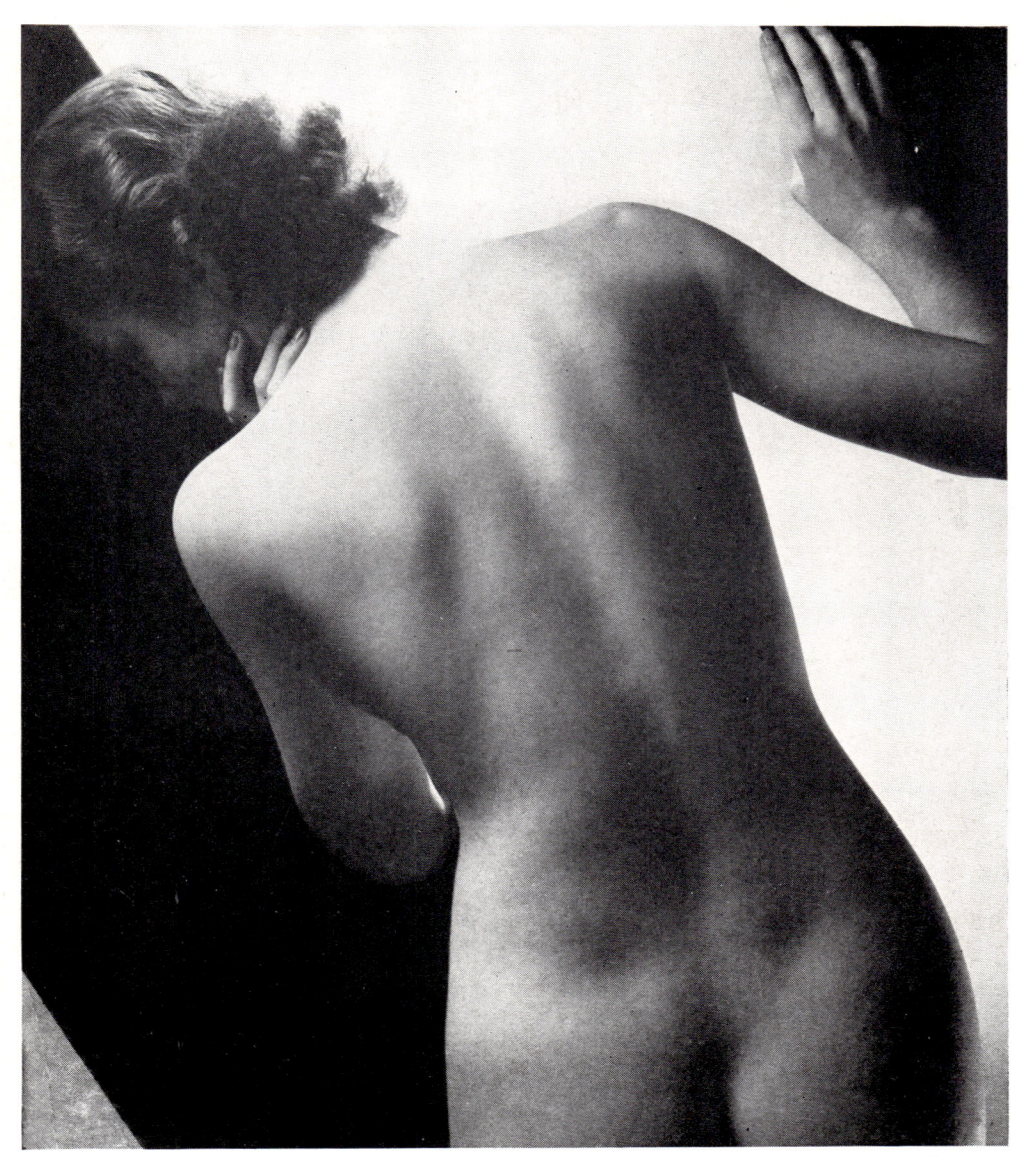

GRAYS AND WHITES against black, shaded torso against white, yet the whole as unbroken as a Gauguin figure, shows with what artistry camera masterpieces are made. Rubens and Renoir hardly treated the human torso more sympathetically. An inspiring creation that combines the appeal of the human figure with the abstract attraction of a fine organization. (*Edward Steichen for Cannon Towels; courtesy of N. W. Ayer & Son, Inc., Philadelphia.*)

While retouching on the negative is directly connected with photography, the retouching of a positive print by airbrush, brush, or crayon is not photography proper. It is rather within the scope of the artist or designer who prepares the prints to enable the engraver to obtain better results in his halftones.

THE STUDENTS AND FACULTY OF THE ABRAHAM LINCOLN HIGH SCHOOL CORDIALLY INVITE YOU TO ATTEND THE EXERCISES TO BE HELD ON MONDAY, FEBRUARY 12, 1934, AT 10:00 O'CLOCK IN THE MORNING. THE GENERAL ORGANIZATION OF THE SCHOOL WILL PRESENT THE LINCOLN AWARD TO HONORABLE SAMUEL SEABURY "TO HONOR HIS DISTINGUISHED SERVICES ON BEHALF OF THE CITY OF NEW YORK."

GABRIEL R. MASON, PRINCIPAL.

Enlarging is a widely used method for obtaining more impressive and distinct prints from small hand camera and midget camera negatives and oversized details from ordinary studio pictures. The menace of heavy *grain* (the amount and size of silver particles suspended in the emulsion), which blurs and dulls many an enlargement, has been checked by the increasing delicacy of film coatings. Every student of illustrative photography will find an enlarging machine of great value to his work. The manipulation of the handy vertical models now on the market is very simple and can be easily mastered.

Photograms are creative compositions which are recorded directly on photographic paper without the aid of either lens or camera. They are apt to seem peculiar to the average onlooker. Their present use is not, therefore, very extensive. Experimenting with photograms, *drawing with light*, is often a good start in instruction or self-education before going over to the intricacies of lens and film. To make a photogram, chosen objects are placed on or near a sheet of sensitized paper. According to the artist's visualization, the paper is then exposed

PHOTOGRAPHIC POSTERS. The restful vista of the Dinan poster and the bold photomontage of the Ciutadà summons invite comparison as to the effectiveness of composite and straight photography. (*French poster photographed by Le Boyer for the Chemins de Fer de l'Etat, Paris; Spanish poster by Juan Seix, printed by I. G. Seix y Barral, Barcelona.*) "Glass Bottle." This still life, originally photographed in two colors by a student, shows fine arrangement and textural distinctions. (*Courtesy Graphic Art and Research School, Vienna.*)

FACING PAGE: The effect of a good woodcut was achieved in this folder by making a direct line engraving from an unretouched photograph of a statue. Similar results may be obtained with sharply contrasted photographic prints. (*Abraham Lincoln High School, Brooklyn.*)

DESIGN 135

HIGHLIGHTS REMINISCENT of a Rembrandt painting, even if a bit more generous, deepen the shadows in this character study of a Soviet peasant woman. Its realistic tones contrast interestingly with the silvery pencil effect of Peter Powel's photograph on facing page. (From Sergei Eisenstein's film "The Old and the New"; courtesy of Kultsviaz-Voks, Moscow.) FACING PAGE: "Woman's Head." The compelling expression of the eyes is accentuated by the delicately "drawn" lines of the face and the hands. The whole rendition is of an amazing clarity and finesse; there are no accidental shadows to mar the unity of the composition. (Peter Powel; courtesy of Vendre, Paris.)

to intense or subdued, mobile or steady light, at close range or from a distance, for varied periods of time. The resulting image, carefully fixed, will show transparency and gradations from gleaming white through all the shades of gray to deepest black. The effect obtained has an eerie quality. The intensity of the whites in a photographic print is due to a coating of *baryta* (barium sulphate) containing pigments of chemically and visually purest white, which insulates the emulsion from any impurities that may be contained in the paper base.

Photomontage is a widely used and greatly abused process of mounting sections of one or more photographs next to or over each other to produce a symbolic illustration. It is essential to organize these illustrative units to create a pictorially coordinated composition. To be effective, combinographs of this sort must be used sparingly and composed with judgment. Superfluous details may ruin an otherwise pleasing combination. Clarity, careful planning, precise cutting and pasting, and a preference for bold details are essential. Beyond this, there are almost no limits to the artist's inventiveness in employing this method of photographic illustration, as witness pages 135, 150, 273, and 335.

DESIGN 137

THE PORTRAIT of Georgia O'Keefe by Alfred Stieglitz depends on straightforward presentation and deliberate design rather than on superficial effects and artificial devices. (*Reproduced from "America and Alfred Stieglitz," courtesy of The Literary Guild of America, Inc., New York.*)

SIDE: "Magneto-Gorsk." The photograph of an industrial scene of present-day Russia by Margaret Bourke-White (standing with consul Tolokonsky) was enlarged to serve as a mural. It has the merit of strong composition and the appeal of actuality. As heroic in size as in results. (*Courtesy the Consulate General of the USSR in New York.*)

FACING PAGE: "Cotton Club." An example of candid camera photography by one of its noted practitioners. Bright reflections of light that interplay with the dark of the silhouetted figures form an exciting pattern. (*Remie Lohse of New York, for the publication, "Town and Country."*)

Reversed positives offer striking possibilities. Here, the negative instead of the positive image of the picture is used. The reverse values often prove more powerful and appealing than the ordinary, natural rendering.

Motion picture and *midget cameras* are becoming increasingly popular. It is advisable for the progressive camera artist to become acquainted with the advantages presented by motion picture photography. When the problem is to secure a fleeting movement or facial expression, a motion picture will provide dozens

DESIGN

of sequential but rapidly changing pictures, placing at one's disposal an ample collection of adaptable poses. Still cameras small enough to use motion picture frames for negatives and producing midget-size images are valuable media for studies and experiments as well as for important outdoor and indoor work requiring copious scenes and rapidity of action. Their cost of upkeep is slight. They are convenient and easy and reliable to use. They provide a varied selection of material from which the most appropriate subject can be selected and enlarged to almost any serviceable size.

The *airbrush* or aerograph is a device for applying color to a surface by spraying. It consists of a small pointed tube, the nozzle of which is blocked by a very fine silver needle. By pressing a trigger, the point of this needle can be withdrawn into the nozzle, thus allowing an even stream of compressed air or liquid carbonic gas to pass from a tank through the nozzle, taking with it a spray of thin liquid color which has been previously prepared in a cup attached to the airbrush. The spray can be adjusted equally well to a fine hairline or a broad coverage. Frisket paper or other material that does not curl up under moisture is cut out and rubber-cemented on the drawing to mask out the shapes required by the design. This masking-out is repeated until all nuances of the finished design appear. The airbrush was originally intended for the retouching of photographic negatives and positives or for decorative background work. It was through the experimental efforts of graphic artists that the spray technique was developed into a flexible and effective creative medium. Unique and fine results have been achieved with the aerograph method by some of the leading illustrators and poster artists (Brodovitch, Gronowski, Carlu, Cassandre, Alexeïeff, pages 143, 318, 323, 347, and 352, respectively).

Photography has become a permanently valuable technique in the hands of the artist. The reproductions suggest something of its achievements and, it is hoped, will encourage the graphic artist and amateur to experiment with this unexploited means of expression. It is a medium of such flexibility that its uses are wide and varied. It is important as a graphic and dramatic aid in the dissemination of informative, commercial, educational, and social messages, in advertising, in news, and in the illustration of books and pamphlets. Aside from the arts, photography is invaluable in X ray, telephoto transmission, astronomy, micrography, aerial survey, photostat, blueprint, and photo-mechanical reproduction.

A fine photographic still life is this work by Anton Bruehl, New York. Especially successful are its use of dark and light distinctions to suggest rotundity, and its curved and angular line contrasts. The outline of the tray is thoughtfully repeated in the elliptical lines of its bottom. These spotlight the dominant group effectively. Even in photography artistic conception and good design are more important than mere subject matter. Many a still life in the hands of a would-be Cézanne has been less memorable than this direct statement by a sensitive photographer.

DESIGN 141

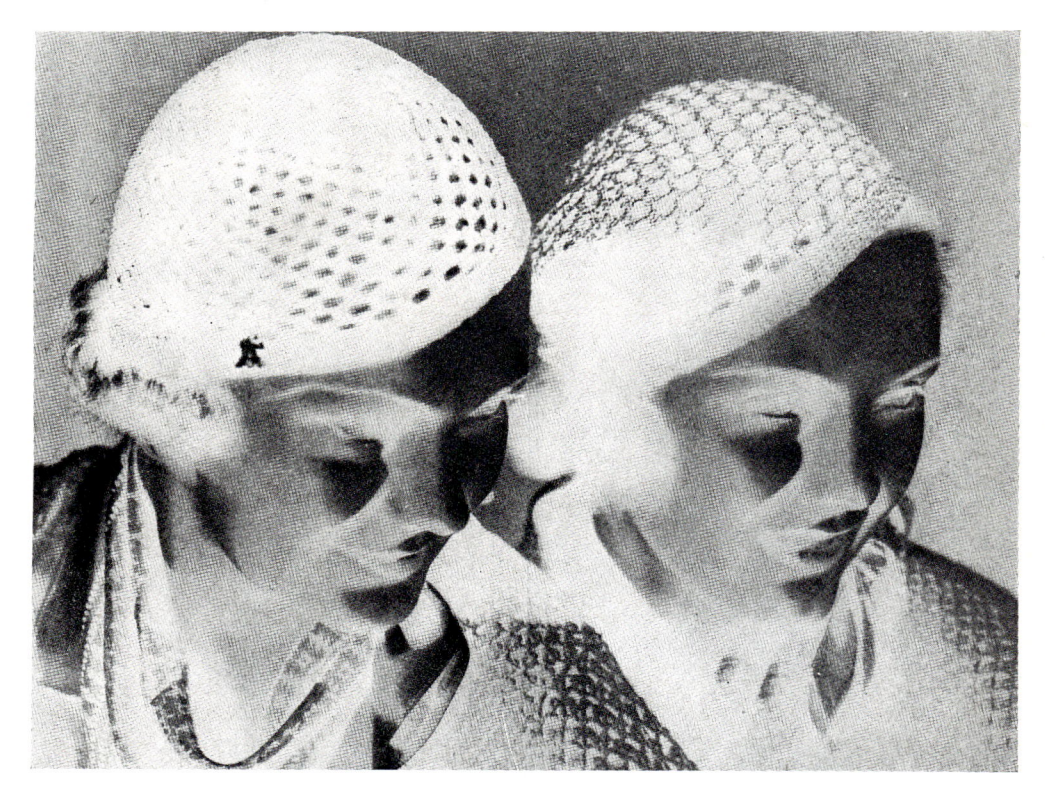

142 GRAPHIC

A PHOTOGRAPHIC presentation of jewelry, sparkling in its realism and beautifully set off against the smooth detail of a manikin. (*Marcus & Company, New York, through N. W. Ayer & Son, Philadelphia.*) SIDE: Cover design for an advertising magazine with text and slogan lettered in on an enlarged, cropped, and slightly retouched photograph. The "Call of Advertising" is well interpreted by the gesture of the figure. (*Ahrlé for Die Reklame, Berlin.*) "Advertising Arts," a cover design in airbrush by Alexei Brodovitch. In its preparation, the artist made no preliminary sketch, merely visualizing in his imagination what he was going to do. Using an airbrush and ordinary showcard black, the artist covered the surface of a piece of Bristol board. He cut a paper stencil of the little man and airbrushed the silhouettes in on the background with white paint. The eye was sprayed through two stencils and the white circles and lines were then drawn in with a compass and ruling pen. The lettering was worked out on tracing paper, transferred to the drawing with a hard pencil, and then filled in with a brush. FACING PAGE: Miniature figures and settings were specially prepared before photographing to convey the texture and the feel of crepe material. (*Lester Gaba for Acele Department, Du Pont, New York.*) A set from the "Balanced and Unbalanced Radio" series, based on a photographic innovation whereby a normal picture is rephotographed through a number of incorrectly adjusted lenses and grotesquely distorted. (*Anton Bruehl for Philco Radio Corporation, Philadelphia.*) The appeal of curiosity aroused by the reverse values of a positive lends interest to a rather usual pose. Such combinations, if not overdone, achieve a most refreshing effect. (*Frederick Bradley for Best & Company, New York.*)

DESIGN ═══════════ 143

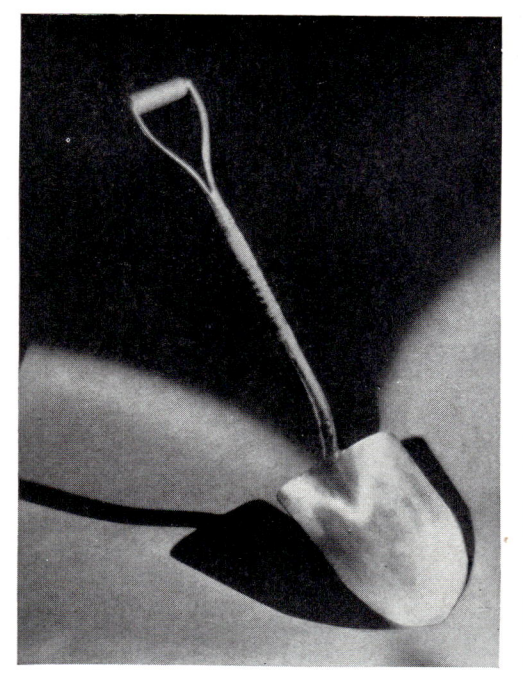

THE EFFICIENCY of the shovel as an instrument for digging is brought out by the diagonal line of this tool and the trench-like shadow. (*Photo by Underwood and Underwood, New York.*) "Porcelain," a modern still life, by its mathematical arrangement, draws attention to the precision and uniformity of quality merchandise. (*Finsler, Zurich, for the State Porcelain Works, Berlin.*) Cigarette advertisements. Details that usually escape observation have been enlarged to reveal the tobacco's quality. The general layout, space for lettering and build-up of composition must be planned before the grouping is exposed to the lens. (*Photography by Grit Kallin; layout by Hadank; Crawford, Berlin, for Haus Neuerburg.*) FACING PAGE: The dramatic effect of power represented by the whirling flywheel of a giant dynamo was achieved by painting with light throughout the exposure time of five minutes. (*Underwood and Underwood, New York, for the America Fore Group of Insurance Companies.*) "Blast Furnaces" is a powerful decorative composition in which modernism is tempered with an understanding of the realistic aspects of the problem. (*Albert Renger-Patzsch in Die Welt Ist Schön, Wolf Verlag, Munich.*) "The Test" is a simple photographic statement that tells volumes about the resistance of Valspar varnish to the extremes of both heat and cold. (*Courtesy of Valentine & Company, New York.*)

144 GRAPHIC

DESIGN 145

AN OVER-SIZE FRAGMENT of the familiar typewriter drives home a forceful message. Such pictures are obtained either by enlarging a photograph of the entire object and then cropping it of dispensable parts, or by masking out the desired section of the negative and then enlarging it to the required size. (*Ralph Steiner for the Oxford Paper Company, through W.L. Brann, Inc.*) Lighting and arrangement of the grinding wheels lend an appeal to the whole that makes it attractive to the layman and the professionally interested alike. (*The Norton Company, New York.*) A well-arranged photograph of packages designed by George Switzer. The two cartons display photographs of the food contained in them as planned parts of the designs. (*Adams Studio, New York, for Advertising Arts Magazine.*)

FACING PAGE: "Silk." Here the lens succeeded in conveying the charm, weight, and expensive finish of the material without the aid of the usual irrelevant figure. A pictorialization whose textural appeal neither words nor anything short of the material itself could equal. (*Courtesy Trude Hamburg, Berlin, for Zeitschrift Ninon.*)

GRAPHIC

SILK, by Trude Hamburg, conveys its message in unmistakable clarity. For description see legend on page 146.

DESIGN 147

THE FLICKER of electric sparks and the suggestion of rolling motion inject life into inanimate glass and metal. (*Photographs by Underwood and Underwood, New York, for the Corning Glass Company and for a manufacturer of piston rings, respectively.*) In comparing these photographs with the photograms on the facing page, it is interesting to distinguish the device used to arrive at these different results. On this page, straight photography has been given an unusual interest by trick arrangements; on the facing page, equal interest has been attained by photography of straightforward but abstract arrangements. However, dependence has not been on tricks alone; artistry has been used.

148 GRAPHIC

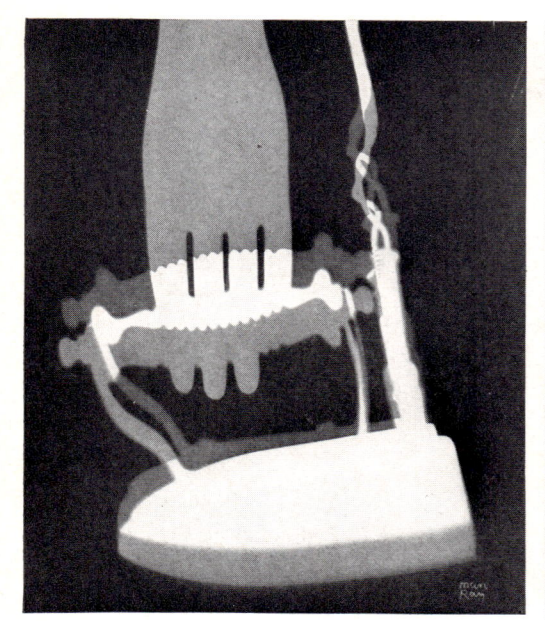

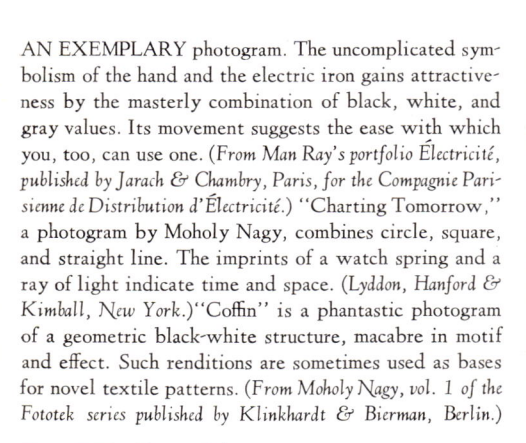

AN EXEMPLARY photogram. The uncomplicated symbolism of the hand and the electric iron gains attractiveness by the masterly combination of black, white, and gray values. Its movement suggests the ease with which you, too, can use one. (*From Man Ray's portfolio Électricité, published by Jarach & Chambry, Paris, for the Compagnie Parisienne de Distribution d'Électricité.*) "Charting Tomorrow," a photogram by Moholy Nagy, combines circle, square, and straight line. The imprints of a watch spring and a ray of light indicate time and space. (*Lyddon, Hanford & Kimball, New York.*) "Coffin" is a phantastic photogram of a geometric black-white structure, macabre in motif and effect. Such renditions are sometimes used as bases for novel textile patterns. (*From Moholy Nagy, vol. 1 of the Fototek series published by Klinkhardt & Bierman, Berlin.*)

DESIGN 149

ABOVE: F. Schmotzer, Graphic Art and Research School, Vienna, evidences a mature viewpoint in his teacup photograph. Our eyes are unavoidably drawn by the lines of the hands to the dark oval center of the composition. BELOW: Segments of two photographs combined into a coherent design. The line along which the prints were cut is obliterated by retouching on the positive. (Paul Furer, student, Abraham Lincoln High School, Brooklyn.)

PROBLEM: Select two or more snapshots adaptable to a similar treatment. Cut out appropriate sections and combine them into a well-arranged unit. If necessary, join the various parts by heavy outlines, as in stained-glass windows. Place emphasis on simplicity in composition, boldness of detail, and clean workmanship. By making some part of the photograph outstanding—dominant—monotony can be avoided.

ALTERNATE PROBLEM: Select a photograph with strong dark and light contrasts and reproduce it as a line cut (see the example on top of page 134).

THE BOOK
CHAPTER 5

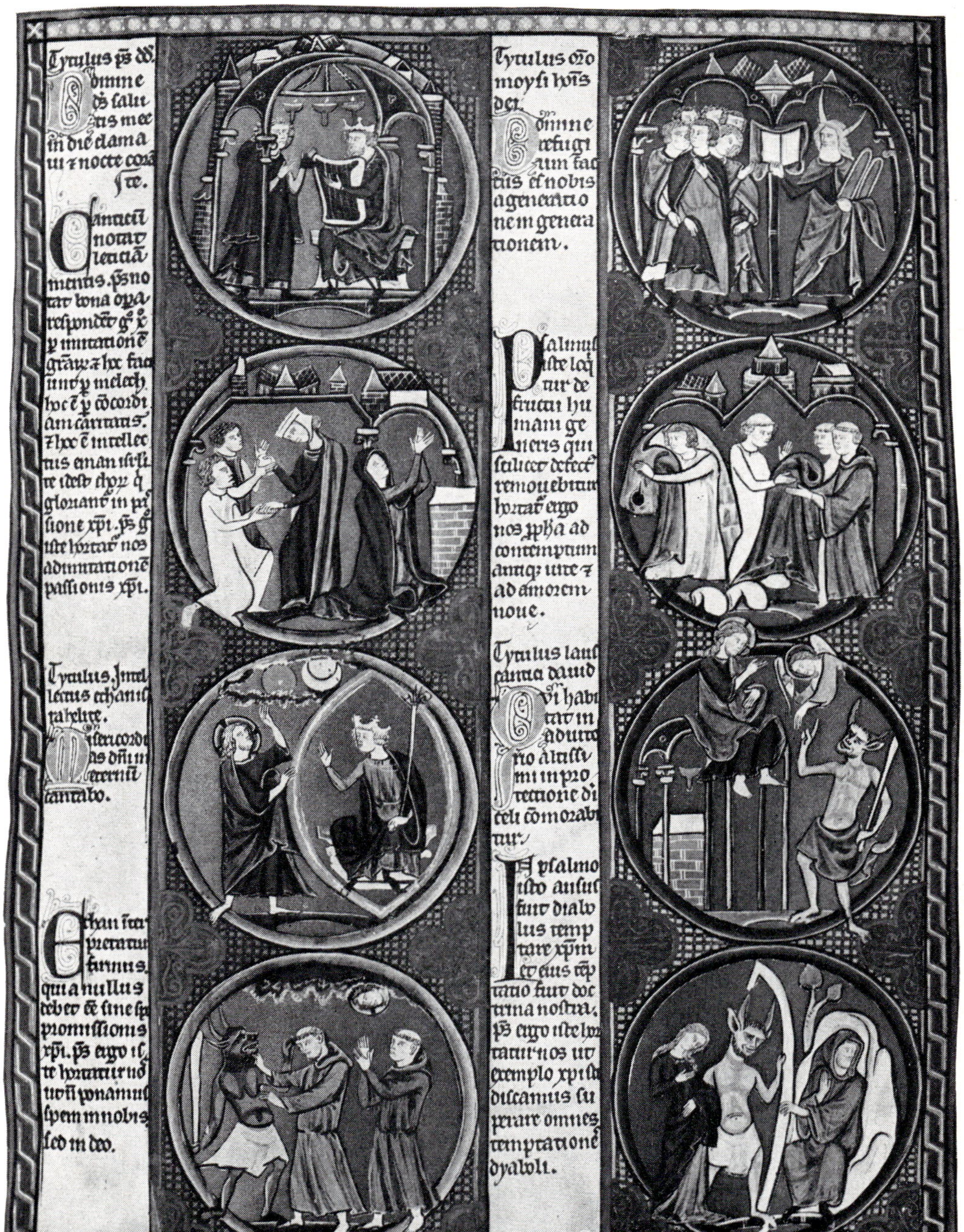

THE BOOK

THE BOOK EMBodies most of the graphic arts. Whether it be lettering or typography, hand-cut illustration or mechanical reproduction, photography or binding, we are likely to see it used in the book. By precept and example, books tell us of the changing philosophies and attitudes of each generation and also of the successive developments in illustration, typographic design, and the graphic arts generally. The successful book has at all times been a harmonious blending of the thought of the author and the good taste of the craftsman.

The prototype of the book format with which we are familiar today existed in Rome as the diptych or codex. These were bound wooden covers with facing surfaces overspread with wax. The writing was done on the wax with a pointed wooden or metal stylus. Primitive as these were, they represented an advance in convenience over the Babylonian slabs of baked clay and the Egyptian, Greek, and Roman rolls of papyrus. Roman codices were later modified from the wooden boards to leaves of vellum or paper arranged in quires and bound in book form. Capital letters exclusively were written across the pages of these tablets, without punctuation of any kind. At about this same period (approximately the fourth century), Roman lettering changed from square capitals to uncial capitals, as was to be expected when the reed and quill became more popular than the chisel and stylus as instruments of writing. An example of fifth century manuscript design is the Alexandrian codex, now in the British Museum, showing two columns of uncial writing. In layout it is not unlike contemporary book design, although the one-column codex of Beza, of the sixth century, and the one-column books of today seem more closely related in plan. Seventh century codices introduced minuscule or small letters, the result of writing old Roman letters with greater speed on vellum, a parchment prepared from the skin of calves, with a finely textured surface that lent itself to speed more readily than did a slab of stone or a layer of wax.

CHAPTER DECORATION: A woodcut by Fritz Richter, Berchtesgaden. CHAPTER FRONTISPIECE: On the illuminated page of a St. Louis Bible (1226) gold leaf and ultramarine predominate. The pictured story was significant even to the untutored, while the limited text gave added information to the few who were able to read.

DESIGN 153

FRESCO PORTRAIT from the palace of Minos (1700-1600 B.C.) representing an early form of illustration. The treatment of the eye reminds us of Egyptian figure drawing where distortion was freely used for its decorative effect and greater illustrative quality. (*Reproduced by permission of Macmillan & Co., Ltd., London, from "Palace of Minos," by Sir Arthur Evans, F.R.S.*) See text on page 161.

The invention of cast-metal types in the fifteenth century was a contribution to book making that has since hardly been improved, though with later inventions it gained facility. The early printers closely followed the traditions of the scribes and with such perfection that, after four centuries of decline, our finest contemporary books are still likely to show the inspiration of ancient models. It can only be hoped that the improved machinery which is available today may give us time for that thoughtful workmanship in the manufacture of our thousands of books that the fifteenth century artisan had for the making of his few.

A substantial innovation in book making was effected not so many decades ago in the field of illustration by the invention of new mechanical processes of reproduction, such as photolithography, line engraving, halftone, rotogravure, etc. These made possible the duplication of profusely colored illustrations which, heretofore, appeared only in manuscript books in the form of original miniatures or tinted block prints.

Papers were originally handmade, and only a few varieties existed. Type faces available to the printing craftsman were as limited in kind and size. And illustrations, for a long time, were restricted to hand-cut blocks whose line character and method of printing (relief) were in keeping with the type. These very limitations made for a unity in effect which careless contemporary manufacturers often lose in their hasty or thoughtless selections from the manifold papers, types, and reproduction processes at their command.

The luxurious leather bindings, both the plain and those that were tooled and inlaid for the medieval aristocratic few, have been progressively supplemented, first by paper covers in the late seventeenth century and then by cloth casings which the publisher Pickering and the binder Leighton introduced in 1822. The inexpensiveness of paper and cloth casings helped to bring the price of books within the limits of the most modest purse. True, the ancient art of binding is still carried on but only to give added distinction to books of unusual merit and as a mark of special pride in a wealthy collector's library. Most contemporary books, and not alone those of temporary worth, remain in cloth casings.

It is encouraging to find a dozen or more books out of each season's publications that indicate a sincere effort on the part of the designer to combine beauty with utility in their manufacture. They lead one to hope that manufacturers will some day emulate the example of the ancient binders and produce book covers that are at least worthy of the author's text. This is latitude, indeed, when one considers some of our modern potboilers. At any rate, the author's lapses ought to be no excuse for the bookmaker's carelessness.

As type has been discussed in a previous chapter, it need not be considered again in the present study of the elements that combine to make a book. Its importance in book make-up justifies its re-examination, however. See Printing Chapter, pages 29 to 70.

TWO ILLUSTRATIONS that belong to the school of simple and sound design and are as modern today as they were when their now nameless artists created them centuries ago. ABOVE: Hieroglyphic figure retaining the Egyptian sense of design and rendered in pen and ink by Professor Lapshin for Ilin's *Black on White: The Story of Books*. (J. B. Lippincott Company, Philadelphia.) BELOW: Centurion and two soldiers, a characterful fragment from the "Passion" cut in wood about 1370 in Bourgogne. (Bibliothèque Nationale, Paris.)

DESIGN 155

Illustration. Many agree with Alice in Wonderland: "'What's the use of a book,' thought Alice, 'without pictures...?'" In fact, it is the universal appeal of pictures that has brought about the wide use of every kind of reproduction process for book illustration. We are all familiar with illustrations that explain and interpret the text by dramatizing it graphically and again with illustrations used in technical books to portray unfamiliar scenes, plans, and features that whole paragraphs of description would reveal with difficulty. We are less familiar, perhaps, with abstract or conventionalized decoration. At least, we more easily understand the storytelling picture of Pocahontas saving Captain John Smith's life, an *illustration*, than we do a formal design using an Indian motif, a *decoration*. Either may enliven the printed text. The appeal of many nineteenth and twentieth century illustrated editions of earlier classics, like *Faust* or *The Arabian Nights' Entertainments*, has gained new interest and added popularity by the use of a different format and new illustrations. Often several editions of a single title are found in one home.

THE *DIAMOND SUTRA*, a Chinese block-printed book, A.D. 868, now in the British Museum, London. Enough text is shown to give some idea of the fine tie-up between text and picture even in this early creation. FACING PAGE: Point of view is possibly the major difference between these two illustrations for Dante's *Inferno*. (See also page 82 for Doré's treatment of the same subject.) Of course, the free rendering of Edy Legrand's lithograph above ("Enfer de Dante," published by Éditions de la Pléiade, Paris) further distinguishes it from the careful design of Luigi Guerrini below ("*Dante*," published by Giulio Giannini and Sons, Florence.) Though both are contemporary, the first suggests the expressionistic point of view of the modern in its attempt to interpret the spirit of the book, while the second emphasizes the literal illustrative quality of the classic school. Legrand's fantastic style is more fitting for this great imaginative story; Guerrini's realistic interpretation brings us back to earth. The tonal color of a line plate that reproduces a design of closely drawn lines is not unlike that of a halftone in its total grayish effect.

Good illustration is design which helps to interpret the author's point of view in a well-conceived and characterful drawing. It combines appropriately with the type, ornamenting the page as it illustrates the text. Also, it provides a vehicle for the imagination of the reader, who is frequently led mentally to complete what is only suggested by the author. But the mere ability of a drawing to illuminate or to make up for the deficiency of text is not the sole criterion of the success of an illustration. It must, on the contrary, throw new light on the subject on the assumption that what does not contribute to the value of the book detracts from it. It is desirable also that the technique and reproduction

LATIN MANUSCRIPT of a psalter written in Germany in the last quarter of the twelfth century. Like most things of the time, it is inspired by religion, but unified in the best principles of contemporary design—common relationship through parallel connecting lines that are barely visible in reproduction. Text and illustration are unified also by "lining up" and by repetition of color in initials and decoration. (*Courtesy New York Public Library.*)

of the illustration be appropriate to the type and paper—preferably woodcut or line cut. The value of reproducing illustrations with actual hand-cut blocks is difficult to overestimate. When, as in most Renaissance and some modern work, the artist cuts his illustration in the wood, he is better able to plan his drawing with a full knowledge of the limitations that affect the finished illustration. He

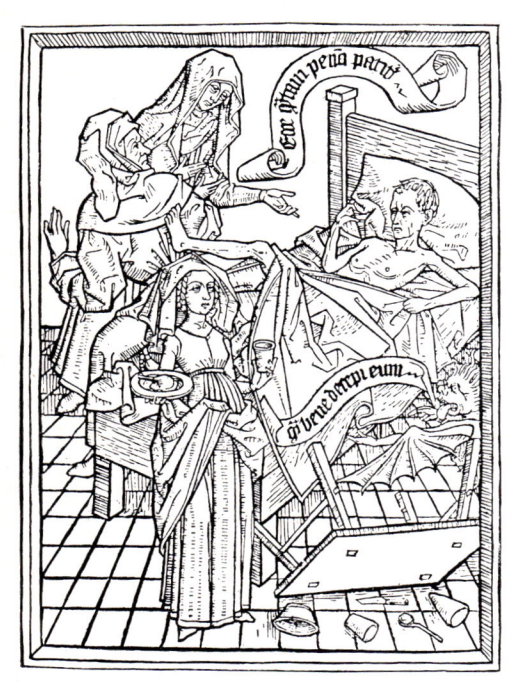

ONE OF THE "TEMPTATIONS" from the *Ars Moriendi* (about 1465), with dialogue, printed on the labels, incorporated in the design. Its pattern is not lost in too-close fidelity to the laws of perspective. CATALOGUE-

LIKE terseness of the woodcut lines in the illustration of *De re militari* of Valturius, printed in 1472, shows something of the background that led up to the "Hypnerotomachia" masterpieces of a later date (see pages 164-165).

avoids unnecessary detail in a drawing that, though sometimes archaic in style, is ever deliberate in design and strong in execution. The work of any illustrator is improved by the directness he gains from the woodcut experience.

The freedom which an artist takes in translating a sketch into a woodcut helps to retain the spontaneity of the original. One has only to compare contemporary reproductions with their originals to see how much may be lost in the processes of duplication, mechanically exact as these processes may be (see page 103).

THE TRANSITION from simple to elaborate initial and from that to book illustration seems to have been a natural one. The modern initial decorations here are by Boris Artzybasheff for *The Wonder Smith*. (The Macmillan Co., New York.)

FACING PAGE: Fifteenth century decorative initials (*from "Die Quelle," a book, published by Gerlach & Wiedling, Vienna*).

DESIGN 159

"FLIGHT INTO EGYPT": The vigorous angular lines of this woodcut by an unknown artist for Turrecremata's *Meditationes* were inspired by Italian frescoes. The lines, broken up either by time or by a careless woodcutter, are nevertheless organized into a clear-cut statement and an impressive design. It is the first illustrated book printed in Italy with movable type (Rome, 1467).

BELOW: First French book illustration for *Le Mirouer de la Rédemption*, Lyons, 1478. The deliberateness of the woodcut line is a happy antidote for the too-facile modern pen line. Forethought and labor preceded each line cut in wood; often, afterthought and white paint accompany the pen stroke. (*From "Le Livre Français," a book by Marius Audin, published by Éditions Rieder, Paris.*)

FACING PAGE: Erhard Reuwich's pyramidal composition for *Peregrinationes* made on his travels with the author, Breydenbach. Half-tone reproduction is purposely used to show the water-color tints that were frequently employed to add charm and individuality to block prints. The protruding foot here and the pointing finger of Edy Legrand's much later sketch (page 156) attempt to break away from the idea that the border of a picture must frame it. (*From the New York Public Library.*)

160 GRAPHIC

Drawing is at least as old as the paleolithic bisons on the walls of the Altamira caves. The frescoes of the Palace of Minos, Knossos, dating to 1700 or 1600 B.C., show drawings which, if transferred to paper, would have much of the quality which we seek in book illustration.* The small decorative paintings in the Egyptian *Books of the Dead* (1500 B.C.) are extremely early applications of the problems connected with book illustration. In Greece and Rome, book illustration has no tangible antecedent. It seems rather to find its roots in book illumination, which was in turn an outgrowth of the humble initial letters of the manuscript writers. The many religiously inspired and gorgeously decorated *Books of Hours*, those illuminated by Paul de Limbourg and his brothers in the early 1400's, for instance, are stepping stones between the illuminators and the illustrators. They had served a like relationship between illuminating and oil painting. Beginning with the School of Paris *Books of Hours* of the fifteenth century, conventionalized and realistic nature—rocks, birds, vines, and trees—began to replace the Oriental and Byzantine influence of abstract geometric design and profusely gilt ornamentation which had entered Europe by way of Florence during the thirteenth century, after the fall of Constantinople in the fourth crusade.

*Palace of Minos, a book by Sir Arthur Evans, F. R. S., published by Macmillan & Company, Ltd., of London.

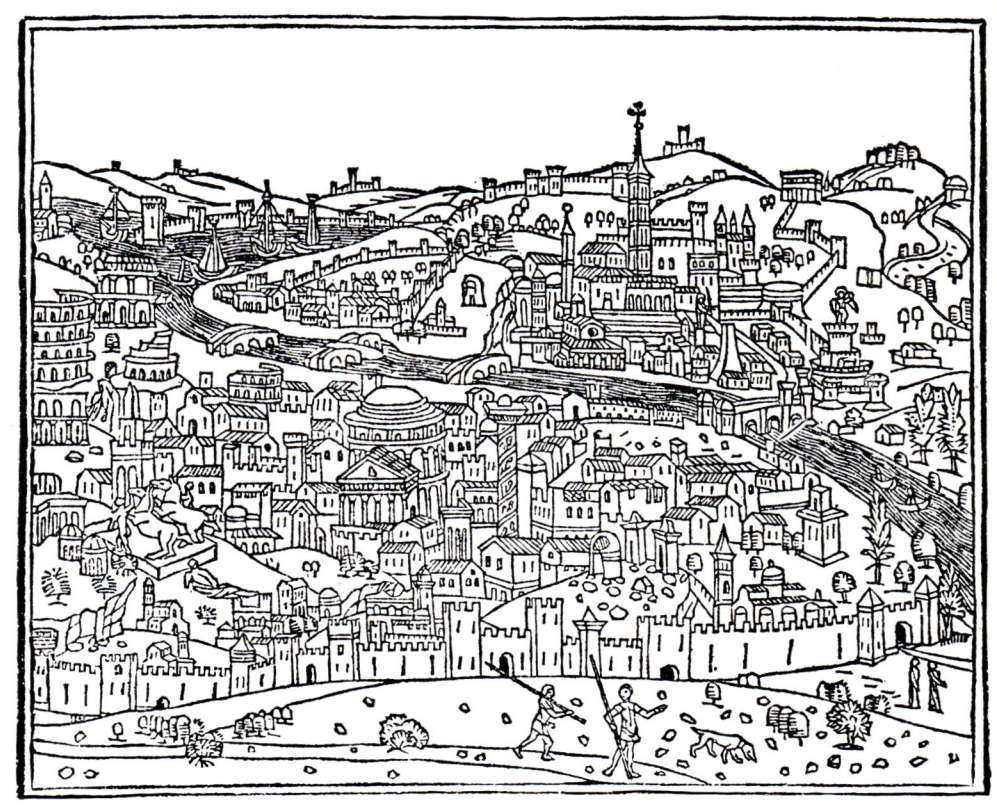

"VIEW OF ROME" from J. P. Foresti's *Supplementum Chronicarum*, B. Rizius, Venice, 1490, could hardly find an equally successful counterpart in contemporary travel guidebooks. Its uniform grayness is much like the color of type matter. The end paper on page 193 offers an interesting comparison. (*Courtesy Victoria and Albert Museum, London.*)

As the book changed from a handwritten copy to a printed one, so illustration changed from a single piece, a miniature painting, to a manifold product, a woodblock impression. In the early examples, type and pictures were cut in the wood, together or in separate blocks. The Chinese *Diamond Sutra* is the earliest block-printed book extant. It was "Printed," the inscription reads, "on May 11, 868, by Wang Chieh, for free general distribution, in deep reverence, to perpetuate the memory of his parents." The beautiful outline drawings keep their sense of design in all-over pattern effects even while they expertly fulfill their illustrative purpose. Of these block books or xylographs, as they are called, the *Ars Moriendi* (*The Art of Dying*) by Ludwig of Ulm is an early European example (1460-1470). Its crude prints show the temptations to which the dying are subjected. Cardinal Johannes de Turrecremata's *Meditationes*, in the British

TWO ILLUSTRATIONS by Jacques Callot (1592-1635) show the excellence that copper engraving of this period had attained. They are free, too, of the ornateness to which such illustrations were commonly heir. PAGES 164 and 165: These two pages, almost exact size, are from Colonna's *Hypnerotomachia Poliphili*, printed by Aldus Manutius in Venice, 1499. The tonal unity of type and illustration can be noted by slightly squinting the eyes. The book is considered by many as the best printed example of bookmaking extant. What do you think? The woodcut has been controlled by the unknown artist to leave only such lines as are consistent with the type that it accompanies. Accidental blacks incidental to woodcutting were removed. (*Metropolitan Museum of Art, New York.*)

Museum, printed in Rome in 1473 after a 1467 edition, with illustrations by Ulrich Hahn, is the first Italian book in which wood engraving and movable type are printed together in a single impression. The books of an earlier (before 1473) Dutch printer are also known to have used woodcut illustrations with type, but these were printed in two separate operations. Some critics, notably Frederick Lippmann, consider the composition of the woodcuts of the *Meditationes* good but the drawing of the faces displeasing. Definitely successful, however, are the catalogue-like outline woodcuts in Valturio's *De re militari*, printed in Verona in 1472 and possibly cut by the medalist Malteo de Pastis. There is little about the vignettes, showing military weapons, to place them in the category of early illustration. They have in them much that is akin to the masterly drawings of later books, the *Hypnerotomachia* for example. The first illus-

ACCVSATOSE POLIA DINANTI ALLA TEMPLA-
RIA DELLA TRANSACTA IMPIETATE. ET CHE AL
PRESENTE TVTA ERA DI ARDENTE AMORE SVF-
FVSA, DIMONSTRANDO POLIPHILO ASTANTE. LA
RELIGIOSA MATRONA CHIAMATOLO AD SE. IL
QVALE SVPPLICANDO STABILIMENTO DI AMBI-
DVI IN VNO RATO PROPOSITO. POLIA DA IMPA-
TIENTE AMORE IN SE INFORTITO INTERVMPET
TE LA RISPOSTA.

PARENDO SEDVLO SENCIA MOR AMEN
to alla uenerabile Sacerdote Poliphilo, expeditamente,
& cum diuote inclinatione se apresentoui costi essendo,
& io cum affectuosi & tonitruali sospiri, Gliquali nel te-
stidunato Tempio sonati, Ecco alle nostre latebrose ore
chie gli rimandaua emula. Et cum gli ochii solo in esso
defixi. Alhora nuda & suilupata di ogni freda duritudine, Ma mitissima
& mansueta & præstabile gli patefeci il patore hiato del mio succeso core.
Et digli suriillici & festeuoli & intenti ochii improcarmé sæpissime fato
domicilio & delicioso diuersorio. Et io como desiderosa, cortesemente il
feci solo di quello digno & emerito Signore, Adiuncto & inseme a posse
dere tuta la uita mia, & me stessa a che ello uolesse arbitrariamente. Ilquale
ad me tanto allhora piu grato præstauase, quanto piu per auanti exoso &
displicibile il teniua, Piu gratioso & efficacissimo rimedio al mio ardente
amore offerentise opportunamente, & molto piu salutare, non apparisco
no ad gli nauiganti lo æstuoso mare cum il cœlo pluuio le lucide stelle di
Castore & il fratello Gemini dalla parte dextra di Auriga sopra Orionte
collocate, & ancora gli optati & sicuri porti.

Onde nellultimo grado damore uulnerata, miraua ello immobilmé
te tuore, cum gratioso intuito, & questo era una dolce congerie & cumu-
lo di iuasiuo foco nel pecto mio. Et lanimo mio percio da ogni altra sol-
licitudine exclusa. Solo esso gli piaceua, Solo esso gratissimo lo optaua.
Solo esso solacio se offeriua. Et ad gli mei insaciabili & desiderosi risguar-
di obiecto delectabile, Dalla uacatione del quale impatiente, & di auidita-
te stimulata, & da immodesto appetito impulsa, & dassi amorosi oblecta-
menti capta & possessa, che quasi externata & in extasi immobile il miraua. Dique gia oltra modo effrenati essendo gliochii mei. Et perche io sen
tiua & experiua, che cosa era il nouello amore, Io miserata ragioneuolmé
te a quegli gli perdonaua la sua scrutaria iportunitate. Ma Poliphilo che
oltra il suo

oltra il suo potere la improbitáte del cæco Cupidine sosteniua, di peruenire la onde ello desideraua anhelante intendeua, Cum summa opera di cōfirmare & stabilire per medio della riuerenda Antista, Dinanti alla quale ello era apresentato, che ambi dui uno solo ligamine tenacissimamente inuinculare facesse. Et del mio aspecto releuato, cum demulcéte eloquio per questa forma letamente ello disse.

Celebre & sacra Matrona, si meritano di essere auditi gli supplici & diuoti seruitori, & deditissimi cultori della Diuina Paphia, dináti il tuo sancto auditorio & tribunale, siano hora pientissima Domina auscultati da te, nel præsente le mie impense prece, & diuotissimi exorati, Cú fiducia pduc̄ti, di cōsequire fauore da, te insigne Templaria. Laquale a questo amoroso acto, ultimo cōfugio arbitro, & alle mie acerbe afflictione reputo efficacissimo Amuleto, Subleuamento, & uera & eximia remediatrice. Imperoche sei a questo loco assumpta, & alle sacrificale Are della sanctissima Cytherea, cú táta sanctimonia, sinceraméte famulando, per adiutare, mediáte la sua gratia, gli inepti & discordi animi, & in uno uolere readunare & consenso, gli amatori. Per tanto alla tua maiestale præsentia son io fiducialmente uenuto, perche sola sei habile di potere patrocinare gli miseri amanti (como io) che languiscono, per iæqualitate del crudele & lictorio lancinare del suo iniusto figlio. Funde le grate prece dunque ad q̄lla Ma-

D

trated French book, *Le Mirouer de la Rédemption de l'Umain lignaige*, was printed in Lyons. It appeared in 1478, five years after the *Meditationes*. In the reproduction shown (page 160), every line is deliberately placed to form an effective pattern. Even the accidental remains of woodcutting have not been permitted to mar the design. Another notable achievement was Breydenbach's *Peregrinationes* (*Pilgrimages*), printed in 1486. Travel replaced religion as the theme in this unusual book, thus widening the field wherein the illustrator could seek inspiration. To Erhard Reuwich of Utrecht, the illustrator and supervisor of printing of the book, was given the unique assignment of traveling to Jerusalem with the author. The illustrations are said to be based on his personal observations. Crosshatching, a doubtful asset in penwork and a definite obstacle in the woodcut, appears for the first time in Reuwich's title page for this book.

   The vogue of copperplate engraving, which had an ill effect on woodcut illustration wherever the two came in contact, is considered to have had its inception in a French translation of Breydenbach's *Peregrinationes*. The precision of line and minute fineness to which the copperplate lent itself were more

PAGE FROM Geoffroy Tory's *Book of Hours*, 1525. The black figure adds a note of contrast to the uniform color of the rest, although it detracts some from the main center of interest, here, the Holy Family. (*From "L' Art du Livre en France," published by Delagrave, Paris.*)

BELOW: Early prognosticators of modern French typography. On the left side is a page from *Figures de Nouveau Testament*, Lyons, 1558; on the right, a page from *Biblia Sacra*, 1569, with the layout by Pierre Eskrich. Both illustrations are by Bernard Salomon.

FACING PAGE: Left, a page from *Theuerdank*, 1517, with its Hans Burgkmair woodcut. The relation of picture and text and the varied but consistent use of swirled lines throughout the book knit the pages into an integral whole. (*Courtesy Gilhofer & Ranschburg, Vienna.*) Right, a page from *Les Simulachres de la Mort (Dance of Death)* by Holbein, Lyons, 1538. It shows the degree of spaciousness that even small woodcuts can convey in the hands of a master. (*From M. Audin's book "Le Livre Français," published by Rieder, Paris.*)

DESIGN 167

TWO MASTERLY representations of birds. ABOVE: "The Titmouse," wood engraving by Thomas Bewick (1753-1828) has the realism of Daglish, although not his deliberate feeling for pattern. ("History of British Birds," 1826.) LEFT: The wood engraving of the "Goldencrest" by Eric Fitch Daglish combines fine pattern with fidelity to nature. The resulting color distinctions have aesthetic appeal independent of subject matter. (From "The Smaller Birds," published by J. M. Dent & Sons, Ltd., London, 1928.)

than offset by the complexity of detail to which it was subjected. The unending flourishes and bewildering tendrils with which copper engraving is associated remind us of early twentieth century handwriting. Its superfluities were as bad. It was, to begin with, an unsuccessful attempt to combine intaglio metal engraving with relief-type printing. The apparent refinement of the copperplate, as Crane* so aptly put it, did not mean extra power or refinement of draftsmanship but merely thinner lines. Jacques Callot (1592-1635), a Frenchman, was one of the few illustrators who did not succumb to and become a slave of the copper plate. His interpretations are ruggedly constructed and well massed. His ability to group a multitude of human beings within a small space foreshadowed the work of Doré. Because Callot (page 163) and Doré (pages 82 and 172) employed different techniques, one may easily fail to note the careful deliberation that preceded work by either artist.

Another avenue for expression was made available to the illustrator when the ornamental title page replaced the colophon—a label at the end of early books naming the scribe or the printer and his work. The substitution was first made in Erhard Ratdolt's *Kalendarium* printed in 1476. The first woodcut initial letters were his also, although several large initials of Fust and Schoeffer's *Psalter* (1457) are considered by many as the first illustrations to be found in a printed book. The finest example of incunabula (books printed

*Walter Crane, *Of the Decorative Illustration of Books Old and New*, published in London in 1896. Still worth reading.

THE ORIGINAL DRAWING and water color of "The Ten Virgins" by William Blake is, collectively, a strong design. As dramatic a theme as Doré's on page 172, but how much more restrained! It very sensitively uses the figures as so many elements in a border repeat, while the line of the trumpeter subtly re-echoes that of the horizon. This is one of the finer examples of the Romantic period. (*Courtesy Miss Carthew, and the Royal Academy, London.*)

before 1500), and possibly of all book design, was Aldus Manutius' *Hypnerotomachia Poliphili*, with its superb outline drawings, printed in 1499. Never have engravings and type combined to better purpose in spirit, delicacy of line,

DESIGN ═══════════════ 169

"THE INNKEEPER" by Gavarni, French illustrator, 1804-1866, uses a dark background to give color and third dimension to the model. The white of the paper becomes a significant part of the picture. RIGHT: "Shepherdess" by Millet, 1814-1875, shows the rugged treatment and sympathy for the worker that characterize all of Millet's peasants. Understanding of the subject is requisite to its most successful delineation as this illustrates. The artist suggests aerial perspective in the design by using a heavy line to bring the figure into greater relief.

or precision of execution. Margins, relation of text to the rectangle of the paper, and the tone quality of the whole, all unite to make the *Hypnerotomachia* (*The Strife of Love in a Dream*) the Parthenon of book design. To carry the simile further, the story of the architecture of the book would have to include Geoffroy Tory's *Book of Hours*, made in 1525. Here, with rare singleness of purpose, Tory is responsible for the shape, size, paper, type, illustration, decoration, and binding. The choice combination of type and ornament—Tory's own designs, by the way—was a pleasant departure from the incongruity and overdecoration that characterized many of the written and printed books antedating him. Incidentally, Tory was equally famous as author, typographer, engraver, and inventor. His broken jar and Manutius' dolphin and anchor are two of the most famous devices in book history. Tory's *Heures à l'usage de Rome*, printed in Paris, is espe-

AUGUSTE RAFFET'S "The Wounding of Captain LeBlanc of the Engineers" proves his fine command of the litho pencil and his effective staging ability—both necessary requisites of the illustrator. As much detail and sentimentality are used as an illustration can bear without becoming too melodramatic. (Bibliothèque Nationale, Paris.)

cially interesting for its illustrations. The use of a black figure in some of the cuts reminds us of Manet's painting *Olympia*, where white and black figures are also cleverly juxtaposed for the color contrast that they make possible.

The examples cited thus far should not be considered as so many accidental stars in as many national firmaments. They characterize more than this. German book illustrations are definitely illustrative above anything else. Following their origin as independent block prints that once preached pictorial sermons to an illiterate populace, German illustrations are invariably literal. They usually show rugged line characterizations and strong contrasts of dark and light. The Italian artist subordinates his illustration to the design of the book as a whole, reconciling the line character of his illustration to that of the type. Restraint and unity are pillars of his illustrations. The work of the French illustrator, even at this early date, shows the moderate use of those little extras—borders, fleurons,

LAOCOÖN-LIKE, too theatrical to be great art, but moving enough to arouse interest in any story, is this illustration by Gustave Doré. (*Metropolitan Museum of Art, New York.*)

BELOW: Another Doré drawing in which the suggestion of action is intensified by the sweeping line of the ladders and the use of sketched figures instead of labored model drawings. (*One of the 425 illustrations in the 1861 edition of Balzac's "Les Contes Drolatiques," published by Garnier Frères, Paris.*)

FACING PAGE: One of the woodcuts by Rethel, 1816-1859, for "Death upon the Barricades." It is similar to Hans Holbein's series in subject (page 166) and not unlike contemporary editorial cartoons in purpose; a masterly job in defense of a highly questionable policy.

172 GRAPHIC

| Wer sie geführt — es war der Tod! | Die ihm gefolgt, sie liegen bleich | Seht hin die Maske that er fort; | Zieht, der Verwesung Hohn im Blick, |
| Er hat gehalten, was er bot. | Als Brüder alle, frei und gleich. — | Als Sieger, hoch zu Rosse dort, | Der Held der rothen Republik. |

curves, color, and similar accessories—which we have come to associate with the French. Artists in other countries have followed, generally, one of these three traditions, differing mainly in the subjects that inspired their illustrations or in the idiosyncrasies that distinguish the craftsman of one country, or one city, from the craftsman of another.

The *Kleine Passion*, printed in Nuremberg in 1512, is a remarkable book chiefly because its illustrator was Albrecht Dürer, the greatest master of the woodcut. He was able to use the resources of wood to the full and to transfer to its surface the keen observation that marked his travels. Simpler and more successful than the *Kleine Passion* in its illustrations was *Les Simulachres de la Mort* (*The Dance of Death*). It was brought out by the Trechsels at Lyons in 1538. The illustrations were designed by Hans Holbein and engraved on wood by Hans Lützelburger, as early, some say, as 1527. The compositional grandeur encompassed in these 2- by 2½-inch blocks has been unrivaled in the history of illustration. Comparison of a Rethel woodcut (see above), a nineteenth century masterpiece, with a

DESIGN 173

174 GRAPHIC

TWO ILLUSTRATIONS repeating similar figures for their major and minor interests. In "Laundresses Delivering Work" by Théophile-Alexandre Steinlen, the massed whites represent the wash in a most flattering manner, without a single unnecessary line. FACING PAGE: "The Jockey," 1899, by Henri de Toulouse Lautrec, conveys a strong sense of third dimension through the exaggeration of the perspective. (*Bibliothèque Nationale, Paris.*)

DESIGN

smaller and much simpler Holbein print shows two things—how great has been the influence of the *Danse Macabre* series and how much even his greatest imitators fall short of attaining that economic spaciousness that was Hans Holbein's special forte.

Another early book that is seldom mentioned, but which is especially interesting because it foreshadows modern French typographic style, is J. de Tournes' *Figures de Nuveau Testament*, printed in Lyons in 1558. The illustrations in *Biblia Sacra* by Pierre Eskrich were published in the same city in 1569 by G. Roville. Examples from both books are shown on page 167. In each case the judicious combination of illustration and widely leaded italic type might very well have been part of a twentieth century best seller.

"LADY GUINEVERE" by Howard Pyle is reminiscent of Albrecht Dürer in its line treatment, but not in color value. The design possibilities of folds rather than rigorous acceptance of accidentals appealed to Pyle. (Reproduced by permission of *Charles Scribner's Sons, New York*.)

Aside from the woodcuts and engravings made independently of book illustration (see also Reproductive Arts), nothing comparable to the high lights of book design so far mentioned was done until late in the eighteenth century. Then Thomas Bewick's (1753-1828) *History of the Quadrupeds* (1790) and *History of British Birds*, (1797) revived white-line wood engraving. It was used to replace copperplate engraving and the black-line woodcut. Copperplate engraving had been in existence since about 1472 and in vogue since about 1550, and, as previously stated, it had assumed much of the overdecoration to which detailed work is heir. The light color of Bewick's cuts was obtained by breaking up the black solids with small white lines or flecks. In so doing he also popularized the use of the graver upon the cross section of boxwood, with an effect which was as different in color from the ordinary woodcut as the Roman type was from the Gothic black face. Bewick's illustrations combined decorative with realistic drawing, showing depth or aerial perspective in the background of his accurately delineated bird pictures. This he accomplished by means of one or two successively lighter planes. Modern illustration of books is considered to have begun with Bewick's work. William Blake's (1757-1827) illustrations for the *Book of Job* were contemporary with Bewick's work but were reminiscent of the xylographs in one particular—design and lettering were again combined on the plate and printed together— although metal was used instead of wood. Blake, who was a mystic, poet, and illustrator, obtained his unusual effects by working in copper in an entirely original manner. He used relief etching whereby words and designs were drawn upon the plate with a varnish, and the background bitten away with an acid. The process is similar to the manufacture of the modern line plate except that the drawing was direct, not photographed, and the routing tool was not used to complete the action of the acid. What coloring Blake used he added by hand. The wholesale use of stencils (pochoirs) in the coloring of books by contemporary French illustrators seems to be but a development of Blake's idea. He is also credited with having started the epoch of romanticism in English literature. Of the man some-

ABOVE: "The Dancer's Reward" by Beardsley is an example of good use of the line cut. It would be stretching a point to have attempted to reproduce the hairlines and dots with wood. Compare the treatment of the folds with that in Pyle's design. BELOW: "Christina Rossetti," engraved on wood by R. A. Maynard after a drawing by Dante Gabriel Rossetti, shows how far the handmade woodcut can go in the direction of mechanical reproduction. ("*The London Mercury*" magazine, London.)

VATHEK: AN ARABIAN TALE

VATHEK, ninth caliph of the Abasside line, was the son of Motassem and the grandson of Haroun al-Raschid. He came to the throne in the flower of his age, and the great qualities which he already possessed caused his subjects to hope that his reign would be long and happy. His countenance was pleasing and majestic; but, when he was angry, one of his eyes shone with such a terrible light that no man could endure its gaze, and the wretch on whom it was turned fell back in confusion and sometimes even expired on the spot. So, for fear of depopulating his country and making a desert of his palace, the prince took care that his anger was but rarely aroused.

THE PREFACE

MY Case is much like Cicero's, when he undertook to write of Philosophy, in Latine; there being then no Books upon that Subject, but what were written in Greek: When some told Cicero, that he would take pains to no purpose, because such as studied Philosophy, would make use of Greek Authors, and not read Latine Books, which treated of it but at second hand; and others, who were no admirers of the Science, would never trouble their Heads, with either Greek or Latin, Cicero reply'd, they were much mistaken; for, said he, the great ease People will find in reading Latin Books, will tempt those to be Philosophers who are none; and they who already are Philosophers, by reading Greek Books, will

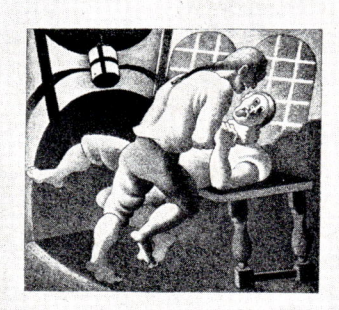

XXIII. - LA MARÉE DESCEND

Le coracle — comme j'eus mainte raison de le savoir avant d'être quitte de lui — était, pour quelqu'un de ma taille et de mon poids, un bateau très sûr, à la fois léger et tenant bien la mer ; mais cette embarcation biscornue était des plus difficultueuses à conduire. On avait beau faire, elle se bornait la plupart du temps à dériver, et en fait de manœuvre, elle ne savait guère que tourner en rond. Ben Gunn

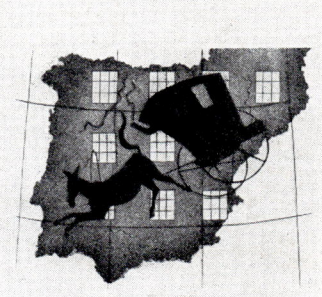

rapidité du voyage me parut étrange. Nous avons voyagé si vite, que nous avons atteint les frontières espagnoles en une demi-heure.

D'ailleurs, maintenant il y

178 ═══════════════ GRAPHIC

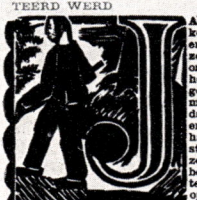

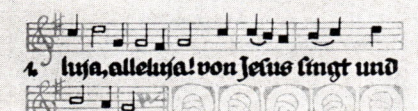

ABOVE: Facing pages with decorations by Joseph Cantré. (*De Sikkel*, Antwerp.) BELOW: A songbook lettered and illustrated by R. Daenert. (*Gerlach & Wiedling*, Vienna.) FACING PAGE. Above: Nonesuch *Vathek* with lithograph by Marion V. Dorn, and Preface from *A Plurality of Worlds* with color stencil by T. L. Poulton (*Designed by Francis Meynell, composed at Nonesuch Press, printed at Curwen Press, London.*) Below: Lithograph by Ben Sussan for *Treasure Island* (*Jonquières*, Paris) and aquatint of a map motif by Alexeïeff for Gogol's *Journal d'un Fou* (*La Pléiade*, Paris.)

DESIGN 179

GROTESQUE CHARACTERS, appropriately colored, are used by G. Tenggren to help kindle the imagination of the readers of this book. It is difficult to overestimate the interest such pictures gain for any story. Reproduction in black and white shows the dark and light basis of the colors used. (*Vespersen og Pios Forlag, Copenhagen.*) FACING PAGE. Above: Edy Legrand's lithograph for Daudet's *Port Tarascon* is characterized by forceful expression and loose handling that leaves much to the imagination of the reader. The two figures in the illustration by Picart Ledoux for Daudet's *Les Femmes d'Artistes* preserve all the spontaneity of the artist's original sketch. (*Librairie de France, Paris.*) Below: Ramiro Arrue's water color for Pierre Loti's *Ramuntcho* shows attention to detail reminiscent of the work of medieval illuminators.(*Éditions G. Crès & Cie., Paris.*) In the illustration of the stylish couple, Charles Martin avoids the pitfalls of the usual commercial fashion plate. (*Librairie de France.*)

thing can be surmised from his oft quoted but rarely observed reflection:*

Thank God, I was never sent to school
To be flogged into following the style of a fool!

The contemporary philosophy of art teaching seems but recently to have accepted the thought conveyed by Blake over a hundred years ago. Only the modern label "Progressive Education" is different.

The French romanticists continued the distinctive note in illustration that Bewick and Blake inspired. Gigoux (1806-1894), who illustrated Lesage's *Gil Blas* (1836), and the many artists who contributed the 450 illustrative gems to *Paul et Virginie* (1838) were some of the shining lights. These illustrators consisted in part of Johannot, Français, Isabey, Huet, Meissonier, Laberge, and

* Charles Eliot Norton, *William Blake's Illustrations of the Book of Job*, published by Osgood & Company of Boston.

Marville. Meissonier, like Raffet before him, specialized in battle pictures, in which he ably supplied all the realistic detail that the camera now obtains for us.

VLAMINCK IS the author and artist of *Tournant Dangereux*. How pleasing seemingly imperfect work may be is instanced by this masterpiece of black and white. It is not lack of drafting ability, but the presence of inspiration that makes this possible. (Librairie Stock, Delamain & Boutelleau, Paris.) RIGHT: The flat poster-like treatment of Piero Bernardini's illustration gives it a restful quality that easily harmonizes with a like quality in the type. Black, gray, and white have been juxtaposed, achieving a wealth of color within limited means. (Bertieri, Milan.)

Gavarni (1804-1866), like Charlet and Raffet, was a popular lithographer. He delineated Parisian types especially and reminds us of Daumier (1808-1879), a contemporary of his, in technique and subject matter. Newspapers achieved the major part of their attention through their cartoons. The most "grandiloquent"* of them all, however, was Doré (1832-1883). His illustrating of over a hundred books necessitated a facility that frequently caused his work to suffer from monotony in rendering. In part, this may have been due to the high pressure under which his engravers had to work to keep up with him, for his conceptions certainly were most varied. Doré was equally successful in his composition of two figures in Hell for Dante's *Inferno* (see page 82) or in his organization of a thousand figures for Balzac's *Les Contes Drolatiques* (page 172). It may be helpful to forget that Doré illustrated either so easily or so profusely but to remember instead that he illustrated exceedingly well.

The most prolific illustrator in Germany and a worthy competitor of Doré in the caliber and number of his illustrations was Adolf von Menzel (1815-

*Frank Weitenkampf, *The Illustrated Book*, a booklet with a succinct history of the subject; New York Public Library.

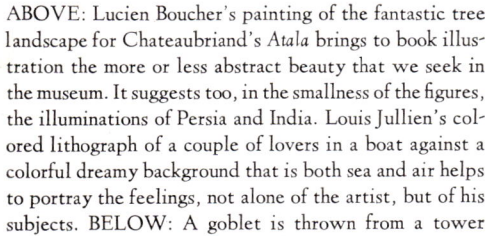

ABOVE: Lucien Boucher's painting of the fantastic tree landscape for Chateaubriand's *Atala* brings to book illustration the more or less abstract beauty that we seek in the museum. It suggests too, in the smallness of the figures, the illuminations of Persia and India. Louis Jullien's colored lithograph of a couple of lovers in a boat against a colorful dreamy background that is both sea and air helps to portray the feelings, not alone of the artist, but of his subjects. BELOW: A goblet is thrown from a tower against a tranquil background, and what a story it brings to mind! It is Ywan Cerf's tempera illustration for Dumas's *Henry III and His Court*. Touchagues' illustration for Berlioz's *Damnation of Faust* gives new form to the well-known opera. (*All four reproductions from a folder by Devambez, Paris, for E. Hoffman-La Roche & Cie.*) Compare these treatments with those shown on pages 186-187. Fine illustrations independently? Yes; but the line character of the woodcuts seems to harmonize better with type-matter.

DESIGN

THE LITHOGRAPH by Mariette Lydis for Montherlant's *Chant des Amazones* indicates in the strength of its drawing something of the idea associated with the title of the book. The crispness of the lines stands in refreshing contrast to the grays. (*Arts et Métiers Graphiques, Paris.*)

THE MILITARY types by Gus Bofa show distortion almost to the point of caricature. The humor of it all is easily apparent in a presentation that is diametrically opposite in treatment to Mariette Lydis's rendering. Both are fine drawings. (*Courtesy of Librairie de France, Paris.*)

1905). To the camera-like realism of a Meissonier he adds a personal and human point of view. Menzel's illustrations for Kugler's *Geschichte Friederichs des Grossen* (1840) — some 500 of them — offer a storehouse of information to the aspiring artist. His work was the incentive for much of the German illustration which followed, but the excellence of his draftsmanship was as discouraging as it might have been inspiring — like the effect of Michelangelo's virtuosity on his would-be followers. A capable contemporary was Rethel (1816-1859). "Death upon the Barricades" and death in other forms and places are the dominant subject of his famous series of woodcuts published at Leipzig in 1849. Like countless other Dance of Death drawings, they owe their inspiration to Holbein's inventions. In the thought conveyed, Rethel's designs (page 173) are surprisingly modern. They might have been culled from the editorial sections of any of the current German publications so far as their treatment, too, is concerned. Incidentally, these macaberesque representations of the power of death were most popular between the fourth and the sixteenth century.

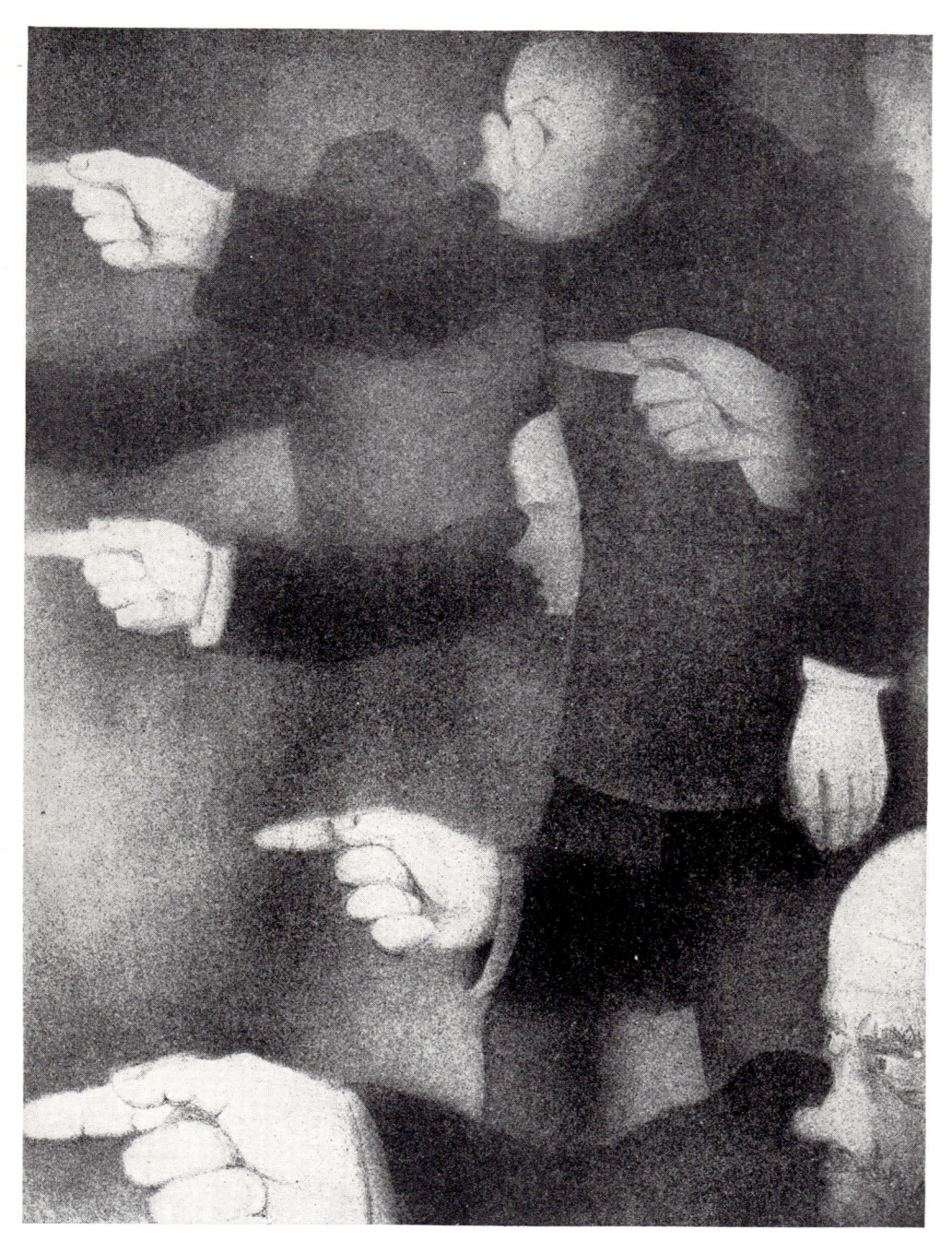

A. ALEXEIEFF'S LITHOGRAPH for Dostoevski's *Les Frères Karamazov* mirrors the feelings of the poor soul who is the recipient of the cross-examiner's rapier-like thrusts. In pattern it is not unlike the repeated design of a textile. The hands attain dominance by repetition despite their seeming smallness, with enough distinctions between hand and hand to avoid monotony. Even the faces do not detract from the single theme. (*La Pléiade, Paris.*)

DESIGN

ABOVE, left: Design by Robert Gibbings for *Samson and Delilah*. (*Golden Cockerel Press, London.*) Note relation of free woodcut with free measure of type lines. Wide margins help to offset the concentrated black of the design. Right: Hermann Paul's clear woodcut for *L'Enfer* is a happy tie-up with the type. (*Léon Pichon, Paris.*) BELOW, left: The values in John Farleigh's wood engraving for G. B. Shaw's *Adventures of the Black Girl in Her Search for God* suggest wood painting. (*Dodd, Mead & Co., New York.*) Right: "La Danse Macabre." Woodcut by Hermann Paul. High lights suggest the ultimate skeleton. (*Léon Pichon, Paris.*)

ABOVE: D. Galanis's woodcut for *Oedipe*, with its mystic charm and its relation to the chaste title page, is refreshingly different. (*Éditions de la Pléiade, Paris.*) BELOW, left: Woodcut for *La Danse Macabre* by Hermann Paul is another masterpiece of the Pichon book. The deliberate placing of spots on the white table and the intense concentration evoked by the card dealer are very forceful. Right: Masereel's woodcuts can almost always be recognized, although by what magic he does this is not so easily discernible. Border lines are blue. (*From Pierre Humbourg's "Le Boy de Sa Majesté," published by Kieffer, Paris.*)

A strong, positive force in bringing a semblance of order and beauty into the chaotic limbo into which nineteenth century bookmaking had fallen was Morris' Kelmscott Press (1890-1896). It succeeded in acquainting people with the "book beautiful," past and present. And it succeeded in making people book conscious despite the fact that the Kelmscott productions were them-

188 GRAPHIC

LYND WARD'S *Wild Pilgrimage* is full of such woodcuts as this one. The sparing use of whites and the elongated shadows contribute mystery to the illustration. (*Harrison Smith & Robert Haas, Inc., New York.*) RIGHT: René Ben Sussan gives an El Grecoesque effect to his figures through exaggeration of their height and by disposition of high lights. (*Jonquières & Cie, Paris.*) BELOW: The monks' frocks stand out in black relief against the gray background. (*Fritz Richter, Berchtesgaden.*) FACING PAGE. ABOVE, left: "The Firing Squad," a Masereel woodcut. There is no irrelevant detail in this composition. (*From Schürmeyer's "Holzschnitt," published by Otto Maier, Ravensburg.*) Right: "Two Nuns." The naïveté of this woodcut by Gino Carlo Sensani for Boccaccio's *Decameron* is most appropriate. The direct statement and the imperfections that one expects in wood cutting are a happy escape from the mechanical. (*A. F. Formiggini, Rome.*) BELOW, left: "The Maze," a woodcut by Blair Hughes-Stanton. In the use of the recurring theme it is close to music. (*From "The London Mercury."*) Right: Paul C. Molnár, Budapest, incorporates in this religious illustration some of the many (too many?) textures obtainable with the woodcut. Mechanical and free lines within the one cut give the illustration its unusual flavor. PAGES 190 and 191: Book layout and illustration by W. A. Dwiggins. The thick and thin lines of his design for the title page of Balzac's *Droll Stories* repeat the thick and thin lines of the type. (*Limited Editions Club, New York.*) Chapter decoration by Eric Gill for *The Four Gospels of the Lord Jesus Christ, King James I Version*, printed at the Golden Cockerel Press, London, with hand set Golden Cockerel type. Union of type and decoration in Gill's work is usually the acme of good taste. He is able to obtain fine decoration without overornamentation.

DESIGN 189

Droll

Stories: thirty tales by HONORÉ DE BALZAC completely translated into modern English by JACQUES LE CLERCQ. *Volume* I: The First Ten Tales.
The Limited Editions Club, *New York*, 1932

PAGES DESIGNED and illustrated by W. A. Dwiggins and Eric Gill, respectively. Description on page 189.

AND
BEHOLD, THERE WAS A MAN
NAMED JOSEPH, A COUNSELLOR;

selves often overornamented. William Morris is said to have initiated the treatment of the facing pages of a book as a single unit. In this he showed rare good judgment. He erred only in failing to attain a happy mean between the attractiveness and legibility of his typography. The vogue fostered by Morris of issuing limited editions of fine books was continued by Joseph Sattler in Germany, D. B. Updike (Merrymount Press) and Bruce Rogers (various presses) in the United States, and other printer artists. "Limited" editions, as understood by these men, referred not alone to the quantity but in most cases to the limited number of imperfections that might be expected to enter into a book that received unlimited inspiration and care. The best illustrations for Morris were those made by Burne-Jones, while the initial letters and typographic ornament which he used were usually of his own design. Other illustrators of this period who

ABOVE: Two illustrations by Robert Lawson for Ella Young's *The Unicorn with the Silver Shoes*. The fine pen work and humor of the drawings are apparent to even the casual observer. Because they are intended for children, they have to be. (Published by Longmans, Green & Company, New York.)

BELOW: Walter Dreesen's drawing is radically different from anything we have seen so far. There is both strength and variety within the length of a single line and the composition itself speaks in terms of angles and space. (Reproduced from Professor Ehmcke's "Das Zelt," Munich.)

ABOVE: End paper by Carlos Sanchez M for Harriet St. Downes's *Philipo the Jongleur*. Its crispness is refreshing, although it would harmonize less with type than its earlier counterpart (page 162). (*Longmans, Green & Co., New York.*) BELOW: Two pages from *Poor Shaydullah*, written and illustrated by Boris Artzybasheff, are certainly out of the ordinary. Delicate lines and robust blacks mark this unusual layout (*Macmillan Company, New York.*)

DESIGN 193

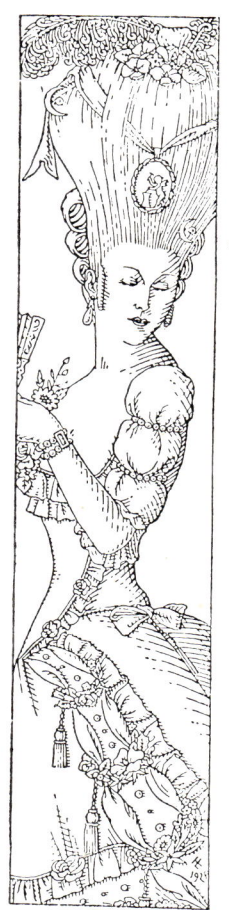

THE WEALTH of variety attainable by wise use of line is illustrated only in part by these drawings. ABOVE, left: This illustration by Duilio Cambellotti for *Le Prime Piume* by M. E. Orano conveys the seriousness of a child's play. Employment of vertical lines and punctuating dark notes gives this decoration its style. (*Published by R. Bemporad e Figlio, Florence.*) Right: Jean Oberlé's drawing of man and dog for Blaise Cendrars's *L'Or* is similar to Cambellotti's in the sparing use of blacks. The lines are freer in treatment, however. (*Published by Henri Jonquières & Cie, Paris.*) BELOW: Thomas Lowinsky's two views of Lady Teazle from Sheridan's *The School for Scandal* originally appear in facing pages of the book. They help to tie the type of the play together as nothing else could. (*Published by Shakespeare Head Press, Stratford upon Avon.*) CENTER: The life and class that can be given to an ordinary recipe drawing are superbly illustrated by this distinctive example of pen and ink technique by Marie Alix for Paul Poiret's 107 *Recettes*, published by Henri Jonquières, Paris.

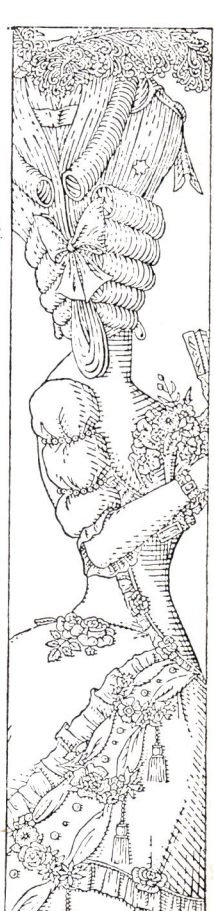

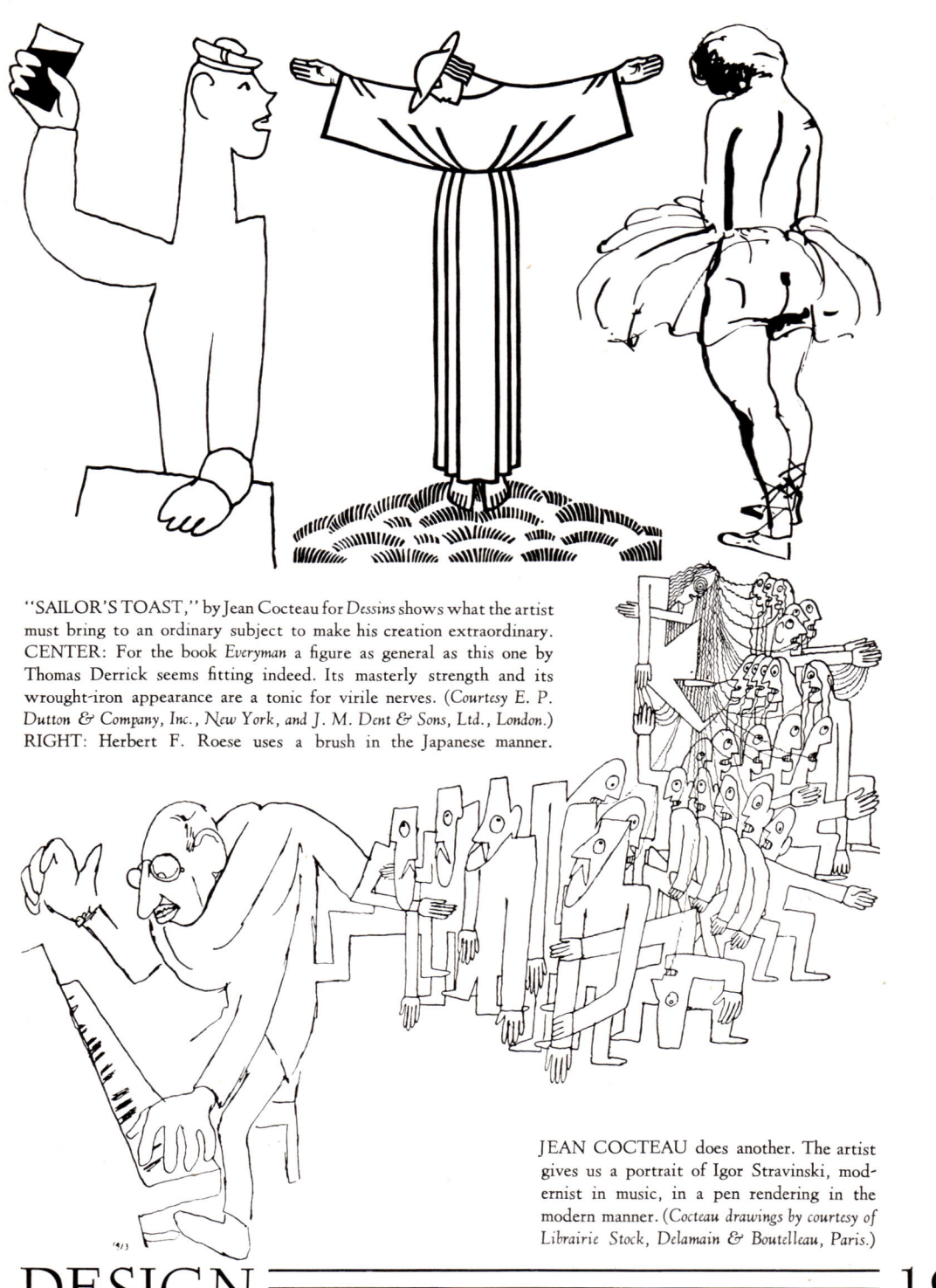

"SAILOR'S TOAST," by Jean Cocteau for *Dessins* shows what the artist must bring to an ordinary subject to make his creation extraordinary.
CENTER: For the book *Everyman* a figure as general as this one by Thomas Derrick seems fitting indeed. Its masterly strength and its wrought-iron appearance are a tonic for virile nerves. (*Courtesy E. P. Dutton & Company, Inc., New York, and J. M. Dent & Sons, Ltd., London.*)
RIGHT: Herbert F. Roese uses a brush in the Japanese manner.

JEAN COCTEAU does another. The artist gives us a portrait of Igor Stravinski, modernist in music, in a pen rendering in the modern manner. (*Cocteau drawings by courtesy of Librairie Stock, Delamain & Boutelleau, Paris.*)

DESIGN

ABOVE: Careful draftsmanship coupled with sparkling pen work makes this work by Rosso Gustavo a gem. Contrast the treatment of the figures with that accorded the room proper. (*From "Confessioni di un Italiano," published by Bertieri, Milan.*) BELOW, left: The composition of the praying figures in this facsimile by Francesco Carnevali reminds us of a Giotto or Fra Angelico. The simple direct line is especially fitting for the subject. (*From "Settimana di Passione," published by Bertieri, Milan.*) Right: What a good time Harry Beckhoff must have had making this drawing, and what a good time this drawing gives the observer! Its unaccented line shows the snap and sureness of a genuine artist. (*Courtesy Society of Illustrators, New York.*) Appropriate line quality was used in each case.

worked for Morris were the Pre-Raphaelites Rossetti, Millais, and Hunt. It is with Aubrey Beardsley (1872-1898), however, that we reach the finest illustrator between the Morris period and the present time. His work shows the influence of fifteenth century Italian illustration and Japanese block prints. Line is used in conjunction with black areas to create a dark and light pattern that is independent of the lighting effects caused by nature. This *notan* (Japanese for light-dark) is a decided improvement over chiaroscuro (light and shade) in the attainment of fine design. It frees the artist from slavish dependence on the accidents of nature. Beardsley's work is possibly the first done to show some recognition of the peculiarities of photomechanical line reproduction.

In England, limited editions were issued at different times by the Doves (Cobden-Sanderson), Ashendene, Golden Cockerel, Gregynog, Nonesuch, Curwen, Shakespeare Head, George W. Jones, and the Pelican presses. T. J. Cobden-Sanderson's work at the Doves Press showed the Morris standard of quality but with less elaboration. Among the German leaders in this effort are the Cranach and the Rupprecht presses, under the supervision of Count Kessler and Professor Ehmcke respectively,

THE ADVANTAGE of good draftsmanship, even within the limits set by a small illustration, is evident in this sketch by Henry C. Pitz. Note with what few lines the man's legs and feet are indicated. (Longmans, Green & Company, New York.)

See
fac-
ing
page

TWO EXAMPLES of students' work indicative of the requisites that furnish the background for successful illustration: fine arrangement, masterful drawing, and transparency of tones. ABOVE: Figure of a workingman by a student of the Graphic Art and Research Institute, Vienna. BELOW: The nude figure in this life sketch is highly simplified and the tonal modeling is very, very economical. Almost anyone could do as well—almost. (*State School for Applied Art, Munich.*) FACING PAGE: What color may add to a line rendering is suggested in these four illustrations. ABOVE, left: The spontaneity of the Forain sketch is exciting. The bold treatment of the advocate furnishes a sparkling contrast with that of the judge. (Librairie de France, Paris.) Right: Flat color and outline are combined in the decorative Foujita water color for *Chansons des Geishas*. Incorporating the white of the paper in the design helps to relate such a page to the white and black of the printed page. (Editions G. Crès & Cie, Paris.) BELOW, left: Charles Laborde's waterfront scene for Pierre Mac-Orlean's *Malice* is, in the original, as happy a combination of line and color as one can find. It is not mere map-like tinting. The careful characterizations of the figures contrast effectively with the freedom of the background. (Henri Jonquières, Paris.) Right: In its sense of color, point of view, and exaggerated drawing, Axel Nygaard's suburban street is purposely child-like in treatment since it is intended for children. It is as whimsical as the subject it illustrates. (Vespersen og Pios Forlag, Copenhagen.)

DESIGN 199

200 GRAPHIC

TWO ILLUSTRATIONS for Soviet juvenile books. ABOVE: V. Lebedev's massive group for S. Marshak's *Board of Social Competition* is as refreshing as a sketch and as well organized as a symphony. No artificial retouching has been resorted to. BELOW: Kukriniksi's illustration for Gershenson's *Pootanitza* employs the technique and humorous characterization that one is accustomed to find in caricatures. It is, therefore, certain to appeal to the child. (*Both illustrations courtesy Kultsviaz-Voks, Moscow.*) FACING PAGE. ABOVE, left: Frank G. Applegate's water color for *Native Tales of New Mexico* looks more French than American. Its freedom is unlike the orthodoxy that is still prevalent in the book arts. (*J. B. Lippincott & Company, Philadelphia.*) Right: Diego Rivera distorts his figures in almost cartoon fashion to obtain what he considers essential to his design. Again, paper plays the role of an important color in the illustration. (*From Stuart Chase's "Mexico," published by The Macmillan Company, New York.*) BELOW, left: Alessandro Cervellati, Bologna, illustrates *The Opera* with humor, color, and enough artistic liberty to make it distinctive. Right: C. LeRoy Baldridge's "Pagan Chieftain's Daughter" is silhouetted against a very interesting background and so made to stand out. (*From "White Africans and Black," W. W. Norton & Co., Inc., New York.*)

DESIGN 201

LEFT: Leonardo da Vinci (1452-1519) numbered caricaturing among his accomplishments. This detail from his "Study of Five Heads" shows the same appreciation for exaggerated forms that caricatures four hundred years later elicit. RIGHT: "Leo Tolstoi," drawn in 1903 by Olaf Gulbransson, is a caricature not far removed from masterly portraiture. It uses color (white) in much the same manner as Steinlen does in his "Laundresses" on page 175. The silhouette has the solidity that we associate with sculptured forms. (*Courtesy of "Simplicissimus," Munich.*)

although the urge to perfection has pervaded such other organizations as the Reichsdruckerei, Poeschel and Trepte, Erasmusdruck, and others. In France, the ideals of fine printing are carried forward by an ever increasing number of bibliophilic publishers and printeries. Pichon, Jonquières, Hazan, La Pléiade, Sans Pareil, Kieffer, George Crès & Cie., and Mornay are some of them. Italian propagators of faith in the beautiful include Raffaelo Bertieri, Giulio Giannini & Figlio, and A. F. Formiggini. De Sikkel Press does the honors in Belgium, and Joh. Enschedé en Zonen and the Zilverdistel Press in Holland. In America, too, the book beautiful has its proponents, although here, as abroad, the private presses are really as numerous as our individual artist printers. Of these we have a generous share. Strong additional factors for good are the various book societies and limited-editions clubs (see also plates in the chapter on Printing).

EXCEPT FOR its use, it would be hard to tell that André Gill's sketch of Rossini's head was anything but a good portrait study. (*Courtesy Éditions de l'Ibis, Paris.*)
BELOW: "Dropping the Pilot," by Tenniel, published Mar. 29, 1890, rewards a moment's observation with a volume of thought. It has been widely reproduced. (*By permission of the proprietors of "Punch," London.*)

Contemporary illustration owes its wealth of variety to the unlimited possibilities of reproduction. Thanks to the camera, line and tone, color and texture, and the fluidity of one or the crispness of another are reproduced with equal fidelity. Masters of line are Howard Pyle and Charles Dana Gibson, Americans; Eric Gill, John Austen, Englishmen; Jean Louis Forain, Bernard Boutet de Monvel, Frenchmen; and a few of the more outstanding cartoonists. Edwin Abbey, N. C. Wyeth, and Maxfield Parrish, Americans; Edmund Dulac, Jules Guérin, A. Grinevski, A. Alexeieff, Frenchmen; and G. Tenggren, a Dane, excel in color. We have the individualists in the field of illustration whose special styles or techniques are so much their own that they cannot be dismissed by a mere mention of names. Such artists are Arthur Rackham, Englishman, with his tinted line; Raoul Dufy, Frenchman, with his transformations of crude color and leadlike lines into beautiful arabesques; and Duilio Cambellotti, Italian, with his well-designed drawings enriched with dark notes. Among the Americans, especially noteworthy are Rockwell Kent, with his severe compositions in the woodcut manner that combine splendidly with type; Ru-

DESIGN 203

"LA DERNIERE MARCHE" by Louis Raemaekers was occasioned by Clemenceau's death. It shows with what sympathy and tact a cartoonist may render character. An intimate personal knowledge of the man by the artist made this possible. Something of the significance and power of the cartoonist's vehicle of expression can be gleaned from the fact that the German emperor put a tremendous price on Raemaeker's head during the World War. His drawings, reproduced throughout the world, moved nations—including, some think, the United States—to join the allies. This is a moot question. The excellence of his work is not. (*Courtesy Dr. Louis Raemaekers, Brussels.*)

PAOLO GARRETTO'S conception of former President Hoover is not a specific portrait of a man as he appears in a moment of accidental lighting, but a generalized portrait that, seen once, will linger for a long time. RIGHT: William Cotton's caricature of Theodore Dreiser accentuates the likeness of the American tragedian by contrasting a carefully modeled face against an almost flat treatment of the rest of the design. Is this caricature or fine art? The colors of the original would have made decision more difficult. (*Reproduced from "Vanity Fair" by permission of the copyright owners, Condé Nast Publications, New York.*)

dolph Ruzicka and Allen Lewis, masters of the colored woodcut; and John Held, Jr., whose playful woodcut imitations and satiric reminders of early American prints seem refreshingly new. W. A. Dwiggins, however, is, in the opinion of the authors, the most successful book illustrator of all the Americans; and Boris Artzybasheff and Lynd Ward are making highly distinctive contributions in the field. The honor roll of artists whose work deserves careful study is a growing one. The following come to mind at once among the English: Randolph Caldecott, Walter Crane, Kate Greenaway, C. Lovat Fraser, Charles Ricketts, Paul Nash, Robert Gibbings, Thomas Derrick, John Farleigh, Thomas Lowinsky, Maynard, and the American-born E. McKnight-Kauffer. French illustrators of exceptional ability are more numerous than those of any other country. Following Daniel Vierge, a Spaniard who worked in France, and Théophile Steinlen, we have the following moderns: Louis Bouquet, Lucien Boucher, A. M. Martin, Charles Martin, Picart Ledoux, Carlègle, Ramiro Arrue, Sylvain Sauvage, Jean Cocteau, Aristide Maillol, Dignimont, Touchagues, Gaston Nick, René Ben Sussan,

Valentin le Campioni, Valentin Bitt, Charles Laborde, Edy Legrand, F. L. Schmied, Gus Bofa, J. E. Laboureur, Hermann Paul, Lalande-Jodel, Alfred Latour, P. Pinsard, Jean Oberlé, Mariette Lydis, Dunoyer de Segonzac, D. Galanis, and many others. Top-notch Italian illustrators, who tend, with few exceptions, to be somewhat more conservative than the French, include Guino Carlo Sensani, A. Moroni, Luigi Guerini, Anthony de Witt, Piero Bernardini, and Sinopico. Among the best work in contemporary German book illustration is that done for the various private presses by the foreigners Eric Gill, Frans Masereel, and Aristide Maillol. Advertising artists who occasionally make sparkling contributions are Professor Fritz Helmuth Ehmcke, E. R. Weiss, and Hans Alexander Muller. Some fine illustrations bear the names of Bruno Skibbe, Ernst Barlach, Walter Buhe, Professor Ernst Aufseeser. Illustrators whose work is much sought after beyond the confines of their own countries are Josef Cantré, Frans Masereel, N. F. Lapshin, J. V. Divéky, Paul C. Molnár, Axel Nygaard, Félix Vallotton, Josef Capek, Vojtech Preissig, Mme. Troyen, Jean Zerzavy, Tadeusz Kulisiewicz, N. E. Edkman, André Van der Vossen, Yngve Berg, P. E. Vibert, Richard Floethe, Marion V. Dorn, and Blair Hughes-Stanton. A word or so about painting is appropriate here because even free painting is not always

FOUR CARTOONS that exemplify the artists' satire of current political, racial, social, and industrial problems. ABOVE: Jacob Burck's massive composition carries the spectator along with the unisonous movement of the slanted bodies. (From "New Masses," New York.) BELOW: The harmony of an impromptu blues tune is molded into languid lines and dark-light planes in the caricature of a dancing Negro couple by Miguel Covarrubias. (From W. C. Handy's "Blues," published by Albert & Charles Boni, New York.) FACING PAGE. Above, left: "You're fired!" A magazine cartoon by William Steig, as fine in its draftsmanship as in its idea. The repetition of the three figures in the massed front of the board of directors confronted with the wise calmness of the wee fellow hilariously punctures the inflated dignity of big business. Note how the lines of the penholders, the horses on the wall and the shadows on the floor all lead the eye in the direction of the boy. (From "The New Yorker," New York.) Right: "The Deadliest Racket in the World," a newspaper editorial cartoon by Rollin Kirby, directed against armament manufacturers. Such cartoons often succeed in creating a clever "type" that is subsequently widely used to represent a collective character. (From the "New York World-Telegram," New York).

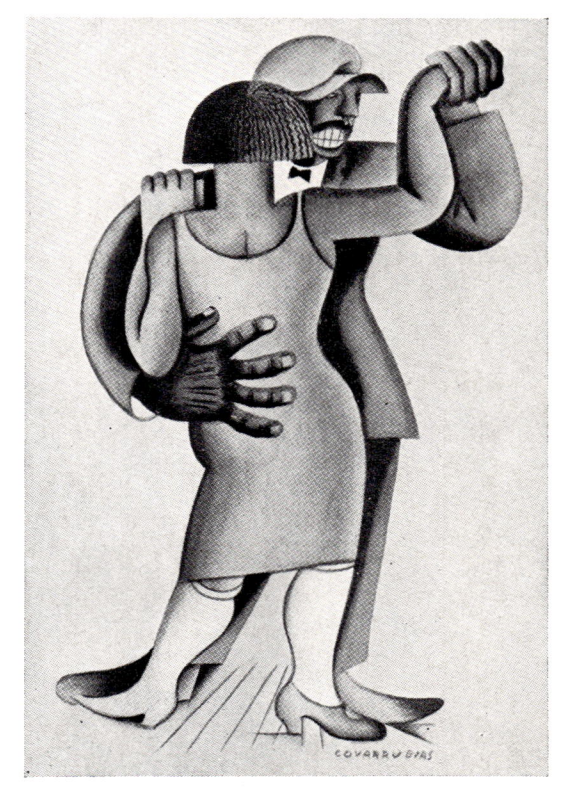

DESIGN 207

easily distinguished from illustration, so called. The work of Edwin Abbey, Toulouse-Lautrec, Marie Laurencin, Maurice de Vlaminck, Marc Chagall, and others can often be defined as either. Painting deals with nuances of a surface, with color and light, and creates an emotion in the observer independent of any story telling quality that it may, but need not, have. Used as book illustrations, paintings tend to become independent representations or pictorial repetitions of what has already been expressed by the printed word. Except in children's books, where the type used is both large and bold, paintings are too heavy for the gray of type matter. At best, they are likely to be independ-

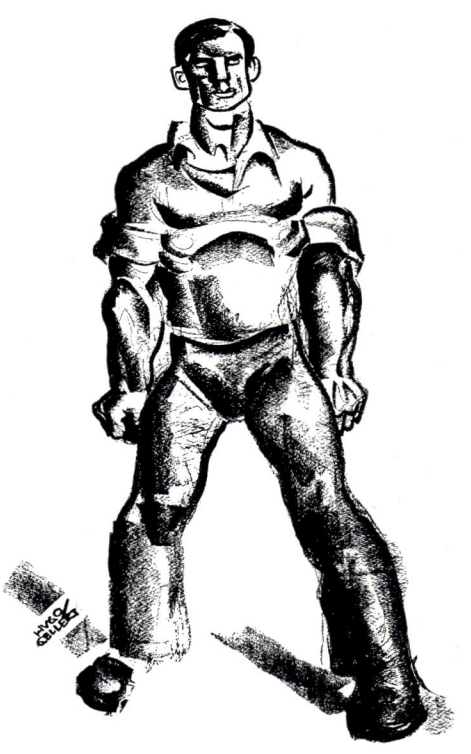

"EUROPE," a commentary on its armament race, by D. R. Fitzpatrick; a blunt indictment in lithographic crayon that suggests by appropriate distortion a powerful body minus the sound mind. (*Courtesy "St. Louis Post-Dispatch."*)

BELOW: The figure of the laborer has the spontaneity of a sketch and the sparkle of a Japanese drawing. Compare this punctuated line that characterizes William Gropper's brushwork with the power of Gellert's broad sweeps of gray on the facing page. (*"New Masses," New York.*)

FACING PAGE. Above: "Europe's Little Men: 'They say we have to have them to protect ourselves from each other.'" With pen, ink, and Ben Day, Strube exposes the irony of these words. (*"Daily Express,"* London.) Below: The worker and his latent power are strikingly portrayed by Hugo Gellert in sweeping strokes of a litho pencil. We see here the strength of Michelangelo's figures presented in a manner original to Gellert. The texture of the lithographic crayon seems to have been preferred by cartoonists since Daumier. (*"New Masses."*)

ent pictorial inserts that dominate the text that they were intended to supplement. Like the halftone, which is the common means of reproduction, a painting does not usually incorporate the paper in its design. Type does. More frequently a halftone or painting appears as an obvious addition, an unassimilated element of the design of a page. Overloading a book with paintings or overloading with pictures of any form tends to make the text so subordinate that additional text is needed to explain the illustrations themselves.

Requirements peculiar to the problems of journalism have brought about the development of a characteristic form of illustration—the cartoon. The basic training for cartoonist and illustrator is much the same, and often a single artist may excel in both forms of expression. Minus a legend, a cartoon and an illustration may

THREE FAMILIAR figures, Chaplin, Grock, and Keaton, as seen by Oleg Zingher, Berlin. Observation of what is most characteristic in people, as illustrated by these sketches, is an essential ability in the strong caricaturist.

look very much alike (see Rethel's "Death on the Barricades," page 173). A cartoon is a graphic comment on some poignant phase of contemporary life. Its origin goes back to the Middle Ages, to the Italian *caricatura*. Its more modern form was developed by such men as Goya, Daumier, Beerbohm, and Cruikshank. To this day, continental Europe cultivates the caricature in place of the Anglo-Saxon cartoon. Although the prevalent cartoon shows humorous or satirical tendencies, it may equally well represent the tragic or the sublime. It has been used to exhort and propagandize, to accuse and defend. Contemporary cartooning can be divided into three fields: newspaper, magazine, and commercial cartooning. The newspaper cartoon has momentary

210 GRAPHIC

value. It concerns itself with such topics of a political or social nature as have achieved enough passing interest to stand out in the spotlight against the blurred background of daily events. The magazine cartoon is more generalized. It exploits the merits and follies of social institutions and customs, of science, of art, and of human traits. The commercial cartoon uses or abuses the inherent and attractive qualities of cartooning in order to create good will for the article advertised. Whole advertising campaigns have been based on and have exploited the possibilities of the laugh-provoking drawing. Pages 292–293.

Caricature and cartoon have been defined as ludicrous exaggerations of characteristic, or allegedly characteristic, features of a personality or an event. Therefore a sleight-of-hand cleverness in arresting a sharp sidelight on popular opinions, customs, or prejudices is just as important as artistic excellence; one must often overlook the disregard of fundamentals of drawing (anatomy, perspective, composition, etc.) for these more telling qualities. The attributes re-

ABOVE: "Toscanini" as an Italian artist, Aldo Mazza of Milan, pictures him. This strip indicates how much research (in this case costume history) even an unpretentious caricature may entail. (*Courtesy of the artist.*) BELOW and facing page: Bits of linear humor by Primo Sinopico for an elaborate liquor book in verse. The gay, brief pen strokes are fit companions for fine wines, women, and songs. (*From a limited edition printed in black and red by Raffaello Bertieri for Davide Campari & Company, Milan.*)

DESIGN 211

JOHN HELD, Jr., does a cartoon in the "good old manner." (Marchbanks Press, New York; courtesy Linweave Editions.)

ENRICO CARUSO could express himself as adequately with few lines as with few notes. Portrait of Antonio Scotti. (From "Caricatures by Enrico Caruso," published by Marziale Sisca, New York.) RIGHT: "O, Henry!" by Pontax. The idea is extremely funny. ("The London Mercury," London.) BELOW: "Truce between Capital and Labor," by George Grosz. The rendering is as spontaneous as a child's, but the disposition of emphasis is that of a master. ("Criterion Miscellany No. 31," published by Faber & Faber, Ltd., London.)

quired of a cartoonist are identical with those demanded of a good news reporter. A sense for news values rather than for pictorial appeal, a practical capacity to observe and condense the observed material into simple drawings easily understandable to a multitude of readers, realism rather than inventiveness, copying from nature rather than an allegoric treatment of the subjects are the desiderata. A certain amount of sensationalism and an understanding of the fetish of all newspapers, *human interest*, com-

DESIGN 213

THE EXAGGERATED hands gain further strength by contrast with a delicately drawn background. Distortion is used for decorative purposes rather than for caricature. Hands inspired, too, the fine lithographic study by Alexeïeff shown on page 185. (Albert Hirschfeld's picture of a Hall Johnson Negro cast, from the Sunday "Herald-Tribune," New York.)

plete the bag of tricks: (A human-interest subject can be described as an incident immediately related to the daily-life philosophy of the unsophisticated, average mortal, expressed in terms of the emotions of humor or pathos.

BINDINGS. LEFT: Hand-sewn binding with flexible back. CENTER: Binding with blind tooling gives distinction to a well-proportioned container. RIGHT: Hand-sewn binding with rounded hollow back. The suggestion of *strength* is part of the design. (*Dorothee Freise, of the Workshops of the City of Halle, Burg Giebichenstein.*)

The more melodramatic the scene is the more general and lasting its appeal is likely to be; "sob sister stuff" is a case in point.)

Happily, at present we can point to a host of cartoonists whose work combines all the requisites of a fine cartoon. These are, to mention a few, Dr. Louis Raemaekers, whose satiric political comments appear in *De Telegraaf*; John T. McCutcheon, whose consistent front-page displays are found in the *Chicago Tribune*; Fitzpatrick, whose lithographed expressions are published in the *St. Louis Post-Dispatch*; Rollin Kirby in the *New York World Telegram*; Boardman Robinson; and Gulbransson, whose vigorous line characterizations are a feature of *Simplicissimus*. The comic-supplement education which some of us receive in our youth is a preparation for the caricatures of human shortcomings, which we see in our maturity. Contemporary cartoonists are worthy followers of Thomas Nast (1840-1902), of whose work Theodore Roosevelt is reported to have said: "I learned my politics from your cartoons."* Nast was also the inventor of the Democratic Donkey and the Republican Elephant, of the square paper cap of labor, the full dinner pail, the Tammany Tiger, and the

* Quotation from the *New York Times Saturday Review* of August 20, 1904.

"THE POET," five panels from a series, "The Nine Muses," by Thomas Derrick. These fine drawings are cartoons only in the sense that they employ artistic license to elicit a laugh. Derrick's versatility is shown by comparing these sketches with the figure of *Everyman* on page 195. (*Reproduced from "The London Mercury," London.*)

DESIGN 215

inflation rag baby of—not 1935—1875. Judged by their leaders, modern cartoonists may be expected to contribute much that is as likely to be quoted and reprinted as Sir John Tenniel's (1820-1914) classic "Dropping the Pilot."* To add to our menagerie, it is often said that Tenniel was the first to use the lion as the symbol of England. Besides the editorial cartoon, there are the saucy flappers of John Held, Jr., the human failings of Peter Arno's bluebloods; the ingenious inventions of Rube Goldberg and Dr. Seuss; the portrait hits of Miguel Covarrubias, William Cotton, and Garretto; the penetrating crayon sculptures of Hugo Gellert; and the hilarious antics of Walt Disney's Mickey Mouse. Of the foreign countries each can match this gallery with an equivalent of its own. Among their better known cartoonists are Tjerk Bottema, Dutchman; Aldo Mazza, Italian; Johnson, German; Low and Partridge, Englishmen. The reader can supplement these names with other great and nearly great caricaturists and cartoonists whose work are his daily or weekly companions and whose dispensations are frequently the only humor in what the reader recognizes as extremely sad states of affairs.

Bookbinding includes the sewing, slips, and boards which are used to bind and protect, and make convenient for use, the pages of the book. Douglas Cockerell, a contemporary craftsman, considers the so-called cloth bindings of the trade, in which boards are covered separately and glued to the book, as *casings*.† The attaching of the

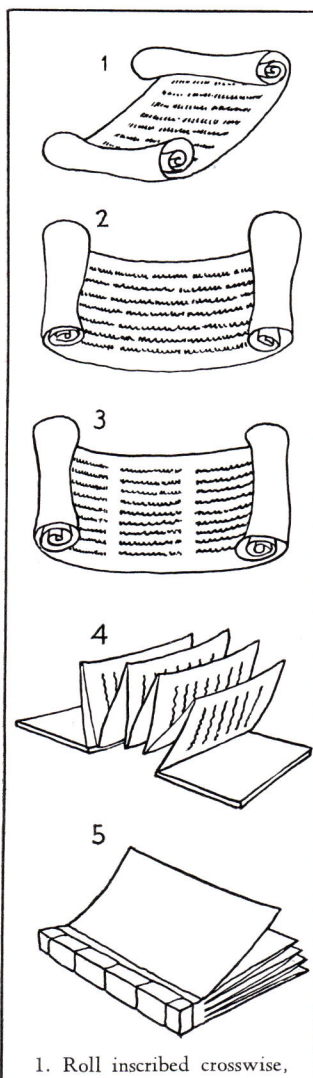

1. Roll inscribed crosswise, read from top downwards. 2. Roll inscribed longitudinally and read crosswise. 3. Roll; lines divided into "pages" as in Jewish scrolls of the law. 4. Roll folded into accordion-like pleating and weighted with boards (Sumatra bark book). 5. Accordion-folded "roll" with writing on one surface and sewed on one end, called *orihon* (Japanese book).

*Published in *Punch*, London, March 20, 1890.
†Douglas Cockerell, *Bookbinding and the Care of Books*, Appleton-Century.

slips to the boards before covering he considers a requisite to *binding*.

The ancient skin, wood, and metal containers of scrolls were the earliest forms of binding. Later, scrolls were wound around a rod and kept in cylindrical boxes. A ribbon protruding from the case gave the title of the scroll. As long ago as 3000 B.C., papyrus rolls, called *volumina*, were used in Egypt. The scrolls of papyri, vellum, or parchment were first inscribed in short lines at right angles to the length of the 15- or 18-foot roll; next, across the full length of the roll; then, in short lines parallel with the length of the roll. The introduction of "paging" into short, readable units was a noteworthy step forward in the purposeful planning of the book. Pleating these pages across the unlettered spaces, accordion fashion, and keeping them in that form between two heavy boards was a still further step toward the familiar volume of our time. It was done about 500 A.D. In books that use semi-transparent paper (e.g., Japanese rice-paper books called *orihons*), this accordion pleating is still used of necessity, although sewing on one end eliminates the need for the heavy covers.

The change from scroll cases to wax tablets and again to binding was a slow one. It was dictated by a desire to make the records more compact and more convenient to read. When, in the fifth century A.D., we have two boards in diptych fashion, covering pages of text, recognizable binding may be said to have replaced the rolled vellum scrolls. Since these early bindings covered rare, sometimes unique, manuscripts, one under-

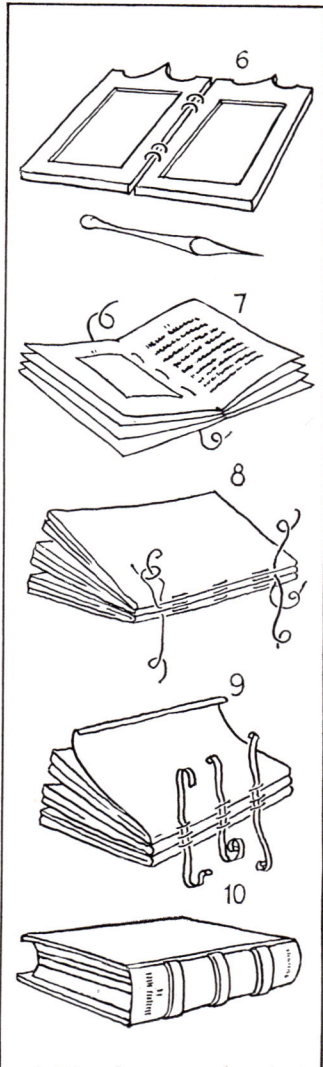

6. Diptych, two wooden tablets hinged together by metal or leather thongs; also stylus. 7. Four doubled sheets fitted into a section called a quaternion. 8. Quaternions with their loose threads tied to each other. 9. Threaded quaternions tied on to transverse bands. 10. Regular heavy binding with tooled leather-covered boards and three bands.

DESIGN 217

BOOKBINDING of about 1050, decorated with metal framework of Limoges enamel and further embellished with stones. The paintings within the metal medallions, added about 1400-1420, are on a red velvet background impressed with unobtrusive flower designs. (*From the Ashburnham collection, courtesy Bernard Quaritch, Ltd., London.*)

PSALTER OF MELISANDA. Ivory carving of the early 1100's. Spots indicate the position formerly occupied by two clasps. The beauty of its low relief and its fine design beggar verbal description. (*The British Museum, London.*)

EARLY ELEVENTH century beechwood cover overlaid with gold, enriched with cloisonné enamel and precious stones. (*Victoria and Albert Museum, London.*) RIGHT: Thirteenth century French champlevé enamel on copper gilt on an oak board. The corner symbols represent St. Matthew, St. John, St. Mark, and St. Luke grouped about the figure of Christ—a popular motif in the bindings of this period. (*Courtesy Victoria and Albert Museum, London.*)

stands why such devotion and craftsmanship were combined to convert protecting boards to works of art. At a time when a book was a costly masterpiece of handicraft and its presence in a household at once a sign of prestige and wealth, the best covers were barely good enough to protect the precious contents of the comparatively few books then produced.

But essentially bookmaking had changed very little from the method used by the Greeks and Romans. Sheets were still ruled for work by indenting them with a blunt instrument. They were doubled and fitted into sections of possibly four folds, called *quaternions*. These sheets were sewed together, and several such sections were tied together by the exterior loose ends of the threads. A book formed of a gathering of original sheets folded once, giving two leaves or four pages, is called a *folio*. In the folio, the long thick lines of the paper, called chain lines (similar to grain lines shown on page 379), are perpendicular to the fold. A book composed of sheets folded a second time, giving four leaves or eight pages, is a *quarto* (4o); doubling such sheets pro-

GROLIER BINDING with the interlaced strapwork of geometric forms that marks most of the books in this famous collector's library. Venice, 1523. (*British Museum, London.*) RIGHT: Bolognese binding for Nicolas Ebeleben, similar in design to Grolier bindings. From the National Library, Dresden. (*Courtesy Seeman Verlag, Leipzig.*)

duces an *octavo* (8vo), with eight leaves or sixteen pages to each section of the book. The chain lines are vertical in the quarto and horizontal in the octavo forms. Folio, quarto, or octavo sizes of books are only relative terms where the sheet folded least is indicative of the largest book—viz., a folio. The signature used in a book can usually be identified by the small letter or figure in the margin at the bottom of each first page of a sheet. Every fourth page is so marked in a folio, every eighth in a quarto, and every sixteenth in an octavo. The identifying marks are used by the binder to help organize the sheets in correct sequence in folding.

Medieval and Renaissance bindings were quite different in appearance from those which we are accustomed to see now. The peculiar construction of the books and bookracks of the time necessitated placing the books with their edges exposed. Consequently the edges were often decorated or written on for identification (fore-edge decoration). The gold-edged pages, which are still used, harmonize most effectively with gold-tooled bindings, and they

DESIGN 221

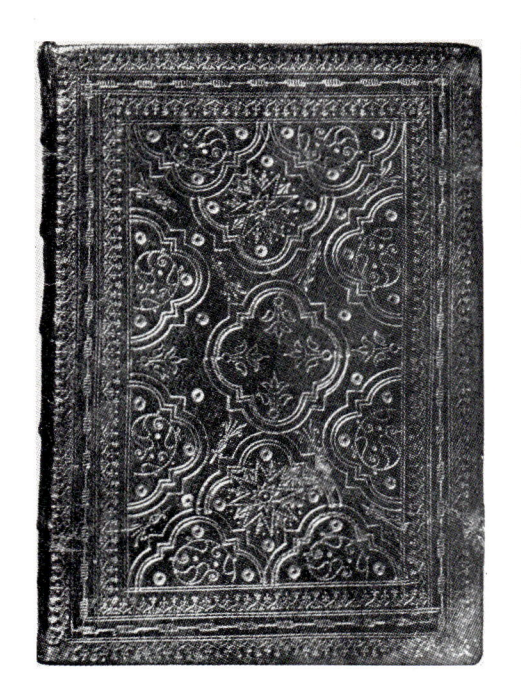

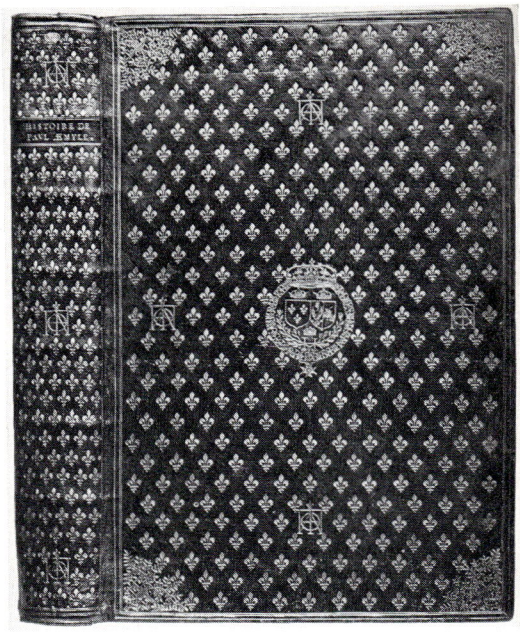

For descriptions of these bookbindings see facing page.

THIS BINDING by Le Gascon, a seventeenth century craftsman, is a near-perfect example of *pointillé* design. It is a good reason for the absence of the book jacket in the early history of binding. People prefer to show beautiful things. (*From the original in the British Museum, London.*)

FACING PAGE. ABOVE, left: Red morocco binding by Clovis Eve. In parts, note the stars, for example, the all-over pattern suggests the *pointillé* work of Le Gascon. (*Courtesy Gilhofer & Ranschburg, Vienna.*) Right: Nicholas Eve's binding for *L'Histoire des Faicts, Gestes, et Conquests des Roys*. The all-over fleur-de-lis design and the floral corners are characteristic of Eve's work. Note attention to even minute matters. (*British Museum, London.*)

BELOW, left: A sixteenth century bookbinding that presents the work of a familiar figure in the printing field, Geoffroy Tory. His broken-pitcher trade-mark is easily discernible. (*Victoria and Albert Museum.*) Right: The embroidered binding for *De Antiquitate Britannicae Ecclesiae* belonged, appropriately enough, to Queen Elizabeth. This adds another bookbinding material to the ivory, metal, wood, paper, and leather that had been used. The freedom of its design is consistent with the material used. Finical detail has been avoided. (*British Museum, London.*)

DESIGN 223

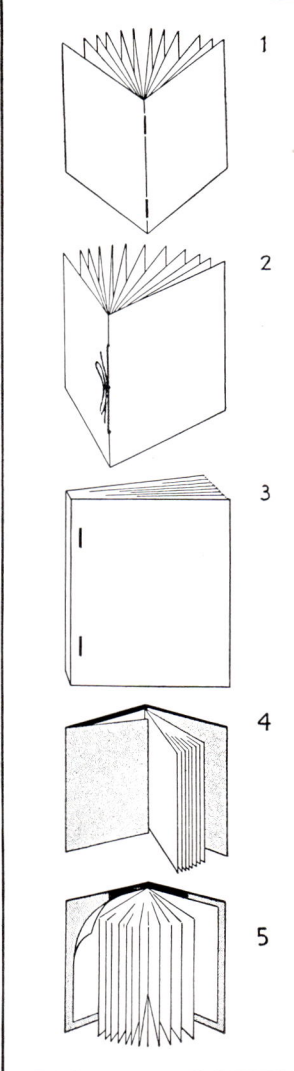

BOOKBINDING METHODS: 1. Saddle-wire stitched book. 2. Saddle-sewed book with bow on the outside. 3. Side-wire stitched book (with cover omitted). 4. Book with a full fly leaf of the cover, folded over one of the leaves of the book. 5. Booklet with a short flap of the cover turned in and an extended cover over which a fly leaf has been pasted.

have the practical advantage of permitting easy dusting of the top edges of upright books. Famous silversmiths created special ornaments and casings for bookbindings, studded them with stones, and laid them in with rare woods or precious metals until the book was so heavy that some considerable physical effort was necessary to read it. The reverence for the intellectual significance of a book was reflected in the care and ingenuity devoted to a binding. Such an example is the elegantly carved ivory covers of the *Psalter of Melisanda* (see page 219) with its text on vellum. The first recipient of the book is said to have been the daughter of a king of Jerusalem. The binding of the thirteenth century French book shown (page 220) is another gorgeous specimen. Limoges champlevé enamel on copper gilt, on an oak board, protected what must have been a book of the Gospels of the Saints. At least, circling the central figure of Christ are the symbols of the evangelists Matthew, Mark, Luke and John. In motif, iconography and use of enamel, it is strikingly similar to a German binding for the *Gospels of St. Luke and St. John* (1290-1300), in the British Museum. The beauty and strength of the covers combine to fortify the contents of such books against the unworshipful. Other splendid examples left by ecclesiastic craftsmen, by the Moors in Spain, by the collectors Grolier (1479-1565) and Maioli (about 1500-1550), and even by the binders of the Baroque period testify to the widespread love for beautiful bindings.

The bindings made for Grolier were not uniform in appearance, although the typical one was

224 GRAPHIC

likely to consist of morocco (goatskin tanned with sumach) with gold tooling. The design of interlaced strapwork of geometric forms was rarely relieved by the free curves of flowers and usually identified by Grolier's note of ownership: "Io. Grolieri et Amicorum" (Grolier's and his friends). A Maioli binding was likely to contain a similar inscription. Bindings made for him were freer and invariably enriched by gracefully curved linework. If Nicholas or Clovis Eve, French royal binders, did the binding, its appearance was likely to show an all-over framework of plant-life design, either alone or with the intervening boxes filled in (*à la fanfare*). Floral corners usually marked the work of these brothers, as can be seen in Nicholas's binding for Henry III, for *L'Histoires des Faicts, Gestes, et Conquests des Roys*. (See page 222. Note the absence of bands; the splendid tooling is attributed to Paulus Aemilius.) The binding for *De Antiquitate Britannicae Ecclesiae* was embroidered on a groundwork of green velvet for Queen Elizabeth. This was most appropriate for a lady. Indeed, lighter binding characterized most of the books from this time on. Removal of the heavy bands from the backs of books accounted for the improvement and also permitted decoration on the spine that harmonized with the decoration on the covers.

Another innovation was the dotted line (*pointillé* design) achieved by Le Gascon (or perhaps Florimond Badier), a seventeenth century Frenchman. The *Historia Belli Dacici: Auctore F. Alfonso Ciacono*, bound by him in 1616, illustrates his style. A more recent master was Roger Payne, eighteenth century Englishman. His love for his

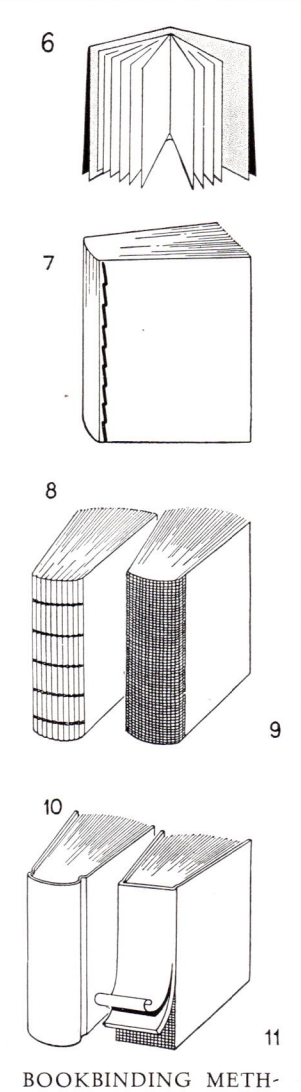

BOOKBINDING METHODS: 6. French-fold cover. 7. Side Singer-sewed book (cover omitted). 8. Smyth-sewed book. 9. Smyth-sewed book, rounded and backed, with super over backbone; second stage of binding. 10. Case-bound book, round back. 11. Case-bound book; square back. (Courtesy of the Champion Coated Paper Company, Hamilton, Ohio.)

226

AN INFORMAL binding for *Geschichte der Herrschaft Gersfeld* by Otto Reichert, Offenbach. The free lettering is consistent with the masculinity of the binding. RIGHT: The *Jahrbuch der Einbandkunst* by Ernest Rehbein, Darmstadt, employs rules ingeniously to obtain decorative results and to get away from the stereotyped in binding. BELOW: Binding in precious wood, ivory, and morocco leather by Rose Adler, Paris, for Mirabeau's *Dingo*. Fine division of space, beautiful play of texture against texture, and wise restraint in labeling mark this fine creation.

FACING PAGE. ABOVE, left: *Euripides*. Roger Payne's work is likely to show as much attention given to the back of the binding as to the sides. Love of simplicity rather than overornamentation is discernible in his bindings. (*British Museum, London.*) Right: One of the bindings by Giulio Giannini, Florence, 1853-1931, which is an example of modern design in the spirit of the sixteenth century. BELOW: The symmetrically conceived binding for *Ein Sommernachtstraum* by Ernest Rehbein, Darmstadt, indicates a fine feeling for large spaces. The *Sommernachtstraum* binding surprises by the economical means with which the strong effects are attained and by its respect for the unworked leather.

DESIGN 227

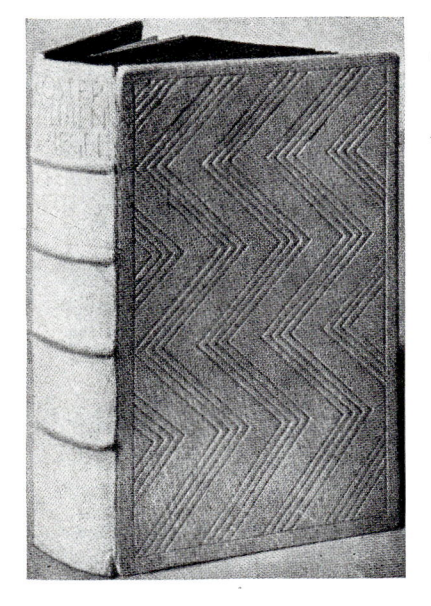

ABOVE: A contemporary Dutch trade binding by S. H. de Roos, Hilversum, architectural in its simplicity. The large "T" harmonizes effectively with the surrounding rules. BELOW: A student's solution to a bookbinding problem for Coster's *Tyl Ulenspiegel*, a professional job in every way. The design uses straight lines in a moving rather than static manner. (*Class of Prof. F. H. Ehmcke, Munich.*)

craft, precision of work, and attainment of good design were exemplary. In a bill which he sent to the Reverend C. M. Cracherode for binding *Eurypides*, printed in Cambridge in 1694, he states: "... one leaf for instance (page 47) took a full day's work" to straighten and strengthen.* His volumes, mostly in Russian leather (originally hides of young cattle from Russia), sometimes showed plain sides and tooled backs, a considerable departure from prevalent taste. Responsible for other noteworthy work, and also writings on the subject of binding, are William Morris, T. J. Cobden-Sanderson, Douglas Cockerell, Englishmen; Giulio Giannini, Italian; Alois Jirout, Czechoslovakian; Rose Adler, young Frenchwoman; and Ernst Rehbein, Ignaz Wiemeler, Elizabeth Ledderhose, and Katharine and Dorothee Freise, Germans.

When books were few in number, they were kept on their sides, protected only by their flat boards. The ornate decorations on the covers were saved from undue wear by highly decorative corner pieces, clasps, and bosses—wooden or metal pieces in relief on the covers. Two very fine specimens are shown on **pages 218 and 220**. As printing increased so did libraries. This dictated a more economical, side-by-side stacking of books. To prevent their being damaged by neighboring volumes, raised decorations in precious stone and metal had to be replaced by flat covers. This was done by decorating

*Henry Benjamin Wheatley, *Remarkable Bindings in the British Museum*, published in London, 1889. Illustrated.

the bindings with color or by hot tooling on the leather ("blind" impression). Beginning about 1470, some years after the fall of Constantinople, the number of bindings with gold tooling à fillet, an importation from the East, increased by leaps and bounds. It is thought that Aldus Manutius first generally employed gold tooling in Europe, although the highest degree of excellence was attained in the work of the French. Rich patterns were pressed, cut, or bronzed into the leather background where additions of metal, ivory, mother-of-pearl, wood inlay, and other beautiful but extraneous matter had formerly lent enrichment.

Although pressing or embossing is now done by machine, many contemporary bindings find the inspiration for their design in medieval masterpieces. Today the artist makes the design. He may suggest the material for the binding and the method or combination of methods necessary to obtain the desired result. Owing to lack of training, however, an artist seldom makes the design *and* completes the binding. He is rarely both the artist and the artisan.

Printing, with its ability to produce an ever increasing quantity of books, spread

ABOVE: Binding in green morocco leather with gilding by Alois Jirout, Prague, for *Basnicí Matkám*. The title, incorporated in the leather, makes up in size what it loses in lack of color. CENTER: Binding designed by J. Stýrský, Prague, and executed by Alois Jirout for *Žal*, a book by S. K. Neumann, whose initials are decoratively arranged on the cover. Gray chagrain leather with platinum and blue mosaic is used. Broad play of light against dark areas and moving lines are combined. BELOW: *Stammbuch* by Elizabeth Ledderhose, Munich. The deckled edge harmonizes with the rough leather.

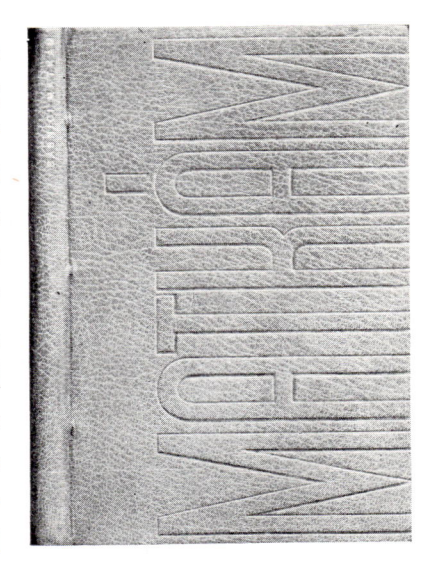

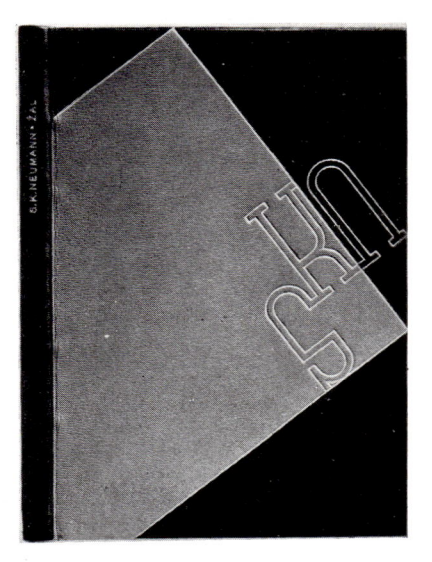

For description of these fine and substantial bookbindings by Katharine Freise, Mainz, see legend on facing page.

ABOVE: For advanced work, the unadorned bindings by Dorothee Freise of the Workshops of the City of Halle offer inspiring examples. Note especially the off-center lettering on the duo-tone binding for *Der Cicerone*. BELOW: This series of small books by Otto Reichert, Offenbach, suggests possible problems for students of lettering and binding. Generous spaces, restrained decoration, fine lettering, and excellent proportions make these books attractive. FACING PAGE. ABOVE, left: Leather and wood covers with silver clasps and blind tooling. Right: White pigskin binding with silver clasps and blind tooling. BELOW: Natural-color pigskin binding with blind tooling. These bindings for religious books are by Katharine Freise, Mainz. Their chaste simplicity is much more in keeping with the unpretentious strength of religion than the ornate bindings with which we are familiar.

DESIGN 231

THE TRANSITION from bookbinding to book casing to book jacket is illustrated by the above two items as compared with the preceding pages. LEFT: *Das Heilige Messopfer* jacket designed by Fritz Kremer, Munich, could not have been reproduced on linen or in leather. The gradation and color of the original halftone and line plate combine to create an unusual setting for a beautiful jacket design. (Published in Switzerland by Benziger & Company, Einsiedeln.) RIGHT: Book casing for *Der Göttliche Dulder* created by an outstanding type designer, E. R. Weiss. These kinds of line and open design lend themselves to easy impression in bookbinding linen and by contrast show, too, why a jacket rather than a casing design was used in the example on the left. (*Insel Verlag, Leipzig.*) BELOW: The jacket by Guido Marussig, Milan, for d'Annunzio's *Ariel Armato* has all the freedom of a muralist's embryonic *croquis*. Movement is successfully suggested by use of diagonals and by the directional line of the figure.

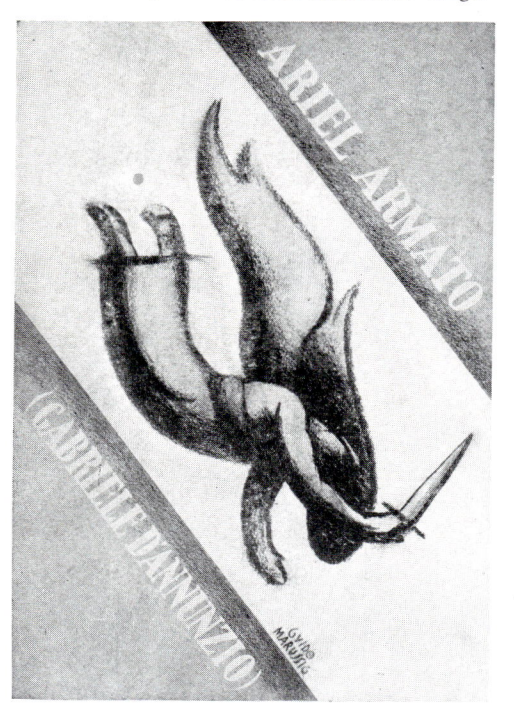

book reading from the scholar and bibliophile to the average man. The book became a mass product. Consequently, the publishers had to look about for a substitute binding that would hold together and protect text pages and yet dispense with the time and outlay required by the more durable leather. Thus originated the semi-leather or French cover with only the spine and corners bound in leather. Emphasis on popular appeal and

BOOK JACKET by Boris Artzybasheff for *Orpheus* in black, silver, and green on a white background. It is an outstanding example of practical beauty. The design is planned as a single related unit with even the panels on cover and spine lining up; a jacket that is not a mere wrapper. (Published by The Macmillan Company, New York.)

widespread production limited the design and the material of the binding to the kind which could be produced by the machine and would be accessible to the pocketbooks of the masses. Cloth usually took the place of leather covers. Linen, pasteboard, and, finally, the paper cover (brochure) bring the sequence of book covers up to date.

Book jacket. The "dust wrapper" (whose name explains its purpose) was originally a plain, unprinted paper used to protect the binding from marks and scratches caused by shipment and shop display. It was usually manila paper. For identification, the book title was later printed on it. Then publishers came to realize that the protective wrapper could serve another purpose. They began to print favorable quotations from book reviewers. It was a short step from plain printing to decorated borders. But only within the last few decades has the technique of the poster been generally used for its display and sales-promotion value. The attention value of a poster, its brevity, dash, and color, have been transferred with little modification to the book jacket. In design, most jackets build their decoration around the title, which appears on the cover and

ABOVE: Jacket for *Jugend Lieder-Buch* by Andreas Niessen, Berlin. Its strong dark and light pattern makes the whole conspicuous. The swinging rhythm of the figures strikes the tempo for the martial character of the songs. FACING PAGE: A challenging jacket is this one by Leo Marfurt for Louis Franck's *Belgisch Congo*. The face, originally in realistic colors, tells much, the title serving only the purpose of identification. (Published by De Sikkel, Antwerp.)

For description of this elemental book-jacket design by Leo Marfurt for *Belgisch Congo* see the legend on facing page.

DESIGN 235

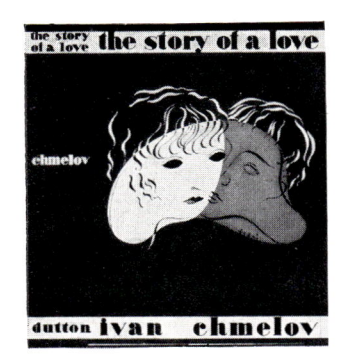

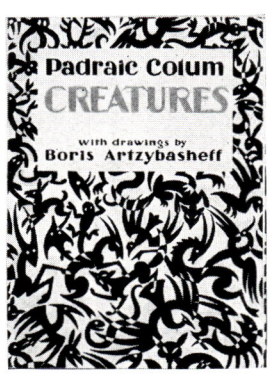

JACKET SOLUTIONS as interpreted by eight artists: Bobri's *The Story of a Love* shows an almost hieroglyphic representation—man, woman and heart. (E. P. Dutton & Co.) A more obvious abstraction is *Das Wunder der Liebe* by Dr. W. Dexel, Magdeburg. In *The Dead Parrot*, Drum mobilizes colors, and hair-raising symbols to provoke attention. (Doubleday Doran & Co.) Grant Wood's painting for *In Tragic Life* juxtaposes character studies to obtain a symbolic pattern. (Doubleday Doran & Co.) Artzybasheff's ornamental silhouette pattern emphasizes the title in a medallion. (Macmillan Co.) A storytelling jacket is Harry Cimini's woodcut design for *Junipero Serra*. (Doubleday Doran & Co.) The fairy-tale motif in *Millions of Cats*, a children's book, is treated sympathetically by Wanda Gag. (Coward-McCann, New York.) In the *Painted Veils* Politzer uses large units within a small area. (The Modern Library, N. Y.)

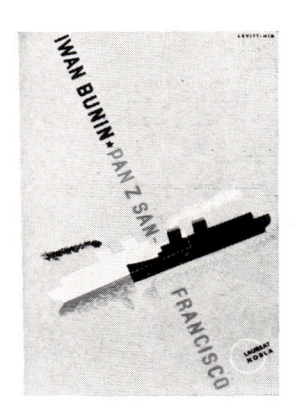

THREE BOOK-JACKET designs from the Levitt-Him studio, Warsaw. In *Garden Party* design and title are unified into an informal eye catcher. For *Opowiadania Dwuznaczne* (*Ambiguous Tales*) the artists fittingly use a black background pierced by a spotlighted patch of white, and in Bunin's *The Gentleman from San Francisco* they show passing ships against much space to suggest the atmosphere of the expansive sea. Collectively these examples show the variety of problems that the jacket designer may be called upon to solve.

SIDE: Samuel Bernard Schaeffer's book-jacket design for *Paul Gauguin* by Becquer hints at the Tahitian background of the painter in the primitive drawing of the decorative unit. Compared with some of the more ornate jackets on the facing page, the simplicity of this one strikes home. (*Courtesy of the artist.*)

spine of the wrappers. This is usually brief, so that it may appear in larger letters within the limitations set by the size of the book. The title gives some definite indication of the type of book, satisfying, in part, the interest inspired by the design. If the reader is urged to peruse the volume, the jacket has accomplished its primary end. Many jackets are so artistically conceived and so expertly executed that, besides protecting and helping to sell the book, they are collected and preserved with as much care as rare prints. Like the poster, book-

DESIGN 237

PAINTING SCULPTURE AND GRAPHIC ART IN THE USSR

238 === GRAPHIC

JACKET DESIGNS distinguished by ample use of white space. ABOVE, left: Design by Rockwell Kent for Zest, wherein title and drawing are held together by a simple border. (Doubleday Doran & Co., New York.) Right: The Modern Movement in Art was designed by E. McKnight-Kauffer to harmonize with the title. (F. A. Stokes Co., New York.) BELOW, left: Lynd Ward's jacket for his Wild Pilgrimage is a virile woodcut. (Harrison Smith & Robert Haas, New York.) Right: Alexandrovsky's cover for a Russian edition of Shaw's Adventures of the Black Girl in Her Search for God shows beautiful spotting of dark and light. (Kultsviaz-Voks, Moscow.) Compare with Farleigh's solution on page 186. FACING PAGE: The cover for Graphic Art in the USSR attains artistic appeal and legibility by using vertical separation instead of the more customary superimposition of lettering on picture.

DESIGN 239

jacket design originated in France and was produced by masters already known in the realm of the poster. Chéret, Steinlen, Daumier, and Gavarni contributed vivid realism in this field. Similarly, in England, Pryde and Nicholson (the Beggarstaff Brothers); and in America, Penfield excelled. Current book-jacket designs are made by many of the artists who have already been listed as illustrators. If, in this field, success has not been so consistent, it is because many who did not dare to essay a poster aspired to do a jacket.

Bookplates are labels pasted inside the covers of books and bearing a device indicating the owner. The label may be enriched with a decoration or illustration symbolic of the tastes or character of the owner, or it may consist of his initials alone. This is a far cry from the devices used before the invention of movable type. Then books were few, and they were inclosed in such individual bindings that ownership could not be questioned. After 1450, scribes ceased to be the sole manufacturers of books. Because they were produced in greater numbers, book covers became simpler in design and less distinguishable in character. The use of bookplates with armorial designs and devices, like a fox to mark Mr. Fox's property, was practical, for the association was within the understanding of even the illiterate. In its contemporary form, the bookplate is said to have originated in Germany. Woodcuts, engravings, and etchings were the common mediums for graphic reproduction. The results, which seem to us almost

BOOK PLATES in which the names or initials of the owners are judiciously incorporated in the design. From top to bottom they are: for the Heuvelpers, by S. H. de Roos, Hilversum; for Schroer and Lauer, respectively, the clever pen-work is by Otto Reichert, Berlin; for Bookplate Association International, the design by Otto Feil, Vienna, suggests in decorative form a collection of book plates. The dot on the "i," red in the original, contributed a note of variety.

exclusively coats of arms, were pasted on the inside front cover or first page of the book. This is the common procedure even now. However, since most people nowadays can read, lettering is often used without pictorial symbols. The processes of reproduction in our time include woodcuts, linoleum cuts, engravings, etchings, and offset. The motif has changed from a limited to a widely diversified one. Only one dictum remains, and that is that the subject and the technique employed be treated in a manner that will contribute to the beauty of the book. The typographic style, the line character of type, should be repeated in the bookplate, and the execution should be such that there is no question as to whether a woodcut or zinc plate is the means of reproduction. Despite the uniformity of purpose that inspires the makers of all bookplates, the results can be as different as the accompanying plates suggest. These will show that the rare efforts of comparatively unknown artists have, in many cases, excelled the average work of those

ABOVE: The design for Warnke by Johannes Boehland, Berlin, is based on a famous printing device that has been used many times, but rarely so well. BELOW: Stanislaw Ostoja-Chrostowski's *ex libris* has much thought matter and organization in its make-up. In its design it is as trim and its verticality is as uplifting as the music of an organ. (*Reproduced by courtesy of "Grafika Polska," Warsaw.*)

SIDNEY HUNT'S design for Bella Landauer gives a comprehensive picture of the owner's interests in a manner that is free from the shackles of traditionalism. (*Courtesy of the New York Historical Society.*) SIDE: The "Westfälischer Wandererdienst" signet by Mallek, Münster, is built around the motif that inspired the so-called first dated woodcut of 1421 (St. Christopher and the Christ Child, see page 74). The suggestion of water by three lines, the design of the hands, and the execution of the figures are in keeping with the lettering. FACING PAGE. ABOVE, left: In the book plate for "O. K. Bücherei," Alfred Winkler, Königsberg, utilizes the crosscut remains of the woodcut as part of the strikingly simple plate. In his design for Kleinfeld, exceptionally fine lettering and a symbol of the owner's vocation have been effectively dovetailed. Right: The linoleum cut for the books of a Boston seaman by Leon Friend, Brooklyn, employs a large unbroken area of black to suggest the depth of the sea. The off-center spacing of "Ex Libris" is an interesting variation from the usual. (*From the "Bookplate Annual for 1925" by Alfred Fowler, Kansas City.*) BELOW, right: John Platt's design for the libraries of the City of Leicester offers a new slant on a time-worn idea, the coat of arms. Its treatment is happily less involved and the spirit of the whole considerably less musty than that of the customary heraldic emblem. (*Leicester College of Arts and Crafts, Leicester.*)

whose names are famous for the number of their bookplates. For the amateur collector it ought to be much more fun to collect bookplates for their artistic merits than for the names of designers that they may bear.

It will be well to recapitulate and to remember that while illustrations, bindings, jackets, and book plates were discussed in this chapter, they are only part of the "makings" of a book. Considered together with these elements must be paper, type, layout, reproductive arts, and printing. Good some of these elements may be individually, yet it requires, in addition, their sound *interrelationship* if we are to create that setting to which fine

BOOK PLATES emphasizing black and designed to serve special purposes. Description in legend on facing page.

DESIGN 243

writing is justly entitled. For this reason let us pause long enough to consider these things together, since only by their synchronization do we attain to that architectural timelessness that is the beautiful book's rightful heritage. (See again text on printing and reproductive arts, chapters 2 and 3.)

PROBLEM:

To employ the information that the student has acquired by contact with the masterpieces in this field, the following problem is recommended. Take an extremely short story, one that can be lettered within the pages of a signature of, say, sixteen pages (octavo). Note again the booklets illustrated on page 231. Then follow these suggestions:

1. Provide for a frontispiece which is to be done with the same tool that is used for the text matter (see pages 6 and 17).

2. Design a simple layout that will tie text with illustration, making provision for an initial letter or two.

3. Score pages with a blunt instrument for lettering.

4. Use the first and last leaf as binders by pasting them into a simple casing. Place under weight for twenty-four hours to keep flat.

5. Design a label with appropriate title and author for the cover.

6. Compare the result with those of your colleagues, with those illustrated in this chapter, and with other books or booklets.

7. Discuss the results; be critical rather than charitable.

ALTERNATE PROBLEMS:

Page layouts; illustration; book jacket, bookplate, initial letter, chapter tailpiece; space filler.

DECORATIVE END PIECE, a picture of an early manuscript book by N. Lapshin for Ilin's Black on White: The Story of Books. (Courtesy of J. B. Lippincott Company, Philadelphia.)

ADVERTISING ART
CHAPTER 6

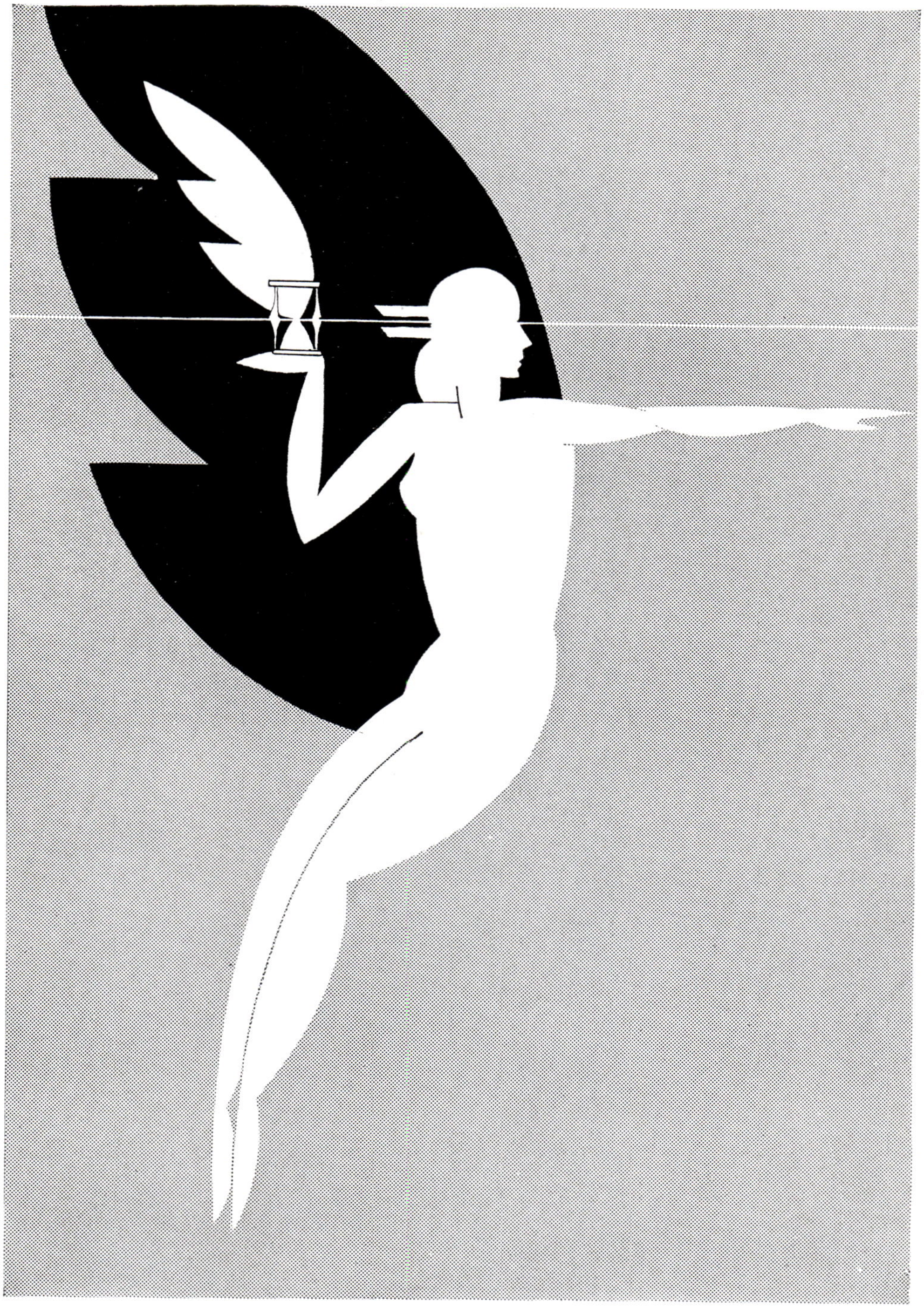

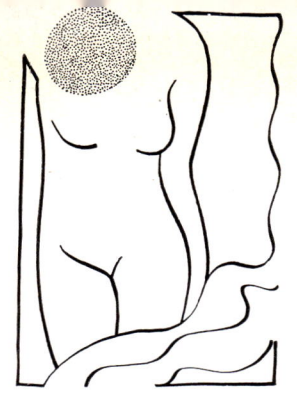

ADVERTISING ART

THE APPLICATIon of graphic design to merchandising has grown tremendously with the rapid development of industry through the last fifty years. Advertising art has become one of the important factors in current civilization. This growing importance of art in advertising increases the responsibility of the advertising artist. He no longer works for personal expression alone. He owes it to his public to make his work as fine and as purposeful as possible, using his opportunity to influence the taste of his vast audience.

Fundamentally, advertising design is a bid of the seller for the attention of the buyer. This is a point that the artist must constantly bear in mind. Since fitness to purpose is one of the primary requirements of all design, the artist's task becomes the reconciliation of the artistic with the practical elements of his problem, to the benefit, in the ideal case, of both.

The beginnings of advertising, if we may consider early attempts to direct public attention toward an object or a person as advertising, can be traced back to earliest recorded history. Symbols extolling the merits of Babylonian rulers have been found impressed in the brick walls of their temples. The famous Rosetta Stone is an advertisement or, more specifically, a publicity story for Ptolemy V Epiphanés, then ruler of all Egypt. The black and black and red wall posters of Pompeii (*graffiti*) and the trade signs of the third century B.C. were early forerunners of pictorial advertising. Even if we limit advertising to *a planned effort to evoke favorable consideration for the advertised purpose*, we can find at least one example in the fifteenth century. Caxton's handbill (1477) advertised his book, the *Salisbury Pye*. It was printed in the form of a small poster, with a footnote in Latin requesting the passer-by not to tear it down. In the sixteenth and seventeenth centuries, we find recruiting agencies, bookshops, patent-medicine vendors, showmen, lottery owners, and innkeepers using graphic art as a means for gaining mass favor. Probably the earliest known newspaper advertisement was a German book review of 1525. In the same year, Correggio painted an

CHAPTER DECORATION from the *Franklin Crier*, house organ of the Franklin Printing Company, Philadelphia. CHAPTER FRONTISPIECE: Classical simplicity of line and layout distinguish this decorative composition in three values by Elmer Tetzlaff, Milwaukee. Curved right line of the figure and jagged left are nicely contrasted.

THE ROSETTA STONE, discovered in Egypt in 1798, is an epochal document that enabled Jean François Champollion (1831) and Robert Young to find the key to the hieroglyphic alphabet. It is a personal advertisement "published" in 196 B.C. by the synod of Egyptian clergy in honor of Ptolemy V Epiphanés on a slab of basalt in hieroglyphic (ecclesiastic script), demotic (business script), and Greek characters. (*Photograph by Anderson, Rome.*)

FACING PAGE: Caxton's handbill, nearly actual size, the earliest British printed advertisement (1477), is a well-designed example of the *si qui* ("If anybody . . .") period of advertising. (*Courtesy of the Bodleian Collection, Oxford.*)

innkeeper's sign, "The Mule Drivers." Holbein painted tradesmen's plaques, and one of Hogarth's cartoons served as an inn signboard (1730). But it was not until the nineteenth century that P.T. Barnum, with his lurid circus bills and other theatrical announcements, demonstrated the commercial value of pictorial embellishment and high-pressure appeal to the emotions. Cruikshank made one of the earliest advertising drawings for an English periodical when he designed the cat-and-boot cartoon for Warren's boot blacking in 1800. Quite unexpectedly Sir John Millais found himself among the early commercial artists when his painting "Bubbles" was purchased for more than $10,000 by the manufacturers of Pears' Soap to advertise their product (1888). These classic examples, with the more recent ones, such as the "Prudential Has the Strength of Gibraltar," Victor's "His Master's Voice," and the "Gold Dust Twins," have for decades gathered good will for their fortunate owners.

Advertising art may be used to initiate, to increase, or to maintain the sales of a product. It may serve to keep an article or name before the public (reminder advertising), to introduce new uses for an old product, or to help to offset competition. But the commercial artist is not limited to the advertising of merchandise. He can help to mold public opinion in educational campaigns that aim to combat disease, show efficient working methods, illustrate social duties, and elucidate pertinent statistics. Advertising art has a definite place in contemporary life. It plays an important part in coloring our likes and dislikes.

The various fields of advertising design may be listed under two classifications: *general advertising*, aimed to appeal to the larger public, and *direct advertising*,

> If it plese ony man spirituel or temporel to bye ony pyes of two and thre comemoracios of salisburi vse enpryntid after the forme of this preset lettre whiche ben wel and truly correct, late hym come to westmonester in to the almonesrye at the reed pale and he shal haue them good chepe

> Suplico stet cedula

distributed to a selected public. General advertising art comprises newspaper and magazine announcements, outdoor and indoor posters, displays, packaging, industrial styling, and the designing of trade-marks, labels, stickers, etc. Direct advertising art includes catalogues and specimen books, booklets, folders, and broadsides, house organs, calendars, blotters, package inserts, and business stationery. In all these forms, success, from the graphicist's point of view, is based on good layout—the proportionate arrangement and relationship of the various parts: headline and text, main illustration, secondary illustrations, and logotype. It is for the layout man to make an advertisement harmonious and striking. An unbalanced, incongruous, or monotonous layout detracts from the advertising message. It is of importance that one element dominate the layout pattern, deliberately inducing the reader to see this item first and the subordinate items subsequently. A good layout will be simple in the contour of its type and illustrative masses. It will employ white space as an inherent part of the scheme, to contrast with the necessary details and to emphasize the importance of the message, thereby facilitating, too, the reading of the advertisement. More time, thought, and money are spent on the art work that goes into our

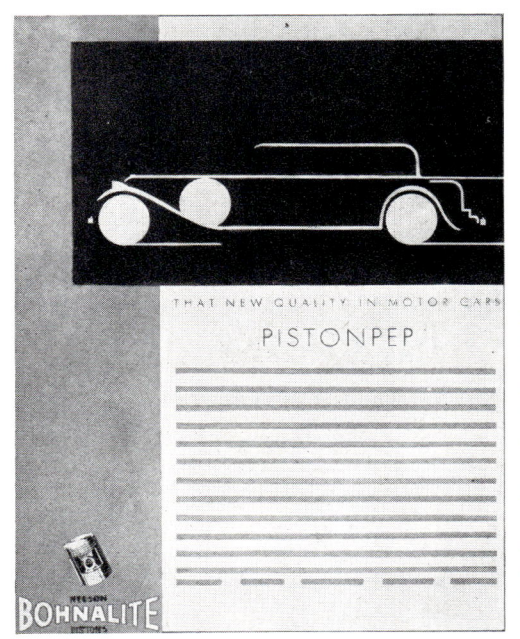

A FULL-PAGE magazine layout. The broad vertical panel supports the illustration and balances the forceful movement of the shorthand-like design of a car in an informal and dynamic manner. The flat treatment of the large areas emphasizes, by uninterrupted association, Bohnalite and its use. In this advertisement there are no irrelevancies. (*Bohn Aluminum and Brass Corporation, Detroit.*)

FACING PAGE: The whole advertisement is purposely tipped off the vertical to obtain a strong suggestion of movement—a happy divergence from the usual if used moderately. The subject of the illustration and the irregular lettering of the headline help to interpret the "Frenzy of Drunkenness." (*Levitt-Him Studio, Warsaw.*)

magazines and newspapers than on the art in all other mediums put together. The large output of such current advertisements compels the artist to be more ingenious than ever if his work is to get attention among the many produced. There is a wide variety of periodicals: morning, evening, and Sunday newspapers; small-town weeklies; mass and class magazines, urban and rural, women's and men's; occupational and club publications. Each has its own requirements and its own public, so that it becomes necessary for the artist to plan the advertisement for the specific needs of the particular periodical, to style it so that its selling points will appeal to the readers to whom it is addressed. The usual aim of an advertisement in a daily newspaper is the immediate consummation of a sale. Its effectiveness is frequently found in its news value. The results expected from magazine advertising are usually the establishment of a sympathetic state of mind and good will toward the object and its advertiser and the stimulation of interest. Such advertising relies on its surprise element or its fresh viewpoint to carry its sales message. To be effective, even a striking idea must be well drawn and well presented.

Direct-mail advertising offers the manufacturer and retailer a means of conveying a sales message to a selected consumer group comparable to that reached by the trade periodical. While the circulation of this advertising may be less than that reached by the popular magazine, the *directness* of its appeal is likely to elicit a larger percentage of response per contact. Only when judged entirely by the number of people reached is advertising in the newspapers or magazines unquestionably the cheapest form. Direct mail is so widely used that it has become necessary for the designer to plan the mailing pieces with a great deal of ingeniousness to arouse the active interest of the recipient.

Poster technique used on envelope or container sometimes accomplishes this. By its dramatic quality it encourages one to read the contents; thus the primary purpose of the mailing piece is fulfilled. On the other hand, direct mail often omits any design or name on the envelope to obtain for its contents the attention given to personal correspondence. In the direct-mail family, the booklet permits the widest range in layout, illustration, and ideas. An element of mystification in the conception and execution of the cover, playing upon our instinctive curiosity, may induce us to open the booklet to "see what's inside." It is advantageous for a booklet or other mailing piece to bear some resemblance to the general graphic make-up of the advertising campaign of which it is part. Its value as a recurrent stimulus thus becomes cumulative. Broadsides and folders have the same problems to solve as the booklet. Their smaller resources and more limited possibilities call for a condensed and simplified treatment of the message. For this reason they demand greater inventiveness in their designing.

The catalogue, as semipermanent reference material, must stand the test of frequent reading. Its purpose is to offer information in a readily available form and to elicit direct favorable interest. It must of necessity be invitingly brief; its items and their specifications must be arranged with clarity; its page layouts must be attractive; and its illustrations must be simple and pleasing. The catalogue challenges the skill and the creative power of the most able

GOOD DRAFTSMANSHIP and arrangement are combined to express smartness. It takes a genuine artist to make so commonplace an association so uncommonly attractive. (*Walter Cole for the American Optical Company, Southbridge.*) FACING PAGE: Panels built up architecturally. The conciseness of the whole emphasizes the beauty and the impressiveness of even small articles. (*René Clarke for Black, Starr and Frost-Gorham, Inc., of New York.*)

artist. Its longer life and its prolonged sales influence justify his best efforts.

The house organ or bulletin fills a place between direct-mail advertising and the general periodical. Its printed salesmanship is based on the assumption that advertising matter is seldom read for its own sake. The house publication, therefore, attempts to interest and entertain the reader, suggesting its sales message only indirectly. Professional or topical information, written interestingly, striking make-up, and clever ideas are employed in an effort to forestall possible lack of reader interest. The effectiveness of this medium depends upon the merit of its text and art and upon the cumulative impressions built up through repetition.

Letterheads, billheads, business cards, stickers, and illustrated letters are important in advertising. The distinguished letterhead imparts dignity and prestige to the advertiser. Distinctive layout, modest decorative effects, and compact, legible information as to name, address, and nature of business add to the value of the letterhead or business card. Good paper stock and printing contribute tone and effectiveness. Another medium in this category is the illustrated four-page letter. Its problems of layout and illustration are usually similar to that of the magazine. In designing a four-page letter, the right and more visible side is commonly used for that item—copy or illustration—that the advertiser desires to feature. Auxiliaries, such as secondary illustrations, testimonials, recipes, and the like, are usually placed on the left-hand page.

Printed slips, miniature folders, or booklets designed for insertion into letters or into packages of merchandise are called inserts and they are economical advertising accessories. They serve as reminders and builders of good will, frequently offering instruction in the proper use of the product. Or they may encourage new uses or cross-advertise allied products of the same manufacturer. A great advantage of an insert as a messenger is that it arrives at an opportune time, backed by the prospect's manifested interest in the merchandise or the letter. The letter with its insert may reach the executive who is "not in" to the salesman. The small size of such inserts calls for a rigidly disciplined layout. Text is usually condensed into slogan-like sentences; the illustrations are clear and bold. A common letter stuffer, the familiar blotter, is in this category.

It is generally conceded that the eye appeal of an attractive package increases the desirability of the merchandise that it contains. The designing or

A FULL-PAGE layout that features the selling points of economy and health in the headline. The arrangement of the components leads the eye from headline, through pictorial appeal, to the picture of the product and the sales copy. (*Brigdens, Ltd., Toronto.*) The amusing line inset stripped into the Orlak Glass page serves as a transitional note between halftone and type matter and adds human appeal to the still life. (*Prepared by Pritchard, Wood and Partners, Ltd., London, for Chance Brothers, Ltd.*) FACING PAGE: The relief figure by Lester Gaba built into a mass of poster-like simplicity enhances an unusual layout for an article of distinction. (*Lesquendieu, Inc., New York.*) A beautiful face finely photographed. Cropping the head is a dangerous device, but is here successfully used to give more emphasis to the face. The clever introduction of white stars saves many words of explanation and the time of the reader. (*Bristol-Myers Company, New York.*) By purposely portraying the sophisticated rather than the pretty type, Darcy's drawing attains a wider appeal. Almost all of us can attempt sophistication; not so with prettiness. The artist wisely places the more or less vertical side of the figure nearer the vertical of the rectangle. (*Guerlain, Inc., of New York.*)

redesigning of a package, wrapper, or container calls for knowledge of the principles of good design; the limitations of economical production; the suitability of size, shape, and nature of the material of the container to the structural qualities of the object; and fitness to its primary purpose of holding and protecting the merchandise. The problem is twofold: to design the structure of the container and to design its surface decoration. The first requires that it be physically adequate as well as attractive; the second, that the decoration be in harmony with the size and form of the container. As far as practicable, the make-up of the container ought to suggest its contents and have sufficient display appeal to invite attention in competitive surroundings (see page 288).

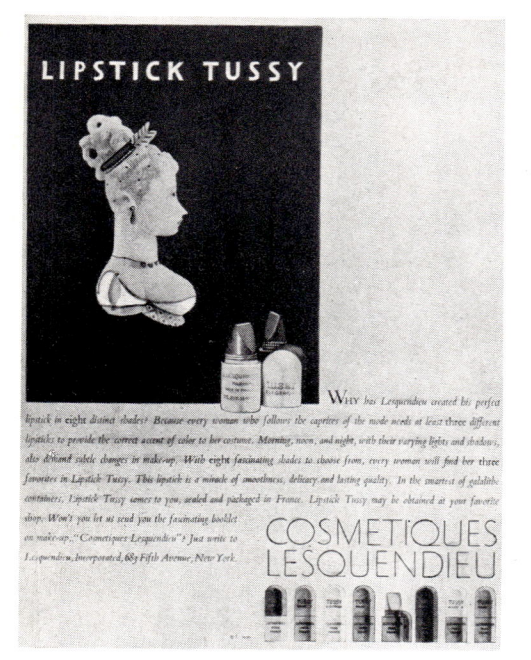

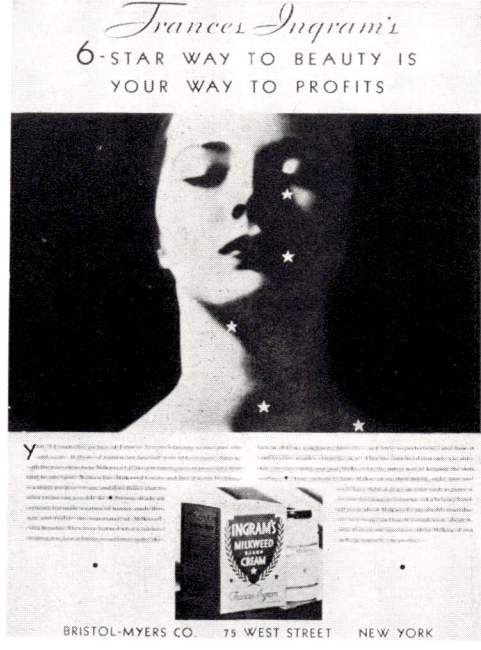

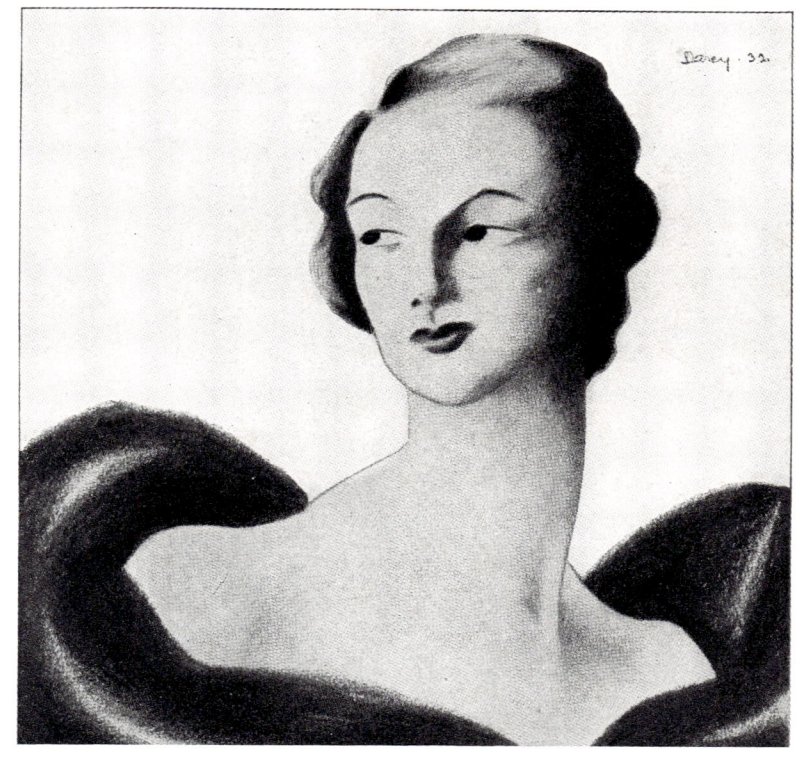

Three advertisements, keyed to feminine appeal, using a sculpture, a photograph, and a freehand sketch in order to attract attention. Description on p. 254.

DESIGN 255

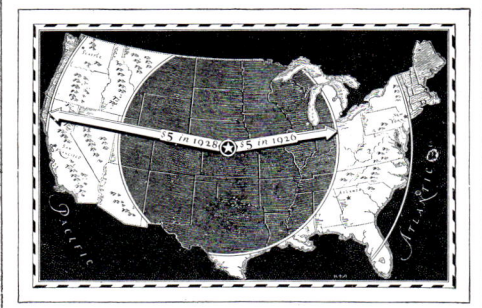

SYMMETRIC LAYOUTS: Strict balance in design adds stability and dignity both to the page advertisement by Rosa Brothers for the American Telephone and Telegraph Company, New York, and to the double-page spread (facing page, top) designed by Lucian Bernhard for the Fleetwood Body Corporation, New York. This device is frequently used to convey something of the dignity and the soundness of long established commercial institutions.

FACING PAGE. Below: Asymmetric layout of pages. Here, equally good and possibly more attention-getting balance is obtained by juxtaposing black, gray, and white areas rather than repeating the same pattern on both sides of an axis, achieving thereby optical instead of symmetric balance. (*Folder by Franklin Printing Company, Philadelphia.*)

Surface decoration cannot excuse the poor construction of a container. The package is intended primarily to hold and to protect merchandise. It should be convenient for the manufacturer to produce and distribute, for the dealer to handle and display, and for the consumer to carry and use. Mere novelties and trick experiments are apt to produce bizarre and gaudy effects that are meaningless and restless instead of structurally sound and inviting. Some containers are designed to augment their advertising value by their usefulness even after the removal of the original contents. To attain this purpose, the designer identifies such containers by shape and color rather than by labels or stickers. Where the appearance of the product itself is attractive enough to stimulate demand, the package can be limited to a protective function. The product can then be made visible either through a die-cut window or by wrapping it entirely in transparent material. Restyling does not stop with the covering. The merchandise itself is often molded into simpler and more decorative but less decorated forms. It is a concession to the public's appreciation of change and novelty. A rejuvenated design enables its producer to capitalize the news value of the change. It encourages the advertising layout man and artist to renewed efforts and the dealer to give it preference in display. This face-lifting results, naturally, in a newly stimulated consumer interest and in additional prestige.

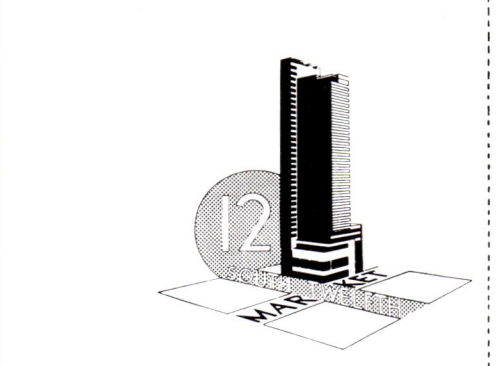

Trade-marks and trade names have a value long recognized. Large sums of money are spent to popularize the symbolic design or name under which a certain brand of merchandise is marketed. Ben Day, Kodak, Simoniz and Flit are

ENRICHMENT IS obtained in this elaborately drawn pen-and-ink design by the strong black areas and the varied patterns. (From a series by T. M. Cleland for International Printing Ink Corporation, New York.)

FACING PAGE: Individual styles of figure rendering. The delicate lines and facile pose of the drawing by Sigrid Grafström for Coty express as much elegance in their way as the sketchy ruggedness of E. Dryden's design for Kayser hosiery does with still another quality of line. (P. K. Frowert Company, New York, and Crawford Advertising Agency, London, respectively.)

as familiar in our everyday vocabularies as are the titles of periodicals. These symbols of acquired good will represent valuable assets to the manufacturer and distributor; for that reason they justify a hesitancy to replace new forms for old. However, the proprietor should weigh his values clearly. If the trade-mark is outdated, he may gain new impetus in sales by redesigning for contemporary appeal. Good trade-marks are brief, clear, easy to reproduce, and easy to remember. These qualities should be the criteria, and, if the trade-mark does not meet them, it should be replaced even at a loss of some familiarity.

Humor is an old and valuable aid in advertising illustration. It calls for more tact and good taste than the designing of a serious advertisement. Even ribald or slightly bizarre humor becomes acceptable when it is employed to advertise an appropriate product. If not used with restraint, the humorous element may easily become offensive, at least to part of the audience. A whimsical witticism, a broad, jolly form of slapstick, and self-ridicule are still the safest ways of offering amusement. It will be found, too, that the advertisements of manufacturers and wholesalers employ humor with restraint, because what may be humor to one section of the country, may be anathema to another, whereas the retailer, in closer touch with the man in his smaller community, is more likely to use an all-humorous presentation.

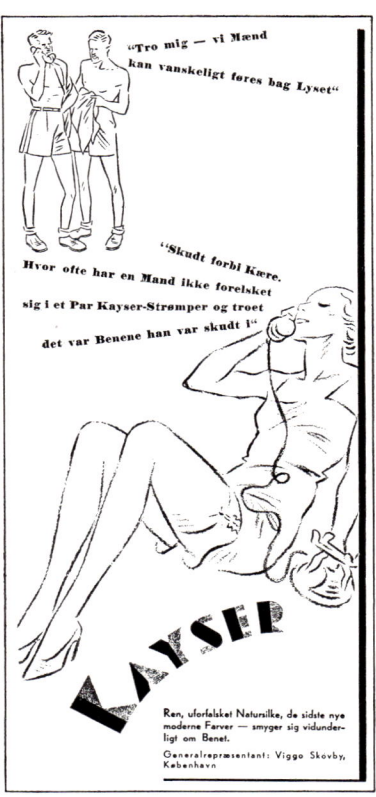

The poster and its art represent characteristics sufficiently distinctive to form an individual class of advertising. Therefore, a separate chapter has been devoted to the subject. Small indoor posters, minor posters (the standard size of a one-sheet poster is 28 by 42 inches), window and car cards, signs and plaques, displays and calendars, too, are its derivatives. Besides being attractive, these must be legible at a reasonable distance to fulfill their advertising mission. However, in poster art as in all art, quality is more effective than size.

Great art, an observant aesthete once wrote, is that work of talented man which evokes a peculiar emotion in the observer. It is the opinion of

FOLDERS. Kind of Folder and Style of Fold: 1. Four page, one fold upright. 2. Four page, one fold square. 3. Six page with flap, three parallel folds. 4. Six page, two parallel folds. 5. Six page, two accordion folds. 6. Eight page, two parallel folds. 7. Eight page, three parallel folds. 8. Eight page, three accordion folds. 9. Eight page, short fold, two folds right angle. 10. Eight page with flap, two parallel and one right-angle folds. 11. Twelve page, three parallel folds. 12. Sixteen page, three parallel folds. 13. Saddle-stitch pamphlet, six-page cover. 14. Side-stitched book with scored cover. (*Courtesy Champion Coated Paper Company of Hamilton, Ohio.*)

the authors that the work of Marie Laurencin, Kees Van Dongen, Rockwell Kent, Eric Gill, Buk Ulreich, and a host of others, when sincerely inspired, is not and need not be less fine because the *raison d'être* for their expression has been, say, an industrial organization rather than a picture dealer. The vendor of pictures who has often dictated the subject and the design of his artists' works with an eye on his public, has been known to be both as disinterested and as covetous as other businessmen.

The title "Advertising Art" has been used in this book to distinguish this special form of graphic expression from the many other kinds of art. Nothing that has been said, however, should be taken to mean that the authors would distinguish this from so-called "fine" art. On the contrary, more and more are alert critics leaning to the opinion that only the art that is "fine" will eventually do duty in behalf of advertising. This, in general, is the belief of the authors and the fact that it is not now true in most cases does not discredit the idea. The condition is due rather to the limited availability or supply of truly versatile artists who can rise to a gamut of occasions and who can work inspiredly within the limitations set by someone other than themselves. The art is not necessarily fine because its author waited patiently for Dame Inspiration. On the other hand, if we may use an extreme example, Michelangelo succeeded, in the case of the Vatican murals, in creating a moving piece of art *to order*, "advertising art" if we please, despite his personal preferences in the matter. What is more, he was able to excel in painting, a form of expression that he considered greatly

DECORATIVE SPOTS, originally used with a body of text. Such units are employed to give freedom to the formality of type matter, as marginal drawings, or in place of ornamental initials. Good drawing is essential in view of the conspicuous position of the spot and the importance of its mission within the limited space. (1. The Bauer Type Foundry, Inc., New York; 2 and 3 by Vladimir Bobritski for the Cunard Line; and 4 by the same artist for Nolde & Horst Sales Company, all of New York.)

inferior to sculpture, the vehicle he preferred. So it is not really the *purpose* that motivates art, nor the *subject* that graces a canvas, nor the absence or presence of anything except the mark of the artist's individuality—spirit, we may call it—that distinguishes fine art from any other kind of art. And advertising art has frequently reached both the pinnacles of the one and the substrata of the other. Again, it is the degree of inspiration and the innate ability of the man behind the brush and the final excellence of the result that must remain the criteria of graphic expression.

It may not be too much to hope that, just as great music has been composed to mark a king's coronation and beautiful architecture raised to honor a nobleman's loved one, so graphic rendition may yet achieve the permanent qualities of truly significant art, even though it be prompted by genre or service promotion. Industry may yet evoke the emotions to that great artistic attainment that militant religion once inspired.

Hackneyed art is not necessarily good advertising because it "sells the goods." Here, we are presupposing things that have not been tested. Has good advertising art been tried at all? This may also be due to the unfortunate fact that the noncritical mass is still larger than the discriminating one, at best a temporary condition. And, finally, the type of articles sold could possibly never have appealed to a group of people of any judgment whatsoever. The future . . . ? Who can tell?

HERE, ROCKWELL KENT'S pen-and-ink lines show the influence of the woodcut technique more usually associated with this artist. They are as precise in their disposition and leave as little to chance as do the lines he gets by use of knife and wood. (*Courtesy A. G. Spalding and Brothers, New York.*)

BELOW: The classic beauty of Harshberger's figure drawing appears novel and impressive. The whole is beautifully related to the rectangle of which it is a part. Kent uses the light and shade that is suggested by nature, Harshberger the white and black (notan) of the artist's palette. (*Hazard Advertising Corporation, New York, for Propper-McCallum Hosiery.*)

FACING PAGE. Above: The crisp contour lines of John Held, Jr.'s famous character Margy speak of the deftness with which this exponent of graphic humor masters the figure. The only solid black spot in the drawing, the advertised ink bottle, attracts our attention by contrast, despite its smallness. (*Courtesy C. M. Higgins & Co., Inc., Brooklyn.*) Below: The free flow and the flexibility of the brush strokes in the figure sketch by Roger de Valerio invite notice of the comfort of the illustrated garment and the softness of its material. (*Courtesy Dévambez, Paris.*)

DESIGN 263

THE FORMAL TRAINING of the artist is evidenced in the structural arrangement of this decorative still life. The only thing commercial about this is the use to which it was put—menu cover. (*Professor Erberto Carboni, Parma.*)

264 GRAPHIC

THREE DIFFERENT layouts designed to appeal to women and characterized by charm, atmosphere, and movement. Notable are the simplicity and directness of the coat drawing by Walter Holz, Berlin; the suggestion of class in the hosiery announcement drawn in wash, pen and ink, litho pencil, and pastel on scrap board by a recent graduate of Pratt Institute, Joseph DiGemma, for Van Raalte; and the strong design and the humor apparent in the make-up of the magazine advertisement for Saks-Fifth Avenue, New York.

DESIGN 265

For description of these drawings by Carolyn Edmundson, Prof. Arpke, and Moe Gross see legend on facing page.

SIX ADVERTISEMENTS serving a related purpose but differing completely in mode of rendition. ABOVE: The importance of woman and her *outlook* is made striking by the contrast of the living figure against the calm of an uninterrupted sky. (*Edwin A. Georgi for McCall's magazine through Calkins & Holden, New York.*) An airy wash by Trias Studio appropriately imparts something of the lightness of femininity and the waft of fine perfume to the cover for Lohse cosmetics printed by Erasmusdruck, Berlin; the five tonal values are effectively juxtaposed.

BELOW: The delicately rendered water-color group by Reuters for Henkell wines associates the name of an established product with the elegance of society on the assumption that, if it is good for the exclusive DeRiches, it is good enough for the more average Smiths. (*Courtesy of Meissenbach, Riffarth & Company, Berlin.*)

FACING PAGE. Above: Rich coloring, fine design, and a textural quality that suggests the richness of a heavy towel are employed in the composition by Carolyn Edmundson for Cannon Towels, New York. Below: Prof. Arpke's imaginative cover design for the almanac of an artists' ball, printed by Otto Elsner, Berlin, is whimsically treated for a gay affair. Fine line quality, draftsmanship, and economy of rendering of a high order mark the spontaneous drawing by Moe Gross, an eighteen-year-old student. What he has left out is as important as what he drew.

DESIGN ═══════════════ 267

THE SWEEP of the line from the girl's head to her hat is nicely repeated by the similar movement in the parasol. The uninterrupted area of the background is the best possible suggestion of the expansiveness of a beach. (*Wash by John LaGatta for Laros Textiles Co., through Fox and Mackenzie, Philadelphia.*)

FACING PAGE: Textile swatches, paste-pot work, and drawing were collectively photographed to create this witty and appealing play on our ego. (*Designed by Jane Miller for B. Altman & Co., New York.*) The amusing quality inherent in the drawing by Melisse for Lord and Taylor, New York, plays no little part in the popularity of this artist's tasteful fashion drawings. Her free treatment of the presentation is consistent with the informality of the daily shopping tour and the breeziness of the younger generation of consumers.

it's a matter of pride

Lord & Taylor
FASHION RELEASE #11

Melisse

- The high muffler neckline... draped in that flung back line.
- Rabbits' hair shot through with gold threads... punctuated with gold cuffs and half belt.
- Bias skirt... slim and tight... with a fine free swing below the knee.

29.75

All in all a pretty important tea time dress for that pretty important person... the young new yorker. Not too ingenue looking and in black only, sizes 11 to 17. And if your dearest enemy sees it first... there are lots of others just as much your type from 12.95 to 49.75

THE YOUNG NEW YORKER SHOP—FIFTH FLOOR

DESIGN 269

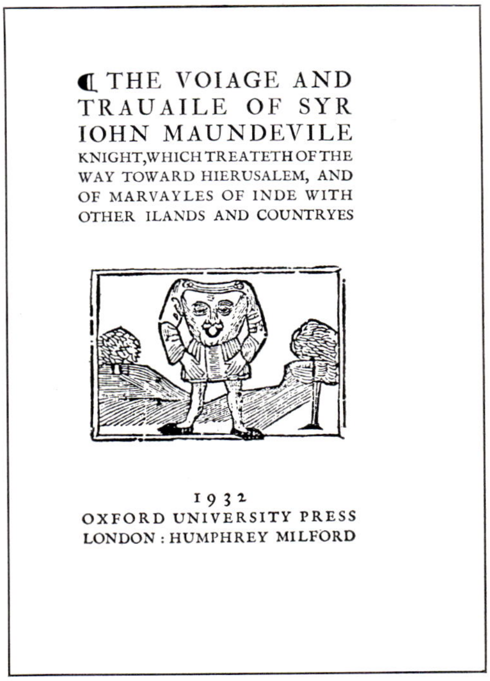
THE VOIAGE AND TRAUAILE OF SYR IOHN MAUNDEVILE KNIGHT, WHICH TREATETH OF THE WAY TOWARD HIERUSALEM, AND OF MARVAYLES OF INDE WITH OTHER ILANDS AND COUNTRYES

1932
OXFORD UNIVERSITY PRESS
LONDON : HUMPHREY MILFORD

CATALOGUE DESIGNED by Trias Studio for Lohse cosmetics. The exceptional clarity of the facing pages strengthened by unassuming pictorialization discourage mere scanning. For cover of this catalogue see page 267. (*Printed by Erasmusdruck, Berlin.*) BELOW: McKnight-Kauffer's advertisement for Aero Shell is unique in layout and in its use of a canvas-like screen. (*Shell Mex and B. P. Ltd., London.*) FACING PAGE. Above: The menu by Grete Aly appears as much a treat for the eye as for the palate. (*Heintze & Blanckertz, Berlin.*) The flavor of sixteenth century typography and illustration is fittingly retained in the unusual announcement for a modern edition of a 1568 travel narrative. (*Oxford University Press, New York.*) Below: Two advertisements in which text and drawings are integral parts of a unified whole, not afterthoughts. In layout they avoid the stereotyped. The piano advertisement is slanted just enough to attract attention but not so much that it interferes with easy reading. Black spot, dynamic tilt, and generous white space give variety. (*Bauer Type Foundry, Inc., New York.*) Rhythmic motion in the horsemen of Ashley Havinden for J. C. Eno, Ltd., London, brings action into the design making the reading of the solid mass of copy comparatively exciting and certainly more easy.

DESIGN 271

IN SIMPLICITY of lettering and symbol, Warren Chapell's composition for *Advertising Arts*, New York, is strong indeed. Coupling the dark note against light with light lettering against dark in one design gains maximum attention value, although breaking the whole into two equal parts is dangerous in that it causes the unit to appear as two different and equally interesting items. Noteworthy are the character and fine proportion of the lettering.

ABOVE: Lifelike photography in the *Corn* booklet for the Caterpillar Tractor Company, Peoria, and inventive photomontage by Walter Breker, Magdeburg, for Wohlfeld Printers are both effective solutions of the respective problems.

SIDE: An ordinary architectural landscape is given extraordinary interest by an exaggerated perspective. (Cover designed by Ribes for the Chemins de Fer d'État, Paris.)

DESIGN 273

GORGEOUSLY CONCEIVED booklets that are made to appeal to a discriminating industrial clientele.

ABOVE: Printed in silver on dark blue, the ingenious lettering of the open French folder suggests the flexibility of the advertised sheet zinc (R. de Valerio for the Compagnie Royale Asturienne des Mines. Printed and embossed by Dévambez, of Paris.)

BELOW. The abstract character of the design conforms to the intangible nature of the service advertised. (H. Harringer for the United States Gypsum Company, Chicago.)

FACING PAGE: Two simple linear forms leading to the message and contrast, in the original, of red, black, and white are employed with striking effect. (Printed by Leon Ullman, Arts et Métiers Graphiques, Paris.)

For description of this colorful and terse booklet cover printed by Leon Ullman, see the legend on facing page.

DESIGN 275

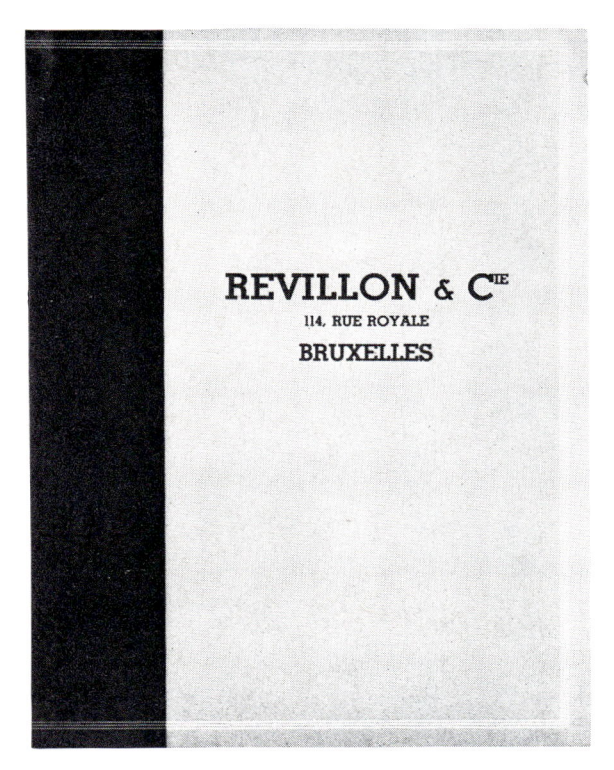

ABOVE: A DIAGONAL MASS, relying on the attractiveness of irregularity, is used to accentuate the design in Ernst Leuschner's cover for a department-store guidebook in Basle. "CRUISE." Freely brushed letters repeating the spontaneity of the sketched drawing help to convey the relaxation and calm atmosphere of the Orient. (*Booklet cover by Howard Trafton for the North German Lloyd, New York.*)

BELOW: Absence of pictorial decoration does not detract from the impressiveness of the catalogue cover printed by Draeger Frères, Paris, for Revillon & Company. The combination of pure type and flat panels carries in itself that suggestion of restraint and dignity that we usually associate with good taste.

ABOVE: The hand motif is successfully incorporated in the cover design by Roger Thivillier printed on highly varnished paper by C. Jacoub & Company, Paris, and in the abstract composition by L'Ibis for *Divertissements Typographiques*, house publication of Deberny et Peignot, printers and type-founders, Paris.

BELOW: The cover design by Patterson and Sullivan for Dollar Steamship Lines offers an interesting contrast with the Mediterranean cruise folder on the facing page. Here the artists have united into a coherent pattern all that one seeks to know in preparation for travel, except perhaps the unappealing element of cost. (Prepared by Lord and Thomas of San Francisco.)

DESIGN 277

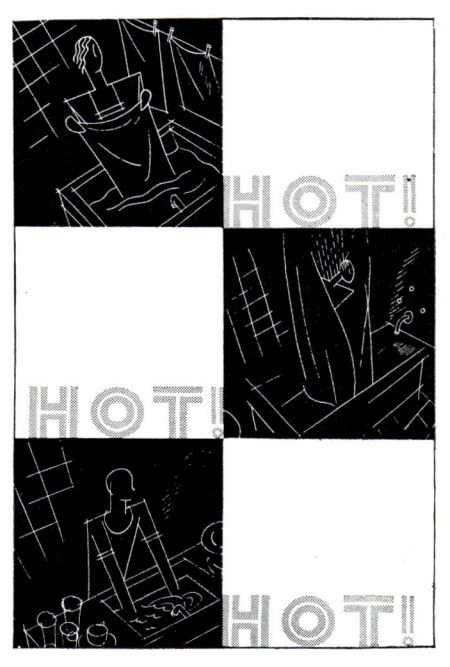

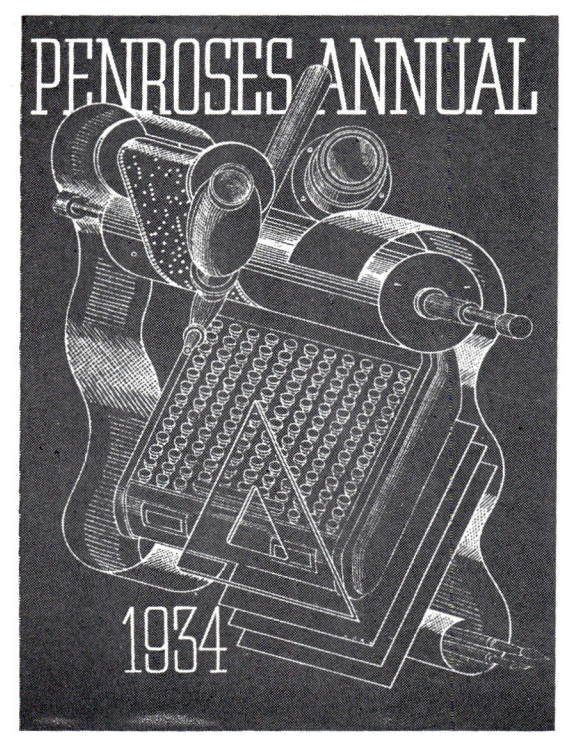

Descriptions of these covers on facing page.

278 ═══════════════════════════════ GRAPHIC

ABOVE: The display card by Erich Schlicht, student of the State Art School, Berlin, is severely architectonic; it has strength, clarity, and legibility. (*Courtesy Heintze & Blanckertz, Berlin.*) R. de Lavererie's placard for Kayser hosiery is smart, whimsical, and economical in its Parisian approach to the problem and in the subtle lines of its drawing. (*Crawford Advertising Agency, London.*)

BELOW: Brief message, small house, and symbols of stormy winds are interwoven on the mailer sent out by the Camden Fire Insurance Association, Camden. The blackness of the background and the weird coils of the storm sound an ominous warning.

FACING PAGE. Above: Booklet covers that employ the dramatic quality of black effectively. The cover for Miss Nahon's School was designed and cut in linoleum by Leon Friend and printed by Marchbanks Press. The mailers "Hot! Hot! Hot!" and "Brass Tacks" were created by Adcraft, New York, for Kings County Lighting Company, Brooklyn. Below: The black and silver cover for *Penrose's Annual* designed by Horn loses something of its striking quality in reproduction. The neatness of its lines was an aid in the mechanical requirements of printing with metallic ink. (*Percy Lund Humphries, Ltd., London.*)

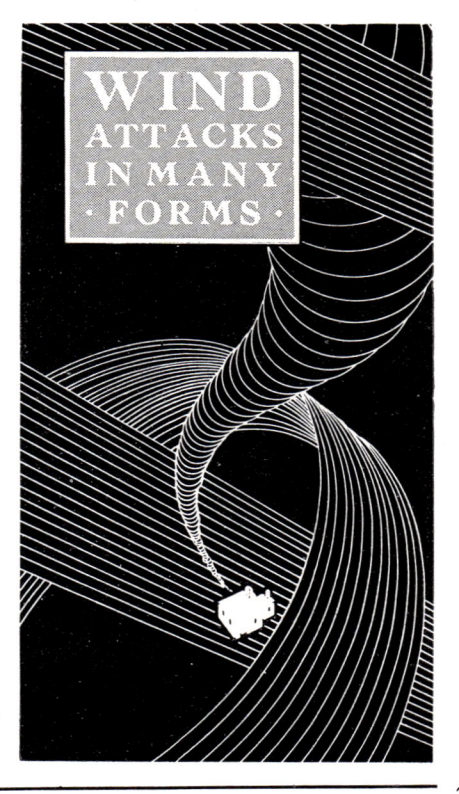

LITHOGRAPHISCHE KUNSTANSTALT
SENEFELDER
LUDWIG RÖTZER & C° GRAZ-STEIERMARK

1932

THE ADDITION of type matter and the purpose they set out to serve often alone distinguish commercial from the fine arts. Only one thing is certain, commercial art must be "fine" enough to sell goods.

280   GRAPHIC

FOUR PAINTINGS in the service of commerce whose basic light and dark (notan) patterns are such that they remain constructionally sound and aesthetically moving even in the reduced black and white reproduction.

THE ROMANTIC THEME of the painting by Edward Buk Ulreich is more artistic than commercial, as is fitting for the service it advertises—music. As prosaic an item as lettering has been beautifully interwoven with the color study. It has not been added on by a "crackerjack" letterer, as distinguished from an artist. Too often it is. (*By Courtesy of the RCA Victor Company of Camden, N. J.*)

FACING PAGE. Above: An expressionistic rendition saturated with color and life decorates the calendar panel designed by Cosimini for Tileston & Hollingsworth Company, Boston. Its appeal is bound to outlast the limit set by the duration of a twelvemonth. Originally intensely but harmoniously colored, the black and white basis of the design is equally sparkling. The dark accenting outlines to the figure and animal forms lend vigor and a sense of rotundity to the dominant parts of the design. Below: A cheerful flowery landscape is the device used to serve a similar end by Hans Wagula for Ludwig Rötzer's Senefelder Company, Graz. "Dog Taking Gun," as intensely colorful as a primitive, is a character study of the Blackfeet Indians by Winold Reiss, New York. The color has been so handled that no line of the characterful drawing has been impaired. It is one of a splendid series of decorative pieces distributed by the Great Northern Railway, St. Paul as a successful aid in attracting tourists. In treatment, it is the antithesis of the rendering by Cosimini.

ANOTHER EXAMPLE of truly fine art serving commerce is the above lithograph by Fred Ludekens drawn to encourage travel by presenting its more romantic aspect—historic associations. The organization of the figures and the arrangement of the vertical lines of the spears are reminiscent of the painting by Velasquez, "Surrender of Breda." The figures have the plastic unity of a sculptured group. They arouse that interest that is a prerequisite to reading and reacting to advertising copy. (*Prepared by Lord & Thomas of San Francisco.*)

FACING PAGE. Above: The New Year's greeting card by W. Dexel, Magdeburg, helped to keep the artist's name and style before the eyes of his clients. Center: One of a series of envelope stuffers decorated with spontaneous pen sketches and mailed by the Bauer Type Foundry, Inc., New York. The thick and thin masses of the black repeat the like quality of the type. Negatively, one can see the need for the dark spot by imagining its absence. Below: Well-designed trade-marks: from left to right, Professor A. Rabenbauer, Munich; Stempel Type Foundry, Frankfort; United Toilet Goods Company, New York; Binder-Germany, Mannheim, for I. G. Wine Cellars, Ludwigshafen; Rudolf Mosse signet by Andreas Niessen, Berlin; Cologne Fair, from Professor Ehmcke's *Das Zelt*. These are advertising pieces whose consistent repetition in association with fine goods or distinctive services has made them synonymous with these things. They beget added confidence for every article that bears their imprint and help to single it out among the many.

BESTE WÜNSCHE ZUM NEUEN JAHRE
W. DEXEL

BAUER BODONI

A living and lovely interpretation of the classic idea, making an immediate appeal to contemporary intelligence and taste.

For description of these interesting black and white or two color mailers and trade-marks see legend on facing page.

DESIGN ══════════════════ 283

TWO WINE labels designed to look like steel engravings. Printed in black and silver, with their trade-mark in color, they help to relate the brands of Kleinoscheg wines in an easily recognizable family. (Rötzer's Senefelder Company, Graz.)

284 GRAPHIC

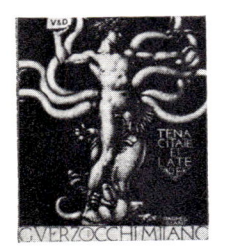

ABOVE: Two heraldic devices that were designed to serve commerce by C. Parmeggiani. Originally, they were part of an expensively printed catalogue distributed by G. Verzocchi, Milan, manufacturer of "V & D" firebricks. RIGHT SIDE: Brilliantly colored embossed cigar-box labels designed by Bittrof and printed by H. & A. Brünig, Hanau. Contrast the composition and draftsmanship of these labels with the gingerbread variety with which most of us are familiar. The effort that entered into their making was not limited by the size of the labels.

DESIGN 285

ABOVE: Theory and practice. The divergence of viewpoints in the conception of the artist and the practice of the industrialist is evident in a comparison of the imaginary "Tobakets" cigarette package designed by George Switzer, New York, with the package of one of the popular brands in actual use. (P. Lorillard Company, Inc., Philadelphia.)

CENTER: Three tobacco and cigarette packs designed by Prof. Ludwig Enders, Offenbach.

BELOW: Tobacco container and packages designed and made by Prof. Ludwig Enders' students at the School of Arts and Crafts in Offenbach. It is interesting to see the results of sincere artistic guidance by a true craftsman and to contemplate its influence on the progress of graphic design.

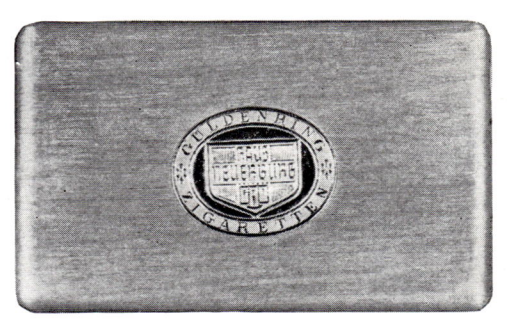

THE FOUR cigarette boxes on top belong to a series designed by Prof. O. W. Hadank for Haus Neuerburg, Cologne. They are gems of taste and simplicity in layout and in actual execution. Equally well conceived and made are the "Liga," "Black-White," and "Club" cigarette boxes of the Greiling Company, Dresden.

BELOW: An American package of the new school designed by Alice McL. Jones for Fairfax Tobacco Company, New York, shows clear planning in layout and a central decorative structure. In fairness to the American cigarette containers it can be said that their contents, at least, are equal to the popular European varieties.

DESIGN 287

288 GRAPHIC

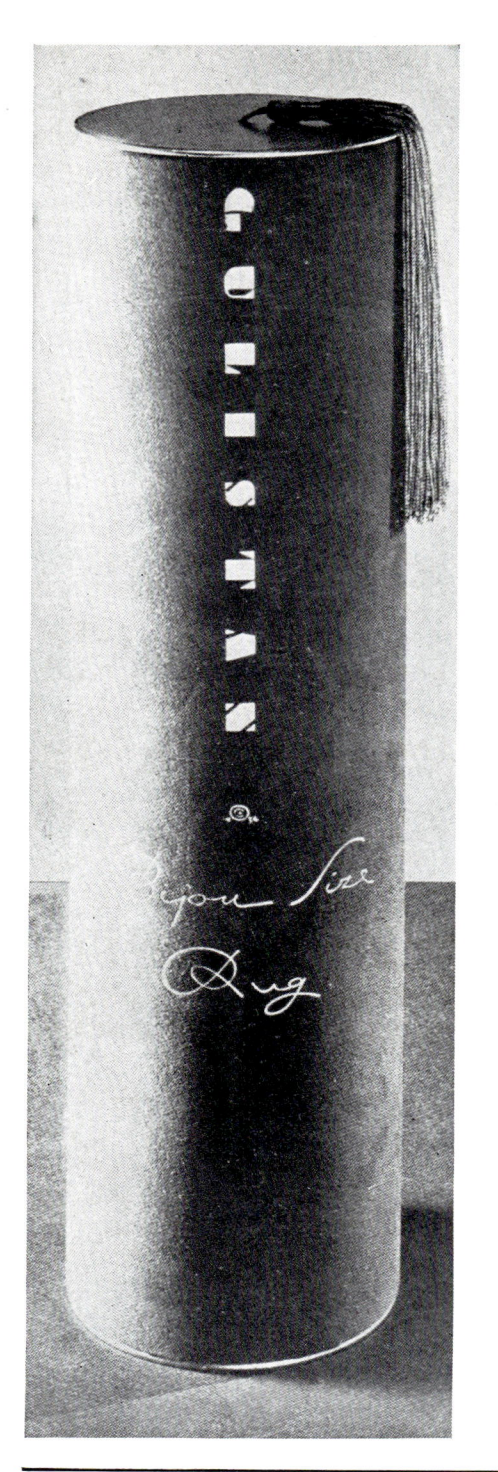

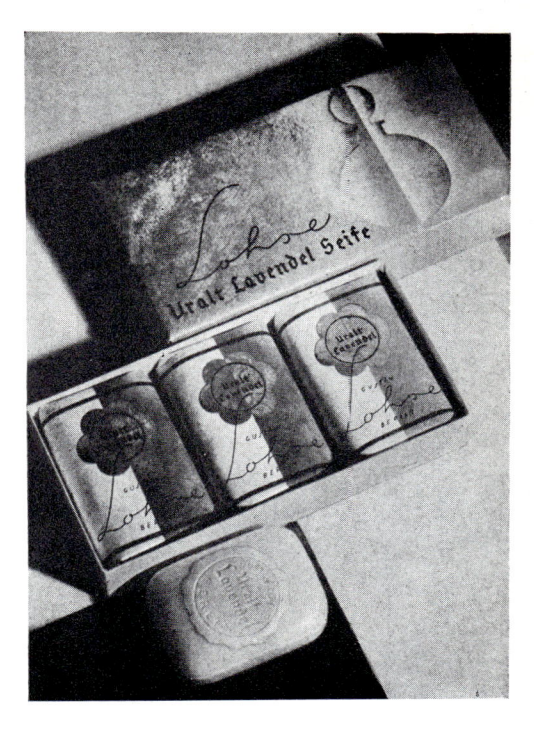

ABOVE: Bottle designs that conform to the rules of sound merchandising as well as to the nature of their material contents. (*Designed by Prof. Ludwig Enders of the School of Arts and Crafts, Offenbach.*)

SIDE: A ticket scale built on skyscraper lines and decorated with architectural restraint and an irresistible "Step on it." (*The New York International Ticket Scale Corporation's Model "S," designed by Joseph Sinel.*)

FACING PAGE: Cylindrical rug container that gives to packaging a distinction extremely rare in commerce. Gold lettering and script against the deep brown suggestion of a fez, properly tasseled for handling, suggest the richness and source of the merchandise it was made to contain. (*Designed by Gustav B. Jensen, New York, for A. & M. Karagheusian, Inc.*) Soap packaging that expresses good taste and refinement is prominently featured in the two advertisements designed by W. Metzig, Hannover, and printed by Erasmusdruck, Berlin, for Gustav Lohse cosmetics.

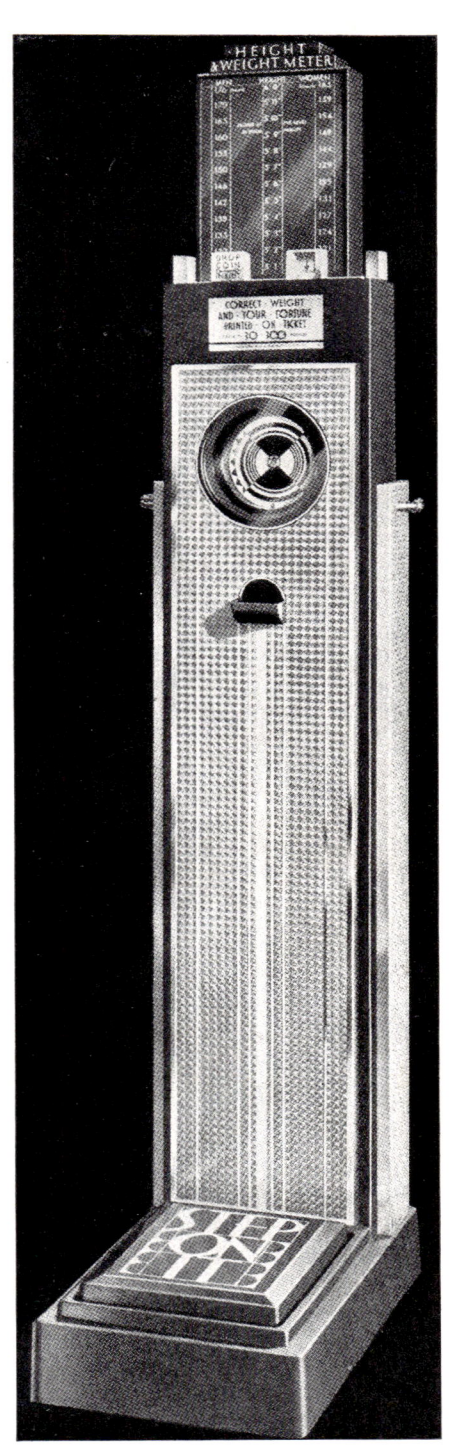

DESIGN 289

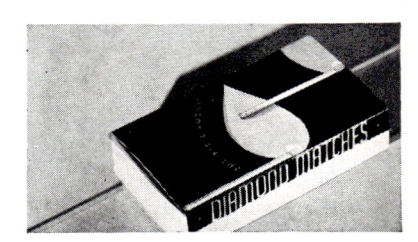

AN EXPOSITION BOOTH designed by Gustav B. Jensen, New York, in behalf of display advertising for Norge Refrigerators and showing the same consideration for purposefulness as used in packaging. The frieze of lettering is used at once to explain and to decorate and the whole is tied together by the radial lines on the floor of the central star unit.

CENTER: The label of a soup can, as redesigned in keeping with the modern trend in packaging, by Joseph Sinel. (*Reproduced by courtesy of Van Camp's, Inc., Indianapolis.*)

THREE BOXES for matches, food, and cosmetics designed with understanding and skill by George Switzer, New York. In the matchbox and the cereal container, the designs are both ornamental and significant of their contents. (*Photographs by Adams Studio, New York.*)

290 GRAPHIC

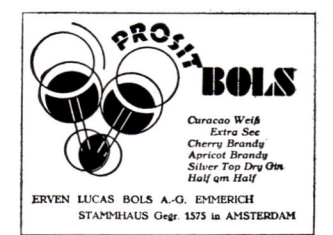

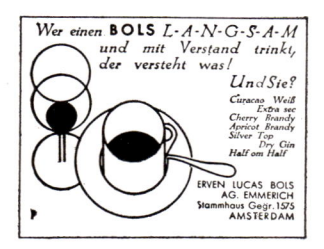

HAMERTON HAS SAID and here the Dorland Advertising Agency, London, has given proof that "the artist shows himself by working within limitation." What good layout and wise distinction between light and dark can do in advertising within even the most limited space is effectively demonstrated in these inserts designed to stand out from a crowded newspaper page. Drawings are by Terence Prentis.

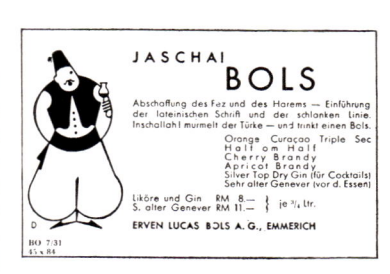

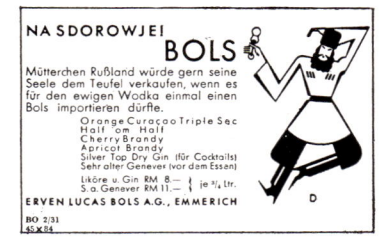

DESIGN 291

EMBARRASSING MOMENTS

When your wife finds you curing your secretary's headache . . . *be nonchalant*

LIGHT A MURAD

JOIN THE GOLD RUSH OF 1933!

Papa, I think we ought to have a sale

Let's see what Macy's did yesterday

A FAIR RANGE of sympathetic and inoffensive satire at the expense of the consumer may be studied in Bertieri's announcement of an addition to his Milan printing office, in Rea Irvin's revelations for Murad cigarettes. (P. Lorillard Company, Inc., Philadelphia), in the Gold Rush and Pop Corn cartoons for R. H. Macy & Company, New York, and in the election scene from a promotional advertisement of *The News*, a New York newspaper.

292 GRAPHIC

HUMOR IS EMPLOYED to aid the sales of two popular brands of coffee. With the domestic scene between Xantippe and Socrates, the artist in the service of Chase and Sanborn's Dated Coffee went back to the files of ancient history. (*Standard Brands, Inc., New York.*) BELOW: Proving the advantage of decaffeinized coffee upon the morphologic trait in man and beast. (*Otto Soglow cartoon for General Foods Corporation, New York, through Young and Rubicam.*)

DESIGN 293

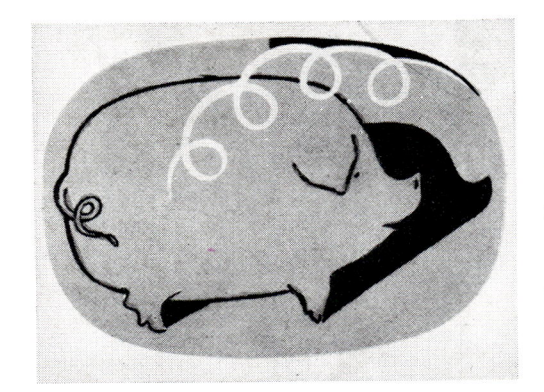

ABOVE: Two covers for travel literature designed by Umberto Zimelli, who also designed the amusing map (on the facing page) as an inside spread for "Gastronomic Italy" to show the epicurean treasures indigenous to that country (Enit, the Italian State Tourist Department, Rome.)

BELOW: A fragment from an advertisement designed by Edward Buk Ulreich for the International Printing Ink Company, New York. There is very little drawing in the ordinary sense, but very much thought in this design.

294 GRAPHIC

For description of this gastronomic map by Zimelli for a travel promotion booklet see legend on facing page.

DESIGN 295

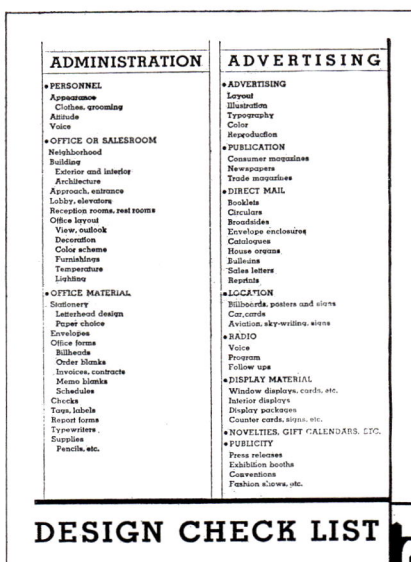

TWO SIDES of a design check list composed entirely of type material by Huxley House for the compiler, Abbott Kimball, New York. It lists the many considerations that are deserving of attention and good design in the furtherance of a well-planned advertising campaign.

THE BEN DAY GRAYS of the drawing by Keith Shaw, New York, make it possible to give a wash effect with line cut on coarse newspaper stock. It shows something of the ability and knowledge of techniques that ought to enter into the creation of even the simplest advertising drawings that confront us daily. It shows also a fine use of whites.

296 GRAPHIC

COMPARISON of current advertisements and an itemized study of their good and poor factors are most helpful in the appreciation of advertising design. Of the two, comparison seems the more important. The greater the number of cases, the more worth while the appraisal of the exhibits is likely to be, although financially the final measure of success must remain the return per dollar invested. The newspaper announcement below, published by the Cunard Line, with a decoration by Vladimir Bobritski, New York, is considered as a design to show a possible method of criticism. Comparison is not used in this case because, publicly, such a device, though an excellent one, is dangerous. Instead, the design of the advertisement as a whole is the criterion. Other considerations are:

The strong decorative spot gives attention value to the copy and distinguishes it from the palm landscapes and speeding steamers that have become the stereotypes of most current travel advertising.

The hand-lettered script acts as a transition from the decorative note of the illustration to the sales talk of the copy.

The gist of the advertisement is condensed into three lapidary lines that set the width for the major part of the layout.

The measure of the type echoes the rectangular shape of the whole layout. The message is conveyed clearly and legibly, with enough white space to set it off from the neighboring advertisements.

The logotype line is possibly the weakest note structurally. As a basis for the body of the preceding copy and the vigorous headpiece, it fails to relate in width or in size to any of the preceding components. Its silhouette is uneven.

140 Arabian Nights and Days on the

FRANCONIA WORLD CRUISE
FARE AS LOW AS $1750

A new itinerary that rivals the storied Arabian Nights in Bizarre interest. Bali, Saigon, (French Indo-China), Canton, Korea, Nikko without extra cost . . . and of course, Cairo, Bombay, Singapore, Hong Kong, Yokohama and every other thrilling world cruise highlight. But more! An optional airplane flight from Bagdad to Babylon . . . a trip to Angkor and thence into the jungles of Indo-China, optional return passage via trans-Siberian Railway.

A matchless world-voyage under the famed leadership of Cunard-Cook, on a ship that has compiled a long record of successful world cruises. Guidance and experience that ensures travellers of every luxury, every comfort so desirable in an extended cruise.

THE FRANCONIA SAILS EASTWARD FROM NEW YORK JAN. 9
Literature from your Local Agent or
CUNARD LINE
25 Broadway, New York
THOS. COOK & SON
587 Fifth Avenue, New York

DESIGN   297

THE PHOTOGRAPH by Eugene Hutchinson and the vignette drawing by W. Mury are combined into a coherent unit. A print of the photograph was cropped to the required oblong shape of the same size as the contemplated reproduction. A layout was then drawn to show the funnel idea and the position of type, headline, and logotype. A negative of the finished line drawing of the vignette was stripped over the negative of the photograph and a combination plate made. Again, knowledge of reproductive arts was necessary. (*Courtesy Bonwit Teller, New York.*)

PROBLEM: Following a similar sequence, cut out a large photographic reproduction from a newspaper or magazine, crop it and work up a combined line–halftone–type advertisement for a popular commodity such as food, cigarettes, or automobiles. A possible procedure might be to: 1. Choose your subject and make a pencil visualization of one or more possible versions. 2. Prepare the layout, using any gray surface of required size to indicate the area and shape of the photograph. 3. Clip and paste down lines of suitable type, regardless of their content, to fill in the text space. 4. Prepare the finished copy by pasting down the cropped version of the selected halftone to suit your design; finish the line drawing, inserting headline and logotype and indicating the body of type matter.

ALTERNATE PROBLEMS: Design a visitor's pass to an exhibition of advertising art work. Impart to the design the distinction you would want associated with your own work. Design a heraldic signet or a modern seal for your school. Select either signet or seal which seems to characterize your school better (e. g. Is it a Gothic or a modern structure?) and incorporate this with name and address into an appropriate letter head design.

POSTER CHAPTER 7

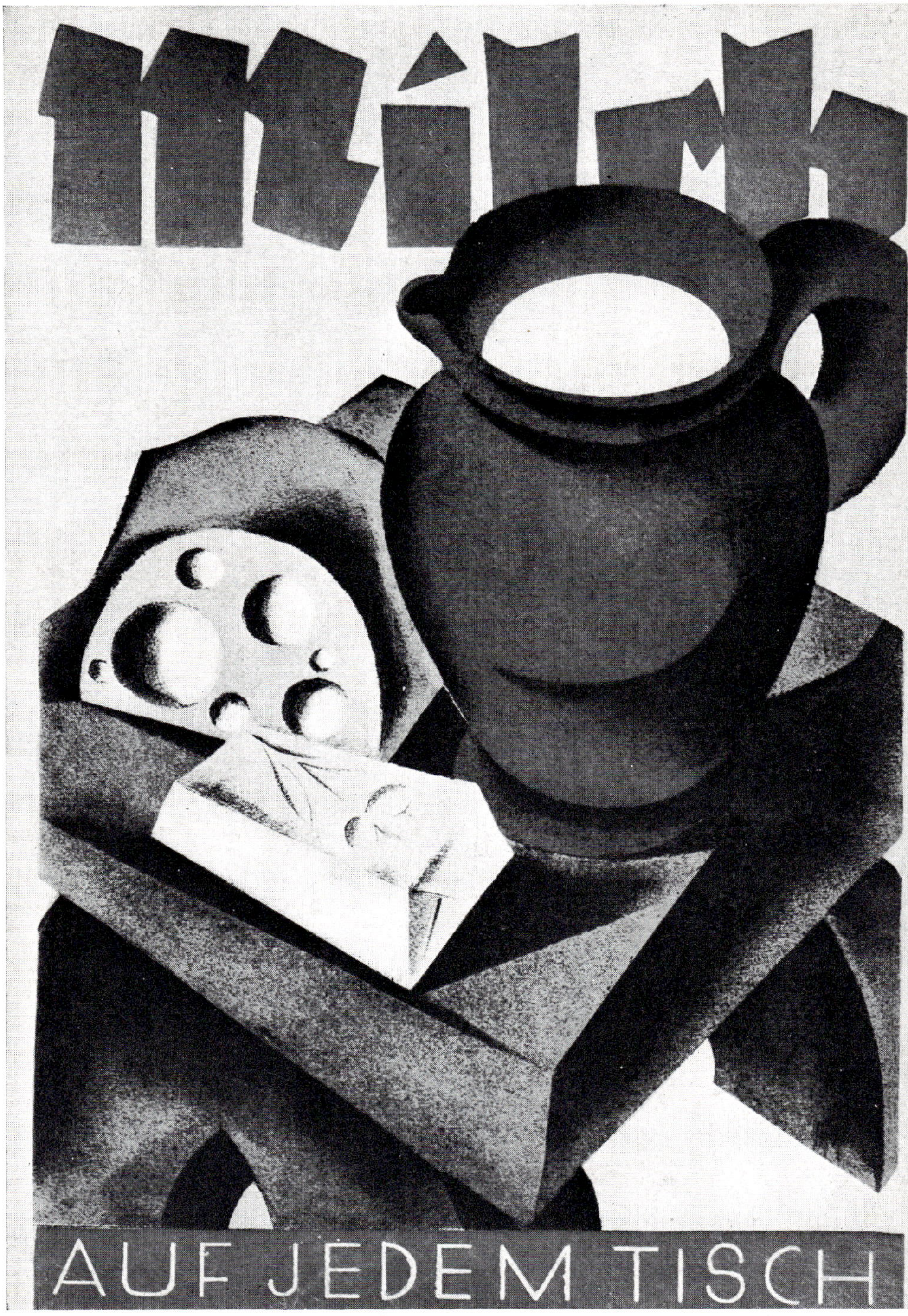
Milch
AUF JEDEM TISCH

THE POSTER

IN THE BROADEst sense, car cards, dash cards, wall hangings, cutouts, outdoor billboards, and window and other displays are considered posters. They are placed conspicuously in the marketing and shopping centers and in popular vehicles of transportation, with the aim of giving information in a manner sufficiently interesting and compelling to promote good will and to obtain favorable action on the part of the observer. Primarily a good poster must attract attention. To this end the artist strives for an original idea, or a novel presentation of an old one. Unusual or striking color is one of his means of making the poster conspicuous. He arranges his most important element of the design as the dominant mass, and subordinate ideas as background for additional interest. Where desirable he makes a specialized appeal to a particular part of the public: to the homemaker, to the motorist, to the ailing. And the poster is placed to the best possible advantage. The artist makes his design simple to catch the attention of the observer quickly and easily and to hold it long enough for the poster to tell its story. Human appeals—humor, pathos, and curiosity—may be employed. An apt and catchy slogan also serves to hold interest and give information, and is a vital factor in making it easily remembered. Repetition and association help, too, to fix the poster and its message firmly in the minds of the public. These results may be obtained only with patience and persistent effort. Unusual care is necessary in planning. The picture, slogan, and message should center at a focal point; by contour, line, and placement one element should lead to the other naturally and easily, so that interest is directed to the important theme. It is vital that the picture and lettering should combine in a unified whole. But *either* the picture *or* the lettering should occupy the major part of the poster area with the other subordinate. The two should not clash for attention. As in all design, equal spacing lacks

CHAPTER DECORATION by Julius Klinger, Vienna. It suggests what the good poster does—attract attention. (*Courtesy Hollerbaum & Schmidt, Berlin.*) CHAPTER FRONTISPIECE: The milk poster by Joseph Binder, Vienna, embodies all essentials of a fine poster—purposefulness, brevity, clarity, and good design. Milk and strength are related; hence there is, significantly, nothing in the make-up of the design that is puny or irrelevant.

DESIGN 301

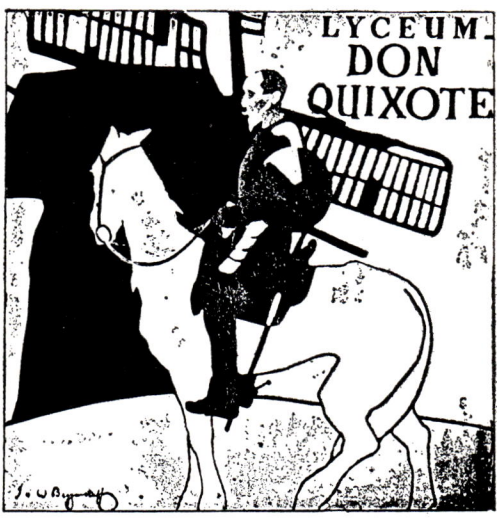

PIONEER POSTERS. Left: The sparkling design by Jules Chéret conveys all the vivacity of Yvette Guilbert. Even then the attention value of slanted lettering was recognized. RIGHT: Contrasted with the verve of the Jules Chéret placard is the strength of the Don Quixote poster designed by the Beggarstaff Brothers of England.

interest. The dominant idea should be expressed simply and directly and shorn of all nonessentials. The poster which can successfully be reduced to postage-stamp size fulfills these requirements. Inversely, the good stamp can stand the test of magnification. Examples on pages 319 and 320 illustrate these points.

The effectiveness of posters is based on the fine juxtaposition of dark and light areas, that can be tested in black and white reproduction. Most posters are further improved with color. By virtue of its own qualities of intensity and luminosity, color is one of the most powerful attraction agents of the poster. In flat areas, the most intense colors carry farthest and attract most, although when broken up into the design of a poster, the use of more than one intense color may impair rather than increase its attractiveness. For far-carrying effects and attention value, contrast of dark and light values is more important than color intensity. The warm colors—red, orange, and yellow—appear to advance toward the eye, while the cool colors—green, blue, and violet—seem to recede. Obviously, by contrasting the more aggressive colors with the more neutral hues, the important parts of the poster may be emphasized. Color, when thoughtfully handled, is aesthetically satisfying and moving, independ-

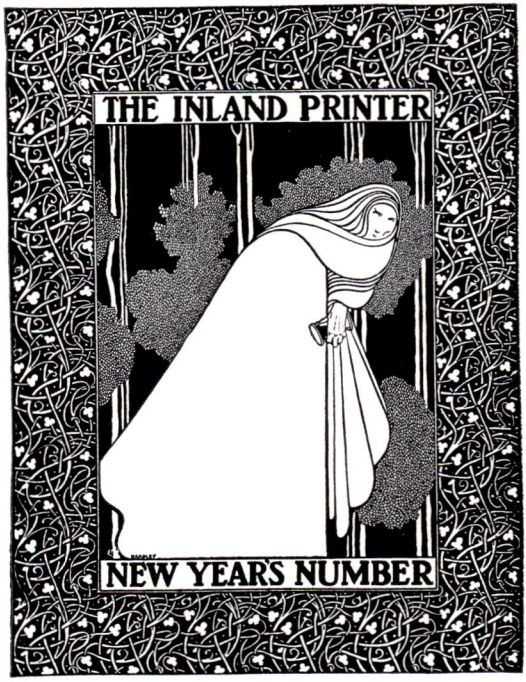

LEFT: Early American poster cover by Will Bradley for *The Inland Printer*, Chicago. The strong color contrast of the dominant figure stands out despite the elaborate border. RIGHT: Fred Walker's design "Lady in White" arouses our curiosity. It suggests depth more than most posters dare and combines just enough realism in the figure and flat pattern in the background to attain variety in the composition of the whole. Fine play of light against dark.

ent of its subject matter. A knowledge of color harmonies is invaluable in obtaining these pleasing effects. The desired result will determine whether the poster shall be done in a monochrome harmony (varying values and intensities of one color), in analogous harmony (related colors), or in complementary harmonies (directly opposed colors). The use of complementary colors as a means of heightening the apparent intensity of each is frequent in poster art. Juxtaposition of different intensities or hues plays an important part in color effects and should be thoroughly understood by the artist so that he may adapt it to his needs. Color may lend its emotional quality to the atmosphere of the poster: lively, high-keyed colors for animation; full-toned, low-keyed colors for richness and dignity; cool blues and eerie violets for tranquillity and mysticism.

In posters, reality of color becomes secondary to effectiveness of color relationship. Combinations of colors may seem quite contrary to nature and yet

DESIGN 303

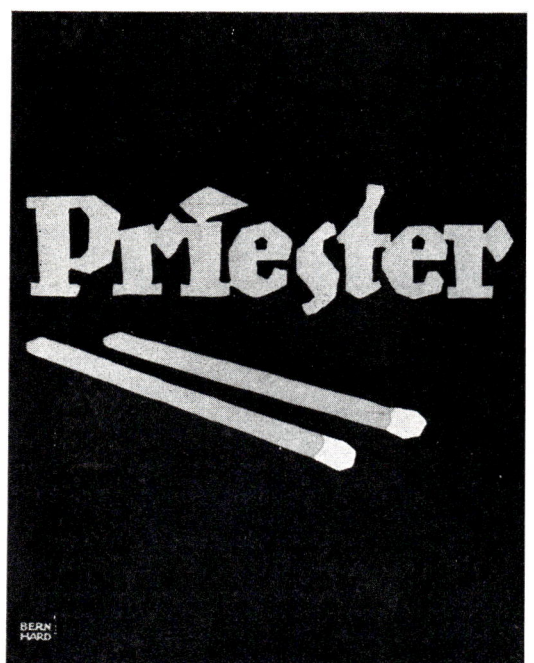

TWO OF THE EARLIEST, and possibly best, posters by Lucian Bernhard. A picture, a word, and strong color contrast are beautifully combined to give appeal to the Bosch spark plug and the Priester matches. The effects are so obvious and direct that a child can read them. Action is obtained in each by restrained use of the slanted line, choicely placed.

FACING PAGE. Fine posters of the early 1900's. ABOVE, Left: Complacent humor, cheeriness, and informality mark Paul Scheurich's early poster for Pilsener Brauhaus. Right: Ernst Deutsch's design for Otero corsets is more pretentious and, appropriately, more feminine in its treatment. BELOW: The poster for Palm cigars by Julius Klinger utilizes the lettering, much magnified, as the center of interest, broadening its appeal by the addition of the amusing figure—altogether, a strong design minus surface prettiness. (*The five posters on these pages reproduced by courtesy of Hollerbaum & Schmidt, Berlin.*)

304 GRAPHIC

DESIGN 305

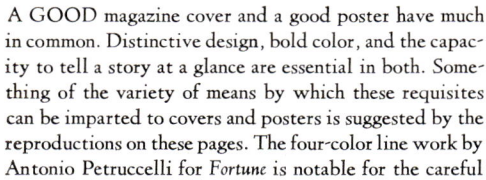

A GOOD magazine cover and a good poster have much in common. Distinctive design, bold color, and the capacity to tell a story at a glance are essential in both. Something of the variety of means by which these requisites can be imparted to covers and posters is suggested by the reproductions on these pages. The four-color line work by Antonio Petruccelli for *Fortune* is notable for the careful arrangement of its figure pattern and the bold black-gray contrast of the background. (*Fortune*, New York.) In the *New Yorker* cover, Kronengold dramatizes a lifeless street corner by strong perspective and enhances it by the free rendering of the architecture. (*The New Yorker*, New York.) FACING PAGE: Pennell's Liberty-loan poster demonstrates the craftsmanship of a master of lithographic art.

furnish a new interest if harmoniously used. All harmonious color arrangements are not necessarily suitable to posters. Greatly modified colors may be too subdued to attract attention. As in music, ingeniously handled color dissonance has a value. But the unskilled should be wary.

Flat color areas, through their absence of detail, carry farther and for that reason are used in successful posters. And, as a rule, neutralized colors are often used in the larger areas, with the most intense colors reserved for the smaller spots. While the *kind* of color used, oil or water, is unimportant, the suitability of the *quality* of the color to the purpose of the poster design must always be considered. Oil color is more frequently used for the finished original of large posters, while small ones are usually rendered in show-card or tempera colors.

Color intelligently handled is one of the most important aids to good poster making. It is our urgent suggestion that every serious student avail himself of its power, not only studying the fundamental principles but also regularly applying them. Because the limitations of space do not permit adequate treat-

JOSEPH PENNELL DEL.
THAT LIBERTY SHALL NOT
PERISH FROM THE EARTH
BUY LIBERTY BONDS
FOURTH LIBERTY LOAN

ment of the several color theories that are in use, the names of several books on the subject are offered in the bibliography.

The poster may be considered as young as Jules Chéret's masterpieces for Sarah Bernhardt's plays. The color contrasts of these posters, however, are reminiscent of earlier Japanese block prints. Mucha's posters are outstanding for their stylized draftsmanship, Steinlen's for his sympathetic animal delineations, while Toulouse-Lautrec, a third Frenchman, is famous for independence of conventions. England's Hassall is known for his droll and appealing humor; the Beggarstaff brothers, Pryde and Nicholson, for flat, two-dimensional patterns. Some of the best original posters in America have come from Bradley, with his strong decorative treatment; Penfield, with his illustrative technique; and Treidler, who excels in bold color arrangements. In Germany, Hohlwein is noteworthy both for his water-color technique and for his composition; Klinger, in Austria, is outstanding in ingenuity and design. Contemporary posters are marked by a high degree of originality, by motion that has an explosive quality, by arrangements that are full of surprises, and by an economy of expression that suggests shorthand.

FORMER GERMAN Chancellor Von Papen leaving a polling place after casting his ballot and *after* having seen some thought-provoking posters. (*Wide World Photos, New York.*) FACING PAGE: A gigantic wall poster in the service of a government for its colonial exposition. Mural-like quality and unerring composition distinguish it from the more usual commercial enterprise. Particularly noteworthy is the artistic rendering of the heads and the hand. Strength is obtained by the architectonic arrangement. (*Designed by Roger de Valerio; printed by Dévambez of Paris.*)

308 GRAPHIC

DESIGN 309

A predominantly lettered poster and a predominantly pictorial one. For description see legend on facing page.

IN "MASUREN," Alfred Winkler, Berlin, uses a part of his lettering pictorially, thereby obtaining interest for his message and variety for his design. RIGHT: In the Ukrainian poster "Kultura," Paul Kowzhun, Lwów, makes message and decoration equally appealing. BELOW: The "Perugina" posters by Seneca, Perugia, utilize line drawings to tie up with the line quality of the one-stroke lettered messages. (*Perugina of Perugia.*)

FACING PAGE. Above: The exhibition poster "Die Schöne Tasse," by Johannes Böhland, Berlin, is an example of freehand lettering dominating the design, with two small decorative units used only to relieve it. Below: "Bouillon Kub," by S. Cappiello, emphasizes the purely pictorial element. Here, lettering is subordinate. (*Dévambez, Paris.*)

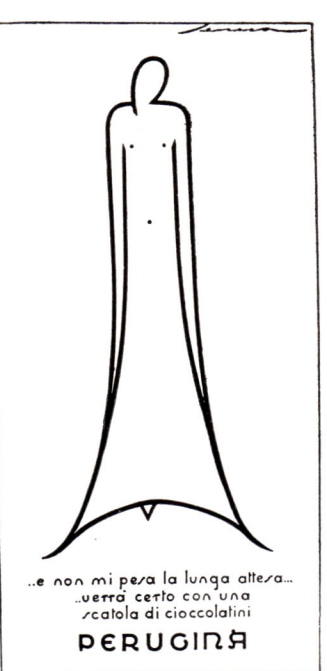

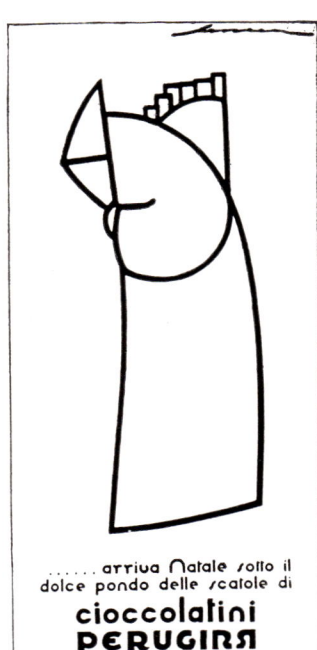

DESIGN 311

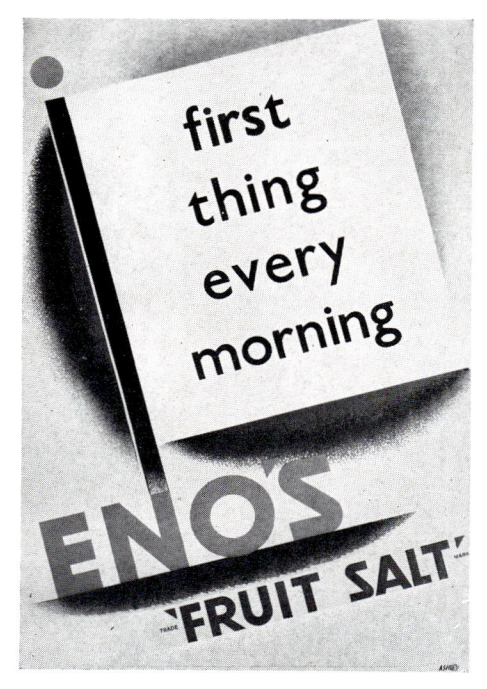

GEOMETRIZED FORMS, brief messages, simple lettering, virile design, and omission of surface detail characterize these posters. ABOVE: The proclamation to buy Austrian goods was designed by R. Heller for the Vienna Chamber of Commerce. (*Courtesy Austrian Consulate General, New York.*) BELOW: "Eno's Fruit Salt" by Ashley Havinden, London, and "Deutsches Turnfest" by A. Bernd, Jr., Kaiserslautern, suggest the variety possible in flag representation. FACING PAGE: The still-life character of these posters is enhanced by the flat pattern treatment of their simplified forms. Above: "Dreher Beer" and "Meinl Coffee" posters are by Bortnyik, Budapest. (*Printed by Korvin Brothers.*) Below: The "Telephone" poster by Frank Newbould is reproduced by courtesy of the General Post Office, London; "Nadszedt Czas," an institutional poster for the sugar industry, was designed by Levitt-Him Studio, Warsaw. The appeal of these posters is based on their strongly simplified forms and inherent good design and not on any human-interest or anecdotal subject matter that is extraneous to their ultimate purpose.

312 GRAPHIC

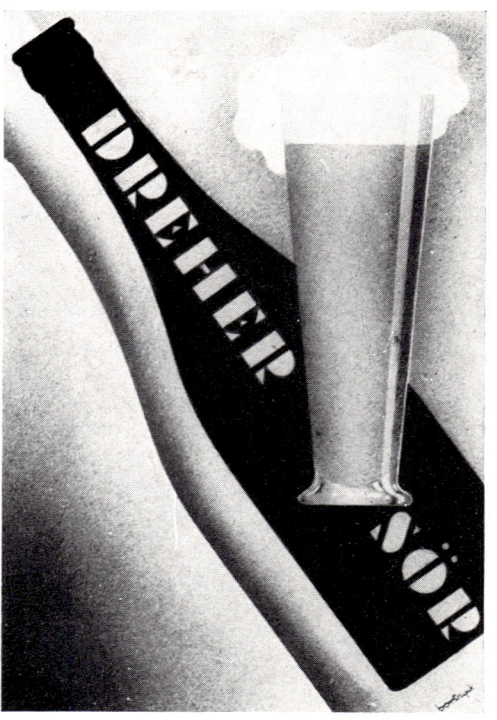

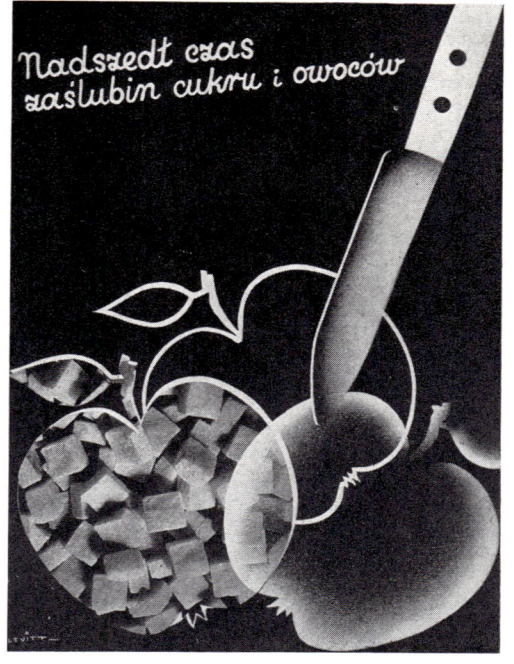

For descriptions see the legend on the facing page.

DESIGN == 313

FOUR POSTERS treating an abstract subject, religion, graphically, well, and without sentimental prettiness. Dignified strength and utmost simplicity characterize the "Oberammergau" poster by Richard Klein (*German Tourist Information Office of New York*), and the film poster "The Cross and the Sword" by José Morell, Barcelona. Contrasted with them are the more detailed, hence not so telling, design for "Chaldon Church" by Herrick (*courtesy Baynard Press, London*), and the enriched, possibly more interesting, exposition composition by F. Gali for "El Arte en España" (*printed by Seix y Barral, Barcelona*). As against the modern drawing of the Passion-play poster, classically composed, we see in Gali's design a classic drawing that has been modernly composed, montage fashion.

314 GRAPHIC

DESIGN 315

For description see legend on the facing page.

CONVENTIONALIZED FIGURES, Grecian in form and beauty, and nudes that would please even the prudish, are the attention-getting devices in these posters. In their generalization and elimination of details, they gain added visibility. ABOVE: The "Vendre" poster, by Gischia, Paris, uses dry brush and cubistic point of view so well that radical reduction does not impair it. RIGHT: The "Perle" poster by Alessandro Cervellati, Bologna, originally blue, brown, and gold, repeats the freedom of the figure in the seeming irregularity of the lettering. The high-lighted dancer is set off strongly against a stage-like background of a flat dark color.

FACING PAGE. Above: In the excellent "Désarmement" stamp, here much enlarged, E. O. Fustier seems inspired in the harmony of his lettering and figure and their disposition. (*Courtesy Swiss Federal Post Office, Geneva.*) Below: The "Exposició del Nu" poster by José Morell, Barcelona, and the "Agrumicoltura" design by Prof. Erberto Carboni, Parma, are equally successful in their artistry and appeal.

DESIGN 317

318 GRAPHIC

DESIGNS CHARACTERIZED by semi-realistic treatment of silhouetted figures. Strong contrast in size or color emphasizes the central theme.

ABOVE: The two anniversary editions of poster-esque postage stamps, here enlarged, and the Pilsudski poster, on facing page, commemorating the tenth anniversary of the Russo-Polish war, are equally effective airbrushed or engraved. (*Courtesy of the American-Polish Chamber of Commerce, New York.*)

BELOW: The film poster "Dzikie Pola" by Osiecki brings the figures out in a spotlight against the dark background. Its strength lies in the absence of distractions and detail. ("*Grafika Polska,*" *Warsaw.*)

DESIGN 319

For descriptions of these posters by Seneca, Aufseeser, Brubaker, and Cooper see the legend on the facing page.

FIGURES SYMBOLIZING labor, farming, and craftsmanship are the themes of these poster designs. ABOVE: "Certamen Nacional" poster by Bartolozzi, printed by Seix y Barral, Barcelona, and "Nitrato di Soda" design by Prof. Erberto Carboni, Parma. BELOW: A Bavarian 15-Pfennig stamp designed by Valentin Zietara, Munich, and a finely drawn exposition announcement for Bavarian handicraft by Max Eschle, Munich. FACING PAGE. Above: A good poster stands postage-stamp reduction. (*Perugina poster by Seneca, Perugia.*) Inversely, a good postage stamp can bear magnification. ("*Deutsche Flugpost*" *stamp by Prof. E. Aufseeser, courtesy Reichspost, Berlin.*) Below: Book poster by Jon Brubaker uses centralized spot of light to gain emphasis. (*Courtesy National Association of Book Publishers, New York.*) The "Keep Cool" poster is by that well-known American designer, F. G. Cooper. (*New York Edison Company.*)

DESIGN 321

HEADS AND FACES are better devices to use in posters than the full figure because a more heroic size can be attained within the identical area. The reproductions on these pages suggest means of escape from stereotype treatments; the drama of facial expression is minimized. Humor and invention take its place.

ABOVE: Both the "Ball de Disfresses" and "Baile de Máscaras" posters are by L. Muntané; the "Baile de Máscaras" poster below was designed by Cenac. (*Courtesy Seix y Barral, Barcelona.*)

FACING PAGE. Above: Masks as poster subjects. In the "La Folle du Logis" poster and the "Gellé Frères" announcement, Jean Carlu uses small bright spots to accentuate the color contrasts. (*Courtesy "Arts et Métiers Graphiques," Paris.*) Below: Two approaches to the man's and woman's face motif by José Morell, Barcelona, in a poster advertising his own services, and by Jean Carlu in a posteresque magazine cover. (*Reproduced from "Vanity Fair," copyright by Condé Nast Publications, New York.*) Forms simplified to barest outlines.

DESIGN 323

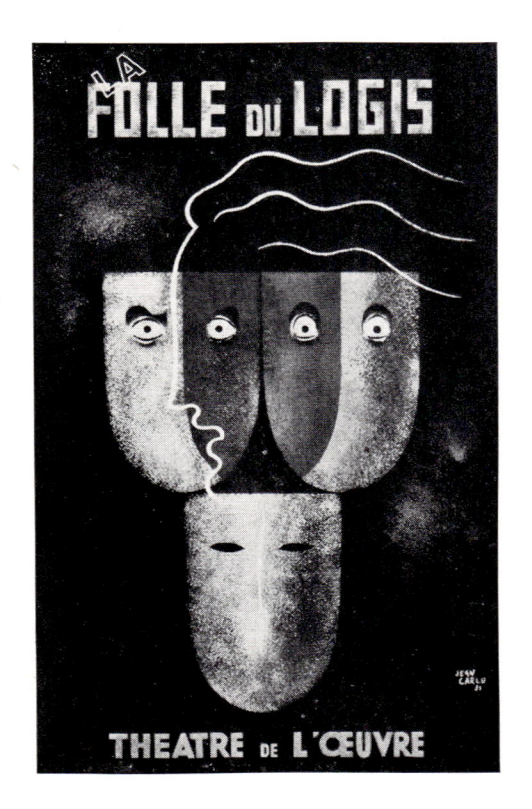

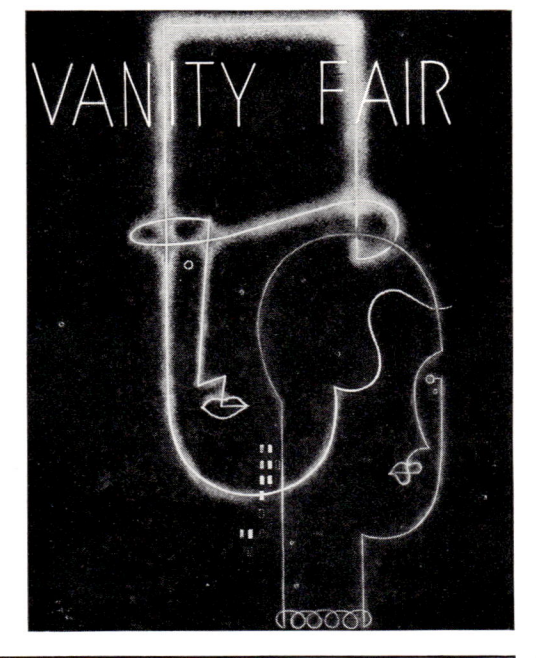

TWO HEADS decoratively treated. The "Widu" poster, above, by Professor A. Rabenbauer, Munich, shows good use of flat masses and tonal relations. The "Augsburger Fest-Spiele" announcement by Göhlert is a rarely successful combination of clear-cut line drawing with punctuating flat areas; it is reproduced here from Professor F. H. Ehmcke's *Das Zelt*, Munich.

FACING PAGE: Posters designed to appeal to the mass and to sway its sentiments. They employ moving repetitions of angles and curves. ABOVE, left, and BELOW: In the three Catalonian League posters, José Morell, Barcelona, generalizes his figures in broad strokes of color against a white background in a spirited way that suggests the restlessness of the thought advertised. ABOVE, right: The "Il Lavoro Fascista" composition by Seneca, Perugia, employs a reversed S shape for the arms, with the main lines of the lettering to harmonize. The rhythmic flow of the line is irresistible.

324 GRAPHIC

DESIGN 325

THE "MOTHER AND CHILD" theme in the poster. ABOVE: The strength of the "Muttertag 1928" depends on its design, not on the appeal of its story. There is nothing irrelevant in its sculpturesque organization. (*Designed by Prof. A. Rabenbauer, Munich.*)

BELOW: The "Désarmement" design by Jean Carlu employs a realistic mother and child that the most ordinary of us can understand, in a geometric shape that is significant of the air torpedo it pictures. (*Courtesy Office de Propagande Graphique pour la Paix, Paris.*)

FACING PAGE. ABOVE, left: The sentimental "Münchner Nothilfe" by Valentin Zietara, Munich, was a widely circulated poster. Its destitute figure knocking at the heart of a city carried a strong appeal for a charitable purpose. Right: A. Bernd, Jr., Kaiserslautern, uses a stylized figure and strong, dark-light contrasts in his health-resort poster for Teplitz-Schönau. BELOW: Two Perugina posters of a series designed by Seneca, Perugia, for a chocolate manufacturer; they speak well of the manufacturer's appreciation of the taste of his buying public. The moving rhythmic power of the figures is intensified by their utmost simplicity in rendering.

DESIGN 327

POSTER TECHNIQUE applied to figure drawing.

ABOVE, left: The "Modiano" design by Seneca, Perugia, and his two "Buitoni" posters on the facing page give the feeling of three-dimensional form in the rotundity of his geometric figures. The lettering in all instances follows the moving pattern suggested by the figures. Right: "Doyen Zigaretten" is a dashing poster where everything, from idea to lettering vibrates with activity; it is a refreshing change from the hackneyed use of the pretty girl in the furtherance of cigarette sales. (*Designed by Cortý for the Adler Company, Dresden.*) BELOW: "Proveinase Midy" by Levitt-Him Studio, Warsaw, is a photographic poster designed to sell pills. Its plastic quality and sense of humor make its suggested action almost pleasurable.

FACING PAGE: "Lait Gallia" by S. Cappiello combines realistic models in an imaginative way and conveys its message clearly by strong contrast of light against dark. (*Printed by Dévambez, Paris.*) Neither realistic nor three dimensional is Valentin Zietara's "Backt mit Hefe." Its angularity suggests instead the quality of a child's toy and is as appealing. Originally white, black, and colors.

328 GRAPHIC

DESIGN 329

THE POSTERS on these pages are alike in being more realistic in presentation than those that preceded. Part of their attention value is lost because they introduce too much detail. Their main interest lies in the attractive treatment of the subjects they convey, not in their posteresque representation. "Scotland" by Dora Zinkeisen for the London and North Eastern Railway and "Barcelona International Exposition" by Canals, printed by Seix y Barral, Barcelona, are a fine illustration and a Goya-like painting respectively. However, they are not overstrong as posters.

FACING PAGE: "Visit Italy" comprises two of a series by S. Bompard. (*Courtesy Enit, Rome.*) The "Hapag" poster by Prof. Otto Arpke contrasts nicely a busy and interesting area with a plain one. (*Hamburg-America Line, New York.*) The "International Overseas Exhibition" designed by Desmeurs makes good use of a circular composition in its relation of figures. (*Robert Lang, Paris.*)

VISIT ITALY IN SPRING

VISIT ITALY IN AUTUMN

HAPAG
MITTELMEER-UND ORIENTFAHRTEN
HAMBURG-AMERIKA LINIE

INTERNATIONAL OVERSEAS EXHIBITION
ROUND THE WORLD IN ONE DAY
PARIS 1931

See facing page.

DESIGN 331

THE "INDUSTRIAS QUIMICAS" poster by Jan for Seix y Barral, Barcelona, and "Tours" by A. Selensky for Intourist, New York, treat rugged subjects appropriately—in free and rugged fashion, the one in drybrush technique and the other in flat planes. In the first, the crossing diagonal lines of the lettering and the vertical lines of the chimneys act as a climax to the closely knit pattern. They gain intimacy by absence of finish.

FACING PAGE: Four travel posters presenting a variety of techniques, compositions, and outlooks. Above: Two excellent maritime subjects designed by W. Mallek, Münster, for the city of Stettin and by Hans Wagula, Graz, for the steamship "King Alexander" respectively. (*Printed by Rötzer's Senefelder Company, Graz.*) Below: The "Then and Now" poster by A. R. Thomason for the London and North Eastern Railway is a good idea but it is weakened somewhat by the combination of two techniques that have little in common. The "Candebec" scene is well rendered artistically and possibly effective as a poster in the intimacy of a railway station. As an outdoor poster its success is moot. (*By courtesy of the Chemins de Fer d'État, Paris.*)

DESIGN 333

334 ═══════════════════════ GRAPHIC

IN THE AIR-BRUSHED "Vers l'Angleterre" H. Biais utilizes a decorative map-picture combination to sell travel. In the wash "Wilno" by S. Norblin, Warsaw, the beautiful scenery is used as an argument to convince the public that it ought to visit this medieval city. (*Courtesy American-Polish Chamber of Commerce, New York.*) BELOW: In the Russian poster "Vipolnenye Programmi" photomontage is used to lend interest to the inanimate industrial background. Its lettering, however, is too weak in contrast and too insignificant in size to be completely successful. (*Designed by Natalie Pincus; courtesy Kultsviaz-Voks, Moscow.*)

FACING PAGE: "Travel in Italy" contains no profuse explanations. Instead, its masterly design and cheerful colors are its own best invitation to visit Italy. (*Courtesy Enit, Italian State Tourist Department, Rome and New York.*)

DESIGN 335

The architectural motif predominates in the posters on these pages. By Hohlwein, Meyerowicz, Roth, Mallek, and Jan.

THE ARCHITECTURAL MOTIF has to be treated with good taste indeed if it is to succeed without recourse to the human. "Exposición Internacional de Barcelona" by Nogués (*printed by Seix y Barral, Barcelona*) and "Lincoln" by Fred Taylor for the London and North Eastern Railway are similarly broken into a major pictorial and a minor lettering panel. They, and the "Ripoll" poster by José Morell, Barcelona, employ a vista through an arch to frame their backgrounds. The lettering units in the two Spanish posters were apparently planned by the artists; the "Lincoln" imprint seems to have been added independently of the artist. Was it an afterthought?

FACING PAGE. Above: Posteresque covers by Hohlwein, Meyerowicz, and Roth respectively. As against the naturalism of "Germany" and "Würzburg," the "Deutschland" design by Meyerowicz shows in its artistically exaggerated wedge shape a clever attention-getting device. (*Courtesy German Tourist Information Office, New York.*) Below: The "Hannover" design by W. Mallek, Münster, selects the most attractive sightseeing points of the city and creates out of them an impressive pattern. In "De Bohi," Jan gives realistic representation a slanted and somewhat modern twist to gain a dynamic quality instead of a static architectural rendering. (*Seix y Barral, Barcelona.*)

DESIGN 337

ABOVE, LEFT: The "Pressa" poster by Prof. F. H. Ehmcke, Munich, portrays buildings as pure masses of color. Careful composition retains an orderly clarity in the complicated design. (*From Prof. Ehmcke's "Das Zelt," Munich.*) Right: A. Bernd, Jr., Kaiserslautern, in "Stettin" and Hipolito Hidalgo de Caviedes in his "Leon" use airplane views of a building to lend variety and virility to their precise architectural renditions. Superiority in poster design does not prevent Caviedes from also excelling in fine arts, so called. He was awarded first prize ($1,000) in the 1935 Carnegie International. (*"Leon" poster printed by Rivadeneira, Madrid.*)

FACING PAGE: "France," by Ervine Metzl has the appeal of an artist's spontaneous sketch incorporated with classic lettering into a straightforward design. (*Courtesy United States Lines, New York.*) "Charal Entwürfe" is an artist's announcement in behalf of his own business. In its angularity and tonal treatment of setbacks it is somewhat similar to the "Pressa" poster. (*Charal, Berlin.*) The beautiful "Scotland" by Herrick and the playful "Eno's Fruit Salt" by McKnight-Kauffer suggest the flat-pattern color contrast and the distorted perspective of the stage setting. (*Courtesy Baynard Press, London, and J. C. Eno, Ltd., London, respectively.*)

GRAPHIC

DESIGN 339

A MAGAZINE COVER by McIntosh that has all the ingredients of a striking poster. Chaste legible lettering and a generalized bear are combined into a classically pure design with nothing extraneous. ("*Asia,*" *New York.*)

ABOVE: "Europa" and "Spain" by Oleg Zingher, Berlin, suggest the finesse of a Grecian vase drawing and the simplicity of cutout paper figures, respectively. In the "Spain" design, the line from the S through the edge of the cape subtly ties the composition together. BELOW:

The two magazine covers, for the *American Printer*, designed by Huxley House, New York, and for *Gebrauchsgraphik*, by Oleg Zingher, Berlin, show the variety attainable within the limits of simplification. Four attention-getting devices combining realism with imagination.

DESIGN 341

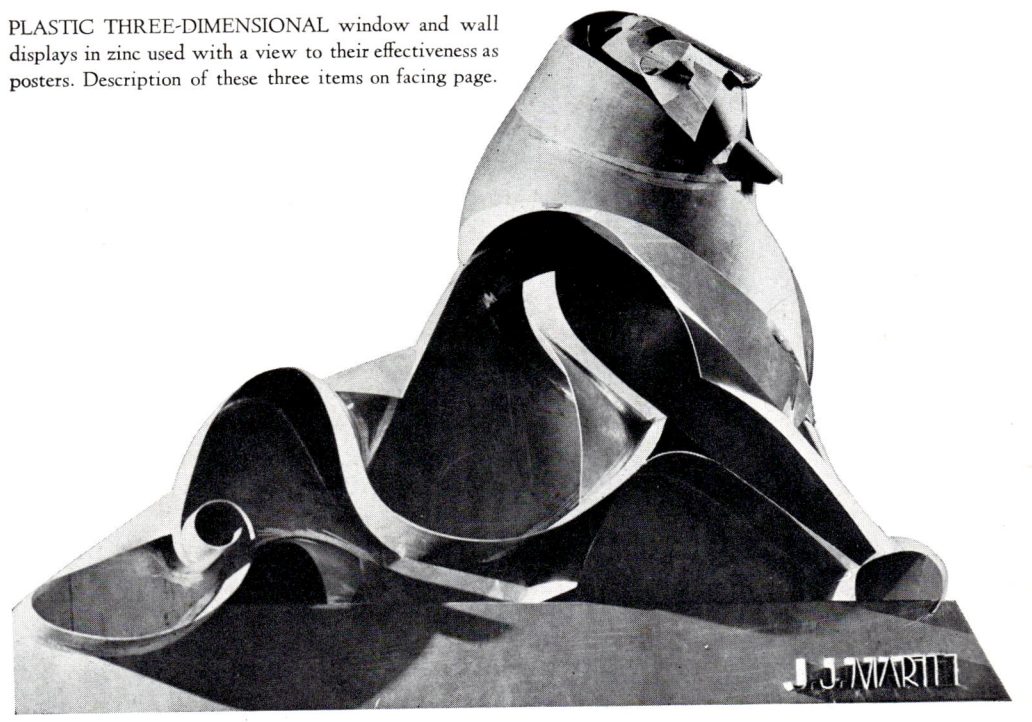

PLASTIC THREE-DIMENSIONAL window and wall displays in zinc used with a view to their effectiveness as posters. Description of these three items on facing page.

342 GRAPHIC

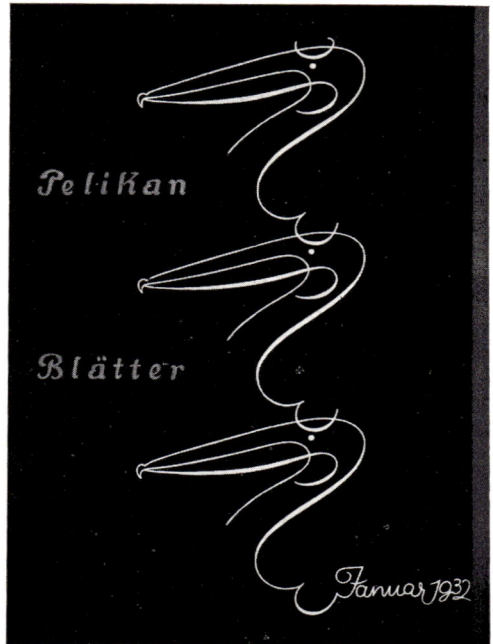

THE POSTER "Das künstlerische Plakat" focuses attention on the small trade-mark of the Union of German Advertising Artists by directing all the lines of the fish to a single object. (*Designed by A. Bernd, Jr., Kaiserslautern.*) The swinging linear repetition of the pelican form in the "Pelikan Blätter" accentuates the trade name the artist is seeking to advertise. (*Designed by W. Metzig, Hannover.*) BELOW: The "Budapest Vásár" poster for a trade fair has an imaginative background to lend vitality to the realistic bird. In the original, orange, black, and the white of the paper were strikingly juxtaposed. (*Bortnyik, Budapest.*)

FACING PAGE. ABOVE, left: "Le Triomphe du Blanc" display contrasts a dark metal horse against a white one and ingeniously overcomes the plastic limitations of sheet metal to achieve sculpturesque form in a posteresque design. Here, the rectangle of the window becomes part of the composition. Right: The circular "Odeon" poster is similarly manipulated for outdoor purposes. Here, again, repetition of the same figure motif adds memory value to the attractive three-dimensional rendering. BELOW: The heraldic lion was constructed for the post office of the city of Belfort. It is an up-to-date version of the traditional and less inventive stone lions. (*All sculptures designed and executed in zinc by J. J. Martel and Jean Carlu. Courtesy Compagnie Royale Asturienne des Mines, Paris.*)

DESIGN 343

CIGARETTE POSTERS. ABOVE: "Club" and "Standard" by Werbekraft Studio fall back on the age-old appeal of the pretty face to gain attention. The typewriter type in "Standard" anticipated by a long time its popularity in American advertising. BELOW: The strength of the woodcut technique, appropriately used in the "Sanct Georg" poster, is a radical departure in treatment from the preceding examples. (*Courtesy Greiling Company, Dresden.*)

FACING PAGE: Posters on the subject of music. "Salzburg" and "Bayreuth" are two of a series by Austin Cooper distinguished by much thought in compilation and good design in organization. (*London and North Eastern Railway, London.*) Johannes Böhland, Augsburg, combines fine lettering with a decorative musical device in his "Bühnenkunst" poster for the advancement of stage art. "Steinway," a reminder poster by von Axsler-Heudtlass, suggests class in the merchandise by appropriate association with society folk and finery. (*Elsnerdruck, Berlin.*)

344 GRAPHIC

DESIGN — 345

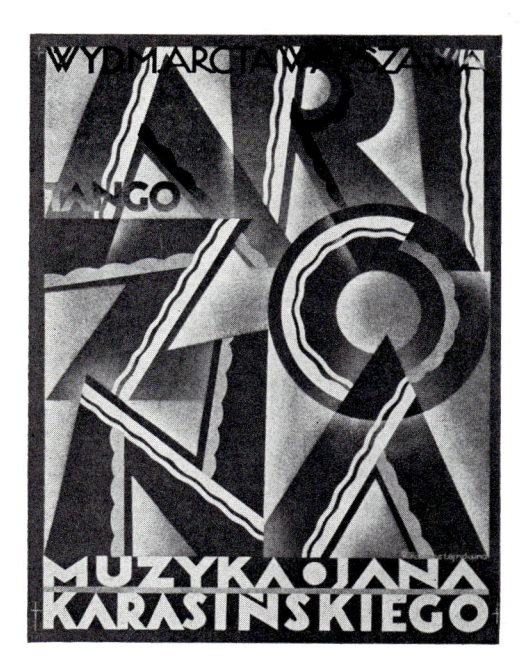

PICTORIALLY TREATED lettering inventions play the main role in the designs on this page. "Arizona," a postery music-sheet cover was designed by R. Rozensztejnówna, a girl student at the School of Fine and Applied Arts, Warsaw. A. M. Cassandre is responsible for the "Deberny Peignot" trade-mark design, which was found equally adaptable to posting on billboards and on the sides of this firm's delivery trucks. The "TVO" design has movement, strength, and color. It was created by the Clement Dane Studio for the British Petroleum Company, Ltd., London. Size and slant of letters suggest power. (*Printed by the Baynard Press.*)

FACING PAGE: The classic design, "Der Montag" by A. Ehrlich, Elberfeld, originally in blue and silver is a fine newspaper poster which furnishes an embarassing standard for the posters turned out by our own fourth estate to cry its wares. Sports posters, equally effective but varied in technique, are A. M. Cassandre's "Lawn Tennis" design, published by the Alliance Graphique, Paris, and based on the always attractive bull's-eye device; Aleksander Deineka's "Discus Thrower," based on the appeal of an athletic female (*courtesy Kultsviaz-Voks, Moscow*); and Jan's "S'Agaró" with the swaying line of his figure set off against a bird's-eye perspective. (*Courtesy Seix y Barral, Barcelona.*)

346 ══════════════════════════════ GRAPHIC

DESIGN 347

BILLBOARD POSTERS. The "U. S. Tires" twenty-four-sheet outdoor poster is a prize-winning design by Leonard London, art director of Outdoor Advertising, Inc., New York. The three "Chevrolet Trucks" designs are visualizations by the staff of Outdoor Advertising, Inc., New York. They illustrate how much thought and effort go into poster creation preliminary to the finished and accepted design. How unfortunate that such dynamic embryos should so rarely reach fruition—and the public eye.

FACING PAGE: The "Tek" panel is one of the very few car cards that can stand the association of fine posters. (*Courtesy Collier Service Corporation, New York.*) The refreshing three-panel "Dubonnet" poster by A. M. Cassandre employs a novel idea that is hard to catalogue. In less skilled hands, the poster might have fallen into three separate parts. It is interesting to observe that, although the little fellow lacks ravishing beauty and sex appeal, he has carried the trade name and the merchandise of his employers clear around the world in thousands of flat and plastic reproductions. (*Alliance Graphique, Paris.*) "The Big Parade" by Fred Ludekens is obvious and direct in statement and bold in design. (*Campbell-Ewald Company, Detroit.*)

348 GRAPHIC

DESIGN 349

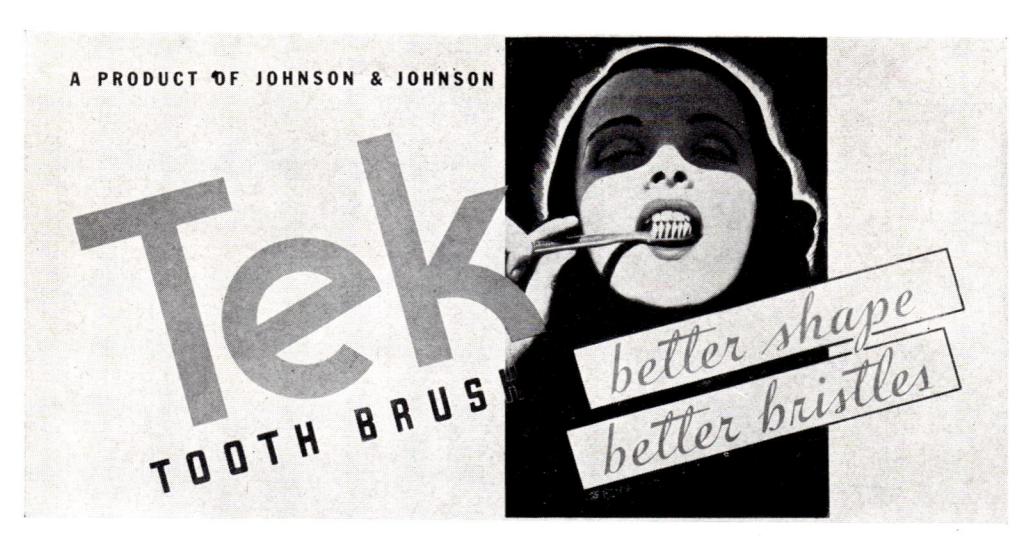

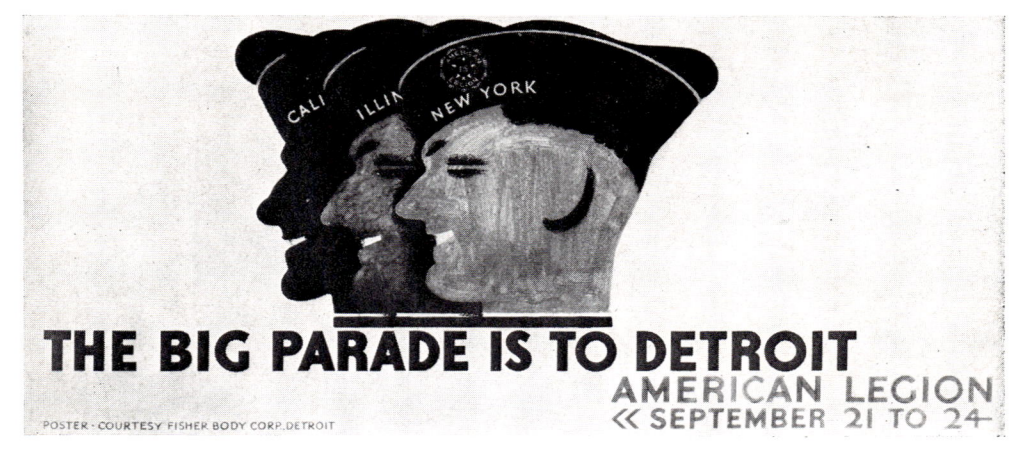

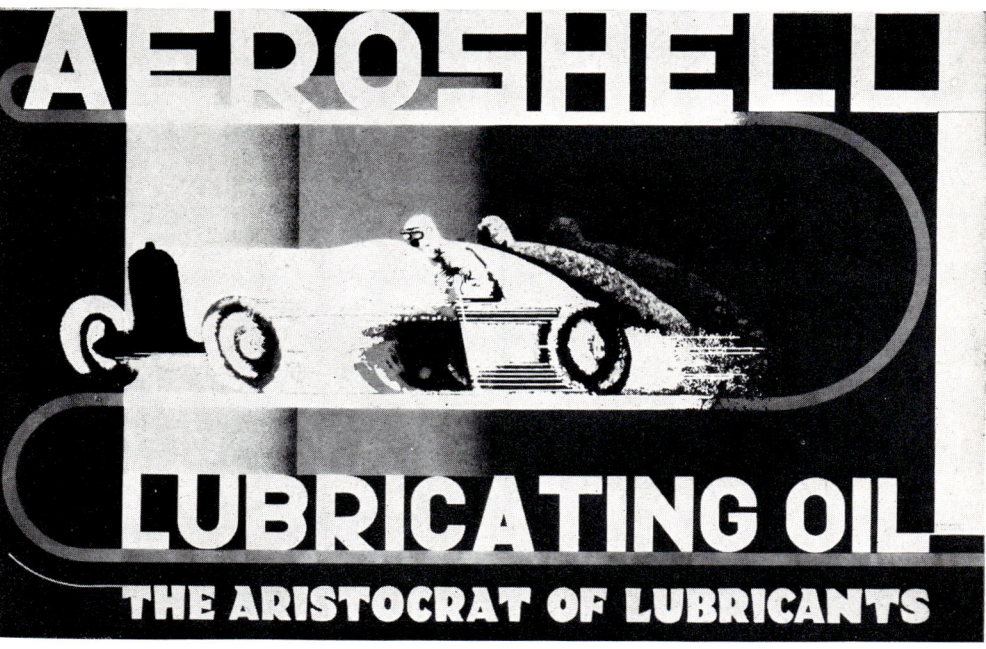

ENGLISH BILLBOARD posters; four of an attractive series. The above, by McKnight-Kauffer, represents two treatments by the same artist. The flow of oil, we take it, is about as smooth as the flow of line in the "Aeroshell" composition, and the rich browns and warm blacks of the original "New Forest" lure the motorist out of the city.

EVERYWHERE YOU GO

LONG MAN OF WILMINGTON — By Denis Constanduros

YOU CAN BE SURE OF SHELL

LAVENHAM

SEE BRITAIN FIRST ON SHELL

TWO MORE examples: "Everywhere You Go" by Denis Constanduros and "See Britain First on Shell" by Edna Clarke Hall convey their different invitations tellingly. Where the former lures the lover of the outdoors, the latter appeals to those who appreciate the quaint countryside. (*Courtesy of Shell-Mex and B. P. Ltd., London.*)

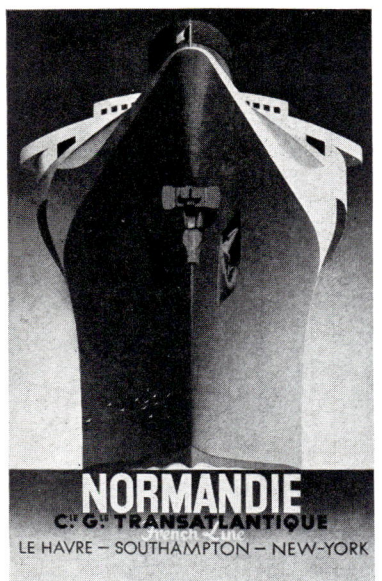

THE NIGHT SCOTSMAN
Leaves King's Cross nightly at 10.25.

NORMANDIE
C.ie G.le TRANSATLANTIQUE
LE HAVRE — SOUTHAMPTON — NEW-YORK

TRAVEL IS MADE to appear romantic indeed in Alexeïeff's "The Night Scotsman." Its decorative quality and masterly lithographic technique are unlike anything we have seen in a long time. (*London and North Eastern Railway, London.*) BELOW: The poster by A. M. Cassandre exaggerates the verticality of the ship to convey something of the massiveness of the "Normandie." The lettering of the word "Normandie," lined up with the sides of the boat, helps to suggest balance and to emphasize the impression of height. (*Courtesy French Line, New York.*)

FACING PAGE: In the highly commended outdoor poster, "Buick VIII," Frederick Stanley's appealing realism is happily relieved by expert staging. (*Campbell-Ewald Company, Detroit.*) Otis Shepard's "Chevrolet" design shows a close coordination of all it takes to make a good poster. His stylized presentation of the figure is radically different from the painstaking brush photography of Stanley. (*Campbell-Ewald Company, Detroit.*) In the "Help" poster, Joseph Binder, Vienna, unites geometric equivalents of objects with harmonious lettering in a decorative design that makes a melodramatic appeal quite superfluous.

GRAPHIC

DESIGN 353

Four posters by students; see page 355 for legend.

354 GRAPHIC

THE FLOWER MOTIF used by a Dutch and a German poster artist. The inventiveness of Machiel Wilmink's "Holland" design (*courtesy Official Tourist Information Office for Holland, The Hague*) and the delicacy of Charal's "Gartenbau Ausstellung" are marked. BELOW: Department-store poster for Austin Reed, London, by Tom Purvis, a master of the posteresque figure. Flat areas dominate.

FACING PAGE: Four posters designed by students of a Polish, American, French, and German school, respectively. The unspoiled freshness and appealing naïveté in these untraditional compositions are difficult to recapture after the student has come face to face with the standardized requirements of the advertising business. "Poznań" is a lithograph by H. Frankowski of the Graphic Industries School (*Szkola Przemyslu Graficznego*), Warsaw; "Bazaar" was composed in cut paper and textile by Moe Gross of the Abraham Lincoln High School, Brooklyn; "Yoghourt Maggi" was rendered in tempera by H. Lodenius of Léon Gischia's and Fernand Leger's Grande-Chaumière Academy (*Académie de la Grande-Chaumière*), Paris; "Deutscher Muttertag" is by a student of Professor Preetorius Munich. (*Staatsschule für Angewandte Kunst.*)

DESIGN 355

"THE TOWN CRIER" a poster trade-mark designed by Walter Dorwin Teague for "Timely Clothes." Keller-Heumann-Thompson Company, Rochester.) It is expressive and concise and hence easy to remember. It is picturesque enough to appeal to a varied audience, and original enough in utilizing an early American motif rather than more abstract conceptions. The figure was reduced to simple outlines, making it adaptable to a variety of reproductive processes and a wide range of sizes. Half-inch business-card emblems to six-foot animated displays of this design were used without forfeiting its effectiveness, as can be seen in the above examples.

PROBLEM: Design a one-sheet poster, vertical or horizontal, advertising an abstract or intangible commodity, such as graphic art, electric current, or hygiene. Use only two simplified symbols of the subject matter (a hand and an eye for graphic art, for example) and limit the color range to four flat colors. Limit lettering to either an appropriate phrase or word.

ALTERNATE PROBLEMS: 1. Develop a posteresque trade-mark or signet for a product or an organization. Render the finished drawing in three different mediums on the assumption that it will be reproduced in varying sizes on all kinds of stock, from coated paper to rough newsprint, in black and white and in full colors, in electric neon signs, and in three-dimensional displays. 2. Redesign one of the current posters or car cards you saw, endeavoring to organize its pattern, to arrange the text in proper relation to the design of the whole, and to improve its visibility. Display it on the wall next to your neighbors' designs; next to some actual car cards. Compare and discuss your findings. Test your color combination in natural light; in artificial light. What do you find to be the most common weaknesses?

GRAPHIC ARTS EDUCATION
CHAPTER 8

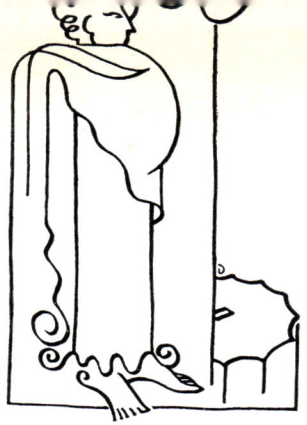

GRAPHIC ARTS EDUCATION

IN THE GRAPHIC arts field, education of the apprentice and creation by the professional go hand in hand. Such internationally known graphic artists as the Americans Goudy, the late Pennell, Boardman Robinson, and the recently naturalized Grosz; the Austrians R. von Larisch and J. Binder; the Germans Ehmcke, Koch, Tiemann, and Weiss; the Frenchmen Fernand Leger, Cassandre, and Carlu; and the Englishmen Johnston and Hewitt have also been teachers in their respective specialties. The opportunities that personal instruction by such men offer are far greater than those made possible by the training that bookwise teachers, with whom most of us are familiar, can give.

For the student selecting his professional training an important criterion ought to be not alone the reputation of his prospective school but the practical ability of his future teachers. More and more schools are beginning to realize the advantage of actual professional help over mere pedagogical advice. Comparison of the faculties of a typical school's 1926 and 1936 catalogues shows the progress that has been made in this direction. Considering their number and the wealth, variety, and intensity of their training, the German *Kunstgewerbe* schools were until recently the outstanding leaders. World-renowned organizations such as the Reimann School of Berlin, the Technikum für Buchdrucker and the Staatliche Akademie of Leipzig, the Staatsschule für Angewandte Kunst of Munich, and others of similar grade were largely responsible for this general degree of efficiency. Some idea of the thoroughness of the training in these schools can be obtained from an appraisal of the caliber and maturity of their students, from a study of their catalogues, from observing their laboratories and noting the manifold opportunities that they offer (pages 360, 377), and from examining their work. While education in the United States was, until recently, very successfully directed toward raising the standards of taste of the great mass of Americans, education in England, France, Germany, Austria, and Poland emphasized the preparation of their craftsmen. The good taste of Americans and the fine craftsmanship of Europeans are shown in those examples of art that we have seen used in this country but labeled with a foreign land of origin. Fortunately, a happier balance between training for appreciation and training for creative production characterizes present-day American graphic arts education. As found in a number of the better schools, this education includes a cultural background and art training, coupled with an engraving and printing apprenticeship. Neither theory nor practice is neglected. The common procedure is to give actual work for the business world to the more advanced graphic arts students. This work is graded according to difficulty, and the assignments are distributed according to the preparation and talents of the students. Reproductions in this book show that it is not unusual for student work obtained in this manner to equal that of professionals. Such preparation

CHAPTER DECORATION by Hertwig for the Reimann School, Berlin. FACING PAGE: A woodcut in which the background spaces—what is left—are as important as what is cut. This and other students' work in the book show the hairline distinction between amateur and professional. (*Wilhelm Oesterle, Reimann School, Berlin.*)

DESIGN 359

360 ═══════════════════ GRAPHIC

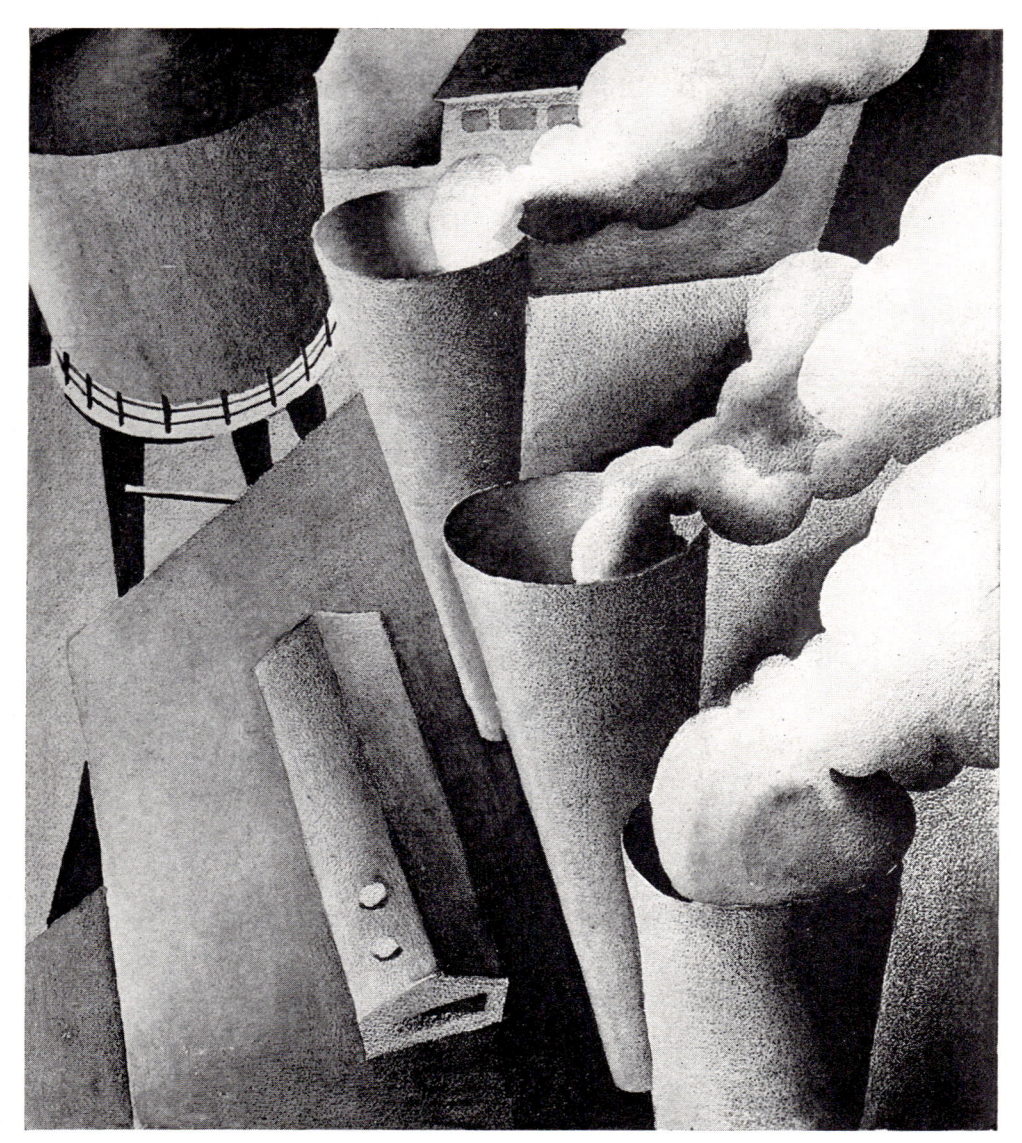

A COMPOSITION with uncommon perspective by George Daigle of the Cass Technical High School, Detroit, awarded first prize in 1932 Scholastic competition. (*American Crayon Company, Sandusky.*) FACING PAGE: Two art groups in the Reimann School, Berlin. Above: The instructor, who is also a practicing artist, criticizes the students' work, suggesting several possible solutions. Below: Packages, posters, trade-marks, etc., are prepared here with a degree of efficiency that even the reduced photograph makes apparent. Originality is encouraged.

has the additional advantage of making less obtrusive the distinction between learning and doing, between the problem of completing a school exercise and that of making a living As a result, there is no chronological border line.

DESIGN 361

Specialization, so prevalent in America, may be an aid to business, but it is an obstacle to a well-rounded training. Here one may become a good compositor, a successful stoneman, an efficient router, or an accurate photographer. The so-called artisan, however, may not aspire to do more than a small detail of the job. The rare man of general training—one who in Europe would be the artist—becomes an art *director* or an art *promoter*. In that capacity he may influence the work of other artists, but he seldom creates or makes practical application of his own knowledge. The director's job is to synthesize the work of idea man, layout artist, artist, photographer, stripper, etcher, router, mounter, retoucher, printer, etc. When these specialists collectively create a work of art, it is a stroke of luck. In Europe, a work of art is the product of one artist. This product, therefore, is more likely to be a consistent whole.

As things are at present, the average American student has the choice of a theoretic education *or* a course of training with the emphasis on the "shop" phase of his chosen profession and little more. Even the fine work of the International Typographical Union and the United Typothetae of America in the printing end of graphic arts education has not completely rectified matters. Rarely are shop and theory combined to the extent of encouraging the whole craftsman—one who thinks his job through to the end. Indeed, as Lord Riddell has so aptly said, following a visit to the United States: "My first impression whilst in your country was the great number of schools in which some section of the printing industry is taught. In no instance, however, did I find a school teaching the whole of the crafts embraced in the great industry to which we belong..."* Little improvement has been made thus far.

The method of graphic arts education abroad explains in part why the Continental student and the professional can be so progressive or even daring in their attempts to solve their problems. Having learned the basic fundamentals of good lettering, the student can experiment in Rudolph Koch fashion, for instance, and still maintain the legibility of the classic alphabet. By working with a successful practicing artist teacher, the student can always be up-to-date. This is especially difficult in commercial art where no textbook ever parallels what is really the latest development in the profession. By contact with a doer, the student gets a drive that critic-teachers who are the product of an over-

*An Open Letter to instructors of printing in America. An uncharitable but accurate appraisal of the situation.

POSTER BY STUDENT E. Tomás of the Académie de la Grande-Chaumière, Paris, of which Léon Gischia and Fernand Leger are directors. The fine dark and light basis of the colored original loses little in reproduction.

DESIGN 363

PRINTS. ABOVE: Two wood engravings from an English school using recurring themes reminiscent of musical motifs. In placing and in treatment, the lettering is an integral part of the designs. (*Arthur E. Broadbent of the Liverpool City School of Art, Liverpool.*) LEFT: Woodcut distinguished by an unusual point of view and a fine disposition of dark and light areas. (*Russell D. Hamilton of the New York School of Industrial Arts, New York, G. K. Gombarts, Principal.*)

364 GRAPHIC

TWO ILLUSTRATIONS in wood. In each case the treatment exploits to the full the possibilities of the technique employed.

ABOVE: A wood engraving, originally in colors, by Prof. Hans Alexander Müller of the Staatliche Akademie, Leipzig, for a school-published edition of a Knut Hamsun novel, cooperatively produced.

BELOW: A woodcut by Paula Jordan, from the magazine *Der Holzschnitt*, published by students of the Staatliche Akademie, Leipzig.

DESIGN

academic training cannot hope to give. After all, a theoretic education in the graphic arts can supply all the information that is available on the subject without helping the student to design even the smallest example of it. In the absence of such practical training some graphic artists have supplemented their educa-

1. EVERY job should start with a plan that gives the exact size of each type block. Have the layout man compute with care the number of letters in each piece of copy and you will save many costly hours of trial and error when you come to set it. No work can be better than the plan on which it is based. If the plan be vague or badly done, the result is quite sure to fall short of its mark. Give a man a good plan to follow and proper tools with which to do it and he will bend his best effort to the work. Deny him these and you tie his hands; you rob him of the joy which every honest man feels in looking upon his finished task and knowing it is well done. There is

2. ```
Every job should start with a plan that gives the
each type block. Have the layout man compute with
ber of letters in each piece of copy and you will save
hours of trial and error when you come to set it. No
better than the plan on which it is based. If the pla
badly done, the result is quite sure to fall short of its
man a good plan to follow and proper tools with whic
he will bend his best effort to the work. Deny him the
his hands; you rob him of the joy which every hones
looking upon his finished task and knowing it is well d
```

3. `Every job should start with a plan that gives the ex-`

FORECASTING THE NUMBER OF PAGES in a magazine. Take any printed matter employing face and size of desired type, but wider in measure (width) than you contemplate using in your layout. (Linotype Estienne in this case.) Cut width of Fig. 1, as shown by gray line, to that which you intend to use in the new layout. Then typewrite ten lines of trial paragraph (Fig. 2), transposing letter for letter and line for line. Find average length of lines by dividing the total number of letters and spaces (here 526) by 10. The vertical line in Fig. 2 was drawn to facilitate tabulation; each line to the left of it has 49 characters and spaces. Set marginal stops of typewriter to 53 and typewrite all copy to this new average (52.6 or 53), using as many lines to the sheet as the magazine will have to the page. Each typewritten sheet will now be equivalent to a printed page. To forecast number of pages, add full-page illustrations, blanks, advertisements, etc. For a more professional method see page 68. FACING PAGE: This illustrates a signature or section of a student-designed and student-printed book (quarto). The tonal harmony of the layout is due to the use of similar line in type and decoration. (*Staatliche Akademie, Leipzig.*)
```

DESIGN 367

tion with work in print shops and engraving plants. At best this offers a splendid opportunity and encourages an appreciation of the various activities which together constitute the graphic arts. At its worst, when the aim of the employer alone is permitted to dictate the character of this training, monotonous work, wasteful of much valuable time to the student and productive of much undeserved profit to the shop, is likely to be the rule.

Any book such as *Graphic Design* may be used to supplement, in a small measure, the training now generally accessible to students of the graphic arts. Not only do its chapters show many of the more successful professional expressions in the various media, but they picture exceptional student solutions as well. If the reader will study these and essay to do the problem with which each chapter terminates, always comparing his solution with the similar works of outstanding professionals, he is likely to be satisfied with nothing commonplace or amateurish. Exposure to work of high standards will stimulate the youthful artist to the best within him. Comparison with the efforts of his possibly less talented classmates, on the other hand, helps the mediocre alone, since a student's satisfaction with his own work is rarely conducive to the highest creative attainment. To the sensitive student the reproductions in *Graphic Design* should serve as strong stimuli to better and more professional work.

The graphic arts course that follows is the first one to have been offered in the academic high schools of the city of New York. Publications of various kinds have been used as the center around which the course is built, because in their production most of the activities considered as graphic arts may be employed. The plan of study is but a beginning that the authors hope may evolve into a more ambitious course than is usually permitted by the limitations of an academic system. It at least has been an attempt to relate theory with practice and school work with professional outside activities.

PHOTOGRAPHIC cover design in red and black for *Photography Sees the Surface*, a book designed and produced cooperatively by the students of the State Graphic Arts School, Prague, Czechoslovakia; Ladislav Sutnar, director.

BOOK ORNAMENTS designed by students. 1. W. Ohme, DeWitt Clinton High School, New York. 2. W. Dreesen, Ehmcke Kreis, Munich. 3 and 5. Students of the Graphic Industries School, Warsaw. 4. Student of the Liverpool City School of Art, Liverpool. 6 and 7. E. Tierney and N. Super, respectively, of the Abraham Lincoln High School, Brooklyn. 9 and 10. W. Taubin, Abraham Lincoln High School, Brooklyn. 8. F. Büttner, Ehmcke Kreis, Munich. 1, 2, and 4 are black and whites, 5 and 8 were originally color drawings, 6, 7, 9, and 10 are linoleum cuts, and 3 was a silhouette clipped from colored papers; varied solutions to similar problems.

DESIGN

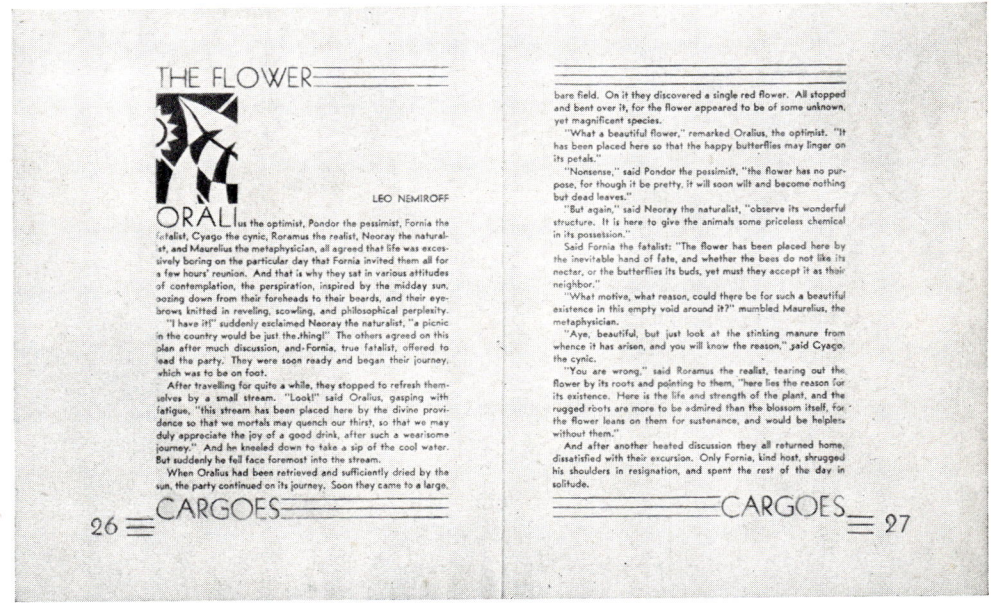

IMPORTANT PROBLEMS of a successful graphic arts course. ABOVE: Magazine cover; because it is the first thing seen, a cover must attract the prospective reader. (*Designed and cut in rubber by Alex Steinweiss, Abraham Lincoln High School, Brooklyn.*) BELOW: Book layout; here, two pages definitely designed as one unit are made attractive by combining type rule with hand-cut initial decoration, by Morris Goldscholle, of the Abraham Lincoln High School, Brooklyn. FACING PAGE. Illustrations. ABOVE, left: Realistic decorative treatment with India ink and pencil on rough paper. (*James Alexander, DeWitt Clinton High School, New York.*) Right: Imaginative, symbolic drawing with lithographic crayon on surfaced board by Abe Marckason and, below, a rhythmic charcoal drawing by James Fisher, both students of the graphic arts course, Abraham Lincoln High School, Brooklyn.

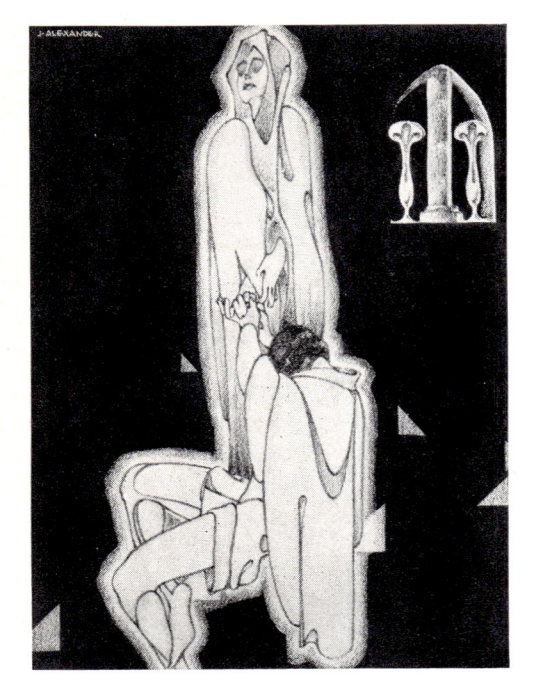

DESIGN 371

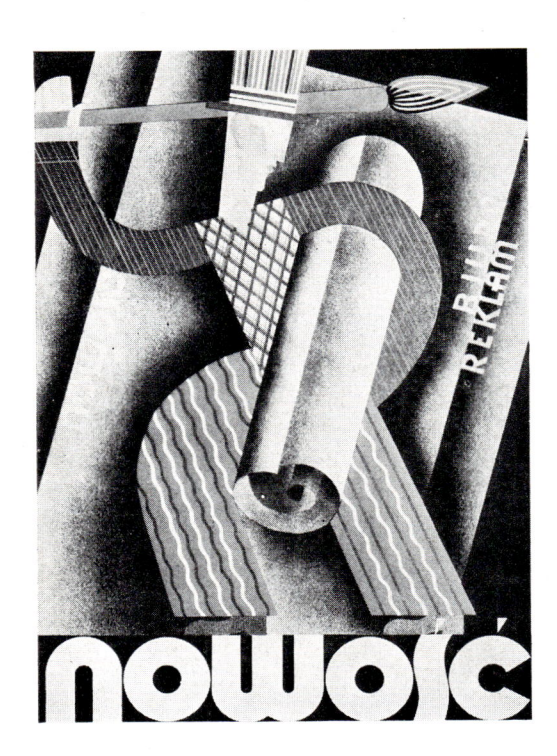

Student designs of professional caliber. For description of these designs by Polish art students see page 373.

LIVELY END PAPER, or wall paper for children's room, designed and printed in six colors by students of the Graphic Industries School, Warsaw. BELOW: End paper in black on India stock designed by an English student. (*Courtesy of Leicester College of Arts and Crafts, Leicester.*)

FACING PAGE. ABOVE, left: Poster by J. Batycki that might serve as a medium for publicizing a school activity. Right: A modern poster-esque interior by E. Manteufel containing all the elements of a moving design. BELOW: A box top originally composed in the vivid colors that are associated with peasant art. (*All three designed and printed in the Graphic Industries School of Warsaw.*)

PROOFREADER'S MARKS

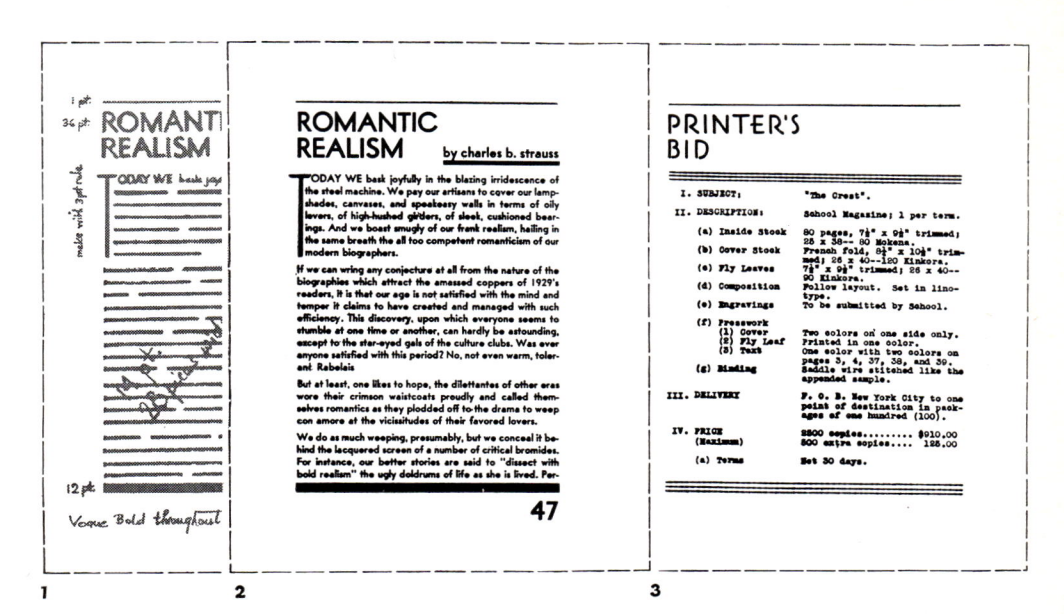

∧	insert here correction indicated in margin	¶	paragraph; with "no", no paragraph	stet	let it stand; retain
✕	defective letter	⊙	insert period	out s.c.	see copy for omission
///	straighten lines	⁀,	" comma	tr.	transpose words or letters
∨	correct spacing	⁀:	" colon	℞ or l.c.	lower case
※	insert space	⁀;	" semicolon	caps	put in capitals
⌣	less space	⁀'	" apostrophe	s.c.	small caps
⌒	no space; close	" "/" "	" quotation marks	ital.	italics
⊥	push down space	/?/	" question mark	rom.	change to Roman letter
[or]	move word or letter to left or right etc.	(!)	" exclamation mark	w.f.	wrong font
⌐ or ⌙	elevate or lower word or character	/=/	" hyphen	Qu.	query (to author)
◌́	indent 1 Em-quad space	a/2/ or	" superior letter or figure	cap	EXAMPLE
ꝯ	turn reversed letter	/a/2/ or	" inferior letter or figure	⌒	In actual practice mistakes are under⌒scored in the proof and indicated with appropriate symbol in⌒the margin. The use of a ~~colored~~ pencil helps the compositor to⌒ locate errors with economy of time⌒and effort.
⌀	take out; delete	(/)	" parentheses	✓⊙ stet	
∼	under letter or word it means "bold face"	[/]	" brackets	⊥	
O	spell out	1/m or 2/m	1 em or 2 em dash		

For explanation of both the printer's bid and the proofreader's marks see legend on bottom of facing page.

374 GRAPHIC

DEVICE FOR JUDGING POSTERS

Grade each item horizontally in order of preference: 1 for best, 2 for second best, 3 for next best, etc. Allow as many points and use as many vertical columns as there are posters (five in this example).

The lowest score is best; inversely, the poorest poster has the highest total. The lowest total score possible for a poster that is rated first best (1) in each of seven items is 7.

	A	B	C	D	E
In the ideal Poster (1) DECORATION is combined with (2) LETTERING to produce a unified (3) DESIGN that will give (4) INFORMATION. It is so (5) COLORFUL and MOVING that it demands your attention. It is so (6) SIMPLE and BRIEF that "he who runs may read." (7) POINT OF VIEW and SLOGAN are respectively so arresting and appealing that the message lingers and leads the observer to favorable action or good will.	( ) ( ) ( ) ( ) ( ) ( ) ( )	( ) ( ) ( ) ( ) ( ) ( ) ( )	( ) ( ) ( ) ( ) ( ) ( ) ( )	( ) ( ) ( ) ( ) ( ) ( ) ( )	( ) ( ) ( ) ( ) ( ) ( ) ( )
TOTAL	( )	( )	( )	( )	( )

FACING PAGE: THE BID. To be complete, it ought to include the students' layout, the printer's interpretation, and a cost estimate based on definite considerations, together with a dummy to show actual size and stock. By using tracing paper or carbons, the layout may be duplicated for two or three competing printers. BELOW: Proofreader's marks ought to be familiar to the graphic arts student. They save volumes of words and much trouble.

THE COURSE OF STUDY

*Aim**

1. To give an opportunity for creative expression to talented students.
2. To raise the standards of appreciation of the general student body by exposing the students to the creative work of their contemporaries.
3. To make art problems real, vital, and purposeful.
4. To develop greater appreciation of the printing arts.
5. To integrate more closely the related arts which together make possible a fine publication.
6. To provide the knowledge, tools, and skills necessary to create a worthwhile publication.

Scope

The course in *art in publications* should offer those opportunities that are essential to familiarize students with the fine examples of the printing arts. More specifically, it should acquaint the students with the history of printing and with style, paper, type, layout, printing, color, reproductive processes, binding, decoration, proof marks, production costs; with illustration and with the tradition of the craft and with all those devices that collectively help to launch the publication.

Prerequisites

Evidences of superior ability as shown by students' art work and the completion of one year of art training are recommended.

Time

Five periods, of 45 minutes each or, where possible, three double periods per week for one year are desirable in a high school, although for professional preparation three or four years may be a minimum requirement.

Research Work

Notebook records of visits and of work done that show the student's reactions should supplement the plates made during the term of study.

---

* These are the recommendations of a committee appointed by Forest Grant, Director of Art of New York City, of which Leon Friend, chairman, was assisted by Catherine Griffin and Eunice Roeszler.

FACING PAGE: ABOVE: Young men and women gaining that appreciation for type and type relationship that is impossible with theory alone. (*State School of Applied Arts, Berlin.*) BELOW, left: Young lady experimenting with paste pot and color for an end-paper design. (*State School of Applied Arts, Munich.*) Right: The camera, used with skill and good taste, is a valuable device for student creative expression. (*Courtesy of Reimann School, Berlin.*)

Three activities that contribute variety and realism to a graphic arts course. Description in legend on facing page.

PROBLEMS FOR COURSE IN ART IN PUBLICATIONS. THE SEQUENCE OF THE PROBLEMS WOULD, OF COURSE, BE INFLUENCED BY THE NEEDS OF THE SCHOOL

Discussion topics	*Creative problems*	*Collateral research*
Printing arts: their contribution to business, learning, and improved living conditions. Compare with "fine arts." Any difference? See text on page 261	Make layouts for two facing pages by cutting and rearranging magazine material. Take special note of "type mass" and the particular appeals of the magazine that is being studied	Compare the *Saturday Evening Post* with the *Ladies Home Journal*, *Vogue*, etc. Consider price, appeal, format, outstanding features, and personal reaction
Typography: 1. Movable type; its invention and its influence on lettering; on life.	Trace a large (48-point) sans-serif type; cut up and arrange letters to form a short paragraph showing fine space relationships	Look up contribution of Gutenberg in any good encyclopedia. Compare with old illuminated manuscripts
2. Essentials of a good readable book type. Explain "pt." system and its importance, artistically and economically, in making layouts	A. Develop a simple alphabet, the letters of which (*a*) are legible, (*b*) go well together, (*c*) are uniform in tone, (*d*) are fine in proportion. B. Design a layout for a title page making provision for the use of three different type sizes	Study the influence of the tool in lettering: Trajan Column; hieroglyphics; manuscript writing; steel-pen lettering; etc. Collect examples of advertisements showing fine use of type and good layout
3. Jiggers; their use with type to break monotony of straight type matter, to form interesting and unique compositions (e.g., type-founders' jiggers, paragraph markers, type rule, initial letters, end pieces, etc.)	A. Combine simple geometric jiggers to create new forms suitable for border designs or end pieces B. Design an invitation for a meeting of the Parent Teachers Association, combining jiggers with type	Collect examples of modern advertising to show the use of typographic jiggers Bring to class various forms of printed invitations for comparison and discussion

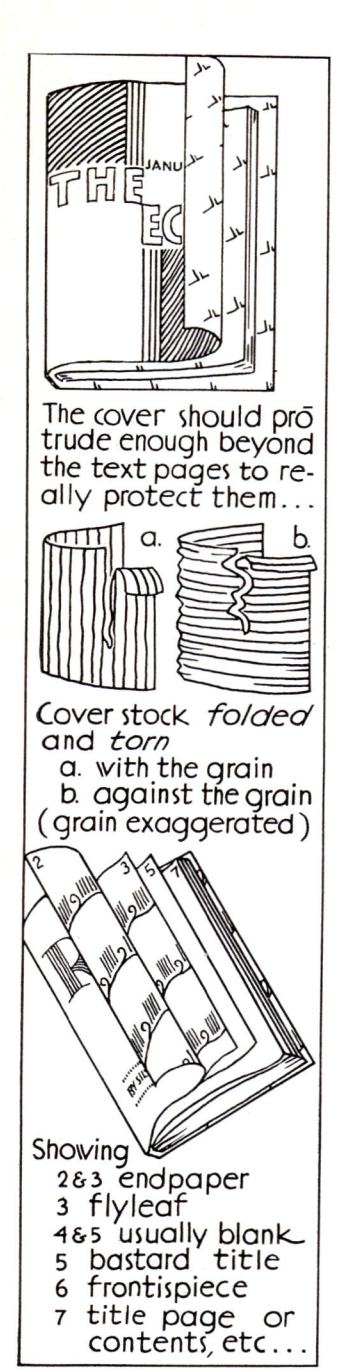

The cover should protrude enough beyond the text pages to really protect them...

Cover stock *folded* and *torn*
 a. with the grain
 b. against the grain
 (grain exaggerated)

Showing
 2 & 3 endpaper
 3 flyleaf
 4 & 5 usually blank
 5 bastard title
 6 frontispiece
 7 title page or contents, etc...

Design of fly-leaf and of end-paper should be continuous. Note combination binding (glued and side-stitch)

Pages are planned as seen—*two at a time*. Page numbers (folio) are placed where they balance each other and are easily found. They should reecho the text-matter in style and in size.

35"x45" paper cuts to two 16 page signatures, each 8½" x 11" *trimmed* minus waste. One such sheet makes a 32 page booklet..

fig.'A' en coated fig.'B' en antique

Additional pressure necessary for uniform printing on rough paper ('B') makes type,'B', darker. This explains why small type prints clearer on coated than on rough paper. On coated stock a 'kiss' impression is sufficient for printing.

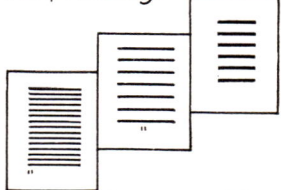

Tone of type-matter depends, too, on
 1. size and family of type used...
 2. weight; light, medium or bold...
 3. space between lines............
 4. background margins and solidity of text area...

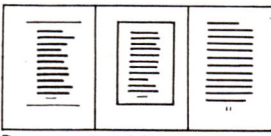

Poetry (and irregularily set material) appears best on a left page or in type border. To maintain rectangle of text, avoid short lines on top or on bottom.

THE MOST POPULAR vehicle for student expression in the graphic arts is the school magazine. These graphic statements illustrate some principles of design and magazine construction that some students know but few magazines objectify. They are worth careful study. Excursions to print shop, engraving plant, and paper house will help.

DESIGN 379

Discussion topics	Creative problems	Collateral research
Reproductive processes: their influence on design: 1. Linoleum (direct and artistic method of duplication)	Design a space filler (for a magazine) in black and white suitable for cutting in linoleum or in composition plate	Look up and distinguish between wood engravings and woodcuts. Study the work of Dürer, Holbein, Blake, Cole, and contemporary artists
2. Line cut (photomechanical method of duplication)	Design a decorative unit in three values, using pen and ink	Visit a photoengraving plant. Collect specimens of fine pen and ink drawings to show the different styles
3. Halftone: lecture by a teacher or a specialist to show its possibilities and its limitations	Take a picture with a camera to show good composition and unusual viewpoint	Cull examples of fine photography: also specimens of trick photography, as photomontage, unusual perspective or lighting effects, composites, etc.
4. Lithography: its use in commercial and fine arts	Using a lithographic crayon on textured paper, design a full-page decoration for a poem. Allow space for mortising the "cut" for the insertion of the type. (Show the possibilities of a reverse plate)	Bring examples of lithography to class for discussion. Report on the lithographic work of Honoré Daumier
5. "Trick techniques." Show how patterned effects can be obtained economically (Ben Day or patterned sheets, surfaced boards, scratch boards, airbrush, dry brush, bleach print, etc.	Design a broadside for a school activity, using fantastic or humorous figures	Show effective use of trick techniques as found in the reproductions of the work of contemporary artists
6. Review techniques	Draw a frontispiece appropriate for the school magazine	Try to associate outstanding artists with the various techniques studied thus far

Discussion topics	Creative problems	Collateral research
Decoration: 1. Illustration: by discussion of outstanding examples, show how different artists have solved problems in composition	Illustrate a story submitted to your magazine. Impart to your design the spirit conveyed by the story	Report on a contemporary illustrator, whose work you admire. Make rapid sketches of unusual designs
2. Imprint or trade-mark: explain its purpose. Discuss color register, separation, superimposition, and influence of background (colored paper stock). Review basic color principles	Design an imprint or trademark for your magazine, to be printed in two colors. (If time permits, students may cut these two blocks themselves, using gelatin or celluloid sheet or offset method for getting color register	Collect and mount or trace fine ancient imprints and interesting modern trade-marks
3. Book jacket: its advertising and protective functions; its relative ease of printing when compared with printing on linen	Design a book jacket using geometric forms. Show how three colors are obtained by superimposing or overlapping two "cuts"	Get book jackets from your neighborhood library or bookstore and arrange an exhibition of the best. Look up the three color process
4. Cover: compare treatment with that of bookjacket and with the covers in other school magazines, house organs, and brochures	Design a cover that is attractive and that has advertising value whichever way the magazine is held	Find and make colored thumbnail sketches of two effective magazine covers
Printing: 1. Paper: serviceability and role of color, texture, weight, deckle edge, and machine cut. Dependence of page proportion on standard sizes of paper	Make a miniature dummy to scale, using a related color harmony. Consider contrast with type	Report on "Paper": the many varieties available and the uses to which they are best suited

DESIGN

Discussion topics	Creative problems	Collateral research
2. Presswork: prerequisites for best results; care of block inking, preparation of paper, "make-ready," pulling of proof, etc.	Experiment with the printing of "cuts" made during the term. (Select two best students to be the liaison workers with the printer of the school magazine)	Visit printshop to observe "stonework" and presswork especially
3. Bookbinding old and new: the purposes and advantages of different kinds. (Side stitch, saddle stitch, sewed and spiral; rounded and squared back)	Organize and bind the term's work (one's own and other students' prints) in a book, folder, or portfolio	Report on term's work, with recommendations for improvement; self-analysis and comparison
4. Costs: consideration of local conditions, timeliness of publication, and allowances for advertisements	Formulation of specifications to be submitted to printers	Get reactions of schoolmates to the magazine
Advertising: poster; discuss a campaign to further the sales of the school magazine	Design a poster that singly or in follow-up fashion will help sell the publication, or use prints of the cover as a poster	Look up business procedure in similar activities

Recommended Minimum Equipment

Portable proof press (the kind used in printshops are better than those made especially for classroom use); some characters of actual type, a full family if possible, and four or five slugs of linotype for demonstration purposes; two brayers (rollers)—use one exclusively for black and one for colors; printing ink (job black and colors); fireproof gasoline container; marble slab (or beveled plate glass); palette knives; assorted carving tools and sharpening stones; fireproof box or cupboard for storing apparatus (wooden box lined with galvanized tin); fireproof waste container. FACING PAGE: A litho pencil on surfaced board achieves a highlight halftone effect with an ordinary line plate. (*Edith Goldkind, student of Abraham Lincoln High School, Brooklyn, N. Y.*)

OTHER PROBLEMS: (1) *Mailing wrapper for magazine;* (2) *proof marks;* (3) *card for installment payments;* (4) *etching processes;* (5) *contour drawing;* (6) *letterhead for publication's use;* (7) *problems in graphic design that are occasioned by the school's needs.*

DESIGN 383

GLOSSARY OF TERMS

The initials after each word denote its graphic art category as represented by the chapters in this book. L—Lettering; PR—Printing; RA—Reproductive Arts; PH—Photography; BK—The Book; AA—Advertising Art; PO—Poster; E—Education. No initials are set for words of general application.

ABRASION, PH. A term applied to the markings marring the surface of photographic paper, caused by breaking, friction, or splitting in the coat of emulsion.

ACTINIC RAYS, PH. The violet rays of the spectrum; also called chemical rays; more active photographically than visually.

ADMAN, PR. Printer who composes advertisements.

AGATE, PR. 5½-point body type.

AIR BELLS, PH. Bubbles originating on the coated side of a photographic print through careless handling of the print in its developing.

AIRBRUSH, PH, AA. An apparatus for applying a fine spray of paint to a surface under pressure from a tank of compressed air or carbonic gas; used creatively and for retouching.

ANASTIGMAT, PH. A lens made of dense barium crown glass and other types of composite glass and produced with a view to eliminating astigmatism and correcting other lens defects. The anastigmic image is almost as flat as the plate image.

ANTIQUE, BK. Rough-surfaced paper.

APERTURE, PH. The width of the opening in the front side of a camera, through which light enters.

APLANATIC LENS, PH. Combination of lenses to produce a sharp image with a large working aperture by counteracting the spherical aberration of light.

APOCHROMATIC LENS, PH. A lens so adjusted that it brings three different points of the solar spectrum to a common focus. Used for three-color photography.

AQUARELLE, RA. Water-color painting made with tints of transparent color.

AQUATINT, RA. Method of biting tones instead of lines into a plate that has previously been prepared with powdered resin for acid action.

ARMING, BK. The stamping of a coat of arms on a book cover.

ART SERVICE, AA. An organization consisting of artists under the management of a business or contact man who attends to the selling of the output of the artists.

ASCENDERS, L, PR. The parts of lower-case letters that project above the waist or main line, e. g., h, d, f, etc.

ASTERISK, BK. A corrected page, marked by a star and supplied to replace an incorrect one, which then becomes a "cancel."

ASTIGMATISM, PH. A serious optical aberration of the lens, which prevents the lens from rendering a simultaneous sharp focus of lines that run in different directions on a flat surface.

AUTOCHROME, PH. Lumière plate used for making photographs in natural color.

AUTOGRAPHIC CAMERA, PH. A camera with a slide attachment, for writing identifying notes or captions directly on the roll of film in the loaded camera.

BACKING, BK. The forming of a groove to receive the boards of a bookbinding; made with a hammer.

BACKING-UP, PR. The registering of two sides of a printed sheet.

BALANCE. A pleasing disposition of masses. Asymmetric or informal balance refers to optical equality of weights; bisymmetric or formal balance to identical division of masses.

BANDS, BK. The cords upon which a flexible book is sewed; also raised ridges across the backbone of a book.

BAREN, RA. Also called FROTTON. A tool for rubbing the back of paper to obtain an impression from a relief block; usually glass, wood, or metal sheathed in a smooth material.

BASSANI HALFTONE, RA. A high-light halftone effect obtained by a Bassani process camera.

BATH, PH, RA. Solutions of photographic chemicals used to develop, fix, or wash negatives or prints. Also a container of glass or porcelain with acid for etching.

BEARD, PR. The beveled metal surrounding the face of a type.

BEARERS, RA, PR. Strips of metal or wood placed at sides of "cut" when proofing or inking it; also type-high runners on a press for rotating rollers.

BED, PR. Part of press in which printing form is locked.

BEN DAY, RA. Process of breaking up of solid areas into grays of dots, lines, or patterns by ordering the appropriate number from a catalogue; name of inventor.

BENZOL, RA. Coal-tar mixture used to remove ink from etched plate; rubbed over paper, it makes it transparent; evaporates without trace.

BEVEL, RA. Sloping edge obtained by filing edges of zinc or copper; also, machined edge used for mounting plate on wooden base.

BILDSATZ, PR.   German expression for decorative figures or pictorial compositions made with geometric or type forms; also called GEOMETRICS.

BILLBOARD, PO.   Structure for posting posters.

BITE, RA.   Action of acid (mordant) on metal.

BLACK-FACE LETTER (or TYPE), L, PR.   Dark or bold form of German text; also called GOTHIC.

BLACK AND WHITE, AA.   Term applied to designate a wash, tempera, or oil drawing rendered in black, white, and intermediate grays.

BLACK AND WHITE LINE FINISH, RA.   Also called FINISHING LINE. Thin black and white line on the edges of a halftone; obtained mechanically by the engraver.

BLEACH PRINT, RA.   Silver print basis on which bichloride of mercury is used to remove the photographic tones after the necessary pen work has been done.

BLEED, RA.   A picture that has been trimmed to permit it to extend to the extreme edges of the page.

BLIND PRINTING, PR, RA.   Printing from the uninked plate to get enriched textural effect where embossed impression differs from the unstamped part (see also GAUFFRAGE).

BLIND TOOLING, BK.   Tooling of bookbindings with the bare instruments, without gold leaf

BLISTER, BK.   A loose spot on a book cover, where the cover material does not adhere solidly to the boards or the stiffening.

BLOCK, RA.   Wood or metal base for a plate; a "cut."

BLOCKING FLUSH, RA.   Block in which the bevel has been removed to permit close-up with type.

"BLOW-UP" PLATE, RA.   Newspaper halftone like high-light halftone in appearance.

"BOARDS," BK.   Cardboard made of many thicknesses of paper and used as covers.

BODKIN, BK.   A steel point used to perforate boards of a bookbinding so that slips may be drawn through.

BODY, PR.   Size from top to bottom of the face of type.

BOLDFACE, PR.   The dark form of a type family as against its *light* and *medium* forms.

BOLTS, BK.   The closed edges of folder signatures.

BOND, PR.   Tough, thin, translucent rag or sulphite paper.

BOOK PAPER, BK.   Papers suitable for book pages.

BOOK PLATE, BK.   Also "ex libris"; label with the name of the owner for posting on the inside cover or flyleaf of a book.

BOOKLET, AA.   Pamphlet bound in paper covers.

BOOK OF HOURS, BK.   Also "Horae" or "Hours of the Virgin"; popular hand-written and illuminated fifteenth century small books containing the epistles and lessons for the mass.

BORDERS, PR.   Type decoration cast in units or strips and suitable for panels, boxes, etc.

BOSSES, BK.   Protruding metal ornaments attached to the sides of books for protecting the tooled covers from undue friction.

BOX, PR.   Rules used to frame text or illustration.

BRAYER, PR.   Handled roller used to ink a cut.

BREVIARY, BK.   Religious book containing psalms, prayers, or readings from Scripture and the lives of saints.

BRISTOL BOARD.   A fine, tough, flexible, one- or several-ply cardboard used for illustration.

BROADSIDE, AA, PR.   An announcement printed on one side of a sheet of paper.

BROCHURE, AA.   An elaborately bound pamphlet.

BRONZING, PR.   Brushing metallic powder onto newly printed matter to which it adheres, usually over a base.

BUFFING, BK.   Roughening leather with emery paper or other polishing material preparatory to bookbinding.

BUILT-UP LETTER, L.   Letters first drawn in outline and then filled in.

BULK, BK.   The thickness of a bound book or of the cover material.

BURIN, RA.   Also GRAVER, tool used by the engraver to remove metal.

BURNISHER, RA.   Highly polished oval-shaped steel tool with tapering point; used to "erase" or lower etched or engraved parts of plate.

BURNISHING, BK.   Glazing of a cover edge with agate and bloodstone burnishers.

RA.   Process of polishing a plate with whiting or charcoal preparatory to etching it; also, the burnishing tool used to rub down dots in halftone work.

BURR, RA.   Metal turned up by needle in dry-point "etching"; also in routing of photomechanical plate.

CALENDERED PAPER, BK.   Paper with smooth rolled surface, obtained by passing through a set of chilled metal rolls which fuse the surface fibers into a smooth texture.

CALLIGRAMS, L.   Letters of a word arranged to form a symbol.

CALLIGRAPHY, L.   Art of writing; the parent of printing.

CAMEO PAPER, BK.   A coated paper of a dull smooth finish for obtaining soft effects in printing.

CAMERA LUCIDA, AA, RA.   Projecting machine used to enlarge or reduce drawings.

CANCELED PLATE, RA.   Plate with face scratched with large cross lines to prevent further printing.

DESIGN 385

CANDID CAMERA, PH.   Unposed photographs made with modern rapid-action camera.

CANVAS SCREEN, RA.   Screen that suggests the texture of a canvas; used in halftone reproduction instead of the usual mechanical screen.

CAPTION, AA, PR.   Legend or title.

CASE, PR.   Partitioned tray containing a complete assortment of capitals, lower-case letters, numbers, and special characters.

CASE BINDINGS, BK.   Covers which are made independently and which are then joined to the rest of the book by the use of end papers as linings.

CASED BOOK, BK.   Book made independently of the cover and then inserted into the case by pasting down the end papers; also "casing."

CASEIN, BK.   Albuminous substance for sizing paper.

CATCH LETTERS, BK.   Letters denoting the first and last words in the pages of a reference book.

CATOLICON, PR.   Gutenberg's last (?) work (1560), showing a departure from his usual blackface type and a tendency toward the round open forms of the Roman characters, especially in the caps.

CHALK, RA.   Magnesium carbonate rubbed over halftone cut to show tone contrasts of the plate.

CHALK OVERLAY, PR.   Mechanically obtained make-ready for type or plate forms.

CHAMPLEVÉ ENAMEL, BK.   Enameling wherein cells are cut into the metal plate to hold the enamel; used in early bookbinding.

CHAP BOOK, AA, BK.   Small pamphlet containing block prints.

CHASE, PR.   Metal frame wherein the type and plates are locked preparatory to printing.

CHEMICAL RAYS, PH.   Violet actinic rays.

CHEWED, RA.   Ragged lines in a cut due to underbiting in a poorly protected plate.

CHROMA.   Degree of intensity or brightness of a color from black to white.

CHROMOLITHOGRAPHY, RA.   Also "chromo"; lithography in colors.

CIRCULARS, AA.   Letters, handbills, or broadsides used in advertising.

CLAY-FINISH PAPER, BK.   Paper whose surface has been smoothened by addition of fine clay.

CLIPPED IMPRESSION, RA.   Print with plate mark removed, "clipped" away.

CLOISONNÉ ENAMEL, BK.   Process of enameling whereby a gold strip is soldered to a metal base to form a cell for holding colored enamel in early bookbindings.

COATED PAPER, BK.   Paper coated with finely ground clay mixed with glue or casein; usually shiny or plate finish on one or both sides.

CODEX, BK.   Early form of book consisting of thin wax-covered boards hinged with leather thongs and written on with a stylus.

COLLATING, BK.   Binding signatures in sequence.

COLOPHON, BK.   Statement at the end of early books telling something of the printing; now contained in a book's preface.

COLOR ETCHING, RA.   Etching made by separate plates for each color, or use of a single plate with the colors put on it after it has been inked and made ready for printing.

COLOR FILTER, RA.   Colored glass or gelatin used to absorb specific colors that other colors may be photographed separately for color separation.

COLOR FORM, PR.   Type and plate locked together preparatory to printing the second color in a printing job.

COLOR PROOFS, RA.   Printing of the several blocks of a picture to show effect of good register.

Progressive proofs show impressions of the separate plates in correct printing sequence.

COLOR SKETCH, AA.   Rough visualization of a drawing or layout approximating the final reproduction in size and color.

COMBINATION PLATE, RA.   Line plate and halftone effects combined in a single block, usually by stripping one negative on another.

COMPLEMENTARY COLORS, RA.   The colors opposite on the color wheel—yellow and purple, red and green, orange and blue.

COMPOSING STICK, PR.   Metal tray graduated to the point system and used to set type to a given measure.

COMPOSITOR, PR.   One who composes or sets type.

CONDENSED TYPE, PR.   A narrow type face.

COPPER SPACES, PR.   ½-point spaces.

COPPERPLATE ENGRAVING, RA.   Plates with their designs cut intaglio ("subway").

COPY, RA.   The original drawing, painting, photograph, or text that is to be printed.

COPYRIGHT.   Legal form of registration for text and art work to prevent infringement.

COVER PAPERS, PR.   Decorative papers heavy enough to serve as covers.

CREASING, BK.   Impressing blank lines on book covers and backbone with a heated tool; also bending paper that they will lie flat.

CRIBLE, RA, BK.   Prints from blocks with designs obtained by drilling or punching holes.

CROP, RA.   Process of trimming or cutting the edges of a plate.

CROSSHATCH, RA. Parallel lines drawn to cross other parallel lines to obtain transparent grays.

CROWN, PH. Variety of glass used to make ray-collecting lenses.

CRUSHING, BK. Pressing down the rough grain of leather for bookbinding to obtain a smoothly grained appearance.

CUNEIFORM, L. Wedge-shaped writing used in Babylonia and Assyria.

CURSIVES, L, PR. Joined letters with rounded angles —like uncial letters.

CURVATURE OF FIELD, PH. Defect due to the forming of a photo-image on the convex surface of a lens at first and then its recording on the flat surface of a plate; thus the focus cannot be sharp all over the flat plate, especially deviating toward the edges.

CURVILINEAR DISTORTION, PH. Defect caused in photographing straight lines through a single lens; by the deviation of the rays toward the curved surface of the lens, straight lines may be bent cushion-shaped.

CUT, RA. Photoengraving plate or woodcut.

CYLINDER PRESS, PR. Machine that prints by the action of a cylinder on a flat form.

CYLINDER PROOF PRESS, PR. The stationary-bed cylinder proof press is a device for obtaining proofs in which the cylinder, *not the bed*, moves.

Cylinder press with moving bed: hand-levered press in which the bed alone moves.

D.O.P., PH. Abbreviation for "developing-out paper," designating a variety of photographic paper that does not show the printed image until the print is developed.

DABBER, RA. Pad for spreading the ground on a plate; usually a piece of white kid (from an old glove) with horsehair and cotton-wool filler, covered with worsted, it is used to ink intaglio blocks.

DAMPING, RA, PR. Moistening paper to remove stiffness to make it more susceptible to impression.

DEADLINE, AA, PR. Final date for receipt of copy for printing.

DEAD METAL, RA. Part of plate to be routed away.

DEAD TYPE, PR. Type that is "killed" or found to be in excess of available space.

DECKLE EDGE, BK. Thinned and frayed edge of a hand- or mold-made paper.

DEEP ETCH, RA. Extra bite of open areas of a halftone or line cut to permit printing on fairly rough paper.

DENSITY, PH. Term describing the degree of solidity in the dark parts of a negative.

DENTELLE, BK. Tooling consisting of a border of finely outlined scrolls or spriggs.

DEPTH OF FOCUS, PH. Capacity of a lens to give a sharp image of near and distant objects.

DESCENDERS, L, PR. Parts of the lower-case letters that descend below the main or waist line, e.g., g, j, p.

DEVIL, PR. Usually youngest helper in a print shop.

DIAPER, L. All-over pattern obtained by crossing diagonal lines at regular intervals.

DICING, BK. Ornamental blind lines crossing each other at right angles.

DIE STAMPING. Use of die and counter die (male and female) in printing.

DIFFRACTION, PH. Bending of rays of light away from their course by an external influence.

DIFFUSED LIGHT, PH. Light rays that are arrested in their direct course from source to object and diverted or subdued; a thin sheet of white cloth or ground glass is the most common diffusing medium.

DIMENSION MARKS, RA. Measurement of plate indicated on the copy by arrows outside the picture.

DIPTYCHS, BK. Wooden tablets hinged together by metal or leather thongs—stepping stones in the development of the book.

DIRECT HALFTONE, RA. Halftone made without the picture by direct photography of the article.

DISK, PR. Circular plate on platen press for ink.

DISPLAY TYPE, PR. Large type used for emphasis.

DISPLAYS, AA. Advertising items, such as plastic figures, small posters, mechanical eye catchers, etc., used to attract attention of passers-by.

DISTRIBUTION, PR. Return of type to the cases.

DIVINITY CIRCUIT, BK. Leather bindings with wide overhanging flexible edges that meet if pressed down over the edges of books.

DOUBLE ANASTIGMAT, PH. A system of three cemented lenses, the middle one of which possesses a refractive index that lies between the indices of the two outer lenses.

DOUBLE EXPOSURE, PH. Photographic method of recording two supplementing pictures on the same plate to obtain a symbolic effect. Several exposures may be so recorded on one plate by multi-exposure.

DOUBLE TRUCK, AA, PR. Term designating a body of copy and illustration that spreads across two facing pages of a publication.

DOUBLET, PH. A combination of two supplementing lenses which may be detached and used separately.

DOUBLURE, BK. Lining of a book cover; leather joint of a book.

DRAGON'S BLOOD, RA. Resinous substance powdered on a plate to protect the shoulders of the bitten line form "undercutting" during the successive etchings.

DESIGN

DRIER, PR. Substance added to ink to help drying.

DROP OUT, RA. Etching away or "dropping out" of the high lights of a halftone; also "high-light" halftone when dots of high lights have been eliminated.

DRY BRUSH, RA, AA. Brush only slightly inked and used to draw tone effects for line reproduction.

DRY POINT (POINTE-SÊCHE), RA. Design cut into metal without aid of acid but with sharp instrument like a steel point, diamond, or ruby which raises a burr in the cutting; also print from such a plate.

DULL-FINISH PAPER, BK. Glossless coated paper.

DULL PRINT, PH. Eggshell-surfaced photographic print adaptable to coloring or retouching of large areas.

DUMMY, BK. Plan of a prospective book which forecasts the appearance of the final job.

ELECTROTYPE, RA. Duplicate of a woodcut or photoengraving obtained by electrolytic deposit of copper or nickel on a mold taken from the original block; used to obtain duplicate plates.

EM, PR. The square of the body of any size type; 10 points wide for 10-point type, 18 points wide for 18-point type, etc.

EMBOSSING, PR, RA. Raised printing obtained by means of a plate in which the image is engraved or etched below the surface; see also BLIND TOOLING.

EMULSION, PH. Film of light-sensitive substance on plates or papers used in photography.

EN, PR. One-half em in width.

ENAMELED PAPER, BK. Paper made glossy by coating of clay or other filler.

ENGRAVING, RA. Process of cutting or incising a line into metal or wood.

ETCHING, RA. Refers (1) to process of incising a line in metal by an acid, (2) to the plate obtained photomechanically, and (3) to a proof from an artist's etched copper or zinc plate.

EXPANDED TYPE, PR. Opposite of condensed type.

EXPOSURE, PH. The length of time during which photographic plates or papers are subjected to the action of light.

EYE CATCHER, AA. Also "eye opener"; portion of advertisement more prominently displayed than other components and designed to attract the onlooker's glance instantaneously.

FACE, PR. The top part of a type piece that gives it its style and distinction.

FAIR CALF, BK. Undyed calf leather of a light cream color.

FAMILY, PR. Type faces that make a related group.

FANOUT, PR. Rubbing a pile of paper fanshape to separate the sheets.

FERROTYPE, PH. Enameled metal plate that gives a photographic print a high surface gloss if the print is dried with its sensitized side in contact with the ferrotype plate.

FILTER, PH. An attachment of tinted glass set up on the lens of a camera to subdue the strong action of blue and violet rays and to equalize the effect of the other spectral colors during an exposure. A filter considerably prolongs exposure time.

FINISHER, RA. Also engraver; one who hard-tools, burnishes, or retouches photoengraving plate to remove defects or to bring out high lights.

FIXING, PH. Removal of unaffected silver salts from photographic negatives or positives with the help of a hypo solution.

FLARE, PH. Rim of light around the outlines of bright areas which the ordinary meniscus lens cannot eliminate without a yellow filter.

FLASHLIGHT, PH. Artificial momentary illumination obtained by the violet combustion of a magnesium compound producing a powerful actinic light.

FLAT BITING, RA. Plate exposed to single biting and drawn on with thick and thin needles for gradated lines.

FLAT TONES, AA. Areas of uniform color showing no transitional shadings or gradations.

FLEXIBLE BINDING, BK. Book sewn on raised cords with the thread passing around each cord; binding that is not stiff.

FLINT, PH. Variety of glass used to make ray-dispersing lenses.

FLUSH, PR, RA. To set two items close together—"flush."

FLYLEAF, BK. First or last free leaf next to the cover in every book.

FOCUS, PH. Point on the axis of a lens at which rays of light meet after passing through it.

FOG, PH. Cloud of silver particles deposited on a developed negative, obscuring also parts that should not have been affected by light.

FOLIO, BK. Sheet of paper folded once (giving four pages); also page number in a book.

FONT, PR. Full assortment of type of one size and face, e.g., 12-point Goudy, 14-point Bodoni, etc.

FORE-EDGE, BK. Front edge of the leaf of a book, in the past frequently decorated—gauffered.

FOUDRINIER MACHINE, BK. Invention of the Brothers Foudrinier; machine which makes a majority of modern papers.

FOUL BITING, RA. Etching of a plate in undesired places due to poorly laid ground, air bubbles, etc.

FOXED, BK. Book spotted with brown patches due to chemical impurities in the paper.

FRAKTUR, L. Angular form of Gothic letter as against rounded form (rotunda).

FRISKET. Protecting cover or mask of paper pasted down with rubber cement for airbrush work.

FRONTISPIECE, BK. Illustration facing title page.

FURBISHING, BK. Cleaning and repairing of shopworn or soiled books.

FURNITURE, PR. Wood or metal forms less than type-high used to fill large blank spaces in chase not occupied by printing matter.

GALLEY, PR. Shallow tray used to assemble or store away type and plates.

GALLEY PRESS, PR. Machine for making proofs.

GALLEY PROOF, PR. Proof of type matter that is still in the galley and so is easily corrected.

GATHERING, BK. Arranging a complete set of signatures or leaves in proper sequence for binding.

GAUFFERED, BK. Or GOFFERED; blind decoration hammered or tooled into the edge of books; also fore-edge decoration.

GAUFFRAGE, RA. Blind printing, used in connection with Japanese blocks.

GAUGE, PR. Metal device used to hold sheets in proper position on the press.

GEOMETRICS, PR. Expression for decorative figures or pictorial compositions made with geometric or type forms; also BILDSATZ.

GLAIRE, L, BK. White of egg beaten up, strained off, and used as an adhesive for gold leaf in place of gelatin.

GLOSSY PRINT, PH. Shiny-surfaced photographic print usually preferred for halftone reproduction.

GOTHIC, L, PR. Uniform-stroke letters or type without serifs: also SANS SERIF.

GOUACHE. Painting with opaque colors that have been ground in water and mixed with a gummy substance.

GRAIN, PR. Direction of the long fibers in a sheet of paper.

GRAIN BOX, RA. Box containing resin which is agitated to distribute a film of resin dust on a plate for aquatint etching.

GRAVER, RA. Cone- or diamond-shaped tool for engraving on plate.

GRIPPERS, PR. Metal prongs on a platen press that hold the sheets to the platen.

GROOVE, PR, BK. In binding: rounded and indented part of book on either side of spine where the boards are attached. In type: the space between the feet of a type.

GROUND, RA. Acid resist; wax, resin, asphaltum.

GROUNDING, RA. Process of applying acid resist to cleaned metal plate.

GUIDE, RA, PR. Color sketch to show inks; also pieces of metal on the tympan against which paper is fed in printing.

GUTTER, BK. Margin of pages nearest the binding.

HAIR SPACES, PR. Thinnest strips used in spacing out type.

HAIRLINE, PR, RA. Extremely light lines in an engraving; also thin rule in printing.

HALATION, PH. Bright blurred outline showing on a negative where strongly lighted portions of the object are recorded.

HALF-BOUND, BK. Book bound with leather back and corners.

HALF TITLE, BK. Title at the head of the first chapter in a book.

HALFTONE, RA. Process for reproducing tonal images obtained by photographing copy through a screen.

HAND PRESS, PR. Vertical moving press manipulated by hand for obtaining impressions, e.g., Washington Press.

HANDBILLS, AA. Advertisements distributed to the public by hand.

HARMONY. Pleasing relation of kindred elements of a composition.

HEAD, AA, BK. Title of newspaper matter; top of a book.

HIGH LIGHT. The lightest part of a picture; concentrated reflection of light on a shiny surface.

HISTORIATED INITIAL, L. Ornamentation of initial with illustrative rather than with abstract decoration.

HOARDING, PO. British equivalent of BILLBOARD.

HOT EMBOSSING, PR, RA. Embossing obtained by using hot dies.

HOUSE ORGAN, AA. Periodical publication issued by a commercial concern for circulation among its own employees, customers, or clients.

HYPO, PH. Popular abbreviation for sodium hyposulphite, used for fixing photographic plates and prints.

ILLUMINATION, BK. Leaf or liquid gold, silver, and bright colors applied in decoration of manuscript books.

IMPOSITION, PR. Lockup of page forms in a chase.

IMPRINT, BK. Name of printer or publisher.

DESIGN 389

INCISED LETTERS, L. Letters cut into a die and stamped upon a surface to obtain a raised impression.
INCUNABULA, PR, BK. Books printed before 1500.
INDIRECT HALFTONE, RA. Line plate made from the enlarged and retouched proof of a coarse halftone.
INFRA RED RAYS, PH. Ordinarily invisible component rays of sunlight, which have heat value but no effect in photography.
INLAY, BK. An onlay that has been glued down in a specially blanked area of a book cover.
INSERTS, BK. Plates that require separate treatment, usually pasting, for incorporation in a book.
INSIDE SPREAD, AA. Printed matter occupying both center pages of a publication.
INSTITUTIONAL, AA. Form of advertising that aims at popularizing an entire industry, institution, or branch of commerce, without emphasizing any individual firm.
INTAGLIO, RA. Plate or printing from sunken line.
INTERTYPE, PR. A form of composing machine.
IRIS DIA PHRAGM, PH. Adjustable opening behind a camera lens controlling the diameter of stops.
ITALICS, L, PR. Script-like letters or **type.**

JOB PRINTER, PR. One who prints small commercial matter.
JOG, PR. Shaking of paper to straighten sheets.
JOURNEYMAN. Graduated apprentice.
JUSTIFICATION, PR. The process of spacing out type to a given measure that lines may be uniform in length.

KERN, PR. That part of a type that is prolonged beyond the body.
KETTLE STITCH, BK. Stitch used in hand sewing of books, whereby each signature is firmly affixed to the next one at head and tail.
KEY PLATE, PR, RA. First printed plate of a series (because it contains most detail), used as a guide for color register.
KIOSK, PO, AA. Characteristic European round or square structure erected on sidewalks and squares and used for the posting of bills and posters.

LABEL, AA. Small slip of paper imprinted with the name, manufacturer, and brief description of the commercial product and attached to the latter's container.
LAID PAPER, BK. Paper with parallel watermarked lines.
LAMINATED BOARD, BK. Board built up of several layers glued together with alternating placing of grains.
LANTERN SLIDE, PH. Image printed from a negative on a glass plate coated with a finely grained emulsion, for projection on a screen.

LAPIDAR LETTERING, L. Chiseled in stone and setting up letter after letter, independently.
LARGE-APERTURE LENSES, PH. Lenses of $f/3.5$, $f/2$, etc., constructed for sport, newspaper, and cinematic work, and for poor light conditions and short exposures.
LAYOUT. Plan of an advertisement, a set of book pages, or of any design.
LEADERS, PR. Dotted line used to lead the reader's eye from word to word in tabular matter.
LEADING, PR. Insertion of metal strips of required width between lines of type.
LEADS, PR. Strips of metal for separating type lines.
LEAFLET, BK. Pamphlet of from 4 to 16 pages.
LEGEND, BK. Caption explaining illustrations.
LENS, PH. Circular polished optical glass, single or in multiple combinations.
LETTERHEAD, AA. Printed caption on a sheet of letter paper with name, business, and address of sender.
LIBRARY BINDING, BK. Book bound according to the specifications of the American Library Association.
LIGATURE, PR. Two or three characters combined on a single type body, e.g., ff, æ, ffi, ffl, etc.
LIGHT FACE, PR. Lightest and thinnest form of a type series; opposite of bold face.
LIMIT PAGE, BK. Book page following the bastard title and showing the quantity of the edition or serial number of the book or the set.
LIMP BINDING, BK. Flexible cover and back consisting of binding material without stiffening.
LINE ENGRAVING, RA. Simplest of the photoengraving blocks without the tonal possibilities of the halftone.
LINOTYPE, PR. Line of type set by a machine manipulated in typewriter fashion; also name of machine.
LITFASS-SÄULE, PO. German equivalent for KIOSK.
LITHOGRAPH, RA. Planographic print made from a stone or metal plate.
LIVE TYPE, PR. Printing matter still in use.
LOCK STITCH, BK. Binding stitch in which the thread is knotted after each stitch so it cannot unravel.
LOCKUP, PR. Type matter and plates locked together in a frame preparatory to printing.
LOGOTYPE, AA. Lettered signature of a commercial firm; single type containing a syllable or word, as "and," "the," etc.
LOOSE LEAF, BK. Binding by means of rings or other detachable fasteners.
LOWER CASE or L. C., PR. Small letters usually found in the lower part of the type case.

LUDLOW TYPOGRAPHY, PR. Slug-casting machine in which matrices are hand set.

LUMIÈRE AUTOCHROME, RA, PH. Photographic plate used for direct-color photography and named after the inventors, Lumière Frères.

MACHINE COMPOSITION, PR. Type set by machine, not by hand.

MACKLE, PR, BK. Soiled pages of printed matter—smudged, offset, etc.

MAJUSCULE, L. Large capital or uncial letter.

MAKE-READY, PR. Preparation of type, press, and plate forms with overlay or underlay to obtain uniform impression.

MAKING UP, PR. Adjustment of types and cuts into a form.

MARBLING, BK. Decorating the three outer edges of a bound book with patterns obtained by dipping the clamped books into a liquid, the surface of which has been spotted, sprinkled, or combed with water colors.

MARGIN, BK. Unprinted area surrounding printed text or illustrations on a page. Sometimes contains annotations called "marginalia."

MATRIX, RA. Form of papier-mâché into which is stamped an impression of a cut or a body of type, to form a basis for a stereotype; also MAT or MOLD.

MATS, RA. Short for matrices or molds of papier-mâché and composition.

MEASURE, PR. Width of a column of set type.

METAL FOIL, PR, AA. Printing stock made of metal foil of various thicknesses and colors. Used for novel effects.

MEZZOTINT, RA. Print obtained from a rouletted plate that prints in different values of a single color.

MINIATURE, BK. Once a small picture that illustrated a manuscript; now any small picture.

MINUSCULES, L. Small letters, not capitals.

MISE-EN-PAGE. French for "page layout."

MISPRINT, PR. Typographical error.

MODERN TYPE, PR. Type with strong contrast between the light and heavy strokes and with thin, straight, and clean-cut serif, e.g., Bodoni.

MONOCHROME, RA. Single color but it may be of many values.

MONOTINT, RA. Print made from a painting or drawing with black ink on polished copper plate.

MONOTYPE, PR. Machine for casting individual type as against foundry type.

MONTAGE, RA. Process of stripping in a line drawing over a silhouetted halftone.

MORDANT, RA. Perchloride of iron or nitric, sulphuric, or other acid for etching metal.

MOROCCO, BK. Goatskin tanned with sumach and used to cover boards in binding.

MORTISE, RA. Cutting of area in a plate to permit insertion of type or of another plate.

NEGATIVE, RA, PH. Photographically recorded image in which the light and shade values are the reverse of what they appear in reality; also negative plate obtained by printing from a positive giving a reversed color proof.

NEWSPRINT PAPER, PR. Cheapest paper made of ground wood pulp, medium coarse in texture.

NICK, PR. Shallow slit in a type which helps the compositor to avoid mixing similar types.

NEWSTONE, RA. Coarse halftone suitable for printing on newspaper stock.

NONACTINIC RAYS, PH. Light rays that do not change photographic emulsion chemically.

NONPAREIL, PR. 6 points or type of that size.

OBVERSE, BK. Recto, the front of a book; opposite of reverse or verso.

OCTAVO, BK. Sheet folded three times, giving eight leaves, 16 pages. In size often 6 by 9½ inches. Also written 8 vo or 8°.

OFFSET, BK. Smudge originating from the contact of an unprinted page with a freshly printed one.

OFFSET PRINTING, PR. Impression on a rubber blanket made by a plate and then offset on paper.

OLD ENGLISH, L, PR. Heavy block-faced letters.

OLD-STYLE TYPE, PR. Thick-and thin-stroked letter with wedge-shaped serifs which are especially marked in the lower cases.

ONE-WAY HALFTONE, RA. Halftone using screen composed of parallel lines.

ONION SKIN. Thin, shiny, transparent paper.

ONLAY, BK. A decorative panel glued on to the front cover of a book.

OPEN MATTER, PR. Widely spaced type lines.

ORIGINAL ENGRAVING, RA. Engraving by the original artist, not after another artist's work.

ORTHOCHROMATIC PLATES, PH. Plates sensitive to colors of the spectrum with the exception of the blue and ultraviolet rays.

OVERLAY, PR. Make-ready; addition of layers of tissue under tympan on press to even the impression. Also cutouts of paper mounted over parts of a drawing to obtain changed effect.

OVERMATTER, PR. The portion of set-up type matter which does not fit into the area determined by the layout and which is discarded.

PACK, AA. British term for "commercial package."

PAD. Sheets of paper glued together at one end.

PALEOGRAPHY, L. The science of deciphering ancient writings.

PAMPHLET, BK. A book bound in paper or cardboard covers or other flexible, semipermanent binding.

PANEL, AA. Rectangular section surrounded by a border and containing a part of the copy or illustration.

PANTOGRAPH, AA. Mechanical device used to reduce or enlarge pictures proportionally.

PARCHMENT, L, BK. Lambskin or goatskin prepared for writing or printing; also paper imitating it.

PEBBLING. Graining paper to remove excess gloss.

PEN AND INK, AA. Term applied to designate a drawing made with either pen or brush and India ink for line reproduction.

PENNAL, L. Letters flowing into each other when forming words—derived from the use of pliable pens.

PHOTOENGRAVING, RA. Mechanical process of making duplication plates through the art of the camera.

PHOTOGELATIN, RA. Planographic process (collotype) of printing in which a sheet of plate glass or flexible aluminum, ground and properly treated, forms the plate that prints without halftone dots.

PHOTOGRAM, PH. Photographic print on paper obtained without use of lens; also called "rayogram" after Man Ray.

PHOTOLITHOGRAPHY, RA. Transferring a drawing on a lithographic plate by photography.

PHOTOMONTAGE, PH. Method of illustration based on combining sections of different photographs in a harmonious composition in appliqué fashion.

PHOTOSTAT, PH. Photographic image recorded by a camera so constructed that it photographs, develops, and fixes flat objects directly on paper in negative values.

PI, PR. Dropped or mixed type.

PICA, PR. Printer's unit of measure; 12 points (approximately 12/72 of an inch).

PIGMENT, PR. Coloring matter in paint or ink.

PINHOLE ATTACHMENT, PH. Attachment with one to four pinholes and a focusing aperture that may be substituted for a lens.

PINHOLE IMAGE, PH. Inverted image of objects reflected on a white surface by rays of light passing through a pinhole in a completely darkened box.

PLANER, PR. Smooth block of wood used for proofing and leveling body of text.

PLANOGRAPHIC PRINT, RA. Print from a flat (not intaglio or relief) block, like a lithograph.

PLAQUE, AA. A small-size poster, usually in semiplastic material such as embossed metal, carved wood, enamel inlay, etc.

PLATE MARK, RA. Impression of the beveled edge of an etching plate on paper.

PLATEN PR. The part of the platen press to which the paper is fed.

PLATEN PRESS, PR. A press that obtains an impression by pressing the paper against the type.

PLANO-CONCAVE LENS, PH. Lens with one flat and one concave surface.

PLANO-CONVEX LENS, PH. Lens with one convex and one flat surface.

PLY, BK. Denotes the thickness or number of layers in glued paper, board, or wood.

POCHOIR, BK. Stencil process of applying color; used especially in fine French book illustration.

POINT, PR. Standard of measure used by printers to justify type (72 points equal about an inch).

PORTRAIT ATTACHMENT, PH. Additional lens mounted to slip over the regular camera lens; permits close-ups of the subject and larger images than would ordinarily be possible.

POSITIVE, PH. Print from a photographically recorded negative, which shows light and shade in their natural relationships.

POSTER, PO. Publicly exhibited announcement in which lettering and picture are usually combined into a single design.

PRIMARY COLORS. Yellow, red, and blue.

PRINTING MARKS, PR. Printers' trade-marks; e.g., broken pitcher was Tory's mark.

PROGRESSIVE PROOFS, RA. See explanation of Color Proofs.

PROOF, PR. Impression from a cut or a body of type for examination or correction.

PROOFREADER, PR. One who marks copy for correction with "proofreader's marks."

PROPORTION. Relation of parts; a principle of design.

PSALTER, BK. Psalms arranged for liturgical use in the divine office; source of countless illuminated manuscripts.

PULL A PROOF, PR. Printer's term for obtaining an impression.

PULP. Fibrous material that is used to make paper.

QUAD, PR. Below-type-high metal blank used to space out ends of lines.

QUARTER-BOUND, BK. Book bound with leather back and cloth or paper covers.

QUATERNION, BK. Four doubled sheets fitted into a section for binding together (16 pages).

QUARTO, BK. Sheet folded twice, giving four leaves, eight pages; size about 9½ by 12 inches; also 4to or 4°.

QUILL PEN, L. Formerly pens made from goose feathers; now, special pen for especially fine pen work.

QUOIN, PR. Wedge-shaped forms used in locking up type matter in chase.

REAM, BK. According to the varieties of paper stock, a measure denoting 480, 500, 516, or 520 sheets of paper.

RECTILINEAR LENS, PH. A combination of two single meniscus lenses mounted in a lens tube with the stop between them. Used to overcome curvilinear distortion by neutralizing mutually the barrel and cushion distortions of each lens; also called "rapid rectilinear lens."

RECTO, BK. Right-hand-side odd-numbered pages in a book.

REDUCING GLASS, RA. Double concave lens that makes images seen through it appear reduced.

REED PENS, L. Writing tools made from hollow reeds with nibs cut to slant as in ordinary pens.

REFLECTOGRAPH, RA. An instrument constructed to perform a service similar to that of a camera lucida. A prism and arrangement of lever arms permit the tracing of an image enlarged or reduced on any drawing surface.

REFRACTION, PH. The bending in an oblique direction of the rays of light that pass a surface, as in a lens or a prism.

REGISTER, PR, RA. Correct fitting together of two or more colors of a series of color plates; also backing up of the two pages of a sheet.

REGISTER MARKS, RA, PR. In printing, the devices that help colors to fit into their correct relationship. In engravers' proofs, the crosses that help to obtain register in proofing.

REGLET, PR. 6- and 12-point wooden furniture.

RELIEF, RA. In printing blocks those parts in which the printing surface stands out—woodcut, line cut, etc.

REMINDER ADVERTISING, AA. Advertising matter published at frequent intervals to keep the advertised item before the public.

RESIST, RA. Protective varnish or asphaltum used to protect parts of a plate from the action of a mordant.

RETOUCHING, PH. Changing of details in a negative; softening or deepening of high lights or shadows with brush or pencil.

RETROUSSAGE, RA. French term used in etching for "bringing up" the ink from the sunken lines by means of a soft muslin.

REVERSE PLATE, RA, PH. Plate that is opposite in tone values to the original.

REVERSED PROOF, RA. Offset made from a wet proof on glazed paper and used as a guide to make corrections in the plate.

REVISE PROOF, PR. Proof taken to check corrections made in a first proof.

RIVERS, L, PR. Spaces between words, accidentally coinciding in successive lines and forming a band of unprinted "rivers."

ROCKER, RA. Steel chisel having curved serrated edge with fine teeth, used to roughen plate for mezzotint.

ROLLER PROOF PRESS, PR. Usually an adjustable metal- or felt- or rubber-covered cylinder resting on a bedplate and used to get proofs.

ROLLERS, PR. Printing rollers or brayers.

ROMAN, L, PR. Thick-and-thin-serifed letters that were first used in Italy.

ROSS BOARD. Illustration board with a specially roughened surface that divides crayon or brush strokes into broken textures suitable for line reproduction.

ROUGH, AA. Preliminary visualization of a drawing; layout.

ROULETTING, RA. Use of dot-making tools called "rockers" on metal in preparation for mezzotint.

ROUTING, RA. Method of removing excess metal from photoengraving plates by means of small drills.

RUBBER CEMENT, AA. Semipermanent mounting medium consisting of gum rubber and a solvent of petroleum or benzol.

RUBRICATING, L. Adding red or other color to a lettered mass.

RUBY LIGHT, PH. Ruby-colored electric bulb for use in photographic darkrooms.

RULE, PR. Strip of type-high metal that prints lines.

RULING PEN. Instrument that holds ink between two adjustable blades to permit it to flow in lines of uniform width.

RUNNING HEAD, B.K. Title repeated on the pages of a book.

RUSSIAN LEATHER, BK. Hides of young cattle used in binding—originally from Russian calves.

S. C., PR. Small capitals.

SADDLE STITCH, BK. Binding formed by stitching pages through their middle folds.

SAND-GRAIN ETCHING, RA. "Aquatint" effect obtained by use of sandpaper instead of a dust box.

SANS SERIF, PR. Letters or type without serifs.

SCORING, L, PR. Furrowing of paper by press or with a blunt instrument to facilitate folding; also used as guide lines for lettering.

SCRAPER, RA. Three-sided blade that is used to pare off undesired parts of an etching.

SCRATCHBOARD. Clay-coated paper which is painted black. On this the design is scratched.

SCREEN, RA. Opaque lines on glass, 50 to 300 to the inch, crossing at right angles and permitting light to enter the camera only through the square openings.

SCRIBE, L. Writer or copyist of medieval manuscripts.

SCRIPT TYPE, PR. Italicized type that looks like writing.

SCRIPTORIUM, L. General office of a monastery where manuscript writing was done.

SECTION, BK. That part of a book which is formed by folding a single sheet, usually 4, 8, 16, or 32 pages.

SERIF, L, PR. Fine cross-stroke terminations of letters—usually on top and bottom.

SET, PR. To compose or arrange type.

SETUP, RA. Negatives of line cut or halftone or both rearranged in some new form in the process of stripping.

SHOWCARD, AA. A window or indoor poster for temporary announcements.

SHOWCARD COLORS (POSTER COLORS). Bright pigments based on a dense, quickly and flatly drying, opaque medium.

SHUTTER SPEED, PH. Length of time the shutter remains open for exposure.

SIGN BOARDS, AA. Small hanging signs, usually suspended above entrances.

SIGNATURE, BK. Section of a book, commonly 4, 8, 16, 32, or 64 pages.

SIGNATURE MARK, BK. Letter or number printed in the gutter of a signature to guide the binder.

SIGNET, AA. A seal; a trade-mark.

SILHOUETTE HALFTONE, RA. Also called "outline halftone"; one where the image minus background is shown.

SILVER PRINT, PH. Photographic positive printed on paper sensitized with silver salt. This permits the bleaching of the photograph after it has served as a basis for inking.

SIQUI, AA. Latin for "If anybody"; opening phrase of early public advertisements, now used to designate the advertisements of that period.

SIZING, RA. Treating a rough fibrous paper with gelatin and alum or other filler, especially for color printing; also yellowish ink used as a basis in bronzing.

SLOGAN, AA. Short sentence attempting to summarize the characteristics of a product or service.

SLUGS, PR. Leads 6 points and more in thickness, used to separate lines of type.

SOFT FOCUS, PH. Effect produced by photographing through specially constructed meniscus lenses that reflect an image with blurred, slightly foggy details.

SOFT-GROUND ETCHING, RA. Etching from a plate that has its ground removed by pressure of pencil on a paper overlay.

SOLAR PRINT, PH. Enlarged photographic print made from a negative taken with a solar camera.

SOLID MATTER, PR. Type lines set without leading between lines.

SPACE, PR. Below-type-high blanks used to separate words in type matter.

SPACING, L, PR. Varying the size of the spaces between words to improve the appearance of the line.

SPECTRUM, PH. Band of colors caused by splitting up a beam of white light by means of a prism.

SPEED (OF EXPOSURE), PH. Ratio between focal length and diameter of stop.

SPHERICAL ABERRATION, PH. Irregularity found in a collecting lens that is unable to bring all rays of light of one single spectral color to a single focus.

SPIRAL BINDING, BK. Form of binding by threading a strong wire spirally through a row of holes.

SQUARE HALFTONE, RA. Halftone plate with four straight edges.

STAGING, RA. Painting out with asphaltum parts of plate that need no further etching.

STATES, RA. Prints from the progressively changed etched plates.

STEEL FACING, RA. Electrical deposit of a film of steel on the surface of a plate to harden it.

STEREOTYPE, RA. Plate cast from a matrix or mold of papier-mâché or other material.

STICK, PR. Device for composing type to measure.

STILL LIFE, AA. Pictorial arrangement of inanimate objects.

STIPPLE, RA. Effect obtained by use of a series of dots and flicks on a drawing.

STOCK, PR. Paper.

STOP, PH. Hole punched into a metal plate and placed in front of a lens to regulate the amount of light entering the camera.

STOPPING-OUT VARNISH, RA. Etching ground dissolved in benzol or other solvent used to protect parts of a plate from further etching.

STRAIGHT MATTER, PR. Opposite of display; plain composition.

STRIPPING, RA. Soaking the negative in acetic acid to remove it and to turn it on the glass.

SUEDE, BK. Velvety finish on fabric or leather.

SUMATRA BARK BOOK, BK. Roll folded into accordion-like pleating and weighted with boards.

SURPRINTING, RA. Double printing, whereby it is possible to combine halftone with line reproduction.

SWASH LETTERS, L. Italic caps with projecting flourishes.

SYMMETRY. Harmonious relation of the parts of a picture or type mass to an imaginary axis.

TACK, PR. Degree of adhesion in glue or paste; also the "give" or stickiness of ink.

TAILPIECE, BK. Decorative unit or small illustration used as a space filler at the end of a page.

TAPES, BK. Narrow linen strips or bands used in binding to combine the several sections of a book.

TELEPHOTO LENS, PH. Also "teleobjective." Combination of a negative (dispersing) and positive (collecting) lens, which permits taking large, direct pictures of distant objects.

TEMPERA COLOR. Water-color pigments combined with a medium that renders them opaque.

TEXT, L, PR. Body matter of a page or advertisement.

THERMOGRAPHY, PR. Wet printing that is powdered and then heated to obtain a raised effect.

THREE-COLOR PROCESS, RA. Method of printing colored pictures by use of yellow, red, and blue and their combinations.

TIB, PH. Term formed by the initials of "time," "instantaneous," and "bulb"—designations that indicate the controls of the three automatic shutter speeds.

TINT, RA. Light value of a color obtained by addition of white or reducing agent.

TINT BLOCK, RA. Uncut block used to print a flat color.

TISSUE, PR. Thin paper used in building up a block in make-ready.

TITLE PAGE, BK. Right-hand page giving title, author, and imprint of a book.

TOOLING, RA. Retouching of plate with burin.

TRINDLE, BK. Device for forcing out the roundness of a book edge while cutting the book.

TYMPAN, PR. Sheet of tough paper that covers the platen or cylinder.

TYPE GAUGE, PR. Printer's ruler having inch and point divisions.

TYPE-HIGH, PR, RA. Height of type (0.9186 of an inch); also height of photoengraving when mounted for printing.

TYPOGRAPHY, PR. Art of type arrangement.

U. S., PH. Abbreviation for "uniform system," a listing of stop openings arranged for rapid rectilinear lenses.

ULTRAVIOLET RAYS, PH. Invisible component rays of sunlight, important in photographic exposure.

UNCIALS, L. Kind of majuscule script used before the tenth century A.D.

UNDERCUT, RA. Undermined lines, especially in linoleum cuts or overetched plates.

UNDERLAY, PR. Make-ready; building up of plate with layers of paper to obtain an even impression.

UPPER CASE, PR. Capital letters.

VALUE of a Color. The amount of light or dark in a color.

VARNISH, PR. The substance that is combined with pigment to make printing ink; overprinted on paper, it gives a shiny finish.

VELLUM, L, BK. Thin prepared calf or lamb gut, although any moderately good skin prepared for writing is also so called.

VERSALS, L. Decorative capitals once used with medieval minuscule letters and so called because they began verses.

VERSO, BK. Left-hand-side even-numbered pages of a book.

VIGNETTE. Illustration with irregular silhouetted background.

VISUAL RAYS, PH. Yellow rays, visually the most luminous, but photographically not very effective.

WASH DRAWING. Monotone rendering with brush and water color.

WATER-COLOR DRAWING, BK. Painting with transparent colors soluble in water.

WATERMARK, PR. Paper mark indicating maker or trade name of stock.

WATKINS POWER NUMBERS, PH. System of numbers devised by Alfred Watkins to figure out the f value of a pinhole in a camera.

WHOLE BOUND, BK. All-leather bookbinding.

WIDE-ANGLE LENS, PH. Lens capable of taking a negative that embraces an angle of view greater than 70°.

WOOD ENGRAVING, RA. Illustration cut with gravers and gouges on the end grain of wood.

WOODCUT, RA. Design cut on a plank with a knife; also a print from such a cut.

WORKING DRAWING, RA. Explanatory drawing used to suggest color desired in final printing.

WOVE PAPER, BK. Paper with cloth-like grain.

WRAPPER, BK, AA. Ornamented paper used to wrap packages or books.

XYLOGRAPHY, RA. Wood engraving.

ZINC ETCHING, RA. A photoengraved line plate made on zinc.

DESIGN 395

A WORKING BIBLIOGRAPHY

The list represents books that the authors found helpful. It is suggestive rather than exhaustive. It includes both classic stand-bys and more contemporary publications.

LETTERING . . . .

CHAPPELL, WARREN. *The Anatomy of Lettering.* Instruction in the art of lettering. Loring & Mussey, New York.

CLODD, EDWARD. *Story of the Alphabet.* D. Appleton-Century Company, Inc., New York.

EHMCKE, F. H. *Historische Entwicklung der Abendlaendischen Schriftformen.* Summary of the development of European writing. Illustrated. Otto Maier Verlag, Ravensburg.

HOFFMANN, HERBERT. *Modern Lettering: Design and Application.* Compiled in collaboration with Bruckner, Hertwig, and Koch. 380 alphabets by 121 artists. W. Helburn, New York.

JOHNSTON, EDWARD. *Writing and Illuminating and Lettering.* With diagrams by the author and 24 pages of collotypes. The Macmillan Company, New York.

LARISCH, RUDOLF VON. *Unterricht in Ornamentaler Schrift.* Treatise by an authority on the subject. K. u. K. Hof- und Staatsdruckerei, Vienna.

Lettering. Introduction by H. Degering, 240 plates of European lettering from ancient times to the nineteenth century. Ernest Benn, Ltd., London.

SMITH, PERCY. *Lettering and Writing.* B. T. Batsford, London.

TANNAHILL, PROF. SALLIE B. *P's and Q's.* The art of letter arrangement. Doubleday, Doran & Company, Inc., Garden City, New York.

VAN LOON, HENDRIK WILLEM. *Around the World with the Alphabet.* Good cultural background for the letterer, amusingly presented by an artist-philosopher. Simon & Schuster, Inc., New York.

PRINTING . . . .

GRESS, E. G. *The Art and Practice of Typography.* Development of American period typography, with 600 reproductions. Harper & Brothers, New York.

I. T. U. *Lessons in Printing.* Series of practical printing texts for shop, home, and school. I. T. U. Bureau of Education, Indianapolis.

JAHN, HUGO. *The Dictionary of Graphic Art Terms.* Technical words and phrases in printing and allied industries. United Typothetae of America, Chicago.

JOHNSON, HENRY L. *Historic Design in Printing.* Masterpieces of Italian, French, and German printing of the fifteenth and sixteenth centuries. Reproductions discriminately selected. The Graphic Arts Company, Boston.

JOHNSTON, PAUL. *Biblio Typographica.* Survey of contemporary printing styles. Covici Friede, Inc., New York.

McMURTRIE, DOUGLAS C. *Modern Typography and Layout.* Statement of the principles underlying the modern movement in typography. Eyncourt Press, Chicago.

Monographs on Color. Three booklets on Color Chemistry, Color as Light, and Color in Use; a concise illustrated outline of data on color in printing and in art. International Printing Ink Corporation, New York.

MORISON, STANLEY. *Four Centuries of Fine Printing.* 600 illustrations of fine press work from 1500 to 1914. Ernest Benn, Ltd., London.

———. *Modern Fine Printing.* An illustrated collection of English, American, Italian, Swiss, Czechoslovakian, Dutch, Swedish, and German printing since 1914. Ernest Benn, Ltd., London.

OSWALD, JOHN C. *History of Printing.* A good general presentation. D. Appleton-Century Company, Inc., New York.

PEDDIE, R. A. *Printing.* History of the art written by a different authority for each country. Grafton & Co., London.

Standard Textbook on Printing. A beginner's manual. United Typothetae of America, Chicago.

STERN, PHILIP VAN DOREN. *An Introduction to Typography.* Good bibliography and excellent photographic chapter headings. Harper & Brothers, New York.

UPDIKE, DANIEL B. *Printing Types: Their History, Forms and Use.* 2 volumes. A study in survivals. Excellent history of type and a fine example of bookmaking. Harvard University Press, Cambridge.

REPRODUCTIVE ARTS . . . .

Achievements in Photo-Engraving and Letterpress Printing. Edited by Louis Flader. Informatively illustrated. American Photo-engravers Association, Chicago.

BLISS, DOUGLAS, P. *A History of Wood Engraving.* Possibly the best book on this phase of the subject. 120 fine illustrations. J. M. Dent & Sons, Ltd., London.

COURBOIN, FRANÇOIS. *Histoire Illustré de la Gravure en France.* About 1500 large plates reproducing the most famous prints from the Bibliothèque Nationale, a fine substitute for the originals. Maurice le Garrec, Paris.

CURWEN, HAROLD. *Processes of Graphic Reproduction.* Preface to American edition by Harry L. Gage. Oxford University Press, New York.

GAMBLE, C. W. *Modern Illustration Processes.* Reference book on engraving, printing, rendering tones in printing ink, and color reproduction. Sir Isaac Pitman & Sons, Ltd., London.

GROESBECK, HARRY A., Jr. *Practical Photo-engraving.* Written in the form of 50 letters to help humanize the technical ideas of the subject. Harper & Brothers, New York.

HAMERTON, P. G. *Etching and Etchers.* Formerly a classic and still a good guide to the mastery of etching. The Macmillan Company, New York.

HAVINDEN, ASHLEY. *Line Drawing for Reproduction.* Illustrated explanation of the variety of effects possible in line engraving. Number 4 of the "How to Do It" series. Studio Publications, London.

HIND, A. M. *A Short History of Engraving and Etching.* Archibald Constable & Company, Ltd., London.

Insel Buecherei. A series of picture books with reproductions of old and contemporary masters, such as Holbein, Masereel. Insel Verlag, Leipzig.

LALANNE, M. *Treatise on Etching.* An old classic that is still more quoted than any other book on etching. Estes & Lauriat, Boston.

LANKES, J. J. *A Woodcut Manual.* Practical textbook by a noted contemporary craftsman, generously illustrated with his own work. Henry Holt & Company, New York.

LEIGHTON, CLARE. *Wood Engraving and Woodcuts.* Number 2 of the "How to Do It" series. Studio Publications, London.

LIPPMANN, FREDERICK. *The Art of Wood Engraving in Italy in the Fifteenth Century* by a noted authority. Reproductions of famous prints. Bernard Quaritch, London.

LUMSDEN, E. S. *The Art of Etching.* Complete illustrated description of etching, dry point, soft-ground, aquatint, and allied arts, with technical notes upon their own work by many of the leading etchers. J. B. Lippincott Company, Philadelphia.

Penrose's Annual. English annual with articles on latest developments in reproduction and printing. Percy Lund Humphries, London.

PLOWMAN, GEORGE, T. *Etching and Other Graphic Arts.* Well illustrated and smypathetically written. Dodd, Mead & Company, New York.

WEITENKAMPF, F. *How to Appreciate Prints.* An expert guide. Charles Scribner's Sons, New York.

WEST, LEVON. *Making an Etching.* Photographic step-by-step representation of the process of making and printing an etching. Number 1 of the "How to Do It" series: fine books for beginners. Studio Publications, London.

PHOTOGRAPHY

BAYLEY, R. CHILD. *The Complete Photographer.* Tenth revised edition. A useful manual of pictorial photography. Frederick A. Stokes Company, New York.

CHARLES, DAVID. *Commercial Photography.* Practical handbook of methods and appliances used in commercial photography. Sir Isaac Pitman & Sons, Ltd., London.

FRAPRIE, F. R. *How to Choose and Use a Lens.* Informative descriptions of most lenses and how they work. American Photographic Publishing Company, Boston.

JOHNSON, ROBERT. *The Art of Retouching.* Practical directions for negative retouching and coloring of photographic enlargements. American Photographic Publishing Company, Boston.

Modern Photography. An English annual with some of the year's best photographs. Studio Publications, London.

Photographie. Annual compilation of outstanding photographic creations throughout the world. Arts et Métiers Graphiques, Paris.

Photography Year Book. 1700 exemplary photographic illustrations. Photography, London.

U. S. Camera. American annual of black-white and color photography by leading camera artists. Edited by T. J. Maloney. William Morrow & Company, Inc. New York.

YOUNG, EDWARD DRUMMOND. *The Art of the Photographer.* A thorough guide to portrait, landscape, and still-life photography, from studio equipment to developing and printing. J. B. Lippincott Company, Philadelphia.

THE BOOK

AUDIN, MARIUS. *Le Livre Français.* History of book development in France, with reproductions of fine book pages. Les Éditions Rieder, Paris.

Book of Kells. Description by Sir E. Sullivan Bart, illustrated with 24 color plates. Studio Publications, London.

Buchkunst. Illustrated essays on the development of the graphic arts and the art of the book by professors and professionals. Staatliche Akademie, Leipzig.

COCKERELL, DOUGLAS. *Bookbinding and the Care of Books,* by a noted artisan. John Hogg, London.

DAVENPORT, CYRIL. *The Book: Its History and Development.* D. Van Nostrand Company, Inc., New York.

DESIGN 397

DOW, ARTHUR W. *Composition*. An outline of design, that changed the emphasis from drawing to design. Doubleday, Doran & Company, Inc., Garden City, N. Y.

FLETCHER, W. Y. *Foreign Bookbindings in the British Museum*. 63 classical examples of bookbindings, with introduction and description. Outstanding reproductions. Kegan Paul, Trench, Truebner & Company, London.

Graphic Art. Compilation of authoritative articles on all phases of the graphic arts, included in the fourteenth edition of the Encyclopaedia Britannica. Illustrated. Encyclopaedia Britannica, London.

HERBERT, J. A. *Illuminated Manuscripts*. Illustrations and a good bibliography. Methuen, London.

HUNTER, DARD. *Papermaking Through Eighteen Centuries*. Well illustrated. E. Rudge, New York.

LEHMANN-HAUPT, H. *Fifty Books About Bookmaking*. A critical bibliography, attractively presented. Columbia University Press, New York.

LOUBIER, HANS. *Der Bucheinband*. A profusely illustrated research into the history of bookbinding from earliest times to the eighteenth century. Klinkhardt & Biermann, Leipzig.

McMURTRIE, DOUGLAS C. *The Golden Book*. History of fine books and bookmaking. P. Covici, Chicago.

MORISON, STANLEY. *German Incunabula in the British Museum*. 152 facsimile plates. Victor Golancz, London.

POLLARD, A. W. *Early Illustrated Books*. Illustrated history of book decoration and illustration from the fifteenth century to the end of the Renaissance. Kegan, Paul, Trench, Truebner & Company, London.

POLLARD, A. W. *Fine Books*. One of the best general books on printing and book illustration. Methuen & Company, Ltd., London.

RÜMANN, ARTHUR. *Das Illustrierte Buch des XIX Jahrhunderts*. English, French, and German illustrated books of the nineteenth century. Insel Verlag, Leipzig.

WHEATLEY, HENRY B. *Remarkable Bindings in the British Museum*. Fine reproductions of rare old bindings. Sampson, Low, Marsten, Searle & Rivington, London.

WEITENKAMPF, F. *Illustrated Books of the Past Four Centuries*. Historical outline of outstanding printed books by nationality and dates. New York Public Library.

WESTWOOD, H. R. *Modern Caricaturists*. Foreword by Will Low. Lovat Dickson, Ltd., London.

ADVERTISING ART . . . .

AYMAR, GORDON C. *An Introduction to Advertising Illustration*. Guide book to the practical phases of advertising art. Harper & Brothers, New York.

DWIGGINS, WILLIAM A. *Layout in Advertising*. Illustrated discussion of the apparatus and technique of advertising. Harper & Brothers, New York.

GREER, CARL R. *Advertising and Its Mechanical Production*. Illustrated. The Thomas Y. Crowell Company, New York.

HORNUNG, CLARENCE P. *Trade Marks*. Fine designs by the author. Caxton Press, New York.

MEYNELL, FRANCIS. *The Typography of Newspaper Advertisements*. Display of English, American, French, Dutch, and German type faces. Table for calculating the number of words to fill a given space in any type. Ernest Benn, Ltd., London.

PRESBREY, SPENCER F. *History and Development of Advertising*. Thoroughly written and illustrated resumé of the vast subject. Doubleday, Doran & Company, Inc., Garden City, New York.

SCHUBERT, DR. W. F. *Deutsche Werbegraphik*. An exhaustive, profusely illustrated compilation of German advertising art. Francken & Lang, Berlin.

WESTEN, WALTER VON ZUR. *Reklamekunst Aus Zwei Jahrtausenden*. Illustrated history of advertising in the last two thousand years. Eigenbrödler Verlag, Berlin.

POSTER . . . .

BINDER, JOSEPH. *Colour in Advertising*. Practical application of the laws of color and color harmony to posters, pamphlets, and packages. Studio Publications, London.

HIATT, C. *Picture Posters*. Good reference on the history of the illustrated placard up to the nineteenth century. George Bell & Sons, Ltd., London.

JACOBS, MICHAEL. *The Art of Colour*. A color system based on the theories of Young-Helmholtz-Tyndall. Color mixing, hues, tints, tones, color perspective, and a dictionary of colors. Doubleday, Doran & Company, Inc., Garden City, New York.

KLINGER, JULIUS. *Poster Art in Vienna*. Examples of the work of leading Austrian poster artists. J. Wisotzki, Chicago.

Ludwig Hohlwein and His Work. 150 of his designs. A pictorial story of the most prolific of the poster artists. H. C. Perleberg, New York

McKNIGHT-KAUFFER, E. *The Art of the Poster*. Treatise on the origin, evolution, and purpose of the poster. Albert & Charles Boni, New York.

MUNSELL, A. H. *A Color Notation*. Deals with color as pigment rather than as light: based on long research and study. Munsell Color Company, New York.

Posters in Miniature. Introduction by Edward Penfield. An old book with reproductions of pioneer poster work. A good background of the contemporary poster scene. R. H. Russell & Son, New York.

INDEX: NAMES AND THINGS

Roman numbers denote text references; italicized numbers denote illustrations.

A

ABBEY, Edwin   203, 208
ABRAHAM Lincoln High School   17, *134*, *150*, *354*, *369*, *370*, *371*, *383*
ACID Resist (ground)   86
ADAMS Studios   *146*, *290*
ADCRAFT   *278*
ADLER, Rose   *227*, *228*
ADVERTISING, direct and general   249
ADVERTISING Art   245; layout   249
AHRLÉ   *143*
AIRBRUSH   140, *143*, *318*, *323*, *347*, *352*
ALBERS, Prof. J.   64
ALDUS (*see* Manutius)
ALEXANDER, James   *371*
ALEXANDRIAN Codex   *153*
ALEXANDROVSKY   *238*
ALEXEÏEFF   97, *178*, *185*, 203, *352*
ALINARI, Fratelli   53, *108*
ALIX, Marie   *194*
ALLIANCE Graphique   *349*
ALY, Grete   *270*
ANGELO, Valenti   *54*
"ANNUNCIATION, The," from *Ruskin Hours*   *2*
APPLEGATE, Frank G.   *200*
AQUATINT   87, 88, 90, 105
AQUATONE   112
ARGUS Book Shop   *103*
ARNO, Peter   *216*
ARPKE, Prof. Otto   *266*, *331*
ARRUE, Ramiro   *181*, *205*
ARS *Moriendi*   *159*, *162*
ARTZYBASHEFF, Boris   *159*, *193*, *205*, *233*, *236*
ASHBURNHAM Binding   *218*
ASHENDENE Press   197
ASHLEY (*see* Havinden)
AUFSEESER, Prof. Ernst   *206*, *320*
AUSTEN, John   *103*, *203*
AUSTIN, Robert   *94*
AXSLER-Heudtlass, von   *345*
AYER & Son, Inc.,   133, *143*

B

BACH, Ernst & Company   84
BADELEY, H. I. F.   6
BALDRIDGE, Leroy C.   *200*

BAREN   81
BARLACH, Ernst   *206*
BARTOLOZZI   *321*
BASKERVILLE   43
BATTEN, Barton, Durstine & Osborn   *128*
BATYCKI, J.   *372*
BAUER Type Foundry   47, 50, 62, 66, *261*, *270*, *283*
BAYER, Herbert   *129*
BAYNARD Press   *6*, *21*, *24*, *314*, *339*, *346*
BEARDSLEY, Aubrey   *177*, 197
BECK-Gerlach Specimen Sheet   *45*
BECKHOFF, Harry   *196*
BEERBOHM   *210*
BEGGARSTAFF Brothers (Pryde and Nicholson)   *240*, *302*, *308*
BEN Day   107, 111
BERG, Yngve   *206*
BERLIN State School of Applied Arts   *279*, *377*
BERNARDINI, Piero   *29*, *182*, *206*
BERND, Jr., A.   *312*, *327*, *338*, *343*
BERNER Specimen Sheet   *44*
BERNHARD, Lucian   25, 43, 48, 50, *257*, *304*
BERTIERI, Raffaello   47, 62, *109*, *182*, *196*, *202*, *210*, *211*, *292*
BERTIERI & Vanzetti   *29*, 53
BEWICK, Thomas   *168*, *176*, *177*, 180
BEZA, codex of   *153*
BIAS, H.   *335*
BIFUR Type   *40*
BINDER, Joseph   *300*, *353*, *358*
BINDER-Germany   *283*
BINDINGS, book   154, 216, *217*, *224*, *225*
BIRMINGHAM School of Arts and Crafts   43, *55*
BITT, Valentin   *206*
BITTROF   *285*
BLAKE, William   *169*, *177*, 180
BOBRITSKY, Vladimir   *111*, *236*, *261*, *297*
BODONI Modern   35, 43
BOEHLAND, Johannes   *241*, *310*, *345*
BOFA, Gus   *184*, *206*
BOMPARD, S.   *331*
BONE, Muirhead   *93*, *95*
BOOK, The   151
BOOK *of Hours*   39, *161*, *167*, *170*
BOOK Jacket   *233*
BOOKBINDING   216
BOOKPLATES   240
BORDERS   60, 61
BORTNYIK   *313*, *343*

DESIGN 399

BOTTEMA, Tjerk 216
BOUCHER, Lucien 183, 205
BOUQUET, Louis 205
BOURKE-White, Margaret 116, 138
BOYER, Le 135
BRADLEY, Frederick 142
BRADLEY, Will 303, 308
BRALEY, Berton 34
BRANGWYN, Frank 94, 98
BREKER, Walter 273
BRIGDENS, Ltd. 115, 254
BROADBENT, Arthur E. 364
BRODOVITCH, Alexei 143
BRUBAKER, Jon 320
BRUEHL, Anton 129, 130, 141, 142
BRÜNIG, H. & A. 285
BUHE, Walter 206
BURCK, Jacob 207
BURGKMAIR, Hans 166
BURNE-Jones, Edward 38, 192
BÜTTNER, F. 369

C

CALDECOTT, Randolph 205
CALENDARIUM, Erhard Ratdolt's 39
CALKINS & Holden 79, 267
CALLOT, Jacques 163, 168
CAMBELLOTTI, Duilio 194, 203
CAMBERWELL School of Arts 112
CAMERA, diagram of parts 122; midget 138; photograph of 122; studio 123
CAMPBELL-Ewald Company 349, 353
CAMPIONI, Valentin le 206
CANALS 330
CANCELLATION Stamps 16
CANTERBURY Tales 54
CANTRÉ, Joseph 179, 206
CAPEK, Joseph 206
CAPITALS, Roman and Rustic 4
CAPPIELLO, S. 310, 329
CARBONI, Prof. Erberto 1, 264, 316, 321
CARICATURE 210, 211
CARLÈGLE 205
CARLU, Jean 323, 326, 342, 358
CARNEVALI, Francesco 109, 196
CARTOON 209
CARUSO, Enrico 213
CASINGS, book 216, 225
CASLON 43; Old Face Open 51; Old Style 35, 48
CASS Technical High School 361
CASSANDRE 40, 346, 347, 349, 352, 358
CASSELMAN 120
CAVIEDES, Hipolito Hidalgo de 338
CAXTON 43, 247, 249

CENAC 322
CERF, Ywan 183
CERVELLATI, Alessandro 200, 317
CHAGALL, Marc 208
CHAIN Lines 220, 379
CHALLENGE Machinery Company Proof Press 67
CHANDLER & Price Plate Press 67
CHAPELL, Warren 272
CHARAL 19, 25, 339, 355
CHÉRET, Jules 240, 302, 308
CHMEL, Lucca 126
CIMINI, Harry 236
CLARK, Jefferson 101
CLARKE, René 253
CLELAND, T. M. 62, 258
COBDEN-Sanderson, T. J. 197, 228
COCKERELL, Douglas 216, 228
COCTEAU, Jean 195, 205
CODEX 153; Alexandrian 153; Bezae 153
COLE, Timothy 83, 84
COLE, Walter 252
COLLIER Service Corporation 349
COLOPHON 168
COLOR 302; separation 108
COMPOSITION Cut 80
CONSTANDUROS, Denis 351
COOPER, Austin 345
COOPER, D. 69
COOPER, F. G. 320
COPPERPLATE Engraving 166, 176
CORREGGIO 247
CORTÝ, Dore 328
COSIMINI, 280
COTMAN 92
COTTON, William 205, 216
COURSE of Study 376
COVARRUBIAS, Miguel 207, 216
CRANACH Press 197
CRANE, Walter 168, 205
CRAWFORD Agency 72, 144, 145, 259, 279
CRÈS & Cie. 181, 198, 202
CRUIKSHANK 210, 248
CUNEIFORM 8
CUNEO Press 36
CURWEN Press 24, 178, 197
CYLINDER Press 33, 36

D

DAENERT, R. 179
DAGLISH, Eric Fitch 168
DAGUERRE, Louis Jacques 117
DAIGLE, George 361
DANCE of Death 166, 173, 176, 184, 186, 187

DANE, Clement, Studio 346
DARCY 255
DAUMIER, Honoré 77, 94, 96, 182, 210, 240
DE RE MILITARI 159, 163
DEBERNY & Peignot 40, 60, 61, 64, 123, 277, 346
DEINEKA, Alexander 346
DERRICK, Thomas 195, 205, 214, 215
DESMEURS 331
DEUTSCH, Ernst 305
DÉVAMBEZ 183, 262, 274, 309, 329
DEVICES, printers' 62
DE WITT, Anthony 53, 206
DE WITT Clinton High School 369, 371
DEXAMENOS Cameo 26
DEXEL, Dr. W. 236, 283
DIAMOND Sutra 157, 162
DIDOT 43
DI GEMMA, Joseph 265
DIGNIMONT 205
DIPTYCH (codex) 153, 217
DISNEY, Walt 216
DIVÉKI, J. V. 78, 206
DORÉ, Gustave 82, 168, 172, 182
DORLAND 129, 291
DORN, Marion V. 178, 206
DOVES Press (see Cobden-Sanderson)
DRAEGER Frères 21, 23, 119, 276
DREESEN, Walter 192, 369
DRUM 236
DRYDEN, E. 106, 109, 259
DRYPOINT 90, 95
DUFY, Raoul 203
DULAC, Edmund 203
DÜRER, Albrecht 13, 76, 85, 173
DWIGGINS, W. A. 3, 42, 190, 205

E . . . .
EASTMAN, George 117
EBELEBEN, Nicolas 221
EDISON, Thomas A. 4
EDKMAN, N. E. 206
EDMUNDSON, Carolyn 266
EHMCKE, Prof. F. H. 3, 18, 19, 24, 25, 43, 61, 197, 206, 228, 283, 324, 338, 369
EHRLICH, A. 347
EISENSTEIN, Sergei 125, 136
ELECTRA Type 42
ELEGANT Grotesk 35, 43
EL GRECO 83
ELSNERDRUCK 19, 25, 267, 345
ELZEVIR 43
END-PIECES 18
ENDERS, Prof. Ludwig 286, 289

ENLARGING (see Scaling)
ENSCHEDÉ en Zonen Joh. 202
ENVELOPES, printers' 62
ERASMUSDRUCK 61, 62, 63, 202, 267, 271, 288
ERBAR Grotesk 43; type 48, 63
ERBE 21
ESCHLE, Max 321
ESKRICH, Pierre 167, 176
ESTIENNE 43, 366
ETCHING 85; aquatint 87, 88, 90; sand-grain 91; soft-ground 87, 92
EVE, Clovis 222, 225
EVE, Nicholas 222, 225

F . . . .
FABIAN Tracts 7
FABRICIUS 117
FARLEIGH, John 186, 205
FARRAR & Rinehart 18
FEIL, Otto 240
FETTE Ratio Latein type 66
FINSLER 144
FISHER, James 371
FITZPATRICK, D. R. 209, 215
FLOETHE, Richard 206
FOLDERS 260
FOLIO 220
FORAIN 198, 203
FORBES, Esther 112
FORMIGGINI, A. F. 188, 202
FOSTER, Robert 14, 25
FOUJITA 198
FOURNIER, Pierre Simon 46
FOX & Mackenzie 268
FRANÇAIS 180
FRANKLIN Printing Company 114, 245, 257
FRANKOWSKI, H. 354
FRASER, C. Lovat 205
FREISE, Dorothee 215, 228, 231
FREISE, Katharine 228, 230
FRENCH Sylvan Type 58
FRIEND, Anna 126
FRITZ, Max 17
FROBEN, J. 43; caduceus 62
FROWERT Company 259
FURER, Paul 150
FUST and Schoeffer 42; psalter 36; colophon 62, 168
FUSTIER, E. O. 316
FUTURA, light 47; bold 66

G . . . .
GABA, Lester 142, 255

DESIGN ═══════════════ 401

GABORJANI-Szabó, Kalman 78
GAG, Wanda 236
GALANIS, D. 187, 206
GALI, F. 315
GARAMOND 44; Ludlow 44; Goudy 46; Old Style 49
GARRETTO, Paolo 205, 216
GASCON, Le 223, 225
GAVARNI 170, 182, 240
GELLERT, Hugo 208, 216
GEORGI, E. A. 107, 267
GERLACH & Wiedling 158, 179
GIANNINI, Giulio, & Figlio 156, 202, 226, 228
GIBBINGS, Robert 186, 205
GIBSON, Charles Dana 203
GILL, André 203
GILL, Eric 3, 7, 14, 43, 54, 191, 203, 206, 261
GIMMI & Company 18
GISCHIA, Léon 317, 354, 363
GÖHLERT 324
GOLDBERG, Rube 216
GOLDEN Cockerel Press 54, 186, 191, 197
GOLDKIND, Edith 383
GOLDSHOLLE, Morris 17, 370
GOMBARTS, George 364
GOODMAN 117
GOTHIC Blackface 9, 13
GOUDY, Frederick 3, 43; Garamond 46; New Style 54, 358
GOYA 77, 87, 88, 91, 210
GOZZOLI, Benozzo 108
GRABHORN Press 54
GRAFIKA 112
GRAFSTRÖM, Sigrid 259
GRAIN of Paper 220, 379
GRANDE-Chaumière Academy 354, 363
GRANT, Forest 376
GRAPHIC Arts Education 357
GREEK Cameo 26
GREEK Coin 26
GREEK Script 8
GREEK Seal 7
GREENAWAY, Kate 205
GREETING Cards 59, 283
GREGORII Frates 36
GREGYNOG Press 197
GRIFFIN, Catherine 376
GRINEVSKY 105, 203
GROLIER 221, 224, 225
GRONOWSKI, Tadeusz 318, 319
GROPPER, William 209
GROSS, Moe 266, 354
GROSZ, George 213, 358
GROUND (*see* Acid Resist)

GUÉRIN, Jules 203
GUERRINI, Luigi 156
GULBRANSSON, Olaf 202, 215
GUSTAVO, Rosso 196
GUTENBERG, Johann; Bible 30; printing 31; *Weltgericht* 32; press room 34

H

HADANK, Prof. O. W. 24, 144, 145, 287
HAHN, Ulrich 160, 163
HALFTONE 108, 109, 110; "blowup" 112; highlight 111
HALL, Edna Clarke 351
HAMBURG, Trude 129, 147
HAMILTON, Russell D. 364
HARBOR Press 55
HARRINGER, H. 274
HARRIS, Walt 14
HARSHBERGER 263
HASSALL 308
HAVINDEN, Ashley 99, 270, 312
HAZAN Éditions 202
HAZARD Advertising Corporation 263
HECKMAN, Albert 93, 96
HEINRICHSEN, Friederich 14
HEINTZE & Blanckertz 13, 19, 24, 26, 27, 270, 279
HELD, John, Jr. 205, 212, 216, 262
HELLER, R. 312
HERODOTUS 36
HEROLD, Don 292
HERRICK 314, 339
HERTWIG 357
HEURLIN, Gustav 5
HEUVELPERS 240
HEWITT 3, 358
HIEROGLYPHICS 5, 8
HILLER, Léjaren a 132, 144
HIRSCHFELD, Albert 214
HOFER 99
HOGARTH 248
HOHLWEIN, Ludwig 308, 336
HOKUSAI 82
HOLBEIN, Hans 76, 166, 173, 176, 248
HOLLERBAUM & Schmidt 299, 304, 305
HOLTEN, Otto von 18
HOLZ, Walter 26, 265
HUET 180
HUGHES-Stanton, Blair 188, 206
HUMAN Interest 213
HUMANISTIC Type 53
HUNT 197
HUNT, Sidney 242
HUTCHINSON, Eugene 298

HUXLEY House 296, 341
HYPNEROTOMACHIA Poliphili, Colonna's 164, 165, 169, 170

I

IBIS, L' 277; ditions 203
IDEOGRAPHS, Chinese 8
ILLUSTRATION 156, 157
INCUNABULA 169
INDULGENCE of Nicholas V 35
INITIAL Letters 36, 39, 40, 158, 159
INNESS Alphabet 14
INTERNATIONAL Typographical Union 362
INTERTYPE 33
IRIBE, Paul 21, 23
IRVIN, Rea 292
ISABEY 180
ITALICS 4, 10, 43

J

JACOUB & Company 277
JAN 135, 332, 336, 347
JAPAN Paper Company 48
JENSEN, Gustav B. 288, 290
JENSON 25, 31, 42
JIROUT, Alois 228, 229
JOB Press (platen) 36
JOHANNOT 180
JOHN of Cologne 25
JOHNSON 216
JOHNSTON, Edward 3, 358
JONES, Alice McL. 287
JONES, George W. 24, 197
JONQUIÈRES, Éditions Henri 62, 178, 189, 194, 198, 202
JORDAN, Paula 365
JULLIEN, Louis 183

K

KALENDARIUM 168
KALLIN, Grit 144, 145
KELLER, E. 26
KELMSCOTT Press 188
KENNERLEY Type 68
KENT, Rockwell 79, 203, 239, 261, 263
KENYON & Eckhardt 130
KEPPLER, Victor 128
KERST, Walter 126
KESSLER, Count 197
KEY-Plate 80
KIEFFER 187, 202

KIMBALL, Abbott 296
KIRBY, Rollin 206, 215
KLEIN, Richard 314
KLEINE Passion 173
KLINGER, Julius 299, 305, 308
KNIGHT, Dame Laura 88, 91
KNOEDLER & Company, Inc. 74
KOCH, Rudolf 3, 13, 43, 48, 358, 362
KORVIN Brothers 313
KOWZHUN, Paul 311
KREMER, Fritz 232
KRONENGOLD 306
KUKRINIKSI Studio 201
KULISIEWICZ, Tadeusz 206
KULTSVIAZ-Voks 125, 136, 201, 238, 335, 347
KUMLIEN, Akke 6

L

LABELS, printers' 63
LABERGE 180
LABORDE, Charles 198, 206
LA GATTA, John 268
LALANDE-Jodel 206
LANG, Robert 331
LANSTON Monotype Machine Company 33, 46, 63
LAPSHIN, Prof. N. 155, 206, 244
LARISCH, Rudolf von 3, 358
LATOUR, Alfred 206
LAURENCIN, Marie 208, 261
LAUTREC, Toulouse (see Toulouse-Lautrec)
LAVERERIE, R. de 279
LAWSON, Robert 192
LAYOUT, printing 70
LEAVES of Grass 54
LEBEDEV, V. 201
LEDDERHOSE, Elizabeth 228, 229
LEDOUX, Picart 181, 205
LEGER, Fernand 354, 358, 363
LEGRAND, Edy 156, 181, 206
LEICESTER College of Arts 43, 69, 243, 373
LEIPZIGER Technikum für Buchdrucker 43, 56, 57, 359, 365, 367
LEONARDO (see Vinci, Leonardo da)
LETTERING 1, 10; appropriateness 16; blackface Gothic 13; inventiveness 18–21; origins 8, 9; Roman 12; spacing 15; styles 14; three-dimensional 26; tools 4, 27
LEUSCHNER, Ernst 276
LEVITT-Him Studio 237, 251, 313, 328
LEWIS, Allen 205
LIBRAIRIE de France 181, 198
LIMITED Editions Club 190
LINDISFARNE, Book of 7

LINE Plate 99
LINOLEUM Cut 80
LINOTYPE 33, 67, 366
LINWEAVE Editions 101, 212
LITHOGRAPHY 91, 113
LIVERPOOL City School of Art 364, 369
LODENIUS, H. 354
LOHSE, Remie 139
LONDON, Leonard 348
LONDON School of Printing 43, 56
LORD and Thomas 277, 282
LOW 216
LOWINSKY, Thomas 194, 205
LUDEKENS, Fred 282, 349
LUDLOW Typograph Company 44
LUDWIG & Mayer 61, 63, 71
LUND Humphries, Ltd. 130, 278
LÜTZELBURGER, Hans 173
LYDIS, Mariette 184, 206

M

M. CARLOS Sanchez 193
McCUTCHEON, John T. 215
McINTOSH 340
McKNIGHT-Kauffer, 130, 205, 239, 271, 339, 350
MAILLOL, Aristide 205, 206
MAIOLI 224
MAJUSCULES 7
MALLEK, W. 242, 333, 336
MALLET-Stevens, Robert 26
MANTEGNA, Andrea 76, 77
MANTEUFEL, E. 372
MANUSCRIPT 152, 158, 161, 216
MANUTIUS, Aldus 43, 62, 164, 165, 169, 170, 229
MARCHBANKS Press 212, 278
MARCKASON, Abe 371
MARFURT, Leo 235
MARTEL, J. J. 342
MARTEN, Professor Frans 40, 64, 65
MARTIN, A. M. 205
MARTIN, Charles 181, 205
MARUSSIG, Guido 232
MARVILLE 181
MASEREEL 187, 188, 206
MAYNARD, R. A. 177, 205
MAZZA, Aldo 211, 216
MEDITATIONES, Turrecremata's 160, 162, 166
MEISSENBACH, George 110
MEISSENBACH, Riffarth & Company 267
MEISSONIER 180, 181, 184
MELISANDA, Psalter of 219, 224
MELISSE 269
MENZEL, Adolf von 182, 184

MERGENTHALER'S Linotype 33
MERRYMOUNT Press (see Updike)
MÉRYON 86, 89
METZIG, Wilhelm 66, 288, 343
METZL, Ervine 339
MEYEROWICZ 336
MEYNELL, Francis 43, 178
MEZZOTINT 91
MICHELANGELO 77, 184, 261
MILLAIS, Sir John 197, 248
MILLER, Jane 269
MILLET, J. F. 170
MINOS, fresco portrait of 154, 161
MINUSCULES 7, 9, 153
MIROUER de la Redemption, Le 160, 166
MOHOLY Nagy 124, 149
MOLNÁR, Paul C. 188, 206
MONDAINI 21
MONOTINT (monotype) 91
MONOTYPE (see Lanston; Monotint)
MONVEL, Bernard Boutet de 203
MORDANT (acid bath) 85
MORELL, José 314, 316, 323, 325, 337
MORNAY Éditions 202
MORONI, A. 206
MORRIS, William 38, 43, 188, 192, 197, 228
MOTION Picture 138
MOURON, A. (see Cassandre)
MUCHA 308
MÜLLER, Hans Alexander 206, 365
MUNDUS Antiqua Type 66
MUNICH State Art School 199, 354, 359, 377
MUNTANÉ, L. 322

N

NASH, Paul 205
NAST, Thomas 215
NEGULESCO, Jean 48
NEW York School of Industrial Arts 364
NEWBOULD, Frank 313
NEWS Syndicate Company 120
NICHOLSON (see Beggarstaff Brothers)
NICK, Gaston 205
NIÉPCE 117
NIESSEN, Andreas 19, 24, 234, 283
NOGUÉS 337
NONESUCH Press 178, 197
NORBLIN, S. 335
NORSTEDT and Sons 6, 55
NYGAARD, Axel 198, 206

O

OBERLÉ, Jean 194, 206

OCTAVO 221
OESTERLE, Wilhelm 358
OFFENBACH School of Arts & Crafts 286, 289
OFFSET 39
OFFSETTING 80
OHME, W. 369
ORIHONS 216, 217
OSIECKI 319
OSTOJA-Chrostowski, Stanislaw 241
OUTDOOR Advertising, Inc. 348

P

PACKAGING 253, 286, 288, 290
PARMEGGIANI, C. 285
PARRISH, Maxfield 203
PARTRIDGE 216
PASSION, woodcut from the 155
PASTIS, Malteo de 159, 163
PATTERSON and Sullivan 277
PAUL, Hermann 186, 187, 206
PAYNE, Roger 225, 226
PELICAN Press 41, 52, 58
PENFIELD, Edward 240, 308
PENNELL, Ioseph 307, 358
PENROSE'S Annual 129, 278
PEREGRINATIONES 161, 166
PERFILIEFF, Captain V. 5
PERSIAN coin 26; helmet 26
PETRUCCELLI, Antonio 306
PHOTOGRAMS 134
PHOTOGRAPHY 115; directions 119; enlarging 134; exposure 124; focusing 122; lenses 128; lighting 122; retouching 128
PHOTOLITHOGRAPHY 94
PHOTOMONTAGE 135, 136, 150, 273, 335
PICHON, Léon 186, 187, 202
PICTOGRAPHS, paleolithic 8
PINCUS, Natalie 335
PINSARD, P. 206
PIRANESI 92
PISAN 82
PITZ, Henry C. 197
PLATEN Press 33, 36, 67
PLATT, John 243
PLÉIADE, La 105, 156, 178, 185, 187, 202
POESCHEL & Trepte 62, 202
POINT 32, 35
POLITZER 236
PONTAX 213
POSITIVE Plate 72
POSTER, The 299, 301, 375
POULTON, T. L. 178
POWEL, Peter 137

PRAGUE State Graphic Art School 368
PREETORIUS, Prof. 354
PREISSIG, Vojtech 59, 206
PRENTIS, Terence 291
PRESSES 33, 67
PRINTING 29
PRITCHARD, Wood & Partners 119, 254
PROBLEMS, advertising arts, 298; the book 244; graphic arts education 378; lettering 28; photography 150; poster 356; printing 70; reproductive arts 114
PROOF Press 67
PROOFREADER'S Marks 374
PSALTER 36, 168
PURVIS, Tom 355
PYLE, Howard 176, 203
PYNSON, Printers 49
PYNSON, Richard 24, 43, 49

Q

QUARITCH, Bernhard 77, 218
QUARTO 220, 367
QUATERNIONS 217, 220

R

RABENBAUER, Prof. A. 283, 324, 326
RACKHAM, Arthur 203
RAEMAEKERS, Dr. Louis 204, 215
RAFFET, Auguste 171, 181, 182
RAIMONDI, Marcantonio 77
RAK 112
RANDOM House 54
RATDOLT, Erhard 39, 168
RAY, Man 131, 149
REDUCING (see Scaling)
REGISTER Marks 80
REHBEIN, Ernest 226, 227, 228
REIACH, Herbert, Ltd. 2
REICHERT, Otto 227, 231, 240
REICHSDRUCKEREI 6, 85, 202
REIMANN School 16, 357–360, 377
REISS, Winold 280
REMBRANDT 87
RENGER-Patzsch, Albert 145
RENNER 43, 66
REPRODUCTIVE Arts 71, 73
RETHEL 173, 184, 210
REUTERS 267
REUWICH, Erhard 161, 166
RHODE, H. 13
RIBES, 273
RICHARDS, Fred 24

RICHTER, Fritz 75, 84, 151, 189
RICKETTS, Charles 205
RIDDELL, Lord 362
RIEDER, Édition 160, 166
RIVADENEIRA 338
RIVERA, Diego 200
ROBINSON, Boardman 215, 358
ROESE, Herbert F. 195
ROESZLER, Eunice 376
ROGERS, Bruce 46, 192
RONNEBECK, Arnold 98
ROOS, S. H. de 228, 240
ROSA Brothers 100, 256
ROSETTA Stone 247, 248
ROSSETTI, Dante Gabriel 177, 197
ROTARY Press 33, 36
ROTH 336
ROTOGRAVURE 113
RÖTZER'S Senefelder Company 280, 284, 333
ROZENSZTEJNÓWNA, R. 346
RUDGE, Printing House of Edwin C. 51, 59
RUNIC Inscription 5
RUPPRECHT Press 25, 197
RUZICKA, Rudolph 205

S

"ST. CHRISTOPHER," woodcut 74, 76
ST. ELIZABETH Lettering 6
ST. LOUIS Bible 152
SALOMON, Bernard 167
SANS Pareil 202
SANS Serif 9
SATTLER, Joseph 192
SAUVAGE, Sylvain 205
SCALING 102, 104
SCHAEFFER, Samuel Bernard 237
SCHEURICH, Paul 305
SCHLEGER, Hans (see Zéro)
SCHLICHT, Erich 279
SCHMIED, F. L. 206
SCHMOTZER, F. 150
SCHOEFFER, Fust and 42, 36, 62, 168
SCHONGAUER 74, 76
SCHULPIG 24, 25
SCHUMANN, Willi 14
SCOTT, John 132
SEGONZAC, Dunoyer de 206
SEIX y Barral 59, 135, 315, 321, 322, 330, 332, 336, 337, 347
SELENSKY, A. 332
SENECA 311, 320, 325, 326, 328, 329
SENEFELDER, Alois 91
SENSANI, Gino Carlo 188, 206

SERMONE Della Oratione 37
SEUSS, Dr. 216
SHAKESPEARE Head Press 194, 197
SHAW, Keith 296
SHEP 21
SHEPARD, Otis 353
SIGNATURE 221, 367, 379
SIKKEL Press, De 179, 202, 235
SILK Screen 94
SIMONS, Anna 3
SINEL, Joseph 289, 290
SINOPICO, Primo 206, 210, 211
SKIBBE, Bruno 206
SMITH, Percy 24
SOGLOW, Otto 293
SPACING 15
STAATLICHE Akademie, Leipzig 359, 365, 367
STANLEY, Frederick 353
STEICHEN, Edward 133
STEIG, William 206
STEINER, Ralph 146
STEINLEN, Théophile 175, 205, 240, 308
STEINWEISS, Alex 370
STEMPEL Type Foundry 58, 61, 66, 283
STEREOTYPING 113
STIEGLITZ, Alfred 118, 138
STOCK, Delamain & Boutelleau 182, 195
STONE, Edward L. 30
STROBRIDGE Lithographing Company 118
STRUBE 208
"STRYGE, Le" 86
STUDIO Sun 121
STÝRSKÝ, J. 229
SUPER, Nat 70
SUPPLEMENTUM Chronicarum 162
SUSSAN, René Ben 178, 189, 205
SUWALSKI, W. 22
SWITZER, George 16, 146, 286, 290
SYRO-Egyptian Script 5

T

TAGLIENTE 11
TAUBIN, W. 369
TAYLOR, Fred 337
TEACHERS College, Columbia University 20
TEAGUE, Walter Dorwin 49, 356
TENGGREN, G. 180, 203
TENNIELL, Sir John 203, 216
TETZLAFF, Elmer 246
THEUERDANK 166
THIVILLIER, Roger 277
THOMASON, A. R. 333
TIEMANN, Prof. 62, 358

TIERNEY, E. 369
TOMÁS, E. 363
TOOLS, engraving 76; lettering 4, 27; lithograph 76, 113, 377, 382
TORY, Geoffroy, *Book of Hours* 39, 167, 170, 222
TORY Border 52
TOUCHAGUES 183, 205
TOULOUSE-Lautrec 174, 208, 308
TRADE-Marks 24, 25, 62, 257
TRAFTON, Howard 276
TRAFTON Script 62
TRAJAN Column, letters 8, 32
TREIDLER, Adolf 308
TRIAS Studio 267, 271
TROYEN, Mme. 206
TYPE, blackface Gothic 31; body and display 32; constructivistic 31; designers 43; face 35; major styles 35; method of forecasting 68, 366; rule 35; stick 40; type high 32
TYPOGRAPHY, principles 41-43

U

ULLMAN, Leon 275
ULREICH, Buk 261, 281, 294
UNCIALS 9, 153
UNDERWOOD & Underwood 132, 144, 145, 148
U. S. GOVERNMENT Printing Office 68
UNITED Typothetae of America 362
UPDIKE, D. B. (Merrymount Press label) 63, 192

V

VALERIO, Roger de 262, 274, 309
VALLOTTON, Félix 206
VALTURIUS 159, 163
VANDERCOOK & Sons, proof press 67
VAN DER VOSSEN, André 206
VAN DONGEN 261
VAN KRIMPEN 3
VAN LEYDEN 74
VELLUM 153
VENDRE 137
VERZOCCHI, G. 285
VIBERT, P. E. 206
VIENNA School of Graphic Art and Research 126, 135, 150, 199
VIERGE, Daniel 205
VINCI, Leonardo da 117, 202

VIRGIL, manuscript writing 9
VIRL, Prof. Hermann 17
VLAMINCK, Maurice de 182, 208
VOLUMINA 217
VON HORN, Tony 130

W

WADE, A. Cecil 18
WAGULA, Hans 280, 333
WALKER, Fred 303
WARD, Lynd 79, 189, 205, 239
WARDE, Frederick 59
WARSAW Graphic Industries School 22, 113, 354, 369, 372, 373
WARSAW School of Fine Arts 112, 346
WARSAW School of Graphic Arts 43
WEHR, Julian Frontispiece
WEISS, E. R. 17, 43, 47, 48, 206, 232, 358
WELTGERICHT, Gutenberg's 32
WERBEKRAFT Studio 344
WERKMEISTER, F. 100
WESTMINSTER Press 18, 63
WESTON, Edward 127
WEYL, M. N. 112
WEZEL & Naumann 14, 24
WHISTLER 94
WIEMELER, Ignaz 228
WILLIAMS, Joy 69
WILMINK, Machiel 355
WINKLER, Alfred 243, 311
WOOD, Grant 236
WOOD Engraving 81, 83
WOODCUT 77
WYETH, N. C. 203

Y

YOUNG and Rubicam 293

Z

ZERO (Hans Schleger) 25, 72
ZERZAVY, Jean 206
ZIETARA, Valentin 321, 327, 329
ZILVERDISTEL Press 202
ZIMELLI, Umberto 294, 295
ZINGHER, Oleg 18, 210, 341
ZINKEISEN, Dora 330

COVERS AND LAYOUT DESIGNED BY THE AUTHORS AND PRINTED IN
GOUDY DEEPDENE BY THE MAPLE PRESS COMPANY, YORK, PENNSYLVANIA